THE POLITICS OF HUNGER

Protest, poverty and policy in England, c. 1750–c. 1840

Carl J. Griffin

Manchester University Press

The right of Carl J. Griffin to be identified as the author of this work has been
asserted by him in accordance with the Copyright, Designs and Patents Act 1988.

Published by Manchester University Press
Oxford Road, Manchester M13 9PL
www.manchesteruniversitypress.co.uk

British Library Cataloguing-in-Publication Data
A catalogue record for this book is available from the British Library

ISBN 978 1 5261 4562 8 hardback
ISBN 978 1 5261 6703 3 paperback

First published 2020
Paperback published 2022

The publisher has no responsibility for the persistence or accuracy of URLs
for any external or third-party internet websites referred to in this book,
and does not guarantee that any content on such websites is, or will remain,
accurate or appropriate.

Typeset by Newgen Publishing UK

The politics of hunger

MANCHESTER
1824

Manchester University Press

For Suzanne and Silas, that you may never
hunger for anything but knowledge

Contents

Tables and figures

Tables

Figures

Acknowledgements

This book was first conceived on my arrival at the University of Sussex in the summer of 2013, though several of the ideas herein had a longer gestation. Beginning work at an institution with a peerless reputation for research on rural resistance past and present provided the spur to make sense of what had been a constant presence in my previous writings and as yet remained obscure, both in my thinking and in the wider historiography. How might one begin to research a book on the politics of hunger in the late eighteenth and early nineteenth century? Having written the book I am convinced that no funding council or charity would be convinced of the case. Indeed, much of the material used here was gathered piecemeal whilst working on other projects, going back to the research undertaken for my doctoral thesis at the University of Bristol. This project, then, was only possible because of the slow accretion of materials across a wide range of topics, time periods, locales and archives. The list of the latter is far too long to detail here – indeed not all libraries and archives consulted remain open – but I note with thanks the permission to reproduce figure 4.1 granted by the East Riding Archives and Local Studies. The individuals who have helped to shape my thinking – and hence this book – are legion, but my particular thanks go to Iain Robertson, Briony McDonagh, Roy Jones, Katrina Navickas, Peter Jones, Steve Poole, Rose Wallis, Richard Hoyle, Malcolm Chase, Keith Lilley, Dave Featherstone, Paul Griffin, Keith Snell, Brian Short, Simon Sandall, and the much-missed Alun Howkins. An earlier version of chapter six appeared in volume 42 of *Historical Geography* and I would like to thank Gerry Kearns – the editor of that fine volume on 'Irish Historical Geographies' – for his thoughtful comments and careful editorial work. Chapter two was first aired at 'People, Protest & the Land: A Workshop in Honour of Professor Alun Howkins', held at the University of Sussex in July 2014. I would like to thank the organiser, Nicola Verdon, and the participants of the wonderful workshop for their feedback and encouragement. Sections of chapter five were first given as a paper at the British Agricultural History Society's Winter Conference in December 2017.

Sussex has proved a wonderfully convivial place to think and work. For granting me a term of research leave – the first and only period of my career so far – so soon after my arrival I am hugely grateful to Richard Black and Alan Lester who appointed me. A year after arriving I became, suddenly and unexpectedly, Deputy Head of Department, and then two years later Head of Department. This book was written during these periods and has provided happy respite from administration variably heavy and light. My thanks in particular for the company and comradeship of Simon Rycroft, Divya Tolia-Kelly, Alan Lester, my former Head of School Andrea Cornwall and current Head of School Buzz Harrison. To Suzanne, who has lived with this book, at home and away, for always supporting me and my work. And to Silas. This is for you both, that you might never know of the horrors of hunger but through the pages that follow.

Bangor, August 2019

Introduction: 'The unremitted pressure': On hunger politics

The English landscape speaks a series of truths about hunger that generations of scholars have failed to grasp. In the extraordinarily rich place-name nomenclature of rural and coastal England hunger is writ more subtly and lucidly than in any study. In such enclosure-era names as Hunger Hill (Cheshire and Lancashire), Hungry Down (Aldington, Kent) and Starvation Point (Whitstable, Kent) we see an admission at once sad and satirical that the land was never a promise of plenty to those who farmed it, let alone to those who laboured upon it. If particular fields might prove unresponsive to the landlord and farmers' investment – 'you'll end up poor and hungry if you till this ground…' – the very deliberate point about naming hunger in the landscape speaks to a more profound truth: that the residents of rural England well knew that a plentiful past was no assurance of future abundance. Plenty and precarity walk hand in hand. Hunger persisted not only as a spectre of the past but as an all too real threat in the present. One harvest failure, one drought, one dearth, one failure of law and governance, was enough to plunge much of the population – in rural England as much as the towns – towards starvation. And as such place names as Cold Comfort Farm and Hunger Farm also obliquely attest, hunger might also come from economic failure rendering you poor and unable to afford to subsist when times were tough. As the work of literary scholars has shown, the fear of hunger was arguably one of the defining tropes of Georgian and early Victorian fiction; hunger was written into the imaginative landscape of the realm.[1]

The implications are clear enough: whatever the actual individual and collective experience, hunger in the late eighteenth and the first half of the nineteenth century was not banished from the land but instead writ into the very essence, self-perception and fabric of its being. And yet, so the received line goes, by the early decades of the eighteenth century the peoples of England could truly be said to be beyond the ravages of famine. As Guido Alfani and Cormac Ó Gráda have recently reiterated, England 'escaped' from the clutches of severe food scarcity and famine 'much earlier' than most other European states; southern England experienced its last 'major' famine in the 1590s, northern England a little later in the 1620s.[2]

There is, it would be foolish to deny, not only a quantitative but also a quali-tative difference between the experience and effects of mass famine deaths and the fear of hunger. But the very etymology of European words associated with famine betrays a complex relationship between food, hunger and, ultim-ately, starvation, and these meanings and relationships have changed over time. If we might now accept a definition of famine as the mass inability to access sufficient food leading to excessive levels of mortality from starvation and hunger-related diseases, this is a relatively recent conception. In early modern England, as Ó Gráda reminds us, '*dearth* signified dearness, but meant famine', but when the shared experience of mass famine deaths was no longer held in the collective memory the meanings of dearth and famine became distinct: a lack of food, an absolute and catastrophic want of food. Conversely, *carestia*, the Italian word for famine, connotes dearness, while the closest German equivalent, *Hungersnot*, relates to a scarcity of food.[3]

The relationship between food, hunger and famine is evidently not a simple or static one. We know that in 'post-famine' England – though I will challenge even this idea later – beyond hunger remaining a fear and a threat, poor consumers still rioted to protect their access to food, while politicians legislated and intervened in the marketing of foodstuffs, occasionally acting to ensure popular access to food.[4] Hunger – whether felt or feared – was important enough to the poor that 115 out of 341 working-class autobio-graphical writings analysed by Emma Griffin explicitly mentioned hunger. This is probably an under-representation as some of the writers may have chosen not to write about matters relating to diet and food.[5] By the turn of the nineteenth century even food security was called into question. The war with Napoleonic France and its allies severely limited the ability to import grain in times of dearth,[6] although the mortality rate – in itself not an unprob-lematic measure – as a recent study has reasserted remained broadly similar in the crises of the 1790s and early 1800s to non-crisis years.[7] Further, Rev. Malthus was able to warn of population checks in a nation whose fertility rate outstripped its ability to increase its food stocks,[8] and yet even in the so-called 'Hungry Forties' – the term an invention by supporters of free trade in the late nineteenth century – when famine stalked Ireland and threatened Scotland, England remained free from famine.[9]

As Amartya Sen's influential theory of exchange entitlements suggests, beyond problems in the food supply the mechanisms by which people were precipitated into starvation were many. The failure of a family's ability to exchange their primary entitlement – their labour for food – was in itself made up of myriad contexts and complexities: from ill health and family disaster, through recession, to shifts in social policy and economic restruc-turing.[10] Ergo, if famine was not a product of simple causal relationships, then comprehending the many stages before death from want is vital in understanding not only the experience of everyday life but also the making of famine itself. Fixating on the absolutes of famine, and Malthusian population checks, arguably acts to limit us in asking interesting questions of the period after which 'famine became unthinkable' and in understanding the complexities of what happened before famine. It also acts to temporally foreshorten understandings of famine, focusing attention back on exploring the dynamics of dearth in the medieval and early modern periods. Of course this is not to say that such questions are not unimportant – they are, on which see below – or that medievalists and early modernists should not persist with such studies. Indeed, recent work by Jonathan Healey, Buchanan Sharp and Bruce Campbell shows the value of close, careful scrutiny of the archive in deepening our understanding of the history of famine.[11] Rather, for the 'post'-famine period, we need to acknowledge that famine for individuals and plebeian communities – that is to say, death from want – did not suddenly become 'unthinkable'. Perishing from lack of food remained a constant fear and threat in the late eighteenth and early nineteenth centuries. The peoples of England were beyond the ravages of famine yet far from liberated from the effects and fears of hunger and starvation. It is the consequences of this fear and threat that demand our attention.

The issue, at heart, remains a paradoxical one. This can be understood as follows. The 1840s witnessed hunger and malnutrition in Britain, and mass starvation in Ireland and elsewhere in the empire. The 'Hungry Forties' came, however, amidst claims that absolute biological want had been eliminated in Britain. Rising agricultural production and the development of integrated national and international markets combined with the (supposed) net of the poor laws meant that by the early nineteenth century the threat of hunger as an 'unremitted pressure' (in the words of Rev. Townsend subsequently quoted by Marx in *Capital*) had lifted for the peoples of Britain.[12] Wages and employment had replaced access to food as the critical nexus of politics. This was the age of Malthus: hunger, as James Vernon has put it, provided a 'natural basis for moral order, in forcing the indigent to work and preventing unsustainable overpopulation'. To be hungry, so the discourse went, was to be an object of 'opprobrium, not compassion'.[13] Only in response to the global famines of the 1840s did recognisably humanitarian discourses evolve, new modes of reporting emotionally connecting the comfortable with the sufferings of the starving.[14] For much of the eighteenth century an expression of hunger found form in food rioting, the practice arguably being the defining protest of eighteenth-century Britain.[15] The 'death' of this tradition with the repression of the national waves of food rioting in 1795–6 and 1800–1 did not suddenly mean, though, that hunger and access to food was no longer a political issue for either poor consumers or the rulers of Britain.[16]

Part of the problem is rooted in the often inconsistent relationship between food, hunger and famine as written in histories of industrialising England. These paradoxes are writ through the historiography and yet remain implicit rather than explicit: famine was, as Richard Hoyle has recently put it, now 'unthinkable' in England and yet the period witnessed the rise of food rioting as a national phenomenon in the mid-eighteenth century and, later, the Malthusian obsession with population checks.[17] In many ways this is a reflection of, as Keith Wrightson put it, the enclosure by time period and theme of English social history (though one could also add economic history and historical geography to this mix).[18] Famines belong to the medievalists and early modernists; food riots, after E.P. Thompson, belong to students of the eighteenth century;[19] and, due to the legacy of Malthus and the Great Famine of Ireland, theorising about famine and populations belongs to scholars of the nineteenth century. Yet in all this neat demarcation, hunger is not so much written out as not ever really written in. Indeed, if recent scholarship has advanced our knowledge of the contours, effects and meanings of famine in England (and in England in relation to other countries),[20] the depth and persistence of food rioting,[21] and the engagement between popular politics and consumption,[22] the effects of hunger in the late eighteenth and early nineteenth centuries remain subject to remarkably little study. Peter Gurney's fine paper on the politics of consumption in the 1840s and Griffin's analysis of diet and the experience of hunger in working-class autobiographical writings are the notable exceptions that prove the rule.[23] In part, the questions asked have remained too narrow: 'Did the peasants really starve?', 'Were food rioters really hungry?', 'Did living standards improve?'. Our fixations have been too squarely framed on narrowly causal relationships.[24]

It is betwixt and between these paradoxes that this book exists. Focusing on the period from the late eighteenth century through to the crisis of the 1840s, this study systematically explores what I conceive to be *'hunger politics'*, or rather *'the politics of hunger':* the articulations of hunger as a tool of protest by poor consumers; its framing as a problem in the making of public policy; and its (elite) political languages and the attendant effects of these. There are three interrelated aims and objectives: first, to understand how hunger was mobilised and articulated by poor consumers during subsistence crises, and, relatedly, how the discourse of hunger persisted 'beyond' the food rioting tradition.[25] Second, to examine the ways in which the polity (both local and national) framed hunger as a public policy problem, initially in relation to social policy responses to rising food prices and declining real wages, and then in terms of how the poor were made as biological subjects (and the attendant political projects to manage and regulate pauper bodies). Third, to analyse how hunger was made and used, in elite terms in the making of hunger as a biopolitical force in the period, thinking through the influence of Malthus' writings in the emergence of hunger as a tool of sovereign power,[26] and popularly, through the ways in which the hunger of others – not least the near subjects of Empire in Ireland – informed a relational understanding of hunger.

Considerations of the politics of hunger have almost totally omitted the period from the mid-eighteenth century to the mid-nineteenth century, the exceptions being Roger Wells' magisterial treatment of the hunger crises of the Napoleonic Wars, *Wretched Faces*,[27] and a small body of recent work reassessing the 'Hungry Forties'.[28] Indeed, even the voluminous historiography considering the influence and accuracy of Malthus' dire predictions has tended to focus on the issue of birth rates and demography rather than on the politics of hunger per se.[29] Further, the dynamics for the period beyond the mid-nineteenth century altered, with food – and hence bodily subsistence – now existing in a global context, and hunger thus concurrently, as Vernon puts it, starting to be conceived of as a global social problem rather than an unavoidable natural phenomenon.[30]

This is a book concerned with the totemic spaces of hunger in late eighteenth- and early nineteenth-century England: the (primarily) agrarian communities of southern and eastern England, the places where the nationally dominant occupational group resided and where debates about the nature of hunger and poverty were located and framed. Notwithstanding rapid industrialisation and urbanisation, England in the period remained an essentially rural nation, both in terms of settlement and population – 1851 marks the first point at which the majority of the population lived in towns and cities – and in terms of political identity, with Parliament dominated by landowners and much political discourse dictated by agrarian concerns, not least in terms of poverty.[31] This is not to deny the importance of the experiences of those who lived and worked elsewhere. Indeed, in many ways this is a study about a more-than-rural England, one that has dominant geographical foci but that often draws upon other places and experiences, other circuits and networks, not least in the final chapter, which begins to think about how the hunger of others beyond Britain was understood. But in essence, for much of the period the problem – and hence politics – of hunger remained defiantly told as agrarian. This book reflects these dynamics.

What follows in this chapter is structured as follows. It starts by examining in detail our existing understanding, surveying the ways in which hunger has been told but more often erased from the field, and the legacy of the misuse of hunger as a concept in history of protest. In so doing, it details the key premise of the book, that the politics of hunger was one of the defining dynamics and discourses of the period, something articulated in different ways by those pauperised, by politicians and by theorists alike. The chapter ends by detailing the overall structure and by mapping out the six thematic chapters that follow.

Escaping hunger

'History, it appears, cannot escape hunger.' So Vernon began his *Hunger: A Modern History*.[32] If his book was an attempt to chart how attitudes to hunger changed from perceiving it as either divine providence or fecklessness to instead a collective, social problem, his premise is important here for it explicitly acknowledges that even after England had 'rid itself of famine', hunger 'remained endemic in Britain'. That in the late eighteenth century and early nineteenth centuries Adam Smith and Thomas Malthus respectively first 'establish[ed] the modern political of economy of hunger' is, so Vernon suggests, telling. Hunger needed to be understood, theorised and cured precisely because it remained a problem.[33] Indeed, the heroic story of rapidly rising agricultural productivity – by 1850 the output per acre was higher in Britain than anywhere else in Europe, Belgium excepted[34] – might have acted to banish famine but it did not end hunger. Higher outputs supported population growth which, in turn, made possible industrialisation as those once tied to the land migrated to industrial and urban centres and fed, so the story goes, a virtuous circle of growth and prosperity. Conversely, enclosure, agrarian capitalism and the creation of the factory system all acted to create a precarious market dependence which kept the wage labourer locked in a cycle of perpetual poverty and hunger.

If all of this is to paint with a broad brush, it is necessarily so, for in thinking about hunger in the period historians have tended to reduce the issue to data-heavy aspatial debates about the standard of living, one of the totemic debates of modern British history. 1750 appears to have been something of a watershed for rural workers. Before that point male and female wages were increasing and the cost of goods was declining, thanks to rising agricultural productivity, low and stable food prices, nominal population growth, and competition for labour from the expanding rural industries keeping wage rates up.[35] There are, of course, exceptions. Some rural industrial communities were already in long-term decline: by the 1720s, for instance, the 'golden age' for the serge weavers and combers of Devon was already over.[36] Thereafter, so a broad consensus goes, the standard of living of working people declined. As Griffin has recently asserted, while analysis of the standard of living of working people was once a heterogeneous field split into 'pessimists' and 'optimists', since the turn of the century there has been a narrowing of the methodological approach that privileges the use of quantifiable series and a clear consensus that living standards declined. The impact of 'the inexorable march of statistics' is, so Griffin asserts, now acting to silence the voices of those who suffered want and poor diets, as such quantitative studies are not only too narrowly framed but also almost self-contradictory.[37] Thus even chief pessimist Charles Feinstein's data shows real wages rising by almost 40 per cent between 1780 and 1850. Similarly Gregory Clark's analyses have shown that agricultural labourers wages rose by 50 per cent in real terms between 1800 and 1850 while those for building craftsmen in the same period increased by some 70 per cent.[38] Studies using other measures of living standards beyond real wages, including calorific intake and GDP per capita, have all come to the same partial and problematic conclusions too.[39]

What of the rural situation? And what about the disaggregated experience? We know that in rural areas, notwithstanding continued increases in agricultural output, population growth, while regionally uneven, acted to increase the labour supply and depress wages and increase the risk (and rates) of un- and under-employment. Against this trend we know that employment opportunities in other rural industries increased in the second half of the eighteenth century, although in some places long-established cottage-based industries were in terminal decline. We also know that poor relief became less generous, and parish vestries applied greater stringency in determining relief policy – until structural changes or crises hit.[40] We also know that in parishes subject to enclosure, poor rates tended to increase, inevitably increasing dependency on waged labour and the vagaries of the market and reducing opportunities for 'sources of subsistence other than wages'.[41] In the Lincolnshire parish of Frampton on the enclosure of Holland Fen poor rates tripled, peaking in 1769, the year of enclosure.[42] Poor harvests acted to reduce the demand for (relatively) highly paid harvest work – something that men, women and children benefitted from – and thus the string of poor harvests in the 1750s and 1760s and again in the mid- to late 1790s and early 1800s hit rural families especially hard. Against this dynamic, post-1750 year-long 'living-in' service also declined while employment in agriculture became increasingly seasonal.[43]

Ian Gazeley and Nicola Verdon's analysis of the surveys of Frederick Eden and David Davies conducted in the 1790s also usefully reminds us of regional variations – labouring households in the agrarian south and east were far more impoverished than those living in the Midlands and the north, though experiences might vary from parish to parish – but also tells us that almost every labouring family was living under the 'poverty line', especially if they had to support children but did not yet have the income from child labour.[44] Of course, given that the data was collected in the crisis years of the 1790s Gazeley and Verdon's conclusions might be unduly pessimistic, especially so when compared to relatively good years for labouring families in the early 1810s, mid-1820s and late 1830s. And yet, using a very different approach and archival material, Griffin's conclusions are broadly similar: for rural families in the first half of the nineteenth century, and especially those in the south and east, 'wages and family incomes hardly moved' and their diet was 'insufficient for all the household's needs'. Ergo, in comparison to families in industrialising districts, plebeian agrarian families were more likely to feel the effects of hunger and to live most in dreadful fear of the perma-threat of hunger the most.[45] As T.L. Richardson has shown for Lincolnshire, drawing on a variety of quantitative and qualitative evidence, the war years of the 1790s, 1800s and early 1810s saw a steady decline in labouring living standards, and then as agricultural commodity prices collapsed at the end of the wars after a short respite, wages started to tumble, opportunities for women and children (with some exceptions) declined, and unemployment started to become endemic, with up to a third of labourers in some Lincolnshire parishes being employed directly by the parish by the late 1820s.[46] This situation, as chapter three explores in detail, was broadly true of the south and east.[47] Real wages might have nominally increased for some families in some years but the situation was so uneven, so changeable, so complex that to speak of the experience of *the* rural worker is to ride rough-shod over difference.

Griffin's paper is novel in combining a central focus on living standards with an emphasis on understanding the poor's self-representations of hunger. Indeed, while hunger might be an implicit emphasis in the standard-of-living literature – and even an explicit reference in recent work on calorific intake[48] – it is neither the central theme nor expressed in terms of either plebeian experience or even policy problem. Nor is it something explored in recent scholarship on famine in a European context. It features not in the index of Alfani and Ó Gráda and is mentioned only seven times on five pages in the text: 'hunger-induced disease', 'the worst years of hunger and famine', 'the great hunger', starvation as 'the fault of the hungry', 'four devastating series of "hunger"', 'the "hunger" continued', 'no need to distinguish between the deadly hunger that produced it and normal hunger'. The same also applies to Ó Gráda's *Famine: A Short History*, wherein hunger is mentioned seven times and then only *en passant*.[49] This is not a criticism but rather an observation. Hunger has not been taken seriously by either standard-of-living historians or famine historians: it exists as a context or label not as a category of analysis.

The same is also true for work exploring the impact of Malthusian thought and examining the veracity of Malthus' claims about the impact of the old poor laws – there was never *one* law, hence the plural – on the morals and marriage practices of the rural labouring poor. For instance in Samantha Williams' fine *Poverty, Gender and the Lifecycle Under the English Poor Law*, the latest and arguably most systematic treatment of population and the poor laws, hunger pervades the analysis – indeed it arguably underwrites the critical theme of the changing contours of need – but is not once made explicit.[50] By way of a further example, poor law historian James Huzel's study of the 'popularisation' of Malthus is threaded through with a rich analysis of the radical languages of need and plebeian rights in opposition to the amoral moralities of Malthus' disciples but hunger, again, provides an implicit context rather than an explicit focus.[51]

And yet, as Griffin's suggestive paper shows, hunger mattered enough to working people that they committed their thoughts, fears and experiences to paper.[52] For between being replete, with no fear of want in the future, to death from want there exists a wide spectrum of hungers. Famine forms one – horrific – end of the spectrum but it is not *the spectrum* of human experience. There are, as noted, a small number of other exceptions to this rule. Vernon's splendid *Hunger: A Modern History* provides an ambitious attempt to chart the changing ways in which we have understood hunger and felt about the hungry, focusing specifically on the emergence from the middle of the nineteenth century of the 'modern understanding' of hunger as not (just) an innate part of the human condition but rather something made and socially shared.[53] But Vernon's account, locating the British experience in the wider co-constituting circuits of empire, begins when this study ends.

Likewise, Gurney's fecund *Wanting and Having* picks up where this study ends, and, besides, it is not a study of hunger per se but rather an attempt to, in Gurney's words, 'uncover a genealogy of the modern consumer as well as links between the consumer and changing democratic discourses'. Hunger here is written as consumption's other, the wanting to consumption's having; the hungry are told as consumers denied basic rights by failures in the system (the Corn Laws; the want of the franchise; the New Poor Law).[54] But there is also a deeper history to be told, a history of the way in which early economic historians used hunger as an explanatory category in analysing the stimuli to riot, and of the intellectual legacies thereof. The next section explores this conceptualisation and its historiographies.

'Hunger riots'

Penned in the aftermath of the Midland Rising of 1607, Francis Bacon's short essay 'Of Seditions and Troubles' has left a long shadow over studies of food and subsistence crises.[55] Notwithstanding that he was clerk to the infamous and powerful Star Chamber, Bacon's analysis of the popular politics of dearth was, as Steve Hindle has suggested, remarkably nuanced and sympathetic to the needs of poor rebels.[56] Popular grievances could be understood in relation to two related concepts, 'Poverty' and 'Discontent', the latter 'inflammations' in the 'Politique Body', the former material want. And when the two states co-existed, there was instability and revolt ('seditions'). The triggers of these seditions were many but the remedy was always to remove 'that material cause of sedition … which is want and poverty in the estate'.[57] And the worst sort of 'sedition' was triggered by dearth: 'If this poverty and broken estate in the better sort be joined with a want and necessity in the mean people, the danger is imminent and great. For the Rebellions of the Belly are the worst.'[58]

This is far more subtle than 'empty bellies leads to rebellion', for without, as Hindle puts it, '[p]essimism and frustration among the landed elite' there would have been no revolt.[59] Hunger was a result of a failure of paternalism, evidence of 'discontent' amongst the elites. But for all these sympathies and subtleties, Bacon's analysis has been reduced to a portable and mutable phrase, something devoid of analysis and context, a reflexive take on agency and the working body: 'rebellions of the belly'. Indeed, this misreading (and misappropriation) of Bacon's work was total, coming from members of the establishment and radicals alike. Thus during the 1795 subsistence crisis no less a radical than John Thelwall berated 'foolish dreaming politician' Bacon for proposing a 'sublime policy of reducing ten millions of people to the brink of famine in one country, in order at once to pinch and wring all sedition out of their stomachs'.[60]

The legacy of Bacon's phrase, if not his analysis, is most profound in our conceptualisation of *demotic* responses to dearth. Building upon the

discourse of earlier Malthusian/political economy readings of Bacon –
Thomas Doubleday claimed in 1852 that as population 'morbidly spreads'
the consequence was either mass emigration or 'that worse sort of rebellions,
which the wise Lord Bacon designates 'rebellions of the belly'[61] – economic
historians appropriated Bacon's phrase as in itself a total explanation. To
Donald Barnes, writing in 1930, 'hunger riots' – a telling tag – were prevalent between the restoration and the early nineteenth century but were 'more
or less alike'. In a Cartesian sense, they were the mechanical response of
automata. '[N]othing is gained', Barnes dismissively concluded, 'by giving
a detailed account of each one'.[62] Thomas Ashton and Julia Sykes came to
a similar conclusion. Quoting Bacon, they asserted that while 'rebellions of
the belly' were endemic in the second half of the eighteenth century – 'the
instinctive reaction of virility to hunger' – the effort involved in their study
was 'disproportionate to the value of any generalisation that would be likely
to emerge'.[63] To Walt Whitman Rostow – 'the dean of the spasmodic school',
as E.P. Thompson so memorably put it[64] – the relationship between hunger
and riot was so immediate as for the latter to be absolutely predictable from
the level of unemployment and food prices.[65]

Early scholars of 'public disorder' were no less literal in thinking through
the relationship between bellies and protest. The important foundational
texts of Frank Darvall and, to a greater extent, Max Beloff may have done
much to bring food riots to wider historical attention, but their analysis was
no subtler than that of early economic historians. According to Darvall,
food riots in the 1810s were the actions of 'mobs' acting to secure supplies,
while to Beloff late seventeenth- and early eighteenth-century 'popular
disturbances' were direct functions of poor harvests and the fear of famine.[66]
Even the early works of George Rudé and Eric Hobsbawm published in
the 1950s, while admittedly not studies of popular responses to dearth
per se, did not challenge the by now received wisdom that food riots were
responses to want and hunger. Rudé's otherwise politically sensitive study
of the eighteenth-century London 'mob' acknowledged that the authorities
thought that some 'mobs' were '*prompted* by hunger' (my emphasis), without
challenging their analysis. Hobsbawm's essay 'The machine breakers' similarly asserted that however one tried to understand 'miners riots', ultimately
most were responses to 'high food-prices', the inference being that absolute
bodily need was the ultimate motive.[67] As 'recently' as 1972, Lawrence Stone
in *The Causes of the English Revolution* suggested that the English labourer
did not take sides during the revolution because they had little to grumble
about, their bellies being full. Or as Buchanan Sharp put it, 'it is clear that
[Stone] believes popular revolts to be the product of increasing impover-
ishment – what Francis Bacon in his essay "Of Seditions" called rebellions
of the belly'.[68] Even to R.B. Rose in his important but oft-forgotten first
systematic study of popular responses to dearth, protests were variably
described as 'price riots' or 'hunger riots', the connection again haunted by
the spectre of Bacon's misrepresented ghost.[69]

The shift from conceptualising food riots as 'rebellions of the belly', or at least reactive responses to hunger, to something beyond spasm came with the publication of Thompson's classic 1971 paper, 'The moral economy of the English crowd in the eighteenth century'. Rejecting the 'abbreviated view of economic man' and 'crass reductionism' of the spasmodic school, 'a product of a political economy which diminished human reciprocities to the wages-nexus',[70] Thompson suggested that such an approach:

> may conclude investigation at the exact point at which it becomes of serious sociological or cultural interest: being hungry ... what do people do? How is their behaviour modified by custom, culture, and reason? And (having granted that the primary stimulus of 'distress' is present) does their behaviour contribute towards any more complex, culturally-mediated function, which cannot be reduced – however long it is stewed over the fires of statistical analysis – back to stimulus once again?[71]

Thompson's method, as is well known but bears repetition, was to examine the values that underpinned crowd actions. In so doing, he asserted that it was possible to read some 'legitimising notion' in 'almost' every food riot: food rioters' actions were given legitimacy by their belief that they were defending rights and customs, and in so doing were supported in their critique – if not necessarily in their approach – by the 'wider consensus of the community'.[72]

It is important to note that Thompson's paradigm shift did not deny the importance of hunger as motivational force, acknowledging the 'self-evident truth' that hungry people can protest, and that riots were 'triggered off by soaring prices, by malpractices among dealers, or by hunger'.[73] Subsequent studies have tended though to ignore the issue of absolute material need and hunger either to focus instead on the meanings and practices of food rioting, or, missing Thompson's point, attempting to assess how hungry food rioters actually were. The latter camp is best represented by Dale Williams' 1976 response to Thompson that used demographic data to answer the question 'were "hunger" rioters really hungry'? Acknowledging that the reception of Thompson's paper had focused on the worth of his 'moral economy' concept, the 'basic questions concerning the relationship between deprivation and popular violence' had, as Williams put it, 'so far ... not been brought into the discussion'. The ensuing analysis of the demographic data for 'rioting' and 'non-rioting' communities for the 'representative' subsistence crisis of 1766–7 showed, so Williams claimed, that there were fewer conceptions in months of crisis in both sets of parishes.[74] Ergo, 'there was, no doubt, a desperation fostered by real suffering. But what is equally clear from the similar demographic performance of the rioting and non-rioting parishes is that there was no direct causal relationship between deprivation and protest.' The conclusion? 'Yes, hunger rioters *were* hungry' and 'many ordinary people' faced great difficulty in finding 'sufficient food for their families'. Given this conclusion, and allowing for the existence of Thompson's value system 'which could justify physical protest', 'why', Williams asked, 'was rioting not more general?'[75] Returning to the theme eight years later, Williams suggested that 'serious deprivation' was ultimately kept at bay and starvation avoided in 1766 by 'concessions' and 'vigorous programmes' of poor relief.[76]

This is not to say that Williams' analysis is either wrongheaded or necessarily incorrect. Indeed, notwithstanding subsequent critiques of his approach and conclusions,[77] the role of biological stimuli in popular responses to dearth has resurfaced as a factor in more recent analyses. Using price as a proxy for hunger, John Archer has suggested that while there the relationship between prices and riots was 'evident but not strong' it was 'surely no coincidence that food rioting declined rapidly as a nation-wide phenomenon after 1818, when wheat prices fell'.[78] The title alone of John Bohstedt's *The Politics of Provisions* is suggestive, and his comments on the first page proper of the book are definitive in asserting the relationship: 'For centuries in times of dearth … driven by gut-feelings of hunger and justice, and steered by memory and calculation, English communities sought forcible remedy, declaring *their* will and right to survive, and demanding action from the wealthy and powerful.' Provision politics, Bohstedt asserts, can be 'summed up as common people's collective actions to avert acute hunger, and their ruler's responses.'[79] In essence, though, the supposedly sustained emphasis on hunger in Bohstedt's study is illusory, a function not of rich contextual readings but of the historiographical readings, his analysis repeating the themes of earlier work or, at best, making suggestions as to the importance and complexity of the languages of hunger. Roger Wells' otherwise magisterial study of the food crises of the 1790s, *Wretched Faces*, while pulling no punches in asserting the deep bodily suffering of the poor – hence the graphic title of his book – is similarly oddly reserved in thinking through hunger, too locked in the dominant idioms and debates about famine.[80]

In all of this there is something qualified, something intellectually cautious; something fearful of sounding too much like a Roscowian by even uttering the word hunger in relation to protest. And yet, as we have seen, hunger was an ever-present danger, a genuine fear, something the majority of families in Britain were only one disaster away from suffering, from *feeling* the effects of a biting hunger. None of this is to say that the influence of Thompson's moral economy thesis has been a baleful thing. Analyses of the values and the attendant protest practices and meanings that underpinned popular responses to dearth have arguably been one of the richest and most fertile fields of social historical inquiry over the past forty years. But in the emphasis on malpractice, duplicitous trading, and the interplay between poor, working consumers and the rulers of Hanoverian England, the absolute biological basis of want and need has been unheeded. Hunger has instead been left to become the conceptual context that scholars of living standards want reduced to measures and models – hunger implicit but written out.[81]

Structure and argument

As detailed in the first section of this chapter, this study has three interrelated aims and objectives, which map directly onto the three sections of the book: 1) how hunger was mobilised and articulated by the poor ('The fight against being hungry'); 2) how hunger was framed as a policy problem ('Managing hunger'); and 3) how hunger was made and used by elites and relationally understood ('Theorising hunger'). Each section is divided into two chapters.

Chapter one goes beyond, as E.P. Thompson put it, the 'self-evident truth' that people are more likely to protest when hungry. Instead, it asks how their hunger – and that of their communities – and their fear of hunger was mobilised in the food riots of the eighteenth century. It begins with the first national wave of food riots in 1740 and ends with the catastrophic subsistence crisis of 1800–1.[82] In so doing, it shows that, against official discourses which recognised the hunger of the poor, most protests – and increasingly so over time – resorted to what I label the discourse of starvation. Indeed, the discourse of hunger was rather different, an almost polite, imploring language that spoke deferentially of need, and thus was used in Thompsonian moral-economy 'negotiations' between poor consumers and patrician rulers. Conversely, the discourse of starvation was much more muscular, a deliberately provocative and often viscerally violent threat, an attempt to emphatically assert their right to immediate redress: if you do not act we will act, for we will not let you starve us. In the crises of the 1790s and early 1800s this discourse was increasingly taken up by the radical cause, while, in turn, the language of radicalism increasingly bled into the protest practices and claims of food rioters, not least in terms of the frequency of the claim that protestors would rather starve than submit to tyranny.

The bitter repression of the subsistence protests of the 1790s and early 1800s supposedly led to the end of the of the food rioting tradition, with the fear generated by the trials and hangings combined with the militarised landscapes of Britain during the Napoleonic Wars supposedly extinguishing whatever will was left to openly resist. Poor consumers either now supported by the extension of support (for which see chapter three) or turned to the tools of terror – incendiarism, animal maiming and the sending of threatening letters – to protest their lot. At the same time, wages replaced the price of basic foodstuffs as the critical component in working families' living standards. Not until the 'Hungry Forties' was hunger 'rediscovered'. The 'struggle over the representation of scarcity', as Gurney has put it, was particularly acute in both the politicking of Chartism and the Anti–Corn Law League, but even this failed to truly penetrate the countryside.[83] Chapter two questions this neat teleology, and instead details the ways in which the twin discourses of hunger and (especially) starvation persisted beyond 1801 and into the 1840s. In so doing it analyses the claims made in threatening letters, legal defences, claims made to (and quarrels with) poor law officials, as well as in popular political forms including speeches, broadsides and ballads, and political journalism, not least the writings of that most prolific of radical political proselytisers William Cobbett. It shows that in a variety of contexts and in multiple forms, the articulation of hunger continued to be a central protest discourse of the poor, ultimately underpinning, whether implicitly or explicitly, all forms of protest. Moreover, as the analysis of radical writings shows, this was not something confined to the protests of the poor themselves, but also remained a critical discourse especially amongst agrarian political writers, before assuming wider popular political prominence as Chartist speakers and writers reanimated the politics of hunger. Indeed, protests in industrial and urban England in the 1840s continued to draw on this discourse and on this deep agrarian well of resistance. The issue of food thus provided a material and symbolic bridge between the city and the rural.

Social policy responses to the crises of the 1790s – and to the mass un- and under-employment of labouring families that overwhelmed the agrarian south and east on the end of the Napoleonic Wars – are supposedly so well understood that the 'Speenhamland story' of the introduction of de facto income support looms large over all our understandings of the histories of social welfare and remains a haunting presence in welfare debates in the neoliberal age.[84] Further, what was a response to a problem of the English cornlands had universal material and political effects, from Speenhamland to Sheffield, Stoke and Sunderland, if you will. But while the impact of such schemes has been the subject of scrutiny ever since – from Malthus' critique that they offered 'a direct, constant, and systemical encouragement to marriage' to more recent declamations by neoliberal politicians – the actual mechanisms and subsequent history of 'bread scales' remain little understood, while the history of the application of policy responses to hunger in rural England has been subject to remarkably little systematic scrutiny. Chapter three returns to the intentions and considers these histories. It starts from the understanding that the original intention of the Berkshire magistrates, as well as those elsewhere who quickly adopted similar policy prescriptions, were simple: to alleviate hunger and distress, and thus prevent riot and the destruction of property, the poor needed support depending on the price of bread, with the development of 'bread scales' as a deviation from casual relief to systematised, measured support. The analysis shows that there was not one Speenhamland scale but many Speenhamland-style scales, a variety of formal, semi-formal and ad hoc income support schemes. Subsequent perversions of the initial intentions behind Speenhamland-type payments meant that all agrarian workers became pauperised. Farmers, mindful that the parish would supplement working incomes, cut wages, thereby making need universal. This acted to further politicise poor law provision: in turn, plebeian poor law protests increasingly drew on the discourse of starvation. The further effect of making need universal, so this chapter argues, was that counter-intuitively the system required new modes of surveillance, as the vestry and the overseer(s) initially needed to know about the population of the parish. And as the costs of such schemes became a major burden on ratepayers, so parish officers needed to know about the circumstances of all poor families.[85] This is not to say that parish surveillance was a new phenomenon – it was arguably as old as the poor law itself – but rather that the value judgements made were now based on magistrates and parish officers devising universal *measures* of need. Hunger was now measured and quantified, the poor rendered as an undifferentiated *body*.

Chapter four extends this argument to think about the ways in which the imperative to define and measure informed the shaping and making of the Poor Law Amendment Act of 1834 (aka the New Poor Law) in the form of workhouse dietaries. By dictating what the poor ate, as opposed to what they might eat, it is argued that workhouse dietaries established an absolute biological minimum for bodily survival decided by individual poor law unions within perimeters set by the central state through the Poor Law Commission/Board. As is well known, such dietaries had profound consequences, in terms both of driving popular revulsion of the workhouse and high-profile scandals: for example, the publicising of inmates at the Andover workhouse notoriously gnawing at green bones to supplement their diets led to the replacement of the Poor Law Commission with the Poor Law Board. While the implications of workhouse dietaries have been subject to careful study, not least through the study of workhouse scandals, this chapter takes a broader perspective. It examines the makings of the idea of the dietary, analysing debates and discussion concerning both the physiological and practical science of pauper diet. In so doing, it analyses antecedents operated by separate parishes and pre-1834 poor law unions, before going on to explore the implementation of workhouse dietaries in the new centrally controlled but still locally operated system. It shows that this tension between the ideals of Somerset House – the administrative heart of the New Poor Law – and individual Boards of Guardians, who were almost invariably concerned more by economy and the politics of local provisioning, led to constant revisions and the refining of the model. The chapter also analyses the critiques of the system, exploring both the centrality of critiques to the politicking of radical politicians and to the rise of a particular type of humanitarianism, a concern with the bodily welfare of the poor that mirrored parallel movements over slavery and working conditions in factories and mines.

If chapters three and four analyse the practical politics and science of managing hungry bodies, the penultimate chapter takes a different approach by considering the ways in which hunger was made and used. It argues that by reducing working bodies to, as Giorgio Agamben conceived it, 'bare life', workhouse dietaries can be usefully understood as part of a wider shift of what Foucault labelled biopolitics, a 'new' technique of government that as its primary political strategy sought to administer 'the basic biological features of the human species'.[86] If the dietary was one of 'an explosion of numerous and diverse techniques for achieving the subjugation of bodies and the control of populations',[87] it is was of particular importance in the context of Britain – and therefore the wider British Empire – both because of its scope and because it built upon an established critique of the workings of the pre-1834 poor laws. In particular, the influence of the claim made by Rev. Thomas Malthus in his *Essay on the Principle of Population* (first published in 1798) that Speenhamland-style payments 'afford[ed] a direct, constant and systematical encouragement to marriage, by removing from each individual that heavy responsibility … for bringing beings into the world which he could not support' was especially profound.[88] Malthus' ideas were written into the very fabric of the New Poor Law, both literally in terms of separate male and female wards and figuratively in terms of practising 'bare life'. Twelve years prior to the publication of Malthus' *Essay*, Joseph Townsend in his *Dissertation on the Poor Law* had made the link even more explicit: 'Hunger will tame the fiercest animals, it will teach decency and civility, obedience and subjection, to the most perverse. In general it is only hunger which can spur and goad them [the poor] on to labour; yet our laws have said they shall never hunger.'[89] This went beyond metaphor: the poor, in Townsend's conception, were *actually* beasts. Chapter five explores the genealogy of these intellectual and ideological understandings of bodily need and hunger, ideas that underpinned the systems analysed in chapters three and four. In so doing, it argues that this emergence was informed by, and a counterpart to, the racialisation of 'the poor', the process whereby working people, especially agricultural workers, were conceived and referred to as a distinct and decidedly animalistic race. By conceiving of the poor as a separate race, New Poor Law administrators and others were given moral consent to control the bodies of claimants, to experiment with forms of bodily control and the negation of individual agency in the making of new subjects. None of this is to say that effects of this racialisation for English labourers were the same as for black colonial subjects – the racisms were necessarily different, and the violence modulated in comparison to the total denial of rights that enslavement entailed, something in itself that fed the rise of what Ryan Hanley has called working-class racism[90] – but, rather, that 'the great chain of being' had further sub-divisions.

Theorising hunger was not, so chapter six argues, something only possible through experience and mobilised only through developing new forms of control, but also something understood and mediated through the plight of distant others. In particular, the devastating famine in late 1840s Ireland was critical in shaping political languages of hunger in the Empire as a whole as well as amongst the peoples of Britain. This chapter does not explore the central governmental response to these famines – though this provides a critical context – but instead examines popular responses to the hunger of others in the 1840s. Distance here is conceived as not only those subjects of Empire in Ireland (and beyond), but also the responses of those in metropolitan and southern England to the privations of industrial workers and the Scottish rural poor in the 'Hungry Forties'. In so doing, the chapter examines the discourses of response (and how these helped to shape understandings of hunger) as well as schemes to relieve famine and the distant hungry. It is argued that against the ideologically driven official governmental responses to these different famines, those who were only one act of misfortune away from being incarcerated in the workhouse and only one or two generations away from experiencing absolute hunger were quick to respond by setting up collections and relief schemes. We see in such responses, the chapter goes on to argue, an extension of the protest discourses of hunger explored in chapter two, the popular cultural potency of the fear of hunger reinvigorated by 'bare life' workhouse regimes. The chapter also asserts that such relief schemes mirrored the political critiques of domestic and imperial food policy issued by Chartist thinkers. Hunger, in this way, was understood relationally, as something mediated not just by individual experience but also through the experiences of *imagined* others. This is not to deny the absolute privations and sufferings that were all too real to many English workers in the 1840s. Rather it is to acknowledge that the popular politics of hunger were not bound by the body or borders but were rooted in the uneven contours of solidarity and reciprocity. Nor is it to claim that this was something universal. It was not. 'Shared' experiences underpinned empathy for some people in some places, but did not absolutely break down an entrenched culture of xenophobia: attacks on Irish migrant workers remained a dismal part of working life in rural England.

It is important to note that, in short, this is not just a book about eighteenth- and early nineteenth-century England. As the conclusion asserts, it is a book that speaks directly to the hunger politics of early twenty-first-century England and beyond. If the threat of famine lifted from the peoples of England, the threat of hunger never did. We live in age of profound hunger, an age where an ever-increasing proportion of the population is reliant on food banks and other forms of charitable and third-sector support to simply subsist. The inadequacy of incomes to meet basic living costs, the slow withdrawal of the state from providing a basic safety net of support for those living on the breadline, the structural denial of support from the state for those who do not meet punitive criteria or who are otherwise hidden from the purview of the state, all have striking parallels with the desperate politics of Hanoverian England. For the less eligibility workhouse read universal credit, for the charitable subscription read the food bank, for the cries of hunger read the cries of hunger. For the indigent and feckless of the early nineteenth century read the beggars and work-shy scroungers of Tory Britain today. Hunger was, and remains, the cruellest pillar of policy.

Notes

1 L. Scholl, *Hunger Movements in Early Victorian Literature: Want, Riots, Migration* (London: Routledge, 2016).
2 G. Alfani and C. Ó Gráda, 'Famines in Europe: An overview', in G. Alfani and C. Ó Gráda (eds), *Famine: A European History* (Cambridge: Cambridge University Press, 2017), pp. 1, 11.

3 C. Ó Gráda, *Famine: A Short History* (Princeton, NJ: Princeton University Press, 2009), pp. 4–5.
4 R. Wells, *Wretched Faces: Famine in Wartime England 1793–1803* (Stroud: Alan Sutton, 1988); Adrian Randall, *Riotous Assemblies: Popular Protest in Hanoverian England* (Oxford: Oxford University Press, 2006).
5 E. Griffin, 'Diets, hunger and living standards during the British Industrial Revolution', *Past & Present*, 239 (2018), 92–4.
6 For the classic account see Wells, *Wretched Faces*.
7 S. Broadberry, B. Campbell, A. Klein, M. Overton, and B. van Leeuwen, 'Clark's Malthus delusion: Response to "Farming in England 1200–1800"', *Economic History Review*, 71:2 (2018), 639–64.
8 R. Mayhew, *The Life and Legacies of an Untimely Prophet* (Cambridge, MA: The Belknap Press of Harvard University Press, 2014).
9 P. Gurney, '"Rejoicing in potatoes": The politics of consumption in England during the "Hungry Forties"', *Past & Present*, 203 (2009), 99–136.
10 A. Sen, *Poverty and Famines: An Essay on Entitlement and Deprivation* (Oxford: Oxford University Press, 1982).
11 J. Healey, 'Famine and the female mortality advantage: Sex, gender and mortality in northwest England, c. 1590–1630', *Continuity and Change*, 30:2 (2015), 153–92; B. Sharp, *Famine and Scarcity in Late Medieval and Early Modern England: The Regulation of Grain Marketing, 1256–1631* (Cambridge: Cambridge University Press, 2016); B. Campbell, 'The European mortality crises of 1346–52 and advent of the Little Ice Age', in D. Collet and M. Schuh (eds), *Famines during the 'Little Ice Age' (1300–1800)* (Cham: Springer, 2018), pp. 19–41.
12 J. Chartres, 'Market integration and agricultural output in seventeenth-, eighteenth-, and early nineteenth-century England', *Agricultural History Review*, 43:2 (1995), 117–38; S. King, *Poverty and Welfare in England, 1700–1850* (Manchester: Manchester University Press, 2000); J. Townsend, *A Dissertation on the Poor Laws: By a Well-wisher to Mankind*, ed. Ashley Montagu (Berkeley, CA: University of California Press, 1971), p. 23; K. Marx, *Capital, Volume One: A Critique of Political Economy*, trans. F. Engels, ed. Samuel Moore and Edward Aveling (New York: The Modern Library, 1906), p. 710.
13 J. Vernon, *Hunger: A Modern History* (Cambridge, MA: Harvard University Press, 2007), p. 17.
14 M. Barnett, *Empire of Humanity: A History of Humanitarianism* (Ithaca, NY: Cornell University Press, 2011). On the ways in which this influenced governance see: A. Lester and F. Dussart, *Colonization and the Origins of Humanitarian Governance: Protecting Aborigines across the Nineteenth-century British Empire* (Cambridge: Cambridge University Press, 2014).
15 Randall, *Riotous Assemblies*, esp. chs 4 and 5; E.P. Thompson, 'The moral economy of the English crowd in the eighteenth century', *Past & Present*, 50 (1971), 76–136.
16 Wells, *Wretched Faces*; J. Bohstedt, *The Politics of Provisions: Food Riots, Moral Economy, and Market Transition in England, c. 1550–1850* (Farnham: Ashgate, 2010).

17 R. Hoyle, 'Britain', in G. Alfani and Ó Gráda, *Famine: A European History* (Cambridge: Cambridge University Press, 2017), p. 141.

18 K. Wrightson, 'The enclosure of English social history', *Rural History*, 1:1 (1990), 73–82.

19 E.P. Thompson, 'The moral economy of the English crowd in the eighteenth century', *Past & Present*, 50 (1971), 76–136.

20 Notably Richard Hoyle, 'Britain', esp. pp. 141–65 and see the references in Hoyle, 'Britain', note 11.

21 For the most recent attempt at synthesis see: Bohstedt, *Politics of Provisions*.

22 P. Gurney, *Wanting and Having: Popular Politics and Liberal Consumerism in England, 1830–70* (Manchester: Manchester University Press, 2015).

23 Gurney, 'Rejoicing in potatoes'; Griffin, 'Diets'.

24 P. Laslett, *The World We Have Lost: England Before the Industrial Age* (New York: Scribner, 1971), pp. 107–27; D.E. Williams, 'Were "hunger rioters" really hungry? Some demographic evidence', *Past & Present*, 71 (1976), 70, 71 n.4; J. Burnett and P. Burnett, *Plenty and Want: A Social History of Food in England from 1815 to the Present* (London: Routledge, 1989).

25 On the latter point, for an initial examination of this dynamic in relation to animals see: C. Griffin, '"Some inhuman wretch": Animal maiming and the ambivalent relationship between rural workers and animals', *Rural History*, 25: 2 (2014), 133–60.

26 After D. Nally, *Human Encumbrances: Political Violence and the Great Irish Famine* (Notre Dame, IN: University of Notre Dame Press, 2011).

27 Wells, *Wretched Faces*.

28 See Gurney, 'Rejoicing in potatoes'; C. Boyce, 'Representing the "Hungry Forties" in image and verse: The politics of hunger in early-Victorian illustrated periodicals', *Victorian Literature and Culture*, 40:2 (2012), 421–49.

29 For instance, see J.P. Huzel, 'Malthus, the poor law, and population in early nineteenth-century England', *Economic History Review*, 22:3 (1969), 430–52; S. Williams, 'Malthus, marriage and poor law allowances revisited: A Bedfordshire case study, 1770–1834', *Agricultural History Review*, 52:1 (2004), 56–82.

30 Vernon, *Hunger*, pp. 2–3.

31 On these perceptions and cultural currents see: J. Burchardt, *Paradise Lost: Rural Idyll and Social Change since 1800* (London: I.B. Tauris, 2002); M. Cragoe and P. Readman (eds), *The Land Question in Britain, 1750–1950* (Basingstoke: Palgrave, 2010).

32 Vernon, *Hunger*, p. 1.

33 Ibid., pp. 3–4.

34 G. Clark, 'The agricultural revolution and the industrial revolution: England, 1500–1912', unpublished manuscript, Department of Economics, University of California, Davis (2002), p. 39.

35 K.D.M. Snell, *Annals of the Labouring Poor: Social Change and Agrarian England, 1660–1900* (Cambridge: Cambridge University Press, 1985); L. Schwarz, 'Custom, wages and workload in England during industrialization', *Past & Present*, 197 (2007), 147. A shift from the 1720s away

from paying by the piece to time-regulated day labour was also a factor in increasing wage rates: A. Hann, 'Kinship and exchange relations within an estate economy: Ditchley, 1680–1750' (DPhil thesis, University of Oxford, 1999).

36 J. Rule, *The Experience of Labour in Eighteenth Century England* (London: Croom Helm, 1981), p. 69.

37 Griffin, 'Diets', 72.

38 C. Feinstein, 'Pessimism perpetuated: Real wages and the standard of living in Britain during and after the industrial revolution', *Journal of Economic History*, 58 (1998), 625–58; G. Clark, 'Farm wages and living standards in the industrial revolution: England, 1670–1869', *Economic History Review*, 54:3 (2001), 477–505; C. Clark, 'The condition of the working class in England, 1209–2004', *Journal of Political Economy*, 113:6 (2005), 1307–40. For an important counter perspective see: J. Humphries, 'Childhood and child labour in the British industrial revolution', *Economic History Review*, 66:2 (2013), 395–418.

39 C. Muldrew, *Food, Energy and the Creation of Industriousness: Work and Material Culture in Agrarian England, 1550–1780* (Cambridge: Cambridge University Press, 2011); R. Floud, R.W. Fogel, B. Harris and S.C. Hong, *The Changing Body: Health, Nutrition, and Human Development in the Western World since 1700* (Cambridge: Cambridge University Press, 2011); M. Kelly and C. Ó Gráda, 'Numerare est errare: Agricultural output and food supply in England before and during the Industrial Revolution', *Journal of Economic History*, 73:4 (2013), 1132–63; D. Meredith and D. Oxley, 'Food and fodder: Feeding England, 1700–1900', *Past & Present*, 222 (2013), 163–214; B. Harris, R. Floud and S.C. Hong, 'How many calories? Food availability in England and Wales in the eighteenth and nineteenth centuries', *Research in Economic History*, 31 (2015), 111–91.

40 On these dynamics see C. Griffin, *Protest, Politics and Work in Rural England, 1700–1850* (Basingstoke: Palgrave, 2014), pp. 17–34.

41 J. Humphries, 'Enclosures, common rights, and women: The proletarianization of families in the late eighteenth and early nineteenth centuries', *Journal of Economic History*, 50:1 (1990), 19.

42 S. Hindle, 'Power, poor relief, and social relations in Holland Fen, c. 1600–1800', *Historical Journal*, 41:1 (1998), 85.

43 D. Stead, 'Delegated risk in English agriculture, 1750–1850: The labour market', *Labour History Review*, 71:2 (2006), 123–44; Snell, *Annals of the Labouring Poor*, pp. 20–1 and 74–5.

44 I. Gazeley and N. Verdon, 'The first poverty line? Davies' and Eden's investigation of rural poverty in the late 18th-century England', *Explorations in Economic History*, 51 (2014), 94–108.

45 Griffin, 'Diets', 109.

46 T.L. Richardson, 'The agricultural labourers' standard of living in Lincolnshire, 1790–1840: Social protest and public order', *Agricultural History Review*, 41:1 (1993), 1–19.

47 On this also see T.L. Richardson, 'Agricultural labourers' wages and the cost of living in Essex, 1790–1840: A contribution to the standard of living debate',

in B.A. Holderness and M. Turner (eds), *Land, Labour and Agriculture, 1700–1920: Essays for Gordon Mingay* (London: Hambledon Press, 1991), pp. 69–90; R. Wells, 'Social protest, class, conflict and consciousness, in the English countryside, 1700–1880', in M. Reed and R. Wells (eds), *Class, Conflict and Protest in the English Countryside, 1700–1880* (London: Frank Cass, 1990), pp. 121–98.

48 Notably Floud, Fogel, Harris and Hong, *The Changing Body*, and Harris, Floud and Hong, 'How many calories?'

49 G. Alfani, L. Mocarelli and D. Strangio, 'Italy', p. 26; V. Pérez Moreda, 'Spain', p. 52; D. Collet and D. Krämer, 'Germany, Switzerland and Austria', p. 111; S. Wheatcroft, 'Eastern Europe (Russia and the USSR)', pp. 218, 219, all in Alfani and Ó Gráda, *Famine: A European History*; Ó Gráda, *Famine: A Short History*, pp. 5, 6, 52, 111, 121, 218, 278.

50 S. Williams, *Poverty, Gender and the Lifecycle Under the English Poor Law* (Woodbridge: Boydell and Brewer, 2011).

51 J. Huzel, *The Popularization of Malthus in Early Nineteenth-Century England: Martineau, Cobbett and the Pauper Press* (Farnham: Ashgate, 2006), esp. pp. 47 n.51, 60, 110, 177, 183.

52 Griffin, 'Diets'.

53 Vernon, *Hunger*, pp. 2–3.

54 Gurney, *Wanting and Having*, p. 17.

55 F. Bacon, *The Works of Francis Bacon, Baron of Verulam, Viscount St. Alban, and Lord High Chancellor of England* (London: C. and J. Rivington, 1826). On the timing of Bacon's essay see: S. Hindle, 'Imagining insurrection in seventeenth-century England: representations of the Midland Rising of 1607', *History Workshop Journal*, 66 (2008), 37 and 57, n.101.

56 Contrast Hindle's reading with that of R.W.K. Hinton, who claimed that Bacon's essay represented 'a prescription for ensuring subjection': 'The mercantile system in the time of Thomas Mun', *Economic History Review*, New Series, 7:3 (1955), 281.

57 Bacon, *The Works*, p. 277.

58 Ibid., pp. 276–7.

59 Hindle, 'Imagining insurrection', p. 37.

60 J. Thelwall, *The Tribune: A Periodical Publication, Consisting Chiefly of the Political Lectures of John Thelwall* (London: self-published, 1795), p. 313.

61 T. Doubleday, *On Mundane Moral Government Demonstrating Its Analogy with the System of Material Government* (London: Blackwood, 1852).

62 D.G. Barnes, *A History of the English Corn Laws, 1660–1846* (London: Routledge, 1930), pp. xiv–xv.

63 T.S. Ashton and J. Sykes, *The Coal Industry of the Eighteenth Century* (Manchester: Manchester University Press, 1929), pp. 126, 131.

64 Thompson, 'The moral economy', 77.

65 W.W. Rostow, *The British Economy in the Nineteenth Century* (Oxford: Oxford University Press, 1948), esp. pp. 122–5.

66 F.O. Darvall, *Popular Disturbances and Public Order in Regency England* (Oxford: Oxford University Press, 1969, first published 1934), esp. pp. 95–100; M. Beloff, *Public Order and Popular Disturbances, 1660–1714* (Oxford: Oxford University Press, 1938), esp. pp. 61–70.

67 G. Rudé, 'The London 'mob' of the eighteenth century', *Historical Journal*, 2:1 (1959), 7; E. Hobsbawm, 'The machine-breakers', *Past & Present*, 1 (1952), 59.

68 L. Stone, *The Causes of the English Revolution, 1529–1642* (New York: Harper & Row, 1972); B. Sharp, 'The place of the people in the English Revolution', *Theory and Society*, 14:1 (1985), 76–7.

69 R.B. Rose, 'Eighteenth-century price riots and public policy in England', *International Review of Social History*, 4:2 (1961), 277–92.

70 Thompson, 'Moral economy', 78, 79.

71 Ibid., 78–9.

72 Ibid., 78.

73 Ibid., 77, 79.

74 Williams, 'Were "hunger" rioters really hungry?', 70, 71 n.4.

75 Ibid., 74, 75.

76 D.E. Williams, 'Morals, markets and the English crowd in 1766', *Past & Present*, 104 (1984), 68–9.

77 E.P. Thompson, *Customs in Common* (London: Merlin Press, 1991), pp. 266–8; A. Charlesworth and A. Randall, 'Morals, markets and the English crowd in 1766', *Past & Present*, 114 (1987): 200–13.

78 J. Archer, *Social Unrest and Popular Protest in England, 1780–1840* (Cambridge: Cambridge University Press, 2000), pp. 30–1.

79 Bohstedt, *The Politics of Provisions*, p. 1.

80 Ibid.; Wells, *Wretched Faces*, ch. 1.

81 On this see P.H. Lindert and J.G. Williamson, 'English workers' living standards during the industrial revolution: A new look', *Economic History Review* 36:1 (1983), 1–25. The same dynamic is also evident in the otherwise more socially and culturally sophisticated study by Ian Gazeley and Nicola Verdon: 'The first poverty line?'.

82 Thompson, 'Moral economy', 71.

83 Gurney, 'Rejoicing in potatoes'; R. Wells, 'Southern Chartism', *Rural History*, 2:1 (1991), 37–59; M. Chase, *Chartism: A New History* (Manchester: Manchester University Press, 2007), pp. 99, 204.

84 On this point see F. Block and M. Somers, 'In the shadow of Speenhamland: social policy and the old poor law', *Politics & Society*, 31:2 (2003), 283–323.

85 On this dynamic see S. Shave, 'The impact of Sturges Bourne's poor law reforms in rural England', *Historical Journal*, 56:2 (2013), 399–429.

86 G. Agamben, *Homo Sacer: Sovereign Power and Bare Life*, trans. D. Heller-Roazen (Stanford, CA: Stanford University Press, 1998); M. Foucault, *Security, Territory, Population: Lectures at the Collège de France, 1977–78*, trans. G. Burchell (Basingstoke: Palgrave, 2007), p. 1.

87 M. Foucault, *The Will to Knowledge: The History of Sexuality Volume 1*, trans. R. Hurley (London: Penguin, 1998), p. 140.

88 T. Malthus, *An Essay on the Principle of Population*, vol. 2, ed. P. James (Cambridge: Cambridge University Press, 1989), p. 120.

89 Townsend, *Dissertation on the Poor Law*, p. 27.

90 R. Hanley, 'Slavery and the birth of working-class racism in England, 1814–1833', *Transactions of the Royal Historical Society*, 26 (2016), 103–23.

Part I

Protesting hunger

1

Food riots and the languages of hunger

Were hunger rioters really hungry? The question, as the introduction details, has framed so much scholarship on food rioting that the importance of hunger has, paradoxically, been all but ignored. Invariably initial work on food riots was dominated by essentially causal analyses: immediate bodily need, high prices. Hunger figures here, but rather than asking how hungry people act and how the fear of hunger, of absolute bodily need, makes people act, hunger is relegated to a stimulus that provokes a reflex response. Likewise, work inspired by E.P. Thompson's now famous paper delineating the 'moral economy' of the English 'crowd' has tended to ignore – though the following section examines the nuances in this work – hunger altogether, focusing instead on the values and politics that underlay popular action. This chapter seeks to redress this imbalance, this lacuna. Rather than questioning the nutritional deficiencies of subsistence protestors or asking what hungry people do, it asks how hunger as an idea, a discourse, was mobilised by poor consumers and the rulers of Britain alike. It considers the ways in which the food rioting tradition might usefully be understood not only as an expression of popular understandings of economics and social reciprocity but also as a practical politics of fending off the threat of hunger. Before analysing the way in which hunger was related and mobilised during the subsistence crises between the first national wave of food rioting in 1740 and the supposed end of the tradition with the 1800–1 riots, the chapter starts with a short consideration of the ways in which hunger has been written in work on food rioting since the publication of Thompson's essay.

The one study clearly located in the Thompsonian approach that has carefully considered the importance of absolute bodily need is Roger Wells' magisterial analysis of the food crises of the 1790s, *Wretched Faces*. The issue is, as Wells saw it, that the 'long secular decline' of real wages from the mid-eighteenth century for groups like metropolitan and market-town artisans and agricultural workers meant that on any calculation the majority of the population could not even meet a subsistence diet against the 'mammoth increases in food prices'. This was compounded by other factors. War funding, credit inflation affected by the huge increase in government borrowing, and inflationary fiscal measures triggered 'general inflation' in the 1790s. The subsistence crises in themselves precipitated recessions in the textile industries, already in an economically pre-carious state due to the loss of export markets. This in turn led to widespread, if localised, unemployment, which added to the ranks of other labourers out of work due to the collapse in demand for casual labour.[1]

Given that the grain supply was complex, easy to manipulate, and fra-gile, the response to mammoth increase in prices was necessarily 'famine conditions and famine responses'.[2] Building upon Oddy's typology of famine, Wells usefully asserted that famine was not synonymous with 'deaths with starvation itself' but rather increased levels of mortality 'owing to hunger-related disease'.[3] This was a feature of both the crises of 1794–6 and, espe-cially, 1799–1801, something the Rev. Malthus commented on in the second edition of his *Essay on the Principle of Population* (1803) by noting the 'change witnessed in mortality of late years' in comparison to the absence of 'extra-ordinary mortality' in England since 1700. 1799–1801 represented, Wells posited, a genuine Malthusian check.[4] While this was regionally variable due to differing degrees of fragility in supply between the cornlands and con-sumption centres – the south-west of England being particularly exposed during the 'hypercrisis' of 1799–1801, with even the producing parishes' supplies exhausted by March 1800 – it was a universal problem that 'popu-lation growth had outstripped agrarian productive capacity'.[5] The evidence showed, Wells concluded, that historians had 'exude[d] a cavalier attitude to subsistence problems in the age of industrial revolution'. The protests of the late eighteenth century were not just reactions to, as John Stevenson had put it, 'distress' but reactions to famine.[6]

Notwithstanding John Archer's assessment that Wells' study was 'defini-tive' in its coverage of the food crises of the 1790s,[7] the wider reception for *Wretched Faces*, while universal in praising Wells' archival industry, ultimately rested on Wells' definition and reading of famine. Michael Turner in his review for *Social History* sums up the theme: 'On the Richter look-a-like measurement of famines this period hardly registers at all.' There were famine conditions but 'these were not allowed to mature', so the issue of famine was an 'unneces-sary diversion' which 'obscure[d] the real trauma of that eventful decade'.[8] The issue is thus one of definition and comparison, the argument being in essence that because there were not the levels of 'excess' mortality witnessed in Ireland in the 1840s, Oddy and Wells' relativist definitions were redundant. The problem runs deep. Historians have been loath to describe even the sub-sistence crisis of 1727–30, the second worst mortality crisis between 1541 and 1871 according to Wrigley and Schofield in *The Population History of England*,[9] as a famine: Jonathan Healey asserted that 'The 1720s crisis was not a famine, not in any straightforward sense anyway'.[10]

Debates over the meanings of famine are, of course, vital for placing historical catastrophes and political violence into wider historical and geographical context, but they are unhelpful here. In much the same way that Sir Francis Bacon's analysis – as considered in the introduction – has been taken out of context and reappropriated in contrary ways to render the analysis of popular responses to dearth a matter of biological reflex alone, so the debate over Wells' (and thus Oddy's) definitions and theorisations has acted to obscure Wells' re-emphasis of the importance of understanding hunger and absolute need. Indeed, whatever the response to *Wretched Faces*, the impact of Wells' critical emphasis on hunger was initially mute. This is not to say that studies in the 1990s altogether ignored hunger – or denied its importance; rather, it was again relegated either to a historiographical quirk or something mentioned *en passant*, a matter for footnotes rather than a subject of analysis. For instance, in the text of Adrian Randall's pioneering *Before the Luddites*, hunger appeared either in relation to pre-existing causal understandings of machine-breaking, regarding misreadings of Thompson's moral-economy thesis, or in relation to the ideology of 1790s radicalism.[11]

More recent studies denote a slight shift. Bohstedt's *The Politics of Provisions* places the politics of attempting to secure 'sustenance' at the centre of its analysis, but while the sustained emphasis on hunger is invariably in relation to his historiographical readings and the problem of acute hunger in the early modern period, there are suggestions thereafter of a more complex understanding of hunger. Thus riotous crowds in 1740 used the fear of hunger to publicly legitimise their actions, and in the Black Country during the 1795 crisis a large crowd of women 'cursed' a miller for their children's hunger while a 'radical handbill' protested 'the cruel oppressions of your wicked rulers, whose intentions are to starve us to death'. Together, such cases were evidence that 'hunger [was] woven into reveries of rebellion', 'feelings of hunger and feelings of justice meet[ing] in the gut'.[12] Katrina Navickas, in her study of protest in Lancashire between 1798 and 1815, also notes that the period was marked by both the fear of starvation and what was understood by some members of the authorities to be actual starvation.[13]

Randall's *Riotous Assemblies* offers a similar set of reflections. Anti-Irish riots in London in July 1736 were in part motivated by 'starving' English manufacturers undercut by their Irish brethren, while the revival of the Assize of Bread and other regulations in the early eighteenth century was a response to the understanding that 'hungry Englishmen did not simply sit down and starve. They rioted.' And so on. It is telling that Randall, in addition to adducing several examples of food rioters making claims to starvation, concludes that food rioters were not motivated by a 'desire to cleanse the morals of the market-makers but by the fear of starvation'.[14] Ultimately, he notes, starving people do not riot, for 'they do not have the energy'. Food riots were pre-emptive of starvation, not the consequence.[15] But as a report in the London press put it in relation to the subsistence crisis of 1766, 'Hunger will break through stone walls.'[16]

We might usefully claim, therefore, that however full the bellies of food rioters and those of their kin and communities, the threat and thus the mobilisation of the idea of hunger mattered. But this discourse has not been, as the above examples attest, subject to systematic analysis. Indeed, given the uneasy relationship between historians of the food riot and the word hunger, the relationship has never been explicitly asserted, let alone explored. What follows in the rest of this chapter (and the chapter that follows) attempts to redress this balance. In so doing, it also explores the ways in which the idea of hunger – and especially the supposed absence of hunger – was used by the rulers of Hanoverian England to deny agency and legitimacy to the protesting crowd, and thus as a way of undermining the shared compact of the moral economy.

The uses of hunger

'A mob, which is generally the growth of a redundant population, goaded by resentment for real sufferings, but totally ignorant of the quarter from which they originate, is of all monsters the most fatal to freedom.'

Malthus, *Essay*, 1803[17]

By the early years of the nineteenth century hunger was something that afflicted the other peoples of the world, not the freeborn English. The pages of the provincial press were littered with accounts of the famished French, ravenous Prussians and half-starved Indians, while reporting of seemingly perpetual famine in Ireland solidified in the trope of the starving Irish peasant.[18] A century of agricultural improvement and industrial development had, so the discourse went, lifted Britons out of hunger's grasp. Or so the story goes. As James Vernon has put it, hunger was now portrayed as a seventeenth-century problem, something of the past.[19] Of course, making claims about distant others was as much about imperial positioning, British progress and progressivism against foreign backwardness and political venality, as it was about reflecting the lived realities of Britons. Still, the discourse was remarkably potent in denying public agency to working people. Food riots were increasingly reported not as the actions of the hungry unable to secure fair-quality food at a fair price but instead as the actions of the lawless and feckless, and those led astray by demagogues. And yet 1800 witnessed what was arguably the most severe subsistence crisis since 1766, while the 1790s had seen an unprecedented expansion in the net of institutionalised welfare in the cornlands in the form of Speenhamland-style income subsidies in direct response to the threat of hunger.[20]

Beyond rhetoric, hunger, absolute bodily need, was real enough for many working families. Hunger, as working-class diaries and memoirs tell us, was as English as plum pudding.[21] Beyond periods of actual hunger, absolute bodily need was a constant spectral presence, a mortal fear for most working men and women who were never more than a few days away from not being able to feed their families. To the rich, hunger politics in the eighteenth century had many complex facets and meanings – e.g. eating disorders as depicted in Samuel Richardson's mid-eighteenth-century *Clarissa*,[22] or the hunger for the exotic and luxurious[23] – while also remaining a constant fear as a possible trigger for disorder and sedition amongst the poor. The regular and conscious setting of the assize in most big towns in the eighteenth century was not only motivated by moral economy virtues but also betrayed the fear of, as Randall puts it, 'hungry and angry mobs on the rampage'. This fear was the motivation for the particularly tight regulation of the assize in London.[24]

There was not only a distinction between hunger as a multilayered set of meanings, but also, at least in some contexts, a difference between hunger and starvation as public discourses. Indeed, beyond Vernon's assertion, it is possible to delineate a precise difference between the public meaning of hunger and that of starvation. In essence, hunger lacked starving's hard political edge and association of critique. Indeed, if starvation was a marker of incivility, hunger had functions. As the words of Proverbs 16:26 put it, 'The labourer's appetite works for him; his hunger drives him on.' Beyond labouring members of the community being reminded of this in readings and sermons at church, the moral was important in underpinning social relations and social policy. As the geologist vicar of the Wiltshire parish of Pewsey Joseph Townsend proclaimed in 1786, hunger 'will … teach decency and civility, obedience and subjection, to the most brutish, the most obstinate, and the most perverse'.[25] The Elizabethan poor law, it is important to remember, also embraced the biblical moral. It never intended to eliminate poverty, for poverty and hunger were seen as, in the words of Lyn Hollen Lees, a 'desirable part of the social order'.[26]

Either way, the mobilisation of the terms hunger and starvation had political potency. One way in which this played out was by (unwarranted) representations made on behalf of the poor. During the grain crisis of 1766 both taxation and export bounties provoked public criticism amidst claims that the poor were hungry and that their hunger would have consequences. To 'the Northamptonshire Freeholder', a de facto columnist in the *Derby Mercury*, the continuation of export bounties during the crisis was not just an abdication of responsibility to the poor but also an act to actively keep them hungry, the price of corn already being high enough that notwithstanding their 'utmost industry' it was impossible to 'earn enough to supply their Families with bread'. Such acts meant that the 'Blessings of Providence' were 'counteracted by corrupt, selfish, and wicked men'. If this was really a critique of enclosure, the consolidation of farms and the shift to rearing mutton and beef – by 'over-grown tenants and monopolizing Villains' – the language of the threats of hunger was clear enough.[27] Indiscriminately, an editorial in *Lloyd's Evening Post* proclaimed that all farmers were at the heart of the problem by 'almost starving them [the poor], tho' in the midst of plenty'.

The consequences would soon be, they continued, that the lack of provisions would provoke riots '[and] what is worse than a hungry and enraged mob?'[28]

The alleged causes were many and the solutions diverse, but what mattered in such pleas was a clear understanding that in the public mind (of the middle and ruling classes) claims to hunger and starvation directly equated to the fear of violence and rebellion. This public discourse clearly stretched back to Bacon's 'seditions' and meant that claims by poor consumers to hunger and starvation alike hit a raw nerve amongst the producers, processers, middle men, clergy, magistracy, gentry and nobility. This was, as the following sections attest, a dynamic in the model of the moral economy. In making claims to hunger and starvation there was a complex interplay, much like the moral economy, that was understood by both sides. Poor consumers mobilised the fear of hunger as likely to have mortal consequences for not only themselves but also the rich; the rich acted preemptively in the provision of emergency relief funds by subscription and extended new forms of relief (and surveillance), a theme taken up in chapter three.

1740: 'Better to be killed or hanged than starve'

As Bohstedt has put it, the food rioting 'tradition' was invented in 1740. There had been food riots before, two centuries of food riots no less, claims Bohstedt, but 1740 witnessed the first national wave of rioting. It also marked the emergence of a repertoire of actions and claims that would stabilise in the period up to 1766 rather than repetition of the 'hoary tradition' that preceded. Before this 'formative period', food riots were scattered, both geographically and temporally, and were played out without both the collective bargaining by riot script, and what Andrew Charlesworth has labelled the 'stately gavotte' of choreographed actions of rioters, retailers, dealers and the authorities alike.[29] While claims for a deeper genealogy of the emergence of the moral economy are many,[30] it is, so reckoned Bohstedt, the constant repetition of claims and actions in the food riots of 1740 (and again in 1757 and 1766) that marks the period out as important. Further evidence for the roots of the tradition emerging in the mid-eighteenth century, as Bohstedt sees it, is provided by the fact that after the particularly muscular crowd actions of many of the 45 riots that he has uncovered for 1740, later riots assumed a more 'stately' form.[31]

Central to this assertiveness was a particular emphasis on preventing the export of food as well as the taking – and destruction – of food as justified by claims to starvation. As Randall has asserted, starving people do not destroy food, nor do they riot for they do not have the energy,[32] yet the *discourse* of starvation was central to the riots of 1740 and built upon earlier claims. A wave of food riots in the winter of 1727 centred around Falmouth in Cornwall was precipitated by claims amongst the tinners that they starving, though the Cornish authorities were quick to counter that 'most of those who carried off corn' were well fed.[33] In 1740 the discourse centred on claims that poor consumers feared starvation and were likely to starve if they did not collectively act in their own interest. For instance, at Stockton-on-Tees in County Durham in May a group of women attacked a ship loaded with grain in an attempt to prevent its export, one part of three days of rioting against the export of corn. According to the reporting magistrate, the women 'swear they will dye before any corn shall be exported for that they had better be killed or hanged than starved'.[34]

This was, as Bohstedt has put it, the 'banner cry' of the English food rioter.[35] But it was not just rhetoric. It was both moral justification for riot and a deliberate attempt to provoke intervention by the authorities, to awaken their paternalist senses. The location of this riot is also telling, for Stockton falls into Bohstedt's category of new industrialising communities that had no prior tradition of riot, and where in 1740 both the rioters and the authorities made things up as they went along.[36] But the rioters' claim can be read as evidence that Thompson's moral economy was already alive and well understood in 1740. Or at least it was understood by the rioters, for their provocations bitterly lampooned military and judicial interventions, the very opposite of a functioning moral economy. It is also evidence that the discourse of starvation – claims to hunger not offering a brutal enough juxtaposition with death by dragoon's sabre or gallows – was a critical plank of the moral economy's invocation by poor consumers.

Similar threats and claims were articulated elsewhere during the 1740 crisis. On 21 May, a crowd of some 400 miners – men, women and children – descended on Rhuddlan, Flintshire, from the Mostyn and Bychton collieries and seized a waggon loaded with wheat bound for export. Having heard that corn had been 'stopped in other parts of England from being shipped off', they justified their actions by asserting that they were starving because corn was being sent to 'their enemies, the Spaniards', the war with Spain having started in October 1739. Here the claim that they 'would rather be hanged than starved' was joined by the declaration that they 'would choose to die fighting against them [the Spanish]'. After several further days of rioting (including at nearby Cwm, Trelawnyd, Rhyl, St Asaph and Prestatyn), the seizure of much corn, threats to murder merchant Colley and destroy his cattle, and to raise Rhuddlan to the ground, concessions were made. Four days after the anti-export protests had started, on Sunday 25 May the church bells rang to celebrate the Rhuddlan merchants' promise to end all corn exports.[37]

If the seizing of corn without payment ran counter to one of the central tenets of Thompson's moral economy – the payment of a 'fair' price – the destruction of food was a key feature of 1740. This took several forms resting on the tools of rural terror: incendiarism; animal maiming; and the issuing of malicious threats. Thus the threats to destroy eighteen of Colley's cattle at Rhuddlan, as with many cases of animal maiming, represented not only a clear enough case of targeting the merchants' fleshy capital but also a direct comment that if local working families could not eat the cattle then no one else should.[38] Similarly, at Blewbury in Berkshire, farmer Slade's corn barn was actually set on fire and destroyed. The destruction of corn either feared bound for export or hoarded became a major weapon of later subsistence crises.[39] This connection was made explicit through the actions of the colliers of Kingswood Chase, some four miles to the east of the city. Having pillaged granaries in Bristol in 1709, the Kingswood colliers were already notorious. When they again descended on the city in September 1740 to complain that while they ate well 'hundreds of poor families were starving around them', the mayor's promise that he would take care that he would 'have Justice done you' was no doubt motivated by their reputation. While they were intent 'to not hurt any Man' that day, this had not stopped them from having already threatened to plunder and destroy the premises of miller Read at Hanham. Likewise, other mills (and a dwelling house) had also been the subject of incendiary letters at nearby Bath.[40] Thus claims to starvation were met directly by threats and acts of destruction – including of food if it was not going to end up in the stomachs of local workers.

While seized food was rarely ruined – the riot at Newcastle on 25 June led to widespread damage in the town but not the destruction of food[41] – threats to destroy corn and foodstuffs bound for export were not uncommon. For instance at Colchester on 20 May, the several hundred people gathered 'under the Pretence of stopping Corn, Flower, &c. from being shipped to other Parts', as the *Colchester Journal* put it, stopped two wagons loaded with meal and threatened to destroy them. Only the intervention of a party of dragoons prevented the destruction and allowed the passage of the wagons, to be shipped from a vessel on the river at Hythe.[42]

The novelty of the experience of 1740 was, as noted, a function of the fact that the riots were a national phenomenon and the local experience, as evidenced by the Rhuddlan miners' talk of successes in England, was motivated by riot elsewhere. The centrality of the discourse of starvation as a justification for the seizing of corn and the prevention of exports was also striking if not novel, evidently building on earlier claims such as that uttered at Falmouth in 1727. Yet unlike in Cornwall in 1727, the reaction of the authorities was not to question the status of the rioters' immediate biological needs. Indeed, it is telling that the Kingswood colliers went out of their way to assert that it was not they who were starving – for surely with Randall's maxim in mind the authorities would not have believed them – but their community.[43] Thus claims to starvation were rarely meant literally or taken at face value. Rather, such claims were already understood as meaning that starvation was likely without action. Their utterance either therefore justified, as noted, the seizing of foodstuffs, or acted as a sensational reminder to the authorities of their obligations. To claim a state of starvation, in this context, had a different, more dramatic meaning and set of effects than to claim hunger. To claim hunger was to be deferential, to defer to authority and to beg assistance, whereas to claim starvation was to invoke chaos and misrule.

Hunger was the language of request, of appeal, of mercy. Starvation was the language of resistance.

1756–7: 'Jack Poor, Will Needy, Will Starve, Peter Fearnot'

Beyond 1740 similar dynamics and claims continued. There were localised waves of food rioting after 1740, for instance around Penryn in the autumn of 1748 where the tinners and their families again seized corn bound for export.[44] But it was not until 1756–7 that another national wave of food rioting occurred. Starting in Staffordshire in mid-August 1756, Jeremy Caple has recorded over 100 incidents in some 30 counties occurring in the period up to the beginning of December in the following year. This, however, represents an underestimate of the scale and depth of the protests. Either way, the riots of 1756–7 were the most extensive and severe of the eighteenth century, at least until those of 1795–6. Rapid increases in prices provided the trigger, but the most frequently expressed motivation – and target – was the export of grain, while other duplicitous trading practices were also a major source of contention.[45]

Again, following the pattern set in 1740, many of the protests either occurred in the countryside or involved workers from the countryside entering the towns and quays. This was not just the miners and cloth workers, but also rural artisans and agricultural workers, those workers supposedly with easiest access to corn through direct purchase from their employers or pilfering. For instance in Sussex, not a county with either miners or (by the mid-eighteenth century) significant numbers of industrial workers, of the seven food riots I have identified for the 1756–7 crisis all involved rural workers. Nor were these all small-scale, low-key affairs. Without doubt, some reports may have exaggerated the scale of the protests. Thus in relation to one decidedly partial invasion of Lewes, the Lewes press reported that a body of '200 poor people' had descended on the town seeking redress from the magistrates, while West Hoathly diarist Thomas Turner noted that:

> [A]bout 40 people out of several neighbouring parishes came there today in a kind of riotous manner in order to demand corn of a person who has lately bought up a large quantity, who very readily offered them any quantity they would have at 6s. a bushel, which prevented any further disturbance.[46]

We should not forget, however, that even exaggerated numbers spoke volumes about the impression mobile groups of rural workers invading local towns made on the populace and the authorities. Thus on Monday 6 June 1757 'a mob of about 500 men and 100 women and children rose' in the small market town of Petworth and visited 'one Hampton, a jobber, and offered him a premium for his wheat'. Hampton refusing, they broke open his warehouse and took out seven loads and four bushels and placed it on the green 'when any body took it that would, some in bags, some in their laps, etc so that it was soon gone'. The following day the 'same people' armed 'some with prongs, some with picks, some with shovels, and such kind of weapons', having first called on the justices for support, proceeded to Adversane, near Billingshurst, Pulborough, Arundel, Hardham and other places to search all the mills, seizing more wheat where they found 'quantities'. As the day went on, their numbers greatly increased so that, according to a report in the *Sussex Weekly Advertiser*, ''tis so large now that they talk of dividing into two bodies one to take the west, the other the eastern road' countenanced by 'great Numbers who give them Victuals and Drink as they go from place to place'. The group, supposedly 500 strong, advanced towards Chichester, creating such alarm in the city that a party of dragoons was sent out to meet them. Finding them after they seized a barge loaded with wheat bound for export, the dragoons took five prisoners, dispersed the rest and retook the barge and delivered it back to its owners.[47] Elsewhere, some five miles due south of Chichester at Siddlesham, the 'mob' also threatened to destroy Woodruffe Drinkwater's recently erected tide mill, prompting Drinkwater to plant some 16 or so cannon, small arms and a constant guard on the mill.[48]

The men, women and children whose protests started at Petworth offered no violence, beyond the force necessary to seize corn and flour. Moreover, the archive records no claims made of starvation, though this may simply be a function of archival partiality. Beyond matters of record and method, evidently the Sussex men and women's actions implicitly made claims to the likelihood of hunger and the fear of starvation. As Bohstedt notes of the mid-century protests, riot was beyond all else a way of 'combatting hunger'.[49] And in the context of 1756–7, it is important to remember that for some individuals the experience of the subsistence crisis went beyond the realities of hunger and the possibility of starvation to the actual experience of starvation. Such cases were rare, certainly far fewer than in 1727–8 when there was what Appleby has termed a 'mini crisis' with extremely high levels of mortality in parts of East Anglia and much of the north.[50] Relief systems and, at least for those in the countryside and the urban fringe, opportunities for pilfering, would mean that only the elderly and socially marginal would be vulnerable to starvation. But the power of the fear of starvation meant that *reports* of individuals starving to death assumed a degree of cultural and political potency. Thus a report from Exeter regarding the case of 'a poor woman' who 'craved charity' at St Sidwell's parish, having had her allowance from her native parish fraudulently siphoned off by the carrier charged with issuing her money, was widely – and prominently – reported in the provincial press, including on the front page of the *Sussex Weekly Advertiser*. Having been 'reduced almost to Anatomy' she was sent by the magistrates to the bridewell where she perished. The verdict of the coroner's jury was plain enough: she had starved to death, this 'coming from the Mouth of the Coroner, and to be believed by all, as he is a Gentleman of Character'.[51] In the context of the unfurling crisis, this was explosive, provocative copy.

This discourse of starvation was, at least in Sussex, given explicit form in the context of incendiarism and threatening letters. On 20 February 1757 farmer Miller of Hailsham was targeted by incendiaries. His corn barn, containing some 13 acres of wheat, some oats and tares as well as a new cart and other husbandry utensils, was fired during the time of Divine Service. While this was not in itself entirely novel in the context of subsistence disputes, what was particularly of note was that the fire was alluded to in an incendiary letter sent three days later addressed to the 'Clarge and Gentery, and … all Gentlemen Farmers' of Ninfield:

> As there hath bin, in a neighbouring Parish, a Barn of Corn destroied by Fire, if Wheat be not fell to the Price of 5s. per Bushell, the same Calamaty will happen in this Parish and sevaerl Parrishes ajoyning; for the Thing is decreed, and will soon be put in Execution, if not prevented by the Faul of Corn: Also several Dwelling Houses are conspired against, and I do asure you there will be but very few Barns standing in this Parrish, and many other ajoyning, in a Months Time.[52]

The writer signed off by alluding either to the earlier Lewes 'riot' or some other unrecorded event close by, saying '[f]or as Mobs and Magistrates will not prevail we will run the hasard of our Lives before we will stareve'. Clearly, the earlier decidedly deferential protest had failed, or other such local protests had been suppressed, thereby necessitating a resort to covert protests and adopting the discourse of starvation. A Brighton farmer, the parish then still being dominated by fishing and agriculture, also received a threatening letter couched in similar terms:

> You covetous and hard-hearted farmers, that heap your Stacks and Mows of Corn to starve the poor, if you will not take them in and sell them that we may some to eat, we will put them down for you by Night or Day.[53]

To reinforce the point, the letter was satirically signed 'Jack Poor, Will Needy, Will Starve, Peter Fearnot, And others'.[54]

In such threatening letters we arguably see an extension of the claims made by food rioters in parleys with dealers and the authorities to become something more political, something that went beyond claims about the self and the community to issue global critiques about pernicious marketing practices. Indeed, in many ways these critiques also represented the shift in food rioting practices in 1756–7 and 1766 compared to 1740, with middlemen, as Randall and Charlesworth have suggested, subject to particular ire from 1766. By way of example, in 1765 the *Bath Chronicle* reported that 'papers tending to inflame the minds of the people against corn jobbers' had been stuck up in the nearby market towns. While the content of the offending 'papers' was not reported, it would be surprising were they not couched in terms of market manipulation as the maker of scarcity and starvation.[55] Indeed, crowd actions in 1766 drew on such popular political critiques and directly gave voice to the idea that 'jobbers' were the creators of hunger. In Wiltshire, it was reported that food rioters were 'burning and pulling down the mills' of those known to be sending meal to Bristol for export, 'a term become as shocking as that of a Bounty to starve the poor'.[56]

1766: 'We are all most Starvied and we can die but once'

In the context of the crisis of 1766, the politics of provisions in the western cloth-making area were visible in the combination of scarcity, exasperation with dealers and processors, and the discourse of starvation manifest in both crowd action and the tools of terror. Initial reports of a 'rising' in September at the Beckington turnpike between Trowbridge and Frome painted the episode as a straightforward reaction to the 'high price of wheat'. Cloth manufacturers gathered in a corn mill duly fired on the crowd to protect their property, which provoked those gathered into throwing firebrands at the mill, which – being thatched – soon burnt to the ground. Subsequent reports showed a more nuanced, complex situation. Somerset Knight of the Shire Prowse together with several other 'gentlemen' had met the crowd and admonished them for gathering, and promised to do all he could to relieve them. This proved no salve to their ills, however: the crowd reportedly declared that 'they might as well be hanged as starved to Death … that they had not eat a Morsel of Bread for three Days, but had subsisted on Grains, &c' and that their wives and children were in the same condition. To the reporter in the Sherborne press this was not just posturing. Many appeared so feeble through want of bread that 'they could scarcely crawl'. They were then given some money and the further promise that their parishes would take care of their families, but this had no effect for they restated their deter-mination to march to the mill. The miller was prepared, having both 'proper assistance' and firearms. The ensuing siege lasted eight hours, during which many of the rioters were wounded, one fatally with others thought unlikely to recover.[57]

If the above example was the most extreme, and tragic, expression of the popular idea that death in resisting their lot was preferable to death by star-vation, it was not the only one. A letter to the *Bath Chronicle* published on 30 October from 'A Friend to the Poor' bemoaned that the recent proclamation prohibiting the export of corn was a case of 'shut[ting] the Stable Door when the Steed is stolen'. The 'artificial scarcity' was 'hourly increasing', which – with no means to gain redress – would lead to 'Anarchy and Confusion'. 'Believe me', the letter writer continued, 'there is not much Difference between Hanging and Starving'.[58] Certainly the proclamation was too late to save a hay rick of farmer Bell of Trowbridge from being fired on 4 October.

This followed a threatening letter he had received three days previously.[59] Nor did it save the life of a twelve-year-old boy in Stroud on whose emaciated body the Gloucestershire coroner recorded a verdict of death by starvation in January 1767. The case was widely reported in the press, no doubt in part a reflection of the dramatic copy such cases offered but also a function of the coroner's considered opinion that a similar fate would befall 'many poor People'.[60]

Such cases served as support, as detailed earlier in this chapter, to press editorials and printed letters variously regarding the selfishness of farmers, the nefarious effects of middlemen and dealers, and the evils of export. These mobilisations of starvation, though, always had some other political end – critiquing the government, mercantile policy, enclosure, engrossment of farms – beyond moralising claims about the state of the poor. Their understanding and experience of hunger was always at least one step removed, something driven by politics and ethics rather than personal experience. It is possible, of course, that the writers of some threatening letters were similarly removed and motivated by wider personal and political ends. By way of example, an 'anonimous and incendiary Letter' found in the cellar of Chipping Norton magistrate William Myers on 12 November 1766 was likely not from the hungry poor but from butter dealers aggrieved at market regulation:

> This is to give notice to the justices constables tythingmen and To the honourable Clerks of the Market That if the do not ring the market bell by eleven a Clock and let folks bring in Their butter & & & as usal to serve the Towns people you certainly shall have your Houses burnt down if not prevented as above no more notice will be given but fire will certainly follow if you refuse this request.[61]

Similarly, 30 years later during the subsistence crisis of 1796, an anonymous threatening letter warned Berkshire lawyer John Stanford Girdler against meddling in the grain trade. The previous summer, Girdler had instituted a campaign in Berkshire against forestalling, engrossing and regrating, personally offering a reward of £20 for information towards the prosecution of such practices. After he placed an advert in the Reading press and the *St James Chronicle*, 'informations of illegal practices poured in… from every quarter', and evidently stoked the ire of grain traders. 'Wee no you are an enemy to Farmers, Millers, Mealmen and Bakers and our Trade', the letter writer asserted. '[I]f it had not bene for me and another you you son of a Bitch you wold have bene murdurd long ago'; the threat now was that 'you shall by God be shot and you may deepend your house shall bee burnt down before long so God blast to eternity and fere death'.[62]

What marked the difference between the letters 'representing' poor consumers and the actual missives of the poor were claims not to hunger but to starvation. No doubt the archive under-represents the number of threatening letters sent, but the claims and language of the extant letters sent in 1766 were similar to those of the 1756–7 crisis. Typical was that sent to farmers Lidington and Kingston, the 'theds [*heads*] of the town' at Silverstone, Northamptonshire. A cross-county coalition from Northamptonshire and Buckinghamshire, so they were warned, would set their 'Barns and hovils' aflame unless the price of corn was reduced within a fortnight. Again, not only were claims to starvation made – 'we are all most Starvied' – but the very condition of being 'all most Starvied' meant that the men of Northamptonshire and Buckinghamshire, so the claim went, were beyond fear: 'we can die but once … so we will downe with them as Shure as you are a Live Downe to ashes the shall Come'. Tellingly, and as analysed in detail in chapter five, the writer(s) also implied that their state of submission and starvation, and the lack of value placed on their lives, had reduced them to the state of slaves: 'We poor Slaves of yours we are all most Starvied and we can die but once'. 'Slaves', barns, 'hovils' and grain, property all, would all be destroyed.[63]

As with the Ninfield incendiary letter in 1757, the Silverstone letter also referenced a recent incendiary fire, this time at Finmere, some eight miles south in neighbouring Oxfordshire where a barn full of unthrashed oats had been 'Downd' on 23 November. Ann Thornton, the wife of a Finmere labourer, was arrested on suspicion of writing a further incendiary letter and, unusually, firing the barn in early December and sent to the Castle at Oxford.[64] In these letters we see a clear millenarian influence in references to starvation and the end of days, an influence and discourse that would play out most profoundly in the 1790s.

Less impressive than the threat of the combined forces of Buckinghamshire and Northamptonshire, though no doubt almost as menacing, was the threat made to the mayor of Chester in April 1767 that '100 Men ready Armed' would 'murder you and all the Corporation' and burn his house down. The objection here was that the actions of forestallers went unchecked, meaning that the poor were 'almost starved'.[65] Likewise, the threat that a self-styled 'gang' of thirteen men had entered into a 'most solemn Engagement' to set fire to the houses of several residents of Bucklebury, Berkshire, was laden with portent. That the letter was found the same night as fellow Buckleburian Mr Snell's premises were fired no doubt added to the atmosphere of fear and recrimination in the neighbourhood. It is also possible that the letter – and Snell's fire – was inspired by a series of threatening letters sent the previous October and November to several constables and gentlemen of Abingdon threatening the destruction of their houses. One of these letters also made claims to broader working solidarities, it being 'Wrat by 5 as Veleys [unclear] not Mayor not Jesties [Justices]'.[66]

The second Abingdon letter also employed a recurring motif in food-crisis threatening letters: making claims of enforcing the law. This, Thompson has argued, was rooted in a popular memory of the Tudor Books of Orders, especially around the setting of prices and the bringing of stock to market.

Although this emergency legislation had fallen out of use during the Civil War, Thompson suggests that in industrial communities like the west of England and East Anglia, the actions of cloth-makers in the eighteenth century were rooted in the issue of the Books of Orders in 1630. Moreover, the Orders were republished in 1660 and again in 1758. Thus the warning of the Abingdon letter-writer 'Gintlmen of ye Corporation Take Noties of this my Word is a law and what thes Linis Exspres is trew' could be understood in this vein, not least given the long tradition of food rioting in north Berkshire and Oxfordshire.[67]

   This potency did not just rest on the politics of an idealised paternalism but was rooted in the popular understanding that the Books of Orders provided a recognition of the fundamental rights of the poor to get bodily by. Thus in south Kent a doggerel notice posted on the porch of Wye church in 1630 read 'The Corne is so dear / I dout mani will starve this yeare / … Our souls they are dear, / For our bodys have sume ceare / Before we arise Less will safise …'. And here the same sentiments persisted into the eighteenth century. In and around Woodchurch and Tenterden in 1768 notices had been 'fixed up' on church doors and inn-signs rousing the poor to rise. This they did on 30 May and threatened to force the farmers to sell their wheat to the millers or directly to the poor at £10 a load and to destroy the mills of those millers who paid over £10.[68] Again in 1794, David Masters, a parishioner of nearby rural Kennardington, and accomplices from Orlestone and Warehorne were arrested for an insurrectionary scheme to increase the price of labour and limit tradesmen and farmers from holding land with an annual rentable value of more than £10 and £100, and set a cap on clergy benefices. The French, so Masters believed, were to land and support him, which, in turn, would prompt the religious dissenters to rise in support.[69] Six years later, during the hyper food crisis of 1800, another would-be insurrectionist, farm labourer William Scott of Wye, also tried to raise a local force. His first approach to potential recruits was to ask their opinion of the 'dearth of provisions'. Invariably, the opinion expressed coincided with Scott's belief that 'it was very bad on poor people who had large families'. The accord thus established, Scott asked the person if they would sign an engagement 'to meet together in a Mob and to stand by each other in a conspiracy against the Government of this Country' and to effect a reduction in the price of grain. Stepping up his politicking on the rapid implementation of the new Relief [Enabling] Act (enacted on 22 December) that allowed magistrates, after consultation, to force overseers to pay up to one-third of all relief in cereal substitutes, his activities threw the local judiciary into a panic. One Ashford magistrate wrote to ask Portland's advice on how to 'proceed' in the prosecution of Scott in light of the fact that the idea of raising a mob 'was very general in this part of Kent' and that, so he understood, 'numerous agents were employed to take down the names of the labourers in different parishes'.[70]

1790s: 'To starve all the poor of the parish'

Tom. Come, neighbours, no longer be patient and quiet
Come let us go kick up a bit of a riot;
I am hungry, my lads, but I've little to eat,
So we'll pull down the mills, and seize all the meat;
I'll give you good sport, boys, as ever you saw,
So a fig for justice, a fig for the law …
Jack. What a whimsey to think thus our bellies to fill,
For we stop all the grinding by breaking the mill!
What a whimsey to think we shall get more to eat,
By abusing the butchers who get us the meat!
What a whimsey to think we shall mend our spare diet
By breeding disturbance, by murder and riot![71]
             The Riot, or Half a Loaf is better than no Bread (to the tune
                   of 'A Cobber there Was', written June 1800).[72]

In May 1790 between one and two hundred of 'the peasantry' assembled at Petworth with large sticks to complain at the price of flour. Claiming 'that they might as well be killed at once, as starved to death', they threatened that 'they would have flour cheaper (as there was no scarcity) or *they would Grind the Miller*'. Ten years later, 50 labourers gathered at Petworth to complain to the magistrates in deferential terms that 'in consequence of the high price of bread and other provisions their families were nearly starving'.[73] The Petworth 'riots' perfectly captured the persistence of the pattern, practices and language of popular responses to earlier eighteenth-century crises into the 1790s, while at the same time detailing shifting practices *during* the 1790s. As is well established, the 1790s represented both the high point and the denouement of the food-rioting tradition. The intensity and scope of the protests of 1795–6 and 1799–1801 were unparalleled.[74]

Whatever the new intensities, both of the scale of protest and of the muscularity and bitterness of their repression, the language of bodily need persisted and remained true to discourses of the mid-eighteenth century. Even after the repression of the riots of 1795, the power of the ever-present fear of starvation was so strong as to lift protestors from fear. The earlier discourse of 'we are as well to be hanged for rioting than starving to death' remained as popularly potent as before. As a returning 'souldier' writing to MP Benjamin Hobhouse in the summer of 1802 put it:

[Th]e burning of Factorys or setting fire to property of People we know is not right but Starvation forces Nature to do that which he would not nor would it reach his Thoughts had he sufficient Employ we have tried every Effort to live by Pawning our Cloaths and Chattles so we are now on the brink for the last struggle.[75]

Even (some of) the nobility recognised the severity of the situation. The Earl of Warwick not only alluded to starvation amongst the 'lower classes of people' in a speech in the House of Lords but also issued a circular to his tenants compelling them to bring their grain to market on pain of not having their tenancies renewed, to ease the 'miserable distressed condition of the poor, now actually starving'.[76]

Between late 1794 and the plentiful harvest of 1796 famine-like conditions gripped England.[77] The popular response to harvest and market failure was a series of waves of food riots and associated protests throughout the nation unprecedented in scale and intensity. If by any quantitative measure the mid-1790s crisis was not as severe as that of 1800–1, there can be no denying the deep distress that afflicted working communities. The extension of charity, including urban soup kitchens and the subsidising of flour, bread and fuel for many poor families, together with the rapid uptake of Speenhamland-style income-support schemes through the Poor Law – as analysed in chapter three – kept countless individuals from absolute want but others fell through or foul of such institutionalised schemes. Places like Bristol, dependent on both coastal and inland supply networks, were doubly affected by the government embargo on coasting vessels introduced in February 1795, while the successful actions of 'starving' colliers blockaded the rivers Severn and Wye, further restricting supplies.[78]

Beyond scale, and the severity of the repression, what marked these protests out as distinctive from those earlier in the century was both the importance of forms of proto-trade unionism in seeking higher wages to better afford record high provisions prices, and the increased influence of radicalism. The first point is easily dealt with. The dependence on money wages for simple subsistence combined with a sustained period of inflation in foodstuffs post-1760 offered a spur to novel forms of gaining redress. As C.R. Dobson has delineated, while forms of trade unionism emerged in the late seventeenth century, it was not until the end of the eighteenth century that they transcended their birthplace in the industrial communities of the north, to exist wherever groups of skilled men worked together in mills and emergent factories.[79] Reports of strikes amongst shipwrights, papermakers, building trades, clothworkers and other industrial workers were many. Farmworkers too, encouraged by the example of militant craftsmen and industrial workers, also struck work, even though, in the words of Wells, the '1790s was hardly the decade for labourers to suddenly perceive that living standards turned exclusively on wages'.[80] Moreover, attempts to prise higher wages from employers during the crisis of 1794–6 are invariably poorly documented: newspaper reports and letters are cursory in their descriptions; prosecutions focused on acts of riot rather than the claims of those striking from work. Cries of hunger and starvation are therefore not recorded. Yet implicit in the act of throwing off work – a risky strategy even for skilled workers in the context of the heightened culture of political paranoia in the mid-1790s – was the statement either that 'the labourer is worthy of his hire' or that we do not have enough to get by, to feed our family and ourselves. And even the former claim was, in the context of the subsistence crises of the 1790s, a direct response to rapidly declining real wages.

The importance of the strike in 1800–1 was, so the archive suggests, even more profound than in 1794–6. This was a reflection of the reduced (political) opportunities for, and efficacy of, food rioting after the bitter repression of the riots of 1795. It also reflected the yet deeper nature of the subsistence crises that gripped England in late 1799, a crisis that left many poor consumers, in the words of Lord Lilford's steward on his Lancashire estates, 'absolutely starving'.[81] Not all individuals were able to protest their lot through any means, including the children of Wymering workhouse in Hampshire whose rations were being sold by the master and mistress of the workhouse, 'nearly starving them'. On complaining, the emaciated infants were placed in 'vigorous confinement'.[82] Leicestershire 'pauper' John Crask also found himself incarcerated in the Wymondham Bridewell for six months for the temerity of telling clerical magistrate Collyer that he and his brother justice had *'knocked their heads together,* to starve all the poor of the parish'.[83] Riot, though, was far from dead in 1800–1. Indeed, in some places and amongst certain groups – including West Country clothworkers and colliers – with deep community memories of the collective bargaining by riot script, certain traditions and practices persisted.[84] But, in totality, in the late 1790s forms of popular expression shifted, betraying a greater range of political and cultural influences than in the mid eighteenth-century.

The language of proto-unionists' claims in 1800–1 was, with few exceptions, not recorded. What is left is inference. By way of example, at Ardingly, Sussex, a 'number' of labourers having assembled went to prevail upon the parish officers that unless their wages were 'augmented' they could not get bread for their families and 'would in consequence become burthensome'. A coordinated campaign at Thatcham in Berkshire, but also active over the Hampshire border at Highclere, made 'very clamorous' demands for either lower food prices or higher wages that were evidently no less desperate. Both examples are writ through with need, with creeping hunger, but if such claims were explicitly articulated they were not recorded in the archive.[85]

The influence of radicalism, both Jacobinism and the lingering elements of lingering Wilkesian and 1770s Reform 'Associations', on the articulation of hunger was both far more profound and more explicit. This, in part, represented continuity. Attempts by radicals at Bristol in February 1800 to incite support by leaving anonymous notes and blood-soaked loaves about the city as well as by issuing a letter to the mayor asking whether the 'labourous people' were 'to be starved this winter?', with the veiled threat that it was 'better to stand like men than starve in the land of plenty', mirrored similar attempts in neighbouring Bath 34 years previously.[86] Forty miles to the east, a handbill found at Ramsbury made similar pleas: 'Dear Brother Britons

North and South, younite yourselves in one body and stand true. Down with you luxzuaras Government or you starve with Hunger.'[87] A handbill originating in London in September 1800, and also used to mobilise riots in neighbouring Kent, drew upon the same rhetoric: 'How long will ye quietly and cowardly suffer yourselves to be thus imposed upon and half-starved by a set of mercenary slaves and Government hirelings?'[88]

Nor was radical influence always perceived to be in the service of the bellies of the poor. A Wiltshire attorney writing to home secretary Portland in July 1795 to represents his belief that the scarcity of grain was the result of corn 'being brought up by our rascally English Jacobins and hid on pur- pose to starve the people into a Rebellion against Government'.[89] The fear of starvation was also used to motivate loyalist actions, including in the ballad 'Loyal Jone' where the titular character's motivation to enlist to fight the French for his king was because his hamlet was 'clamming and starving'.[90] Such attempts to stir up popular loyalty, including through the so-called 'Paine Burnings' of 1792, helped to inculcate, to quote Frank O'Gorman, an 'apocalyptic climate of fear', which seeped into the popular consciousness. In a village near Hull in February 1795, an old woman conversing with a shop- keeper on the 'hardness of the times' related that 'some wicked person' had lately stolen by night a large number of fowl from her yard. On being asked if she knew who the culprit was, she replied that 'she believed it to be one of your Tom Painers'.[91] Yet such expressions of loyalism hid, as Navickas has asserted, a 'tense unease about the threat of starvation'. Whether 'artificial' or 'real', whether politically or commercially motivated, the ever-present fear of starvation had very real effects.[92]

Threatening letters rather than crowd parleys offer the best expression of radical influences on working people's expression of hunger. While this is not to say that all such letters issued their threats through articulating bodily need and fears through popular politics – for instance an incendiary letter sent to William Dyke of Syrencot in the parish of Figheldean, Wiltshire, in March 1800 relied only upon biblical allusions in encouraging him to 'Indevor to sink the Markers'[93] – the juxtaposition became a defining trope. Some such letters did not use radical rhetoric but instead betrayed a natural-rights influ- ence as filtered through the analysis of Tom Paine. As one letter 'picked up' in the streets of Lewes in March 1800 put it:

> O ye rich genteiman farmers, tis you that uphold all this Dearth; you grow the Corn, you fat the beas & Sheep, & make the butter And cheas, which are the 5 princebel things that a poor pepel wont to bye; And they are so Dear that the poor are all most Starved; & Do you not think that a shame in a land of plenty, if there was not a plenty how Could it be had for money; but tis not so, for they that have Plenty of money, Can have a planty of Ever artkle that they wont ... they men that keep back the Corn so much, & they that bye to make a Dearth, will have no mercy shode them, for that is a Shame; there is maney Dogs that live far before Poor men, & you will

see them Dambed before you will raise their wagers, & how Can they live, this is a nough to make them rise wather they would or not, he may As well fight as to be starved …[94]

Echoing the above-mentioned Bristol handbill, the refrain of the injustice of starvation in a land of plenty precisely mirrored the radically tinged discourses of 1766. But here the juxtaposition of dearth, market manipulation, wages and starvation was clearly also joined by the language of rights. Another public statement in the same town was less subtle but still betrayed the same influences, albeit in a satirical rather than directly threatening way: the skeleton of a cat was nailed to a fence of the Star Inn with the words 'Symptoms of Starvation' graffitied above the expired feline.[95]

In other missives the radical influence was proudly proclaimed. A threatening notice placed upon the Market House at Windsor in December 1800 did not mince its words in proclaiming: 'This is to give notice to king G.3 & all his tyrannical crew that we will have bread at 6d pr. Loaf & meat at 4d. p. lb or we the starved poor are determined he shall be shot.' Not only did it threaten regicide but it also warned the farmers 'and others that hold their corn from market' that their ricks would be burnt 'for we value not our own lives so as we can get rid of these tyrants'.[96] The same discourse ran through a threatening letter sent to a Rye (Sussex) farmer in early 1801. 'We have agreed in 5 parishes we mean to have provisions cheaper or Rescue our lives' was far from novel: it made the now established claim to the muscularity of popular protest. The next line, though, was designed to strike at the heart of establishment paranoia: 'we are Led up by popery and oprestion the same as France was before the war begun'. The solution to hunger was bloody revolution. Not even repentance on the part of the rich would save them. '[Y]ou are agoing to have a fast to offer up prayer to God but it is an offer to the Devil[,] God will never hear the prayer of the unmerciful.' This was millenarianism writ large, the selfishness of the rich bringing upon themselves judgement and damnation: 'the time is short that we must give an account of our work'.[97] As the author of a threatening letter sent to a Lenham (Kent) farmer put it: 'if God was as much a gainst the poor as the rich are we shall have been all starvd before now long agoe.'[98] Similarly, a letter reportedly 'picked up' in the streets of Winchester threatening a publican who had informed against conspirators to riot even found millenarian undertones in Proverbs:

> Sir, This is a matter if serious consequence in wick I think you will suffer Most Infamous you might Depend on it your life his forfeted so far as to be a Done man so Prepare your self for the next World For your life in this is but short as the Proverb says there Is a Time for to Die but I believe You to be a Dead man & I think it is high time you was Out of the world for you whould starve thousands you Damd rascal We will have your life so prepare your self for a Better Place …[99]

The radical politics of starvation: 'Pitt and the Committee for Bread are combined together to starve the Poor'

The radicalisation of popular responses to hunger went hand in hand with their response to the militarisation of provincial England. The popular experience of the role of the military in repressing the food riots of 1795, and the financial, social and cultural impact of troops barracked and billeted in local communities (including their impact on the availability and price of foodstuffs), not to mention the broader fiscal pressure of the war effort and the familial impact of militia ballots, was to irretrievably antagonise poor consumers. As Navickas notes, the 1790s was defined by the experience of living with and negotiating militarised landscapes.[100] While no members of the military were absolutely saved from popular scorn, such rhetoric realised the difference between rank and file soldiers and their officers. Radical attempts to make common currency with soldiers drew upon privates' sense of injustice at wartime fiscal and military policy. This was in part pragmatic politics: without the support of the military Pitt's government would collapse. But the attempt to build a broad, muscular platform was also opportunist politics, a belief that after the involvement of militia soldiers as protagonists in the food riots in the spring of 1795 and the subsequent court martials, rank-and-file soldiers were not far from mutiny. A handbill picked up at Lewes in the immediate aftermath of the court martial of some of the Oxford Militia, responsible for a two-day food riot at Newhaven and Seaford in April 1795, implored that the soldiers should

> with intrepid Hand Grasp Sword and Gun to save thy native land for see your Comrades murder'd, ye with Resentment Swell and join the Rage, the Aristocrat to quell let undaunted Ardor each bold Bosom warm. To down with George and Pitt, and England call to Arms.[101]

Mindful of the revolutionary tone of the handbill, the editor of the *Sussex Weekly Advertiser* wrote to the Sussex Lord Lieutenant, the Duke of Richmond, to ask his opinion as to whether he should copy it in his newspaper. The bill was never publicised.[102]

If the Lewes handbill was rich in bodily symbolism, radical attempts to stir mutiny amongst the soldiers elsewhere explicitly drew on starvation politics. At Sheffield residual sympathy for the plight of the privates allied to the popular fear of subscription was stoked in the form of a handbill circulated about the town on 4 August 1795.

> The People's humbugg'd! A Plot is discovered! – Pitt and the Committee for Bread are combined together to starve the Poor into the Army and Navy! and to starve your Widows and Orphans! – God help ye Labourers of the nation! you are held in Requisition to fight in a bad Cause … Every one to his Tent O *Israel*! Sharpen your weapon, and spare not for all the Scrats in nation are united against your Blood … Behold! good bread at six shillings per stone … Cursed be the Farmers and Promoters of the Corn-bill![103]

Popular mobilisation in Sheffield was driven by several years of antagonism between the democratic Sheffield Society for Constitutional Information (SSCI) – founded in late 1791, and already 2,000 members strong by the following March – and 'Church and King' loyalist sentiment seeded and supported by local Tory elites. As Navickas notes, the battle between radicals and loyalists was both political and representational, an attempt to, respectively, defend and to deny the liberty to meet.[104] Antagonisms ran deep and took many forms. It was believed that 'a Mob' – for which read SSCI members – intended to unite with the recruits in Colonel Cameron's regiment, then being raised at Sheffield, and proceed to riot on pretence of 'some arrears of pay, called bread-money'. On the evening of the 4th, the usual parade of Cameron's recruits was watched by a crowd, which, according to reports, swelled to 'several thousands'. On Cameron's men being dismissed, the populace shouted out 'Halt'. Cameron's further attempt to dismiss his regiment was met by cries of 'Damn him, stab him – stick him – kill him'. Remonstration and even calling out the Volunteers had no effect, the crowd complaining of the scarcity of bread. The Riot Act was then read, but again to no avail. The standoff eventually descended into violence, with members of the crowd throwing bricks and stones met by the order for the Volunteers to fire on the throng, two of whom were shot dead. Subsequent enquiries found that some of the recruits had come to the parade with stones in their pockets, others had exchanged the wood in lieu of flints in their guns for real flints, while another had earlier that day attempted to purchase a scythe for the purpose of 'vindicating himself'.[105] In the context of the fevered atmosphere of the 1790s and early 1800s, the politics of provisions went hand in hand with the battle for the control of public space and the battle for popular representation.

The greatest vitriol was spared for the yeomanries and Volunteers, associations led by the local gentry and nobility and composed of farmers and the middling sorts, the employers of the working poor. Or, as the author of an 'incendiary paper' posted on Andover market house on the night of 24 January 1800 labelled them, 'your Yeoman Cavalry and a Soctaion Begar Killers'. This 'Claret-Faced Crue of Statesmen, Farmers, Mealmen & Shopkeepers' were, so the author asserted, complicit in 'keeping the poore under your Subjection … Not one half doe Nothing but swager about and Stuff their dam'd ungodley Guts; and the other half work hard, Starve and be used worse then Dogs.' Now, the threat went, they have 'a knuff to do to dought Fires instead of quelling Mobs'.[106]

Even if farmer volunteers were thought well of as employers, their role in the yeomanries was enough to make them the subject of popular revulsion. As the author of the aforementioned threatening letter sent to farmer Procter at Rye put it: 'Sir we have no ill against you only your being Captaing over these men that are kept under arms to keep people in Rougery and Slavery all the Days of our Lives.'[107] This dual, contradictory responsibility was perhaps best expressed in a pithy threatening letter affixed to a signpost in Bicester (Oxfordshire) in early April 1800:

All Bicester Gentlemen as calls themselves clever Gentlemen if they don't rise poor mens pay as they can live better we will rose and Fight for our Lives better fight and be killed nor be starved an inch at a Time As for your association Beggar Boys we don't mind no more nor a parcel of Old Women.[108]

To volunteer was to keep the poor in a state of not only subjection but also hunger. That organised popular forces could rise and overwhelm the yeomanries was a common claim. The terror of starvation united all in conquering fear and law. 'Be Ready', implored a notice stuck up in the marketplace at Rye at the same time that farmer Procter received his threatening letter; 'This is to Acquaint the Inhabitants of this town and the Lower Class of people … if they mean to have provisions cheaper to be Ready to join the country.'[109]

Persistences

Throughout the eighteenth century and into the early years of the nineteenth century the dual discourses of hunger and starvation remained as a remarkably persistent way in which poor consumers were able to articulate – and protest – their perilous state in times of crisis. It persisted because, whatever the positive effects of increasing agricultural output and better market integration and efficiency,[110] the *fear* of hunger never lifted for poor consumers, many of whom were only ever a few days of illness or worklessness away from being in absolute bodily need. Indeed, without in any way being callous, whether the poor were actually hungry or reduced to a state of near (or actual) starvation was not – initially – the most pressing point. To ask whether food rioters were hungry is to miss the point. Besides, as Randall noted, being in a state of constant hunger was not conducive to rioting.[111] 'Hunger' rioters were not – always – motivated by hunger per se, rather they were always motivated by the fear of a deep, grinding hunger and ultimately starvation. It was the avoidance of being placed in a state of absolute bodily degradation and immediate calorific need that was ultimately at stake in all forms of protest during subsistence crises, whether moral economy-type practices of *taxation populaire* and anti-export interventions or the sending of threatening letters and the firing of farmers' and dealers' property. The point was not to bodily succumb, the point was to make sure that the household and the community could survive.

Persistence did not mean the discourses were unchanging and not adaptable. Rather, the particular discourse of hunger – the making of claims that being hungry and/or fearful of hunger justified certain modulated actions and demanded a positive response from their social betters – was a pillar of studied, choreographed moral-economy parleys and practices. We are hungry, we might not survive, we speak, we act to implore you to see us righted. This, then, was rooted in a Thompsonian take on the ritual performances of paternalism. The plebeian discourse was firm and clear – and clearly understood by all – with only the inference of the threat of more muscular action if nothing was done.[112] In many contexts, indeed in most crowd-action contexts that demanded restraint and an element of deference, whether faked or genuine, the discourse of hunger was central and fundamental to the protest.

Conversely, to mobilise the discourse of starvation was to scream rather than firmly – but ultimately respectfully and politely – to implore. It was to threaten and justify all forms of direct action and even of overt and covert destruction and terror. Immediately. For to fall into a state of starvation was – and remains, in parts of the Global South[113] – to proclaim the failure of paternalism, the failure of law and the failure of the market, and therefore in the face of death to justify all acts to find subsistence. Given the explicit threat inherent in the discourse it was, by definition, the discourse that underwrote all covert acts – most obviously in the form of threatening letters. Thus the shift from classic moral-economy crowd actions after 1795–6 towards covert acts of terror meant that it became, increasingly, the defining discourse, the way in which the poor spoke to hunger. The discourse of starvation was thus also well suited not just to popular provisions politics, to draw on Bohstedt's concept,[114] but also radical participatory politics. It was notably co-opted and mobilised in the 1800–1 crisis after the abject failure and repression of the protests of 1795–6. Against this, we know that, as detailed above, the more deferential discourse of hunger was co-opted by the authorities to stoke loyalist feeling to counter the rise of Jacobinism. Indeed, *The Riot, or Half a Loaf is better than no Bread* was a blatant piece of loyalist propaganda rooted in this idiom: we understand that you are hungry, we want and will help you, but only if you do not down the mills, seize all the meat, abuse the butchers, and breed disturbance, murder and riot. The next chapter examines what happened to this endemic discourse in the context of the supposed death of the food-rioting tradition after 1800–1, considering if – and how – the popular politics of hunger played out in both the relative quietude of the latter war years and during the crushing, 20-year-long depression that followed the peace.

Notes

1 R. Wells, *Wretched Faces: Famine in Wartime England, 1793–1803* (Stroud: Allan Sutton, 1988), pp. 1, 55, 57–8.
2 Ibid., ch. 2.
3 D.J. Oddy, 'Urban famine in nineteenth-century Britain: The effect of the Lancashire Cotton Famine on working-class diet and health', *Economic History Review*, 36:1 (1983), 68–86; Wells, *Wretched Faces*, p. 54.
4 Ibid., p. 8; T. Malthus, *An Essay on the Principle of Population* (London: J.M. Dent and Sons, 1803, 2nd edition).
5 Wells, *Wretched Faces*, p. 50.

6 Ibid., p. 53; J. Stevenson, *Popular Disturbances in England, 1700–1870* (London: Longman, 1979), pp. 110–12.

7 J. Archer, *Social Unrest and Popular Protest in England, 1780–1840* (Cambridge: Cambridge University Press, 2000), p. 108.

8 M. Turner, 'Review of *Wretched Faces: Famine in Wartime England, 1793–1801*', *Social History* 15:3 (1990), 391, 392. An exception to this is John Bohstedt's review in *Albion*, but while this was uncritical of Wells' approach it claimed that he had advanced no definition of famine: 'Review of *Wretched Faces: Famine in Wartime England, 1793–1801* by Roger Wells; and *Crowds and History: Mass Phenomena in English Towns, 1790–1835* by Mark Harrison', *Albion*, 22:4 (1990), 687–92.

9 E.A. Wrigley and R.S. Schofield, *The Population History of England, 1541–1871: A Reconstruction* (Cambridge: Cambridge University Press, 1981), pp. 652–3, 667, 681–4.

10 J. Healey, 'Socially selective mortality during the population crisis of 1727–1730: Evidence from Lancashire', *Local Population Studies*, 81 (2008), 59. Another, earlier, historian of the same period claimed that the high levels of mortality represented a 'population crisis', but not a famine: A. Gooder, 'The population crisis of 1727–30 in Warwickshire', *Midland History*, 1:4 (1972), 1–22.

11 A. Randall, *Before the Luddites: Custom, Community and Machinery in the English Woollen Industry, 1776–1809* (Cambridge: Cambridge University Press, 1991), pp. 3, 255, 278.

12 J. Bohstedt, *The Politics of Provisions: Food Riots, Moral Economy, and Market Transition in England, c. 1550–1850* (Farnham: Ashgate, 2013), pp. 116, 196, 197, 262.

13 K. Navickas, *Loyalism and Radicalism in Lancashire, 1798–1815* (Oxford: Oxford University Press, 2009), pp. 32, 34.

14 A. Randall, *Riotous Assemblies: Popular Protest in Hanoverian England* (Oxford: Oxford University Press, 2006), pp. 36, 75–6, 97–8, 106.

15 Ibid., p. 98.

16 *Lloyd's Evening Post*, 16–19 May 1766.

17 Malthus, *Essay*, 2nd edition, p. 526.

18 On the reporting of starvation in Ireland see: Charlotte Boyce, 'Representing the "Hungry Forties" in image and verse: The politics of hunger in early-Victorian illustrated periodicals', *Victorian Literature and Culture*, 40:2 (2012), 421–49.

19 J. Vernon, *Hunger: A Modern History* (Cambridge, MA: Harvard University Press, 2007), p. 6.

20 Wells, *Wretched Faces*. On the Speenhamland system see chapter three below.

21 See, for instance, E. Griffin, *Liberty's Dawn: A People's History of the Industrial Revolution* (New Haven, CT: Yale University Press, 2013), pp. 21, 31–2, 65, 67–8, 83; E. Griffin, 'Diets, hunger and living standards during the British Industrial Revolution', *Past & Present*, 239 (2018), 71–111.

22 D. Frega, *Speaking in Hunger: Gender, Discourse, and Consumption in Clarissa* (Columbia, SC: University of South Carolina Press, 1998).

23 For instance see: M. Berg, *Luxury and Pleasure in Eighteenth-Century Britain* (Oxford: Oxford University Press, 2005); L. Weatherill, *Consumer Behaviour and Material Culture in Britain 1660–1760* (London: Routledge, 1988).

24 Randall, *Riotous Assemblies*, p. 76.

25 J. Townsend, *A Dissertation on the Poor Laws: By a Well-wisher to Mankind*, ed. Ashley Montagu (Berkeley, CA: University of California Press, 1971), p. 27.

26 L.H. Lees, *The Solidarities of Strangers: The English Poor Laws and the People, 1700–1948* (Cambridge: Cambridge University Press, 1998), p. 14.

27 *Derby Mercury*, 12 September 1766. Also see *Derby Mercury*, 6 June 1766 (regarding effects of the engrossing of land and the game laws) and *Gazetteer and New Daily Advertiser*, 7 March (letter from 'A Constitutionalist' regarding the tax on beer).

28 *Lloyd's Evening Post*, 16 May 1766.

29 J. Bohstedt, 'The pragmatic economy, the politics of provisions, and the "invention" of the food riot tradition in 1740', in A. Randall and A. Charlesworth (eds), *Moral Economy and Popular Protest: Crowds, Conflict and Authority* (Basingstoke: Macmillan, 2000), pp. 55–61; A. Charlesworth, 'From the moral economy of Devon to the political economy of Manchester, 1790–1812', *Social History*, 17:2 (1993), 210.

30 For instance see: B. Sharp, 'The Food riots of 1347 and the medieval moral economy', in Randall and Charlesworth (eds), *Moral Economy and Popular Protest*, pp. 33–54; J. Walter and K. Wrighton, 'Dearth and the social order in early modern England', *Past & Present*, 71 (1976), 22–42.

31 Bohstedt, 'The pragmatic economy', p. 55. For details of Bohstedt's survey see: http://web.utk.edu/~bohstedt/files/RCIII_1740–1741.pdf (accessed 21 June 2015).

32 Randall, *Riotous Assemblies*, p. 98.

33 The National Archives, London (hereafter TNA), SP 36/4, fos 108–9, Magistrates of Falmouth to Duke of Newcastle, 18 December 1727. For a full account of the Cornish riots of 1727 see: J. Rule, 'The labouring miner in Cornwall c. 1740–1870: A study in social history' (PhD thesis, University of Warwick, 1971), pp. 126–8. There were further anti-export riots in Cornwall in 1737 in and around Falmouth and Penryn when much corn was seized by groups of tinners: Ibid., pp. 130–1.

34 TNA, SP 36/50 fos 425 and 432, Information of Henry Brown, Alderman William Sutton and William Barker, merchant, all of Stockton upon Tees, taken before magistrates John Hedworth and George Vane, 23 May 1740, and Sir William Williamson to the Bishop of Durham, 24 May 1740.

35 Bohstedt, 'Pragmatic economy', p. 64.

36 J. Bohstedt, *Riots and Community Politics in England and Wales, 1790–1810* (Cambridge, MA: Harvard University Press, 1983); Bohstedt, 'Pragmatic economy'.

37 K. Lloyd Gruffydd, 'The vale of Clwyd corn riots of 1740', *Flintshire Historical Society*, 27 (1975–6), 36–42; Bohstedt, *Politics of Provisions*, p. 116.

38 Gruffydd, 'The vale of Clwyd corn riots', 38.

39 TNA, SP 36/50 fo. 88, Petition of John Webb, Vicar, the churchwardens, overseers and others, Blewbury, Berkshire, 12 February 1740.

40 *Ipswich Journal*, 27 September 1740; *Gloucester Journal*, 30 September and 7 October 1740; S. Poole, 'Scarcity and the civic tradition: Market management in Bristol, 1709–1815', in A. Randall and A. Charlesworth (eds), *Markets, Market Culture and Popular Protest in Eighteenth-century Britain and Ireland* (Liverpool: Liverpool University Press, 1996), pp. 91–114. Also see: R. Malcolmson, '"A set of ungovernable people": The Kingswood colliers in the eighteenth century', in J. Brewer and J. Styles (eds), *An Ungovernable People: the English and their Law in the Seventeenth and Eighteenth Centuries* (London: Rutgers University Press, 1980), pp. 85–112.

41 On 19 June a large group of keelmen descended on the city. Having insisted that they had rye at 2/6 per bushel, wheat at 3/6 and oats at 1/3, Alderman Ridley persuaded the merchants to agree to such terms. However, on the factors breaking the agreement on the morning of 25 June a 'vast number of keelmen' entered the town with their colours flying and accompanied by a drum. They first liberated from the gaol those arrested on the 19th, before assaulting Ridley. In turn, some gentlemen of the town opened fire on the men, resulting in one man being short dead, which provoked the men to attack the gentlemen and ransack the guildhall chamber and the town court. The riot carried on throughout the day, though the troops' fixing of their bayonets eventually dispersed those who had not already been taken prisoner. TNA, SP 36/52, fo. 19, Cuthbert Fenwick, Mayor of Newcastle-upon-Tyne, to Newcastle, 9 August 1840; *The Scots Magazine*, 6 July 1740.

42 *Colchester Journal*, n.d. copied in *Ipswich Journal*, 24 May 1740; TNA, SP 36/50, fo. 454, John Blatch, Mayor, and magistrates of Colchester, to Newcastle, 28 May 1740.

43 Randall, *Riotous Assemblies*, p. 98.

44 Rule, 'The labouring miner', pp. 131–3.

45 J. Caple, 'Popular protest and public order in eighteenth-century England: The food riots of 1756–7' (MA thesis, Queen's University, Canada, 1978); J. Caple, '1756–7', in A. Charlesworth (ed.), *An Atlas of Rural Protest in Britain, 1548–1900* (London: Croom Helm, 1983), p. 86.

46 *Sussex Weekly Advertiser*, 2 February, 9 May, 13 and 27 June, 15 August; *Salisbury Journal*, 13 June 1757; D. Vaisey (ed.), *The Diary of Thomas Turner, 1754–1765* (London: CTR Publishing, 1994), pp. 82 and 107.

47 *Sussex Weekly Advertiser*, 13 June; *Salisbury Journal*, 13 June 1757. Ten days later, a further protest happened at Rook's Hill, two miles north of Chichester, when a 'mob of women' 'seized' a wagon loaded with flour and carried off seven sacks: *Sussex Weekly Advertiser*, 27 June 1757.

48 *Sussex Weekly Advertiser*, 20 June 1757; H.W. Haynes, *Sidlesham Past and Present* (Brighton: Southern Publishing, 1946), p. 79.

49 Bohstedt, *Politics of Provisions*, p. 126.

50 A. Appleby, 'Epidemics and famine in the Little Ice Age', *Journal of Interdisciplinary History*, 10:4 (1980), 643–63. As Jonathan Healey has put it, 'in terms of deviation from background levels of mortality, the years from 1727 to 1730 rank as the second worst crisis between 1541 and 1871, outdone only by the terrible epidemics of the 1550s'; 'Socially selective mortality', 59.

51 *Sussex Weekly Advertiser*, 20 December 1756.

52 *Sussex Weekly Advertiser*, 28 February 1757.

53 *Sussex Weekly Advertiser*, 7 February 1757.

54 *Sussex Weekly Advertiser*, 7 and 28 February, 7 March and 20 June 1757.

55 Randall and Charlesworth (eds), *Market Culture*, p. 14; *Bath Chronicle*, 25 March 1765.

56 Cited in Randall and Charlesworth (eds), *Market Culture*, p. 14.

57 *Sherborne & Yeovil Mercury*, 22 and 29 September 1766.

58 *Bath Chronicle and Weekly Gazette*, 30 October 1766.

59 *Bath Chronicle and Weekly Gazette*, 16 October 1766.

60 *Sherborne & Yeovil Mercury*, 2 February; *Leeds Intelligencer*, 27 January 1767; *Oxford Journal*, 31 January 1767.

61 *Oxford Journal*, Saturday 15 November 1766.

62 J.S. Girdler, *Observations on the Pernicious Consequences of Forestalling, Regrating, and Ingrossing* (London: H. Baldwin and Son, 1800), p. 289; *Reading Mercury*, 30 May 1796.

63 *Leeds Intelligencer*, 9 December 1766.

64 *Oxford Journal*, 6 December 1766. As John Archer has shown, agrarian incendiarists were with very few exceptions young men: *'By a Flash and a Scare': Arson, Animal Maiming, and Poaching in East Anglia 1815–1870* (Oxford: Clarendon Press, 1990), pp. 179, 214.

65 *Leeds Intelligencer*, 14 April 1767.

66 *Bath Chronicle and Weekly Gazette*, 27 March 1766; *Oxford Journal*, 8 November 1766.

67 Thompson, 'Moral economy', 109–10; *Oxford Journal*, 8 November 1766. On the tradition of food rioting in the area see: W. Thwaites, 'Oxford food riots: A community and its markets', in Randall and Charlesworth (eds), *Market Culture*, pp. 137–62; Thompson, 'Moral economy', 110–11.

68 *Kentish Gazette*, 28 May 1768; *Calendar of Home Office Papers, George III, 1766–1769*, vol. 2 (London: HMSO, 1879), p. 342.

69 TNA, Assi 94/1387, Calendar and indictments of Masters, Barling, Beale and Cruttenden, Kent Lent assizes 1794; *Maidstone Journal*, 11 February and 25 March; *Kentish Gazette*, 2, 11 and 14 February 1794.

70 TNA, HO 42/49, fos 454–7 and 42/61, fos 22–4, Rev. Breton and Robert Mascall, Ashford, 1 January 1801, enclosing depositions of William Browning, Wye, no occupation stated, 31 December 1800, James Allard, Wye, labourer, 1 January, and Thomas Pellett, Kennington, shoemaker, 1 January; and Robert Mascall, Ashford, 5 January, to Portland, enclosing deposition of John Arthur, Willesborough, labourer, 5 January; *Kentish Gazette*, 6 January 1801. For the impact of the Relief [Enabling] Act see: Bohstedt, *Riots and Community Politics*, pp. 194–5.

71 *The Riot* was a tract by Hannah More, deliberately populist in style and published by the 'Cheap Repository for Moral and Religious Tracts': H. More, *The Riot, Or, Half a Loaf is Better Than No Bread* (London: J. Marshall, 1795).

72 This version was copied in the *Ipswich Journal* (11 October 1800), presumably as a warning against rioting.

73 *Sussex Weekly Advertiser*, 10 and 17 May 1790, 24 February 1800.

74 Thompson, 'Moral economy'; Wells, *Wretched Faces*; Bohstedt, *Politics of Provisions*, ch. 5.
75 TNA, HO 42/65, fo. 172 'A souldier' to Benjamin Hobhouse, 26 July 1802.
76 *Newcastle Courant*, 22 November; *Ipswich Journal*, 22 November 1800. Not all members of the nobility were so active in attempting to ease hunger. On 21 March 1801, the Attorney General presented a petition from the Whitehaven (Cumberland) overseers complaining that the Earl of Lonsdale's repeated quashing of poor rates on 'trifling informalities' had meant that the parish had had to borrow £1,000 to support the poor. Their lines of credit now exhausted, 500 paupers were in danger of starving. *Exeter Flying Post*, 26 March; *Salisbury and Winchester Journal*, 30 March 1801.
77 Wells, *Wretched Faces*, pp. 36–7.
78 Poole, 'Scarcity and the civic tradition', p. 102.
79 C.R. Dobson, *Masters and Journeymen: A Prehistory of Industrial Relations, 1717–1800* (London: Taylor & Francis, 1980). As I have argued elsewhere, given that many skilled 'industrial' workers lived in the same communities as other artisans and rural and town labourers, we need to acknowledge that the spirit – and knowledge – of combination undoubtedly quickly transcended narrowly industrial trades so that a 'culture of combination' became far more pervasive than we have hitherto acknowledged: C. Griffin, 'The culture of combination: Solidarities and collective action before Tolpuddle', *Historical Journal*, 58:2 (2015), 443–80.
80 R. Wells, 'Tolpuddle in the context of English agrarian labour history, 1780–1850', in J. Rule (ed.), *British Trade Unionism: The Formative Years* (London: Longman, 1988), pp. 114–15.
81 Lancashire County Record Office, DDLi, box 57, Steward Hodgkinson to Lord Lilford, 22 March 1801, cited in Navickas, *Loyalism and Radicalism in Lancashire*, p. 34.
82 *Salisbury and Winchester Journal*, 10 November 1800; *Hampshire Chronicle*, 10 November 1800.
83 *Morning Post*, 19 January 1801.
84 By way of example, on 20 October 1800, 300 colliers from the Timsbury and other Mendip pits descended on Bath to seek relief from the mayor, stating that their only 'object was to be instructed how they were to get bread for their starving families': *Sherborne & Yeovil Mercury*, 27 October 1800. On the subject of persistences and traditions in the 1790s see: Bohstedt, *Riots and Community Politics*, ch. 2.
85 *Sussex Weekly Advertiser*, 21 April 1800; *Reading Mercury*, 16 June 1800.
86 Poole, 'Scarcity and the civic tradition', p. 107.
87 TNA, HO 42/50, Meyrick to Portland, 12 June 1800, cited in Randall, *Before the Luddites*, p. 274, n.75.
88 *Chester Chronicle*, 19 September; 1800; Wells, *Wretched Faces*, pp. 128–31; *Kentish Gazette*, 19 September; TNA, 42/51 fos 152–3 and 278–9, J. Kennedy, Rochester, 15 September, and Lord Romney, The Mote, to Portland, 19 September 1800.
89 TNA, HO 42/35, fos 197–8: J. Garnett Attorney, Kilperton, nr Trowbridge to Portland, 18 July 1795.

90 Manchester City Library, broadside ballads, BR f.824.04.BA1, vol. 4, p. 155. 'Loyal Jone', printed by J. Haddock, Warrington, cited in Navickas, *Loyalism and Radicalism in Lancashire*, p. 76.

91 F. O'Gorman, 'The Paine burnings of 1792–1793', *Past & Present*, 193 (2006), 111–55; E.P. Thompson, *The Making of the English Working Class* (London: Penguin, 1968), p. 430; *Hull Packet*, 27 February 1795.

92 Navickas, *Loyalism and Radicalism in Lancashire*, p. 32.

93 *Salisbury and Winchester Journal*, 24 March 1800.

94 *Sussex Weekly Advertiser*, 24 March 1800.

95 *Sussex Weekly Advertiser*, 28 April 1800.

96 TNA, HO 42/55 fos 69–71, Colonel Manningham, Windsor to Portland, 14 December 1800.

97 TNA, HO 42/61, fos 141–5, T. Lamb, Rye, 14 February 1801, to Portland, enclosing threatening letter sent to farmer Procter.

98 TNA, HO 42/61, fos 5–6, Mr Lloyd, Lenham, to Portland, 2 January 1801.

99 TNA, HO 42/52, fos 151–3, George Earle, Winchester to Portland, 4 October, including enclosed threatening notice, dated 24 September 1800.

100 On the popular effects of militarisation in the 1790s see R. Wells, *Insurrection: The English Experience, 1795–1803* (Stroud: Alan Sutton, 1983); Navickas, *Loyalism and Radicalism*, p. 193.

101 TNA, HO 42/35 fos 29–31, Duke of Richmond, Goodwood, to Portland, 22 June, enclosing Mr Lee, editor of the *Sussex Weekly Advertiser*, Lewes to Richmond, 15 June 1795.

102 Ibid. On the Newhaven riot see: R. Wells, 'The militia mutinies of 1795', in J. Rule (ed.), *Outside the Law: Studies in Crime and Order* (Exeter: Exeter University Press, 1982), pp. 35–64.

103 *York Courant*, 17 August 1795.

104 K. Navickas, *Protest and the Politics of Space and Place, 1789–1848* (Manchester: Manchester University Press), pp. 28, 47–9, 52.

105 *York Courant*, 10 and 17 August 1795.

106 *Hampshire Chronicle*, 27 January 1800.

107 TNA, HO 42/61, fos 141–5, Letter sent to Mr. Procter, farmer, Rye, 12 February 1801.

108 *Oxford Journal*, 12 April 1800.

109 TNA, HO 42/61, fo. 145, note stuck upon the Market Place, Rye, on the morning of 14 February 1801.

110 M. Overton, *Agricultural Revolution in England: The Transformation of the Agrarian Economy 1500–1850* (Cambridge: Cambridge University Press, 1996); J.A. Chartres, 'Market integration and agricultural output in seventeenth-, eighteenth-, and early nineteenth-century England', *Agricultural History Review*, 43:2 (1995), 117–38.

111 See note 33, above.

112 Thompson, 'Moral economy'; E.P. Thompson, 'Patrician society, plebeian culture', *Journal of Social History*, 7:4 (1974), 382–405.

113 R. Bush and G. Martiniello, 'Food riots and protest: Agrarian modernizations and structural crises', *World Development*, 91 (2017), 193–207.

114 Bohstedt, *Politics of Provisions*.

2

The persistence of the discourse
of starvation in the protests of the poor

On his ride down the valley of the Avon in Wiltshire during the blistering hot summer of 1826, the grand old man of English radicalism William Cobbett calculated how many families the produce of Milton Lilbourne parish would support were it not for the demands of 'idlers who live in luxury'. Beyond Cobbett's makeshift calculus, the case was simple enough. Why should those that 'raise the food' be subject to begging for relief, emigration schemes, and gaols and transportation vessels for taking what they produced, when 'no project is on foot … for *transporting* pensioners, parsons or dead-weight people!'[1] To the grand old rural radical, such scenes were, as Ian Dyck noted, reminiscent of France before the revolution of 1789. The only way to save the produce of plenty from the incendiarist's torch was for the farmers to make common cause with their workers.[2]

This was not just bombast. For, as with all of Cobbett's fierce rhetoric, behind his words lay a hard reality. If dearth, market manipulation and the effects of the war had combined to produce the most grinding of scarcities in 1795 and 1800, the possibilities and fear of genuine hunger never went away. Those who laboured – men, women and children – were only ever one crisis away from absolute bodily need. Many in the towns and country alike continued to live in a state of constant hunger, their diets inadequate to sustain their toiling bodies.[3] Rural workers, especially in areas with few alternative sources of employment and those in the western counties where the cloth trade was in steep decline, were particularly vulnerable. Wages had failed to keep up with spiralling food prices – this relationship was *the* determinant of the standard of living – while the extension of poor relief in the form of Speenhamland-type payments progressively became less generous and subject instead to ratepayer manipulation (as chapter three explores).[4]

And yet historians of rural England have paid remarkably little attention to the politics of hunger in the decades beyond 1800. This is not to say that rural historians have been blind to the issues of hunger. In neighbouring

Ireland and, to a lesser extent, Scotland, this period was the absolute nadir of hunger politics: the wretched famines of the 1820s and 1830s followed by the devastation of the 'potato famine' of the late 1840s dominate the historiography of rural hunger.[5] As related in the introduction, historians of early modern England have also long been alert to the political impacts of hunger and famine,[6] while references to the cries and effects of hunger by rural workers can be found interspersed in the works of such eminent rural historians as Alun Howkins and Keith Snell.[7] The more culturally inflected poor law historians have also alluded to the political importance of hunger,[8] while no study of the 1840s is complete without reflecting on the critical importance of hunger lived and politically constructed in shaping that decade.[9] But in all such writings on rural England, hunger is a context rather than the focus, a dynamic in rural social relations rather than something analysed in its own right.

In part, as the next section explores, this is a function of a particular (and arguably perverse) reaction to E.P. Thompson's moral-economy thesis. Moreover, concurrent with the supposed death of the food-rioting 'tradition' after the national wave of food rioting in the 1790s as explored in the previous chapter, wages rather than food prices and availability became the key factor in labouring living standards and, ergo, in determining rural social relations.[10] With this in mind, and with the understanding that hunger is invariably articulated in the archive by way of protest – broadly defined – this chapter seeks to explore the ways in which hunger persisted as an important protest discourse of the rural poor in the early nineteenth century. Or rather, as the analysis shows, the language of the poor was framed not around articulations of hunger, though that was necessarily implied, but the more urgent, visceral starvation. The bodily state of hunger, and the associated plebeian discourse of starvation, I contend, was not 'rediscovered' as a political force in the mid-1840s, but was persistently given voice through the protests of the poor and through radical politics in the decades before.

Starvation beyond subsistence crises

Reprising an argument first rehearsed in an influential, if controversial, paper published in the *Journal of Peasant Studies* in 1979, Roger Wells argued in his seminal *Wretched Faces* that the national wave of food riots during the subsistence crises of 1795–6 and 1800–1 represented the 'end' of the food-rioting tradition. The combination of military intervention, increasingly militarised landscapes, trials and court martials with the subsequent hangings and transportations supposedly extinguished whatever will was left to openly resist. If Thompson had already identified the 1790s as a turning point in popular responses to dearth,[11] Wells' thesis placed a greater emphasis on shifting welfare regimes and forms of popular protest. The extension of parish poor relief during the 1795 crisis, typified in the cornlands by Speenhamland-style income support schemes, provided an important palliative when bread prices rose, but many still fell through (or foul of) networks of institutionalised welfare. Rather than turning to collective bargaining by riot, their grievances were either ameliorated through turning to crime, especially poaching and pilfering, or were expressed through a resort to covert tools of terror. The 'moral economy' was not dead; it just had to be articulated in different ways using different tools of protest.[12]

The crisis of 1810–12 was, supposedly, decisive. To Bohstedt, previous historians' focus on 'class, Luddism, and radicalism' in the 1810s 'obscured' the fact that this decade witnessed a critical turn in the politics of provisions.[13] Going beyond Randall's claim that in the 1810s 'problems of food supply were superseded by an issue that struck deep into moral economic attitudes of industrial workers: machinery', Bohstedt suggests that 'the Luddite years' were not only marked by machine-breaking, armed attacks and assassinations, but also, by 1818, a turn to regionally coordinated strikes.[14] Thus while the crisis of 1810–12 and the harvest failure of 1816 were marked by some food riots, these were 'a matter of political opportunity', symbols of 'rural desperation, archaic community politics, or urban pandemonium'.[15] Wage levels, as Fox Genovese suggested, had replaced the price of basic foodstuffs as the fundamental component in plebeian living standards and were now the key stimulus to popular protest.[16]

Bohstedt's *longue durée* study of subsistence riots offers a useful corrective for the period after 1801: some limited resort to food rioting continued, but 1801 still marked the demise of the era of 'provisions politics'.[17] But such a conclusion seems premature given that in the 1840s hunger was 'rediscovered' as a political force, the 'struggle over the representation of scarcity', as Peter Gurney has put it, being central to the politicking of Anti-Corn Law League (ACLL) and Chartism alike. 'Hunger', he continued, 'had no obvious, straightforward meaning or political effect, but, as in other contexts, was itself culturally and discursively constructed'.[18] In short, Chartist and ACLL leaders had good reason to 'rediscover' and mobilise hunger in their claims and discourses. But notwithstanding their assertions that they represented the interests of the nation, their messages were essentially urban, geared not to the field workers but to the factory workers and operatives. Even Chartist broadsides against the food served to the inmates of New Poor Law workhouses failed to help the movement truly penetrate the rural south, east and west.[19] But food was not a popular political problem relegated to the towns and the Celtic fringe.[20] It is the contention of this chapter that after 1801, 'provisions', or rather the lack thereof, remained an acute popular political force. Why else did reformers place such symbolic value in 'the big loaf'?[21] Hunger, it is asserted, was articulated in different ways than the 'classic' food riot, finding persistent voice in threatening letters, protest parleys, incendiarism, court room claims, satire and radical politics.

Protest and survive

If to labour without complaint was stoic and heroic, hunger had no honour. The alternative to protest was clear:

> Richard Richardson, who, as we stated in our last, was found dead on the downs, in the parish of Alceston [Alciston], is supposed to have fallen a sacrifice to fatigue and want. He was in the habit of going every morning to the distance of four miles from home to work, at 12s. per week. On the fatal day he got up at his usual hours, and was about to start for his destination without taking any victuals with him – for all the food he possessed in the world consisted only of a three-penny loaf, and which he would fain have left for his family, as it was the only article of subsistence in the house, and he had no money or credit, and had been refused, as we understand, parochial support, when his wife, by repeated solicitations, induced him, though most reluctantly to accept the loaf, with which at length he departed. On his return, at night, it is supposed, he sunk exhausted, as he was found lifeless on the downs, with the loaf, almost untouched, in his bag, intending no doubt, to restore it to his half-starved wife and six children. The verdict returned was '*Died by the visitation of God*'.[22]

The Sussex labourer Richardson's case is perhaps apocryphal, but this 1815 report underlines that the cries of hunger normally went silent (and thus unrecorded) and provoked little in the way of public protestations. Even at the parish vestry, labouring families were more likely to perform the deferential logic of proclaiming need rather than expressing their hunger: the latter approach was a de facto critique of the policies of the parish paymasters. Anyone familiar with the language of pauper letters and the wording of vestry and select vestry books will know that *explicit* declarations of hunger were exceptional. A search through the indexes of the five volumes of Pickering and Chatto's excellent *Narratives of the Poor* notes only one entry for 'diet, starvation', in a pauper letter from a Samuel Parker of Kidderminster to the Uttoxeter overseers of the poor complaining that he was travelling thousands of miles for work 'with an Hungry Belly sore feet and an Aching Heart'. There is much in these volumes that makes representations of 'need', 'necessity' and lacking the 'necessities of life', but not hunger or starvation.[23]

As Samantha Shave has shown, even in criticising the Cannington (Somerset) overseers' relief policy, recently widowed pauper Ann Dunster only alluded to her hunger through the discourse of 'need':

> I am sorry to receve such a measage from/ you that I am to have four Shillans of/ my Pay taken of I hope you will not/be so hard harted as to take it from me/ as I stand in more need of having some.[24]

This is the exactly the same tone and form of language as that identified by Steve Hindle – a 'shift' rather than 'having some' – for the early years of the poor law two centuries previously.[25] Beyond the persistence of needy deferential tropes, the report of Richardson's demise and Dunster's letter serve to remind us that the experience of everyday life for working families in the early nineteenth-century English countryside was one of constantly being in bodily need. Even gout-afflicted, archaeology-obsessed Camerton clergyman John Skinner understood it, and recorded meeting with the starving in his diaries.[26]

Given the everyday need of avoiding direct conflict with the vestry, it is not surprising that public articulations of hunger tended to be given voice as acts of protest. In a position of subjection, the public performance of hunger was bound to be deferential, the language softened, the claim less threatening, the rule of power with, as Thompson put it, its acts of 'ostentatious display' and occasional acts of 'class appeasement' reciprocally demanding forelock-tugging recognition of their (hegemonic) liberality. But the language of need was just that, a playing out of the rituals of cultural hegemony. The protest voice was different, expressed in terms not of need or hunger but of starvation, a visceral discourse of shock; to pick up Thompson's analysis, a deliberate dialectical antagonism.[27]

The most obviously articulated expressions came in the form of threatening letters and in utterances made by protesting crowds. The former was a continuation of the practice from the high point of the food 'rioting' tradition, the sending of threatening and incendiary letters being a practice that went hand in hand with riot during every major wave of food rioting in the eighteenth century.[28] A few days after an arson attack on the property of one of the parish paymasters at Newport on the Isle of Wight on 8 September 1804, a threatening letter was posted on the door of the church, striking symbolically at the heart of power in the parish:

> A coucen for the farmers and those that was the incegation of the unnecery rise upon flower and Bread we dp hereby declear and give public Nodice that if you dont lore the price as before we will put fire to every Wheat Rick within our Reach.

So much was standard fare, but it continued: 'For we think it necessary that the Rich should starve as well as the poor and so you may depend upon this as truth.'[29] Here was the trope that would become central to radical political discourse, the idea of hunger amidst plenty (itself a revision of the earlier critique of 'artificial' scarcity that underpinned much moral economic action).[30] The timing at the end of the wheat harvest was no coincidence.[31]

In a slightly different context, the same trope was used in a threatening letter sent to Bradford-upon-Avon clothiers Thomas and Mawbey Tugwell during the so-called 'Wiltshire Outrages' of 1802, the protests against the introduction of finishing machinery by Wiltshire clothiers. Following the firing of a hay rick earlier that night, the threatening letter was placed under the door of Tugwell's workshops and found on the morning of 26 June. It followed a similar, if more graphic, theme:

> Death or Glory to you T & M Tugwell We will Burn you and your Horseis we will Cut your heart out and Eat him you ot to have Dam heart out of your Body you will go to Hell for starveing the poor thee Shot Shaw by night for some of you.[32]

The same discourse was a common theme in threatening letters beyond the immediate memory of the food riots of the 1790s. Magistrate Thomas Biggs of Pedmore (Worcestershire) received two threatening letters, the first in September 1812, the second the following January, of a decidedly moral economic tone:

> We right to Let you no if you do not a medetley See that the Bread is made cheper you may and all your Nebern farmers expect all your Houses rickes Barns all Fiered and Bournd down to the ground you a gestes and See all your felley Cretyrs Starved to death Pray see for Som alterreshon in a Mounth or you shall see what shall Be the matter.[33]

Somewhat different was the aforementioned 'big loaf' rhetoric adopted by the wider reform movement that also penetrated and informed Luddite thought. As the Derbyshire ballad 'Hunting a Loaf' put it:

> For Derby it's true, and Nottingham too,
> Poor men to the jail they've been taking,
> They say that Ned Ludd as I understood,
> A thousand wide frames has been breaking.
> Fall al, &c.

> Now it is not bad there's no work to be had,
> The poor to be starv'd in their station;
> And if they do steal they're strait sent to the jail,
> And they're hang'd by the laws of the nation.[34]

It was at times of crisis that such cries were most voluble. Thus, notwithstanding the collapse in agricultural commodity prices at the end of the Napoleonic Wars, the concurrent decline in wages and the swelling of un- and under-employment intensified both the long-term decline in real wages and the precarity of existence for many labouring families.[35] No less a formal publication than the Board of Agriculture's 1816 *Agricultural State of the Kingdom* stated that labourers in Lincolnshire were 'starving for the want of employment'.[36] Similarly, an anonymous letter writer to the Home

Office reported that during the 1816 subsistence crisis he was 'frequently
… shocked by the imprecations of men and women on the authors of their
present starving condition'.[37] Even before the formal proclamation of peace,
campaigning against the proposed new corn law provoked protests in the
rural south – contra the claims of J.R. Wordie – amidst claims of likely starvation.[38] At Portsmouth a meeting in May 1814 noted that the 'lower classes'
had 'already suffered by the pressure of the times' but that the proposed bill
would mean that:

> [the] poor would be unable to procure bread, and then they would rob,
> and in fact they would have no other means of living – so that this new law
> would infallibly either reduce people to *starvation*, or compel them to be
> *hanged*.[39]

Arguably the most obvious popular articulation of the discourse in the
immediate post-Napoleonic period gave its name to the localised 'rising'
of agricultural and industrial workers in East Anglia in the spring of 1816,
'Bread of Blood'. Not only did the protests involve the classic moral-economy
forms of seizing of bread and flour but the demands made also invoked the
protestors' families' immediate bodily need. The day after demanding from
the magistrates 'Cheap Bread, a Cheap Loaf, and Provisions cheaper', a
group of men and women again gathered and submitted a petition threatening
'Bread or Blood in Brandon this day'. Not winning any concessions, they
gathered again for a third consecutive day of protests on 16 May with a
banner proclaiming the same words, 'Bread or Blood'.[40] The symbolism and
inferences are obvious and yet the sole systematic study of the 1816 protests'
analysis of hunger begins and ends with the assertion that the protestors
existed on Spartan fare.[41] It is evident that the protests combined the practical
measures to alleviate need – attacks on flour mills, the looting of butchers'
shops and mills, and taxation populaire – with the symbolic. The destruction
of threshing machines, pleas for higher wages to match the increased price
of flour, and setting fire to wheat stacks were all deliberate comments about
their being hungry amidst such abundance.[42]

That the East Anglian protests have been afforded the 'Bread or Blood'
tag is in some ways unhelpful, rendering a heterogeneous set of protests as
seemingly homogenously concerned only with getting by. It is important to
remember that this was a rapidly deindustrialising region. The woollen and
weaving districts of Essex and East Anglia had been in long-term decline, but
competition from more highly capitalised and machine-operating Yorkshire
and the massive drop in demand on the cessation of war on the continent
effectively put a total end to the once huge cloth industry.[43] This, combined
with the rapidly deepening agrarian depression and the concurrent introduction of new threshing technologies and other tools of landscape 'improvement' – not least around drainage – represented not only a concurrence of
circumstances but also a clear sense of the fear of the old ways being lost.

Bread here stands not only as sustenance but as also a metaphor for the old world being lost; blood is not only a disembodied threat but also the violent uncertainty of a dystopic future of empty bellies, grain prairies, union workhouses and machines. The deliberate reference to bread was also a direct reference to – and was in all likelihood inspired by – popular politicking over the passage of the Corn Importation Bill that would become known as the Corn Laws. Indeed, claims that labouring people in the corn counties did not protest at the Corn Laws have been shown to be a fallacy. Wherever the archive is examined, evidence of popular opposition is uncovered. And this extended to East Anglia. Bread or Blood spoke to custom, local experiences located in a national context, and national popular politics.[44]

Elsewhere in 1816 the symbolism was more graphic. In common with a 'general discontent' that prevailed amongst working people in the 'western counties' that spring, the 'strongest marks of abhorrence' were made by the 'lower classes' every evening in public houses against the ministers for passing the Corn Law. One morning a loaf drenched in blood with a heart placed alongside was found in the streets of Plymouth. The previous night the walls and 'large dons' had been gratified with (and here the Home Office correspondent probably paraphrased) the words:

> Damn the promoters of the Corn Bill – Bread we must and will have – It is better to die to obtain bread than tamely to perish for want of it – Our blood shall deluge the land or else we will be prevented from starving – Eternal destruction to all those who oppress the poor.[45]

Evidently promoting their own political agenda, the correspondent suggested that only by repealing the Corn Bill and a 'spirit of commiseration' being 'speedily manifested' to the poor could a 'general Insurrection' be prevented.[46]

The 'hungry labourer'

If the bloody loaf combined with anti-government taproom utterances was as much of the 1790s as it was the 1810s,[47] the focus of the protests on the corn loaf attests the continued political potency of hunger (and the fear of the hunger) as well as its imbrication in new political fronts. By the 1820s, and endemic by the late 1830s, a new popular discourse was being used to describe rural workers: the farmworker was no longer just the labourer but instead the 'hungry labourer'. Of course, historians need to be careful in making claims to novelty. After all, farmers and labourers alike were often reminded from the pulpit of the parish church that, in the words of Proverbs 16:26, 'The labourer's appetite works for him; his hunger drives him on'. But this new form of description went beyond earlier tellings of the keen and lusty labourer driven on by a hunger-induced work ethic to something rooted in a radical political sensibility. It also mirrored what Keith Snell has noted was a marked shift in early nineteenth-century artistic depictions of rural workers: earlier representations of labouring in choreographed place gave way to paintings of wretchedness and mobile poverty.[48] As Snell acknowledges, such depictions were not the defining representational paradigm of rural England in the early nineteenth century. Rather, most depictions of rural workers, as John Barrell has shown, placed them either in chaste and sober domestic settings or so far into the distance that they remained non-threatening but neither evidently at work nor haggard.[49]

Still, this shift, however partial, also mirrored broader trends in the politics of representation. For instance, Percy Bysshe Shelley's poems in the early 1820s frequently returned to the theme of famine and starvation. Shelley's poetry is undoubtedly Janus-faced in its intended audiences – a select group of elite literary aesthetes and 'the people' with whom he identified and often tried to position himself as a voice of – while Shelley also proclaimed to Thomas Medwin that he did not wish to live near the squalor, hunger and starvation of a 'populous manufacturing dissipated town'.[50] Moreover, the extent to which Shelley really knew of grinding poverty beyond that described in radical journals and that witnessed at a distance and discussed amongst his progressive friends is unknown. That said, there is no doubt in poems such as 'A Ballad: Young Parson Richards' (later renamed by Shelley anthologists as 'Ballad of a Starving Mother'), a tale of clerical moral duplicity, as to what Shelley's sentiments on the *lived* politics of hunger were:

> Young Parson Richards stood at his gate
> Feeding his hound with bread;
> Hunch after hunch, the mere beast ate…
>
> A woman came up with a babe at her breast
> Which was flaccid with toil and hunger –
> She cried – 'Give me food and give me rest;
> We die if I wait much longer.–[51]

That the child is the Parson's progeny is the root of the satire in the piece but the social commentary is most savage in relation to the juxtaposition of the profligate consumption of the rich and the absolute bodily need of the poor, well-fed fido against the withering babe. For such writings there was evidently a market, but this radical political sensibility of representing hunger was at odds with a wider sensibility in 'polite' society which, given voice in journals and before parliamentary committees, recognised the privations of the poor in the temperate language of charity and need rather than starvation. In this way hunger was still political – being mobilised as evidence for the need for political reform, a reform of morals and manners of the poor, and reform of the poor laws – but in a different register to the discourse of starvation. Hunger had uses, it served political ends.[52]

The spoken and written discourse of the 'hungry labourer' was integral to anti–Corn Law campaigning (including in the rhetoric of the ACLL),[53] and was writ through the rhetoric and writings of early Chartism,[54] but it also took on a wider resonance in the countryside. A report in the *Wiltshire Independent* in December 1838 promoted good garden (and allotment) management in the cultivation of beans as a way of feeding the 'hungry labourer after he has returned from his day's toil'.[55] If allotment management was not outwardly political, more obvious was a letter to the *Cambridge Chronicle* in January 1822, just predating the wave of threshing-machine breaking and incendiarism in East Anglia that year. '[We are] in a starving condition, yet surrounded by plenty; complaining or repining at the bounty of an all-wise Providence for the super-abundance we *ought* to enjoy.' If the landlords and occupiers of land 'cannot live upon the immense track of soil they have been in the habit of cultivating', then, so reckoned the letter writer, the starving poor should be let from two to ten acres to keep a cow, breeding sow, a few poultry and to grow crops, hay, vegetables and fruit.[56]

This was also William Cobbett's solution – and also at the root of his critique. 'In every view of the matter … it is desirable that the families of which a nation consists should be happily off', decreed Cobbett in the introduction to *Cottage Economy*, his guide to labouring household management. To be happy, he continued, 'a family must be well supplied with *food* and *raiment* … [t]he doctrines which fanaticism preaches, and which teach men to be *content* with *poverty*, are calculated to favour tyrants by giving them passive slaves.' This was the basis of labouring rights:

> To live well, to enjoy all things that make life pleasant is the right of every man who constantly uses his strength judiciously and lawfully. It is to blaspheme God to suppose he created man to be miserable, to hunger, thirst and perish with cold in the midst of that abundance which is the fruit of his labour.[57]

The labouring body denied and controlled by the parish paymasters rendered the labourer – and by extension labouring families – 'land-slaves'.[58] But it was the very condition of hunger, unemployment and, by the late 1820s, a heightened political consciousness that gave Cobbett hope that rural workers might throw off their shackles.[59]

The juxtaposition of hunger with plenty was both one of Cobbett's defining leitmotifs and one of his most powerful weapons in teaching labourers to see the tyranny of their enslavement. This was at its most powerful in his *Rural Rides*, first published in his *Political Register* and *Two-Penny Trash*. In this text Cobbett's politics are placed in the context of the spaces of everyday labouring existence. Outwith the barren heaths and 'villainously ugly' forests ('a poorer spot than this New Forest, there is not in all England; nor, I believe, in the whole world'), everywhere Cobbett journeyed he was met by plenty.[60] But beyond a few places where enlightened landlords supported farmers to support the labourers, plenty was the product of the ragged, haggard poor; their labours, in Cobbett's mind, invariably fed the 'infernal WEN'.[61]

To Cobbett the politics of food were clear, though there were contradictions in his position. As a farmer, and pertinently as a farmer's son, he believed in the fundamental agrarian capitalist tenets of private property, a free labour market and the farmer's right to the land. He was, in short, not an Owenite by disposition. But there were important qualifying conditions. If the young Cobbett was a supporter of enclosure, the older Cobbett was ardently opposed. A Sunday stroll on and around the common at Horton Heath in south Hampshire in 1804 convinced him of the economic and cultural worth of commons to rural workers.[62] Moreover, economic value accrued not just to the commoner but also to the wider community. Enclosure might increase wheat production, the *staple* of the labourers' diet, but it would markedly diminish honey, meat, milk, and vegetable production thereby diminishing variety (and perhaps even calorific intake) in the commoners' diet. Similarly, poaching to feed the family was not to be reproved. On his 'rural ride' between Highworth and Malmsbury in Wiltshire, he came across thirty men engaged in spade husbandry by the overseer. Calculating the married men's wages to be about 4s 6d a week, the single men on rather less, Cobbett suggested that simply to live they must have more food 'either by *poaching* or by *taking without leave*'.[63]

Cobbett thus realised that there was a wretched materiality to food. While labourers were often on meagre and unvaried diets, *they* were the ones producing food, every day surrounded by the abundant products of their labour. This irony was not lost on Cobbett. Rural riding in the Avon Valley of Wiltshire, he noted:

> The stack-yards down this valley are beautiful to behold. They contain from *five* to *fifteen* banging, *wheat-ricks*, besides *barley-ricks*, and *hay-ricks* … A very fine sight this was, and it could not meet the eye without making one look round (and in vain) *to see the people who were to eat all this food*; and without making one reflect on the horrible, the unnatural, the base and infamous state, in which we must be … I saw in *one piece*, about four hundred acres of wheat-stubble, and I saw a sheep-fold, which, I thought, contained *an acre of ground,* and had in it about *four thousand sheep and lambs* … This is certainly the most delightful farming in the world … [I]t seems impossible to find a more beautiful and pleasant county than this, or to imagine any life more easy and happy than men might here lead, if they were untormented by an *accursed system that takes the food from those who raise it, and gives it to those that do nothing that itself is useful to man.*[64]

Similarly, in journeying through the cloth-making valleys of north Wiltshire, Cobbett observed:

> Of all the countries that God, in his goodness, ever made for the enjoyment of man, even in this the most favoured land, this seems to be the most

delightful, and its extent the most valuable. Rich land, beautiful woods, water bubbling from the hills in all directions, coal in abundance at a short distance, stone and slate the substratum of the bound these winding and ever varying valleys, where climate is so mild, and the gardens so early and so blessed with products. Yet this spot ... has become the abode of gaunt hunger and raving despair.[65]

The rise in crime, particularly theft, was singularly attributable to this contrast. Crime was hunger materially manifest as resistance. As one Dorset labourer admitted in court in December 1828, he poached because he was poor: 'unless I take [up] a gun now and then; I must starve'.[66] The situation was especially acute in the Weald, where labourers openly declared that so long as there was anything to eat they would steal it so as not to starve. To this end, rural workers were 'all now confederates, so that detection is scarcely possible'.[67] In rallying against the game laws in 1823, Cobbett had suggested that labourers had cause to rebel, stating his resolve to see 'every inch of property' given over to the poor. These were strong words, if not truly reflective of his broader position. Still, Cobbett consistently argued that hunger was justification enough for the poor to take from the most prosperous farmers: '[a society] in which the common labourer ... cannot secure a sufficiency of food and raiment, is a society which ought not to exist; a society contrary to the law of nature'.[68] Many labourers agreed. As an extraordinary letter addressed to the *Suffolk Chronicle* from 'The poor labourers' of the Hundred of Cosford lamented, 'our class are starving weigh'd down with oppression and worn out with vexations'. 'We shall', the letter continued, 'shortly fight for ourselves[. W]e count it an absolute right for us to rise for support for our wives and beloved children ... our side is strong and hang as it were by a thread ready ripened for a revolt.'[69]

This discourse of hunger was central to the Swing quasi-insurrection of 1830 in several ways. Attacks on labour-saving machinery in the countryside were not new but before 1830 they drew little comment from Cobbett. The grand old radical was silent on the use of threshing machines (one positive comment in 1816 aside) until during Swing.[70] And yet attacks on labour-saving agricultural machinery, not least threshing machines, were not new phenomena and had long been explained in terms of hunger, a recognition of the irony that 'once we could eat that which we threshed, but now that we don't thresh the grain we cannot'. These claims were writ through both the 'Bread or Blood' protests and the lesser-known 1822 'East Anglian Riots', both low points in the post-Napoleonic depression,[71] but were most explicitly articulated during the crisis of 1829–31 and in particular by Swing activists. At Melksham, a place with a long history of opposition to machinery dating back to at least 1740, during the summer of 1829 a steam carriage en route from London to Bath was pelted by a volley of stones. The 'concourse of persons' who gathered explained that they believed 'a steam carriage was calculated to reduce manual labour', and cried: 'We are starving already, let's have no more machinery', 'Down with the machinery', and 'Knock it to pieces'.[72] During Swing the connection was also made explicitly in relation to the operation of threshing machines. Around Havant in south Hampshire machine-breakers were reported to have explained: 'We are out of employ – we have no work – Break the machines – we will have bread – we will not starve'.[73] Some of those involved with the Elham gang of machine-breakers in Kent told local MP and patrician Tory grandee 'they would rather do anything than encounter such a winter as the last'.[74] The plea of those assembled at Sutton Scotney, another major centre of machine-breaking in the Dever Valley of Hampshire, was similar, if more conciliatory: 'We are half starved; we are willing to work, let us be paid what we earn, that's all we want!'[75]

Starving Swing

Making a link between popular political writings and the starvation discourse of Swing activists is necessarily complex. While the direct influence of Cobbett's writings on hunger is impossible to definitively prove, we do know that Cobbett's writings (and lectures) provided a direct inspiration for many Swing activists. Indeed, Cobbett deliberately went on a lecture tour of southern England at the height of Swing to deliberately (and directly) provide inspiration.[76] We also know that the discourse of hunger permeated the wider reform movement; for instance, a reform petition sent to the King from Corsham in Wiltshire pleaded that the 'evils afflicting the country' including the 'starvation of the poor' and 'gaols filled by crime due to misery and the game laws' be removed.[77] A pro-reform editorial in *Keene's Bath Journal* at the height of Swing likewise attested that the condition of rural workers was proof enough of the need for reform:

> [T]he poor are sunk to the lowest grade of existence – potatoes and salt being often their only sustenance [this a motif of Cobbett]. And who is prepared to say, that they ought to preserve their moral character through such trying difficulties? – When a poor man's means of maintenance at home is more miserable than that of a gaol, what terror has the law? When his labour will not enable him to maintain his family, whom he is continually doomed to see half starved around him, what impulse has he to industry?[78]

We also know, thanks to the late Ian Dyck's labours, that Swing was not only predicted by Cobbett but also had 'advance billing' in rural songs of the 1820s. Over and above complaints about threshing machines, parish make-work schemes and migrant workers, these songs also explicitly bemoaned the fact that rural working families were starving. As the ballad 'What Will Old England Come To?' put it:

> When the harvest had used to come, O that was the working-man's joy,
> But for now to reap & mow, it's strangers they all do employ,
> A man that stops in his own parish has scarce any work for to do,
> While his family they are half-starving,
> O what will old England come to?[79]

With this in mind, what is telling is that many of the claims to hunger in Swing's archive not only assert starvation (as opposed to the less politic- ally charged hunger) but were also made in the context of broader popular political critiques. In the vicinity of Maidstone (Kent), Swing was manifest through the actions of highly mobile groups walking from parish to parish led by two radical shoemakers, Robert Price and John Adams. Both were quick to make political statements and draw on radical critiques when challenged by the rulers of rural England. On 29 October when Adams' group was met by a combined military and civil force at Boughton Monchelsea, he attempted to address the magistracy, led by the Mayor of Maidstone. However, the Riot Act was read. Incensed, Adams accused the government of being 'privy to the outrage ... as an excuse for sending soldiers to spill the blood of these half- starved men'. On this, Adams and two others, Pitman, a fellow Maidstone shoemaker, and Holloway, a Southwark tailor, were seized. Others in the group also complained to the magistrates that their families were starving.[80]

Put simply, Swing was inherently political but at heart it was a 'bread and butter' – or more appositely just a bread – movement. As Sir Edward Knatchbull, East Kent grandee and chair of the local quarter sessions, related to home secretary Peel: 'They [the machine-breakers] would rather do any- thing than encounter such a winter as the last.'[81] As a Sevenoaks corres- pondent to the *Rochester Gazette* reported in relation to the wave of incendiary fires in the north-west Kent in the late summer of 1830 – fires that were con- current with the start of threshing-machine breaking in the Elham Valley at the other side of the county: 'The expressions of the mob are dreadful: they said "Damn it, let it burn, I only wish it was a house: We can warm ourselves now: We only want some potatoes, there is a nice fire to cook them by!"' The desire to cook potatoes was a deliberate allusion to their absolute state of degradation, a fire to cook famine food.[82] Swing was hungry desperation writ large, a collective desire to suffer no more. Indeed, at nearby Lenham no popular political utterances were reported but the men processed around the parish with a banner declaring that they were 'Starving at 1s. 6d. a week' and demanding food.[83] Likewise at Hicksted in mid-Sussex, those gathered barricaded the farmers in the Castle Inn, and berated them for starving the poor while they were always 'boozing' at vestry meetings. If the juxtaposition between want and plenty was not already clear, that night overseer Sharp's corn barn was set alight.[84] The connection was made even more bluntly in graphic threatening letters sent to a Horsham farmer and to Reverend Woodward of Maresfield. The former was accused of 'gorg[ing] upon the vitals of the poor half starved labourer till he has sworn to wear the chains of slavery no longer'; the same letter also warned that the 'Parson Justices' ought 'make your Wills'.[85] The letter received by Reverend Woodward was even more vitriolic:

> Sir, we have enquird into your tithe and find you join in eating the country up … what business have you with the others ought not the poor labour to right have it that works for it who you starve you old Canible take it if you dare and we will rost you and your daughter in your bed.[86]

Whatever the realities of the dietary relationship between labourers, farmers, clergy and the magistracy, such claims were rooted in a reality the rulers of rural England recognised. As Lord Carnarvon's Highclere steward put it, 'the whole rural machine is going wrong'. Most labourers were 'not half employed', those who were received only seven shillings a week, 'little better than a mere saloop from starvation'. Farmers too were half-ruined, while shopkeepers 'suffer from the poverty of their country customers'. The country was 'rife for change', needing 'only a spark to set it off '. A 'revolution', he concluded, 'is quite possible'.[87] Dorset MP Edward Portman also remarked that a group of machine-breakers active in and around the Blackmoor Vale in north Dorset were 'half-starved and half-naked and desperate'.[88]

After Swing

Whatever the effects of the repression of Swing and the concessions made to many labouring families during the rising, reprisals and continued protests in the ensuing months were still informed and shaped by the discourse of starvation. A 'Swing' letter received by farmer Humphrey at Donnington near Chichester in January 1831 threatening to burn his premises if he used his threshing machine was wrapped in a handbill entitled the 'Starvation of the Poor'.[89] William Lee, 'a miserable looking biped' in the words of the Tory *Bridgwater and Somersetshire Herald*, was even brought to trial for 'sedition' at the Devon Epiphany Quarter Sessions in 1831 for uttering:

> that if the mob were to come there to Stoodley, he would join them, if he were to be hung the next hour, for he had a wife and four children and not half-work, and it was as well to be hung as to starve.[90]

Arguably of greater importance, given the huge upturn in incendiarism after 1830, was the threat made to Henry Drummond, the Surrey magistrate who had committed labourer James Warner to stand trial for firing Albury Mill: 'We fired the mill; starving and firing shall go together.' Or as another report put it: 'It was me who fired the Mill – starve and fire go together.'[91] Much like the prevention of exports during earlier food riots, this was a clear statement that if the hungry poor could not eat what they had grown, no one else would.

Animal maiming, like incendiarism, was also often a simple enough case of destroying that which rural workers had reared (or produced, in the case of incendiarism) but would not be able to eat. It was a classic inversion of meaning. The following case is especially instructive. In January 1848 198 sheep of gentleman farmer Erlysman Charles Pinkney were killed by being fed copper sulphate at Berwick St John, Wiltshire.

On a reward of 100 guineas being offered and a handbill stating the facts of the case being circulated in Salisbury and the surrounding countryside, labourer James Blanchard was arrested on suspicion. Having been dismissed from Pinkney's employ in 1840 for misconduct, Blanchard threatened 'to do for' him, for which he was arrested and bound over to keep the peace. Blanchard again applied to Pinkney's steward for work in July 1847, but on being refused again threatened to have his revenge: he would shoot Pinkney and would poison the sheep when they came off the downs in the winter and 'would be d_d if he did not'. On being challenged by the steward, Blanchard responded, 'If I live, and you live, you will see; there will be mutton enough for many.' Blanchard was again arrested and placed in custody, but on his sending Pinkney a contrite letter, the gentleman decided not to seek his prosecution. There were limits to Blanchard's contrition, though, for he confessed to a fellow prisoner that on his release he would poison the sheep 'when all were in bed and asleep' and that hundreds would die. The evidence presented at the Wiltshire assizes was only circumstantial, however, and Blanchard was found not guilty and duly acquitted. Either way, the sentiment is clear enough: why should others profit and be able to eat that which we cannot?[92] Not as dramatic but no less provocative was the case of a pony belonging to Captain Moneypenny of Rolvenden, Kent, that was symbolically locked in a cold room where it starved to death, the place of incarceration again being deeply symbolic.[93]

To Cobbett the tools of rural terror were merely symptomatic of the problem rather than being the solution. Indeed, both before and after his trial for sedition in 1831 – the government's immediate motivation for which was apparently his influence on labourer Thomas Goodman's turn to incendiarism at Battle, Sussex – Cobbett's writings betrayed an ambivalent relationship with covert protest. By the early 1830s, Cobbett's occasional radical revolutionary words had hardened into a genuine belief that the only way to fill the bellies of the poor – building upon the *Cottage Charter*'s demand of bread, bacon and beer – was to overthrow the system of landlords, clerical parsons, stockjobbers and sinecurists.[94] But the Great Reform Act of 1832, celebrated at Cobbett's Chopsticks' Festival at the Swing village of Sutton Scotney during which the grand old man symbolically spent his time devouring roast beef, begat the New Poor Law which begat further desperation. If by the time of his death in June 1835 very few new Poor Law Unions had been formed, Cobbett knew perfectly well what the consequences would be: a society decisively divided both on class lines and in terms of adequacy of diet. This was reason enough for the labourers to declare absolute ownership of the land so they were able to feed themselves.[95] The Swing Riots had been the start. If the ruling classes were quick to point the finger at Cobbett and other urban radicals and 'demagogues', the grand old man of English radicalism was in no doubt as to the cause: 'The millions have, at last, broken forth; hunger has, at last, set stone walls at defiance, and braved the fetters and the gallows; nature has, at last, commanded the famishing man to get food.'[96]

Whether Cobbett's words were at the forefront of the minds of those who claimed hunger and starvation in mitigation for their stealing food and breaking into shops and pantries is perhaps a moot point, but from the late 1820s, and especially from the mid-1830s, this was a notable trend.[97] As John Rule has stated, John Beattie's evidence for eighteenth-century Sussex and Surrey suggests that most rural crimes were driven by hunger, with the connection still strong in the early nineteenth century.[98] However, the coming together of the acute economic pressures of the period, popular and radical discourses of hunger, and, after 1834, the experience of and opposition to the Poor Law Amendment Act, created a different dynamic. Indeed, as Wells has suggested, opposition to the New Poor Law in the countryside was tied up with hunger, and hunger frequently evoked in its opposition.[99] One of the satirical names attached to the Act by radical politicians was not without basis – or effect: 'the Starvation Bill' or, in its longer form, 'the Whig Poor Law Starvation Bill'.[100]

Examples are legion, but the following cases detail the claims made. Robert Poole of Bolney (Sussex) regularly sought relief or work from the Cuckfield Union relieving officer. Even his refusal to enter the workhouse on being so ordered did not stop him again from trying to claim relief. As Wells notes, Poole's 'weekly contrivances transformed relief days into a public farce'. On one occasion, claiming starvation, he lifted three pounds of cheese, challenging the relieving officer ('whom he threatened to knock "Arse over Head"') to prosecute him. Two Eastbourne workhouse inmates prosecuted for the theft of turnips pleaded hunger, and in support exhibited a 'very small modicum of bread' and an ounce 'of unappetising cheese' in proof. At Hellingly, meagre portions provoked a demonstration in the street, the paupers carrying their bread allowances, and in one case dramatically impaling their bread on the turnpike gate.[101]

These flames of opposition were fanned by the numerous scandals that engulfed the Poor Law Commission in the 1830s and early 1840s.[102] Chapter four considers these scandals in detail, but certain points are pertinent here. Before the notorious exposé of the inhabitants of the Andover workhouse being reduced to gnawing the green, fetid bones they were supposed to be grinding for fertiliser to supplement their meagre dietary, *The Times*, the radical press and other anti-New Poor Law newspapers gleefully reported such abuses, thus fanning the flames of opposition. To give but two examples from Sussex alone: children were found to be exhausted and starving in the Ringmer workhouse, with the coroner reporting a verdict of want of diet and medical attention on the one child who died; and labourer Thomas Pentlow of Angmering hanged himself for want of securing relief to feed his young family.[103] As a letter to the *Brighton Patriot* detailing abuses in the Eastbourne Union put it, families had to be starving before even thinking of entering the new union workhouses.[104] The 'Starvation Bill' brought absolute privation and protestation together more intimately and inseparably than before. So close was the relationship that the motivation of hunger went without saying in many labouring protests in the late 1830s and early 1840s.

Popular political prescriptions

This 'struggle over the representation of scarcity', to return to Gurney's phrase, was undoubtedly acute in the 1840s.[105] Indeed, it is with good reason that the 1840s later assumed the tag the 'Hungry Forties', the privations of the time thus continuing to live on in folk memory.[106] The effect of the European Potato Blight – most devastating in Ireland but causing famine-like conditions in much of England due to repeated bad cereal harvests – and depressions in industry and agriculture alike meant conditions were more devastating than in any decade since the 1790s.[107] If rural unemployment remained defiantly worse in the south and east, the pattern was uneven. Rural 'industrial' workers in the north suffered dreadfully from short-time employment and desperately inadequate relief. Many workers in Cumbria, according to R.N. Thompson, were close to starvation,[108] while the peculiarities of employment practice in Norfolk plunged labourers into a particularly grinding poverty that was given voice in countless threatening letters and an unprecedented wave of incendiary fires.[109]

The decade also witnessed Chartists and the ACLL battling over the causes of (and thus the political prescriptions for the cure of) hunger, the former offering political reform and universal manhood suffrage, the latter resting on Adam Smith's claims that only an unrestrained corn market could prevent 'the miseries of famine'.[110] This battle over representation between competing Chartist and ACLL critiques and prescriptions even filtered into other popular media forms, the ACLL's 'cheap loaf' rhetoric becoming a dominant theme in ballads of the early 1840s. But the battle was not just fought on class lines. As Charlotte Boyce has noted, 'column upon column of newsprint was dedicated to the topic' with access and entitlement not only a critical political issue but also a defining feature of early Victorian print media. New illustrated periodicals attempted to 'realise the chronic, and often life-threatening, hunger that beset the socially and economically vulnerable without offending middle-class sensibilities'.[111] Indeed, one of the first editions of the *Illustrated London News* included a story and supporting illustration of a food riot in Galway on 13 June 1842, tellingly entitled 'The Galway Starvation Riots'. The framing of the report attests that while the editor, Ingram, a reformer but by no means a radical, might not wish to offend middle-class sensibilities, those sensibilities had by the 1840s altered sufficiently that the discourse of starvation could shift from the pages of radical journals and the words of the poor to the pages of mainstream print.[112]

Protests in industrial and urban England in the 1840s continued to draw on this established discourse. The trope of hunger was not just apparent in the ACLL's rhetoric but was also – as will be explored in more detail in chapter four – writ through much Chartist language. As Gurney has shown, Chartism drew directly on 'earlier traditions of plebeian consumer consciousness and action, which … had been key parts of the eighteenth-century moral economy'.[113] Further, Chartist popular politicking often invoked a rich seam in which food (and hunger) symbolically tied everyday urban lives to the surrounding countryside, spaces central to the movement given that Chartist meetings were so often held beyond the urban sphere and that drills were held in the hills and moors that surrounded northern towns.[114] The discourse of starvation and the wider politics of hunger acted as a bridge between the city and the country, between the labourer and the operative.

While the influence and penetration of the ACLL and Chartism in the countryside has arguably been underplayed,[115] it is important to note that their shared promise of an end to hunger simply fed into the protest discourse of hunger that was alive and well in rural England. Undoubtedly there was some influence of their rhetoric in rural protests over hunger in the 1840s. The claims and threats of shepherd and animal maimer Blanchard at Berwick St John were evidently infused with the language of the ACLL. But, as David Jones has asserted, the blame attached to the ACLL and Chartism as 'outside elements' for incendiarism in the 1840s countryside was essentially groundless.[116] Instead, what we see in the rural protests of the Chartist and ACLL period, not least in incendiarism and threatening letters that defined rural social relations, is continuity with the protests of the late 1820s and early to mid-1830s. What was different was the tone. There was a sense not of possible solutions but of escape from starvation, escape from dependency on the whims and fancies of large farmers who, in the words of *The Times*, 'look[ed] on the labourers as a mere crowd, hungry, and dependent' but who were either powerless to help or indifferent.[117] As the writer of a threatening letter found at Stowmarket put it: 'Loock at the people standing daley around your market place, loocking you full in the face as much as to say, we want work, we are starving.'[118] At nearby Burgh, labourer William Medlar, who was sentenced to fifteen years' transportation for firing farmer

Thorne's shed, proclaimed in mitigation that Thorne starved his family by, 'neither g[iving] him work, nor suffered others to do so'.[119]

But such cries of starvation were not rhetoric but pathetic reality. Time after time in the depositions and courtroom testimonies of alleged incendiarists we see something beyond a sense of despair. The brief promise of Swing and reform had been truly vanquished – leading to a sense of abandon. On not being paid in full for hop-picking in John Bourne's gardens at Brede, Sussex, labourer Henry Dine was reported to have threatened that 'I will set a stack on fire, or steal a sheep or a duck for my supper.' Besides, he later continued, he would be 'much better off if transported than he was while running about the country in a state of starvation'. Minutes later an oat stack was on fire. Dine neither denied nor explicitly confessed to the fire and was found guilty, but judge Lord Abinger, wanting to deny Dine his wish, sentenced him to two years in prison with hard labour.[120]

Ultimately, the fact that the ACLL and Chartism, whatever the difference in their claims and prescriptions for ending hunger, still drew upon the long-established wellspring of starvation discourses speaks to the persistence of the fear of hunger in England. It also speaks to the reality that this fear was manifest in lived realities: 'we are but one disaster away from perishing from want'. The expression may have changed since the heyday and ultimate denouement of the food rioting tradition in the 1790s, but the persistences are striking in terms of tone, language and symbolism. Indeed, to claim that the death of food rioting – itself overplayed – represented the end of hunger as a popular force before it was rediscovered in the 'Hungry Forties' is evidently nonsense. It was not rediscovered because it never went away. The spectre never lifted, the threat never passed. Rather, hunger became mediated and told in different ways: the poor law, as chapters three and four consider in detail, became the battleground in which hunger was mitigated, made and ultimately experienced. That radicals, poets and balladeers made hunger the subject of their oeuvre in the 1820s and 1830s attests to a profound importance that has hitherto been overlooked. We might need to dig deeper into the archive to find evidence, and this evidence might be more diffuse, but the discourse of starvation remained wretchedly live.

Notes

1 *Cobbett's Weekly Political Register,* 16 September 1826.
2 I. Dyck, *William Cobbett and Rural Popular Culture* (Cambridge: Cambridge University Press, 1992), p. 159.
3 See, for instance, E. Griffin, *Liberty's Dawn: A People's History of the Industrial Revolution* (New Haven, CT, Yale University Press, 2013), pp. 21, 31–2, 65, 67–8, 83.
4 On these dynamics see: R. Wells, 'Social protest, class, conflict and consciousness, in the English countryside, 1700–1880', in M. Reed and

R. Wells (eds), *Class, Conflict and Protest in the English Countryside, 1700–1880* (London: Frank Cass, 1990), pp. 121–98; C. Griffin, *The Rural War: Captain Swing and the Politics of Protest* (Manchester: Manchester University Press, 2012), ch. 2. On the declining western cloth industry see A. Randall, *Before the Luddites: Custom, Community and Machinery in the English Woollen Industry, 1776–1809* (Cambridge: Cambridge University Press, 1991).

5 C. Ó Gráda, *Famine: A Short History* (Princeton, NJ: Princeton University Press, 2010); C. Kinealy, *This Great Calamity: Charity and the Great Hunger in Ireland: The Kindness of Strangers* (London: Bloomsbury, 2013); D. Nally, *Human Encumbrances: Political Violence and the Great Irish Famine* (Notre Dame, IN: University of Notre Dame Press, 2010); J. Crowley, W.J. Smyth and M. Murphy (eds), *Atlas of the Great Irish Famine* (Cork: Cork University Press, 2012). For a useful comparative study see: L. Newman (ed.), *Hunger History: Food Shortage, Poverty and Deprivation* (Oxford: Wiley-Blackwell, 1995).

6 See: A.B. Appleby, *Famine in Tudor and Stuart England* (Stanford, CA: Stanford University Press, 1978); J. Walter and R.S. Schofield, 'Famine, disease, and crisis mortality in early modern society', in J. Walter and R.S. Schofield (eds), *Famine, Disease and the Social Order in Early Modern Society* (Cambridge: Cambridge University Press, 1989), pp. 1–73; R. Hoyle, 'Famine as agricultural catastrophe: The crisis of 1622–4 in east Lancashire', *Economic History Review*, 63:4 (2010), 974–1002; J. Healey, 'Land, population and famine in the English uplands: a Westmorland case study, *c.* 1370–1650', *Agricultural History Review*, 59:2 (2011), 151–75.

7 A. Howkins, *Poor Labouring Men: Rural Radicalism in Norfolk, 1870–1923* (London: Routledge, 1985), pp. 32, 92; A. Howkins, *Reshaping Rural England: A Social History 1850–1925* (London: Routledge, 1991), pp. 84–5, 103–4, 123; A. Howkins and I. Dyck, '"The time's alteration": Popular ballads, rural radicalism and William Cobbett', *History Workshop Journal*, 23 (1987): 22–3, 30, 32; K.D.M. Snell, *Annals of the Labouring Poor: Social Change and Agrarian England, 1660–1900* (Cambridge: Cambridge University Press, 1985), pp. 123, 128 n.98, 384–5.

8 On readings of hunger by poor law historians see: Lees, *The Solidarities of Strangers*, pp. 14, 37, 88, 156.

9 For the classic study of rural England in the 1840s see: D. Jones, 'Thomas Campbell Foster and the rural labourer: Incendiarism in East Anglia in the 1840s', *Social History*, 1:1 (1976), 5–37.

10 E.P. Thompson, 'The moral economy of the English crowd in the eighteenth century', *Past & Present*, 50 (1971), 76–136; E. Fox Genovese, 'The many faces of moral economy: A contribution to a debate', *Past & Present*, 58 (1973), 161–68; R. Wells, 'The development of the English rural proletariat and social protest, 1700–1850', *Journal of Peasant Studies*, 6:2 (1979), 115–39.

11 Thompson, 'Moral economy', 128–31.

12 Wells, 'The development of the English rural proletariat'. Adrian Randall offers a different take, suggesting that the experience of 1795 showed that the 'justices' instrumental power in the market had greatly waned'. 'Gentlemen'

again failed to 'uphold their side of the moral economy' when crisis hit Britain in 1800, the result being a 'fracturing of the old moral economy': *Riotous Assemblies: Popular Protest in Hanoverian England* (Oxford: Oxford University Press, 2006), p. 239.

13 J. Bohstedt, *The Politics of Provisions: Food Riots, Moral Economy, and Market Transition in England, c. 1550–1850* (Farnham: Ashgate, 2010), p. 241.

14 Randall, *Riotous Assemblies*, p. 239; Bohstedt, *Politics of Provisions*, p. 245.

15 Bohstedt, *Politics of Provisions*, pp. 247, 249–50.

16 Fox Genovese, 'The many faces of the moral economy'.

17 Bohstedt, *Politics of Provisions*, ch. 5 and esp. ch. 6. For an articulation of the persistent ways in which the same community politics that underpinned food rioting in the English west continued to inform other forms of collective action and trade unionism, even finding manifestation in food rioting as late as the 1820s, see: C. Griffin, 'The culture of combination: Solidarities and collective action before Tolpuddle', *Historical Journal*, 58:2 (2015), 443–80.

18 P. Gurney, '"Rejoicing in potatoes": The politics of consumption in England during the "Hungry Forties"', *Past & Present*, 203 (2009), 101.

19 R. Wells, 'Southern Chartism', *Rural History*, 2:1 (1991), 37–59.

20 For which see: Nally, *Human Encumbrances*.

21 D. Binfield, *Writings of the Luddites* (Baltimore, MD: Johns Hopkins University Press, 2004), pp. 133–5, 255, n.75.

22 *Hampshire Courier*, 28 August 1815.

23 Staffordshire Record Office, D3891/6/100, Letter from Samuel Parker, Kidderminster, to the overseers of the poor, Uttoxeter, 21 July 1833, in A. Levene (ed.), *Narratives of the Poor in Eighteenth-Century England, Volume 1: Voices of the Poor: Poor Law Depositions and Letters* (London: Pickering and Chatto, 2007), p. 267.

24 Somerset Record Office, D\P\Can13/13/6, Ann Dunster to Mr. Allen (Cannington overseer), [no day or month] 1821, quoted in S. Shave, *Pauper Policies: Poor Law Practice in England, 1780–1850* (Manchester: Manchester University Press, 2017), p. 1.

25 S. Hindle, *On the Parish: The Micropolitics of Poor Relief in Rural England c. 1550–1750* (Oxford: Oxford University Press, 2004), ch.1.

26 For instance on 21 November 1831 Skinner recorded that he had encountered 'a sister of Moon's wife … [who] was on the way to his Parish (Holcombe, I believe) to get relief, for they were absolutely starving, not being able to work, either himself or his boy': H. Coombs and P. Coombs (eds), *Journal of a Somerset Rector, 1803–34* (Oxford: Oxford University Press, 1984), p. 464. On the wider context see: R. Thompson, 'A breed apart? Class and community in a Somerset coal mining parish, c. 1750–1850', *Rural History*, 16:1 (2005), 137–59.

27 E.P. Thompson, 'Eighteenth-century English society: Class struggle without class?', *Social History*, 13:2 (1978), 150–1. On this dynamic also see: K.D.M. Snell, 'Deferential bitterness: The social outlook for rural proleteriat in eighteenth- and nineteenth-century England and Wales', in M. Bush (ed.), *Social Orders and Social Classes in Europe Since 1500: Studies in Social Stratification* (London: Longman, 1992), pp. 158–84.

28 C. Griffin, *Protest, Politics and Work in Rural England, 1700–1850* (Basingstoke: Palgrave, 2014), ch. 5; E.P. Thompson, 'The crime of anonymity', in D. Hay, P. Linebaugh, J. Rule, E.P. Thompson and C. Winslow (eds), *Albion's Fatal Tree: Crime and Society in Eighteenth-Century England* (London: Allen Lane, 1975), pp. 255–344.

29 *Hampshire Telegraph*, 1 October 1804; *Salisbury and Winchester Journal*, 15 October 1804.

30 On which see Thompson, 'Moral economy', 131–3.

31 E.L. Jones notes the harvest of 1804 was 'deficient' and the crop 'inferior'. However, the weather in late August in southern Hampshire was excellent and the crop 'fair average': *Seasons and Prices: the Role of the Weather in English Agricultural History* (London: Allen and Unwin, 1963), p. 157; *Times*, 28 August 1804.

32 *Salisbury and Winchester Journal*, 12 July 1802; A. Randall, *Before the Luddites: Custom, Community and Machinery in the English Woollen Industry, 1776–1809* (Oxford: Oxford University Press, 1991), p. 158.

33 *London Gazette*, 27 February 1813.

34 'Hunting a Loaf', Broadsheet Collection, Derby Local Studies Library, box 15, cited in Binfield, *Writings of the Luddites*, pp. 135–6.

35 N. Gash, 'After Waterloo: British society and the legacy of the Napoleonic wars', *Transactions of the Royal Historical Society*, 28 (1978), 147; Griffin, *The Rural War*, ch. 2.

36 Board of Agriculture, *The Agricultural State of the Kingdom* (Bath: Adams and Dart, 1970/1816), pp. 156–7.

37 TNA, HO 42, fos 61–2, 'Friend to his Country', Plymouth to Sidmouth, 18 May 1816.

38 Wordie's claim that labouring people in the corn counties of the south and east did not protest at the passing of the 1815 Corn Laws has been shown to be far from the mark: J.R. Wordie, 'Perceptions and reality: The effects of the Corn Laws and their repeal in England, 1815–1906', in J.R. Wordie (ed.), *Agriculture and Politics in England, 1815–1939* (Basingstoke: Macmillan, 2000), pp. 37–8; C. Griffin, 'Placing political economy: Organising opposition to free trade before the abolition of the Corn Laws', *Transactions of the Institute of British Geographers*, 34:4 (2009), 492.

39 *Hampshire Courier*, 30 May 1814.

40 A.J. Peacock, *Bread or Blood: A Study of the Agrarian Riots in East Anglia: 1816* (London: Victor Gollancz, 1965), pp. 77, 79.

41 Ibid., p. 25.

42 Peacock's *Bread or Blood* remains the only systematic study of the 1816 protests, though Andrew Charlesworth's comparative study with later rural protests offers a useful analytical advance and Rose Wallis' ongoing work likewise offers critical comparison: A. Charlesworth, 'The spatial diffusion of rural protest: An historical and comparative perspective of rural riots in nineteenth-century Britain', *Environment and Planning D: Society and Space* 1:3 (1983), 251–63; R. Wallis, 'Prosecution, precedence and official memory: Judicial responses and perceptions of Swing in Norfolk', in C. Griffin and B. McDonagh (eds), *Remembering Protest in Britain since*

1500: Memory, Materiality and Landscape (Basingstoke: Palgrave, 2018), pp. 159–85.

43 Peacock, *Bread or Blood*, pp. 27–9.

44 Wordie, 'Perceptions and reality', pp. 37–8; Griffin, 'Placing political economy', 489–505.

45 TNA, HO 42, fos 61–2: 'Friend to his Country', Plymouth to Sidmouth, 18 May 1816.

46 Ibid.

47 Wells, *Wretched Faces*, ch. 9.

48 K.D.M. Snell, 'In or out of their place: The migrant poor in English art, 1740–1900', *Rural History*, 24:1 (2013), 73–100.

49 J. Barrell, 'Sportive labour: The farmworker in eighteenth-century poetry and painting', in B. Short (ed.) *The English Rural Community: Image and Analysis* (Cambridge: Cambridge University Press, 1992), pp. 106–7. This shift in representation was a reflection of a concern that the actuality of rural life should be represented, and part of a wider – and internationally focused – assertion of British identity and values. Thus the increasing seriousness in depictions of agricultural workers – from the earlier eighteenth-century trope of comedy and idiocy – was in part an attempt to assert British progress, productivity and harmony. As Barrell notes, at the turn of the nineteenth century 'the image of wage-labourers, of a rural proletariat, selflessly and irremissively engaged in the back-breaking work of the fields was everywhere hinted at in paintings of farmworkers, but was very hard to represent' given that the actuality was hungry, haggard and dirty men. Thus the solution was to place the working body at a distance where it was tiny and powerless. Ibid., pp. 126, 131.

50 M.H. Scrivener, *Radical Shelley: The Philosophical Anarchism and Utopian Thought of Percy Bysshe Shelley* (Princeton, NJ: Princeton University Press, 2014), p. 52.

51 P.B. Shelley, (ed. W. Heck), *Ballad: Young Parson Richards* (privately printed, Iowa, 1926), reproduced in J. Donovan, C. Duffy, K. Everest and M. Rossington (eds), *The Poems of Shelley: Volume Three: 1819–1820* (London, Routledge, 2014), pp. 489–90. On the later name change see: J. Bieri, *Percy Bysshe Shelley: A Biography: Exile of Unfulfilled Reknown, 1816–1822* (Cranbury, NJ: Rosemont, 2005), p. 152.

52 On these wider currents see Vernon, *Hunger*.

53 For instance see ACLL reports in: *Morning Chronicle*; 2 March 1839; *Hertford Mercury and Reformer*, 30 October 1841.

54 As the text of the first petition (July 1838) put it: 'The land itself is goodly, the soil rich, and the temperature wholesome … [yet] our traders are trembling on the verge of bankruptcy; our workmen are starving; capital brings no profit and labour no remuneration; the home of the artificer is desolate, and the warehouse of the pawnbroker is full; the workhouse is crowded and the manufactory is deserted.' British Library, London, Place Ms., 27,820, f. 374. My thanks to Malcolm Chase for this point.

55 *Wiltshire Independent*, 27 December 1838. A similar sentiment pervaded a speech by founding member of the Dorset Labourer's Friend Society Rev. W.B. Whitehead in 1846: 'Those who possessed the better things of this life might go on revelling in their luxuries – they might continue in the enjoyment of their worldly possessions, careless of the starving population around them, but such a state of apathy was little in accordance with the sentiments of a man who loved his country and his fellow creatures – [and] totally inconsistent with the obligations of Christianity': cited in J. Burchardt, *The Allotment Movement in England, 1793–1873* (Woodbridge: Boydell and Brewer, 2002), p. 81.
56 *Cambridge Chronicle and Journal*, 25 January 1822.
57 W. Cobbett, *Cottage Economy* (New York: Cosimo Classics, 2007/1821), p. 6.
58 Quoted in I. Dyck, 'William Cobbett and the rural radical platform', *Social History*, 18:2 (1993), 195.
59 For the genesis of Cobbett's prediction of a rural revolt see: Griffin, *The Rural War*, pp. 67–8.
60 W. Cobbett, *Rural Rides*, ed. I. Dyck (London: Penguin, 2001), p. 425.
61 For instance see *Political Register*, 22 February 1823 ('To Mr Canning').
62 Dyck, *William Cobbett*, p. 19; *Political Register*, 26 May 1804.
63 Cobbett, *Rural Rides*, pp. 441–2.
64 *Two-Penny Trash*, December 1830, pp. 126–7.
65 *Two-Penny Trash*, July 1830, pp. 11–12.
66 *Times*, 10 November 1828, cited in K. Bawn, 'Social protest, popular disturbances and public order in Dorset, 1790–1838' (PhD thesis, University of Reading, 1984), p. 141.
67 *Brighton Guardian*, 14 October 1829.
68 Dyck, *William Cobbett*, p. 208.
69 Quoted in J. Archer, *By a Flash and a Scare: Incendiarism, Animal Maiming, and Poaching in East Anglia 1815–1870* (Oxford: Oxford University Press, 1990), p. 88.
70 *Political Register*, 8 June 1816.
71 Peacock, *Bread or Blood*; P. Muskett, 'The East Anglian agrarian riots of 1822', *Agricultural History Review*, 32:1 (1984), 1–13.
72 *Salisbury and Winchester Journal*, 3 August 1829.
73 TNA, HO 52/7, fos 101–2, Henry J Leeke JP, Westleigh near Havant to Peel, 21 November 1830.
74 Centre for Kentish Studies, Maidstone, U951 C177/28, Sir Edward Knatchbull, Mersham to Peel (draft), 6 October 1830.
75 *Southampton Mercury*, 20 November 1830.
76 See R. Wells, 'Mr William Cobbett, Captain Swing, and King William IV', *Agricultural History Review*, 45:1 (1997), 34–48; Griffin, *The Rural War*, ch. 7.
77 *Keene's Bath Journal*, 18 October 1830.
78 *Keene's Bath Journal*, 29 November 1830.
79 Dyck, *William Cobbett*, pp. 162–4. 'What Will Old England Come To?' is part of the Madden Broadside Ballad Collection held at Cambridge University Library.

80 TNA, TS 11/943, Prosecution Brief prepared by the Treasury Solicitor in the cases of the King v. John Adams, 1830; *Kent Herald*, 4 November 1830.

81 TNA, HO 52/8, fos 276–7, Knatchbull, Mersham to Peel, 6 October 1830.

82 *Rochester Gazette*, 14 and 21 September 1830.

83 *Kent Herald*, 28 October; *Kentish Gazette*, 29 October 1830.

84 *Brighton Gazette*, 25 November; *Sussex Advertiser*, 29 November; *Times*, 24 November; *Brighton Herald*, 27 November 1830.

85 TNA, HO 52/10, fos 653–7, William Tribe, Worthing to Melbourne, enclosing two threatening letters, 3 December 1830.

86 TNA, Assi 94/2073, Indictment of William Bish, Fletching, and Henry Bish, Newick, Sussex Winter Assizes 1830.

87 Hampshire County Record Office, Winchester, 75M91/E26/10, J.R. Gowen, Christian Malford to Lord Porchester, Lynmouth, 18 November 1830.

88 Dorset History Centre, Dorchester, D124/242, Ilchester Papers, E.B. Portman, 26 November 1830. Contrast Portman's language here with the sober language of the landed elite used in parliament and before parliamentary committees, the desperation of the Swing activists mirroring Portman's (and others') panic in the face of rural revolt.

89 *Sussex Advertiser*, 31 January 1831.

90 *Bridgwater & Somersetshire Herald*, 12 January 1831.

91 TNA, HO 52/12, fos 363–4, George Walton Onslow, Chairman of the Guildford Bench to Melbourne, 8 January; *Kentish Gazette*, 14 January; *County Chronicle*, 18 January 1831.

92 *Hampshire Advertiser*, 20 May and 19 August; *Hampshire Telegraph*, 19 August 1848.

93 *Sussex Agricultural Express*, 26 November; *Rochester Gazette*, 29 November 1842.

94 See Howkins and Dyck, '"The time's alteration"'.

95 Dyck, *William Cobbett*, p. 209.

96 *Political Register*, 4 December 1830.

97 It is important to note here that this might, in part, be a function of improved reporting practices, but either way the fact that newspapers gave publicity to such claims by printing them is suggestive of a wider public interest in the politics of hunger.

98 J. Rule, 'The manifold causes of rural crime: sheep-stealing in England, *c*. 1740–1840', in J. Rule (ed.), *Outside the Law: Studies in Crime and Order, 1650–1850* (Exeter: University of Exeter Press, 1982), p. 103; J. Beattie, 'The pattern of crime in England 1660–1800', *Past & Present*, 62 (1974), 47–95. See also: J. Beattie, *Crime and the Courts in England, 1669–1800* (Oxford: Oxford University Press, 1986).

99 R. Wells, 'Resistance to the New Poor Law in the rural south', in J. Rule and R. Wells, *Crime, Protest and Popular Politics in Southern England 1740–1850* (London: Hambledon, 1997), pp. 91–126.

100 For instance see: *Brighton Patriot*, 5 April 1836 (regarding a tea party organised by women opposed to the introduction of the New Poor Law in Brighton) and *Brighton Herald*, 18 June 1836 (regarding a meeting of the Marygate Benefit Club, Brighton, concerning the New Poor Law).

101 Wells, 'Resistance to the New Poor Law', p. 109.
102 For two of the best studies of pre-Andover scandals see: S.A. Shave, '"Immediate death or a life of torture are the consequences of the system": the Bridgwater Union scandal and policy change', in J. Reinarz and L. Schwarz (eds.), *Medicine and the Workhouse* (Rochester, NY: Rochester University Press, 2013), pp. 164–91; R. Wells, 'Andover antecedents: Hampshire New Poor-Law scandals, 1834–1842', *Southern History*, 24 (2002): 91–227.
103 *Times*, 30 June 1842; *Weekly Dispatch*, 18 February 1838.
104 *Brighton Patriot*, 12 February 1839.
105 Gurney, 'Rejoicing in potatoes', p. 101.
106 On which see: Flora Thompson, *Lark Rise to Candleford* (Oxford: Oxford University Press, 1945).
107 Gurney, 'Rejoicing in potatoes', p. 99
108 R.N. Thompson, 'The working of the Poor Law Amendment Act in Cumbria, 1836–1871', *Northern History*, 15 (1979), 117–37.
109 Jones, 'Thomas Campbell Foster'; Archer, *By a Flash and a Scare*, ch. 5.
110 A. Smith, *An Inquiry Into the Nature and Causes of the Wealth of Nations*, vol. 2, ed. E. Cannan (Chicago: Chicago University Press, 1977), p. 33.
111 C. Boyce, 'Representing the "Hungry Forties" in image and verse: The politics of hunger in early-Victorian illustrated periodicals', *Victorian Literature and Culture*, 40:2 (2012), 421, 444.
112 *Illustrated London News*, 25 June 1842.
113 Gurney, 'Rejoicing in potatoes', p. 101.
114 For instance see: K. Navickas, *Protest and the Politics of Space and Place, 1789–1848* (Manchester: Manchester University Press, 2015), pp. 223–4.
115 For useful correctives see: Wells, 'Southern Chartism', and A. Randall and E. Newman, 'Protest, proletarians and paternalists: Social conflict in rural Wiltshire, 1830–1850', *Rural History*, 6:2 (1995), 222.
116 Jones, 'Thomas Campbell Foster', p. 24.
117 *Times*, 22 March 1844.
118 *Times*, 14 June 1844, cited in Jones, 'Thomas Campbell Foster', p. 30.
119 Ibid., p. 30.
120 *Brighton Herald*, 23 March; *Brighton Patriot*, 26 March 1839.

Part II

Hunger policies

3

Measuring need: Speenhamland, hunger and universal pauperism

The received history of the English and Welsh old poor law is told in four parts: creation and implementation; 200 years of adaptation; from the end of the eighteenth century, crisis and reform; and, then, passing of the centralising, workhouse-based Poor Law Amendment Act in 1834.[1] More recent work has problematised this neat division. From Steve Hindle and Jonathan Healey delineating the spatially and temporally uneven contours of implementation, or Steve King detailing the varied geography of poor law practices and the contours of (relative) generosity of relief, through to Samantha Shave's unpicking of the complex web and governance of policy-making, we now better understand that there is no one history of the old poor law but rather multiple, overlapping and often contradictory tellings of our poor law past.[2] And yet in spite of recent (vital) revisionism, the importance of the 1790s – the 'Really Hungry Nineties' as we might usefully call the decade – as arguably *the* pivotal decade in poor law history remains. Central to this understanding is the supposed transformational importance of the so-called Speenhamland scale, set out by the Berkshire magistrates meeting at Speenhamland at the height of the subsistence crisis of 1795, whereby if family incomes (as tied to the price of bread) did not reach certain thresholds, the parish would make good the difference from the poor rates. The story has been variously repeated and challenged in poor law studies, never passed over, is always centre stage and yet has been subject to remarkably little systematic study.

Such scales, as is well known, would soon become notorious, most famously in Rev. Malthus' critique that such payments represented 'a direct, constant, and systemical encouragement to marriage'. This claim has been subject to continued scrutiny, with poor law historians variously refuting and supporting Malthus' implicit argument that the amelioration of poverty through such schemes actually created more poverty. The most recent claim, made by Samantha Williams, is that 'it seems highly unlikely that allowances were the cause of early marriages and larger families ... allowances ... were a necessary *response* to the sharply worsened circumstances after 1790.'[3] The notoriety of Speenhamland was cemented when, in his 1944 classic *The Great Transformation*, Karl Polanyi devoted a whole, admittedly short, chapter to Speenhamland. The narrative formed a key component of his analysis of the 'Rise and Fall of Market Economy'. As Polanyi saw it, 'the creating of a labor market in England was prevented through the Speenhamland Law', it being the last act, the last vestige of, as Tim Rogan has put it, 'an expiring humanitarianism', 'of medieval moral scruples concerning conduct in economic life', a 'vain attempt' (in Polanyi's words) to 'forestall the commodification of labor'. If Polanyi's emphasis on the importance of Speenhamland was questioned by historians on *The Great Transformation*'s publication, and his evidential base and interpretation of the geographical scope and the motivation of the Berkshire magistrates was widely challenged, the influence of Polanyi's assertion cannot be underestimated.[4] Indeed, for several generations of critical social scientists Speenhamland has variously acted either as a proxy for all that was wrong with the poor law or as a buffer against the creation of a market economy. Consequently, as the sociologists Fred Block and Margaret Somers have suggested, the 'shadow of Speenhamland' not only looms over much thinking on the English poor laws but also retains a haunting presence in welfare debates in the neo-liberal age.[5] And as syntheses by Lynn Hollen Lees, Steve King and Alan Kidd attest, the 'Speenhamland story' still casts a shadow over much poor law scholarship.[6]

Outside of studies that responded to Malthus' critique and, relatedly, examined the impact of scales and other systems on the cost of poor relief, the workings and subsequent history of the effects of such payments have been subject to remarkably little systematic study.[7] Indeed, beyond pioneering work by Mark Neuman on the context of the passing of the Speenhamland scale in the county of its creation and his subsequent work exploring the subsequent history of poor relief in Berkshire, and by Roger Wells on responses to the subsistence crises of the 1790s, we know remarkably little about the history of the effects of such schemes and how they operated.[8] Further, however the story is told, Speenhamland needs to be understood as a multifaceted, complex response to hunger. It was a humanitarian response to the absolute bodily need, the real, grinding hunger of the poor in the face of hyperinflation and crises in supply during the early months of 1795. It was also a patrician response to the pleas of the poor writ and read in the shared understandings of the discourse of hunger. And yet it needs to be understood as a pragmatic yet paranoid attempt at maintaining order against the power of the mob and the threats implicit in the discourse of starvation. These understandings are too often relegated to mere context in conventional tellings of the 'Speenhamland story', the backstory to the real stuff of poor law reform. Therefore, this chapter seeks to place such de facto income-support schemes into the wider context of the politics of hunger, both in the critical decade of the 1790s and thereafter. Scales, it argues, represented an important shift in poor law thinking, a move away from thinking about individual need to an idealised need; need was now measured against the *population*, against what it was thought a labouring family needed to get by. Such idealised 'support' payments, so the chapter argues, became embedded in the operation of labour markets in the cornlands of southern and eastern England, but the initial intentions of alleviating hunger were perverted to instead systematically shift the cost of supporting labouring wages from just agriculturalists to the wider community of ratepayers. In this way, it argues, all agrarian workers could become pauperised. Poor relief might be universal but that 'universal relief' counterintuitively required new modes of surveillance and knowledge of the poor. This is not to say that parish surveillance was a new phenomenon – it was arguably as old as the poor law itself – but rather that value judgements made were now based on magistrates and parish officers using universal *measures* of need. In this way, hunger was now measured and quantified; the poor were rendered as an undifferentiated *body*.

The crisis of the 1790s

In some locales the harvest of 1793 was poor, in part due to unseasonal rain and hailstorms in late July and August. The consequent sudden rise in the price of butter occasioned a 'serious disturbance' in the butter market at Sheffield on 18 July – though reports from such places related that there had never been 'a more plentiful crop'.[9] The harvest of 1794 was almost an unmitigated disaster, though a subsequent government survey supposedly found some parts of Kent to have had *above* average yields. The problem, at least at first, was exceptionally hot weather. The 1794 harvest started early, as the 'unremittant sun unseasonally ripened immature grains of all varieties'. In most places, while the quality was good it was deficient in quantity. The harvest finished earlier than usual, the grounds were prepared and winter wheat planted ahead of time.[10] However, persistent rain in October followed by almost continual sub-zero temperatures between December and March destroyed or retarded the growth of much of the young crop and all but prevented inland communication: Hull in January 1795 was absolutely cut off from the 'inland parts of the country'. And when the snow and ice thawed suddenly – in late January in the south-east, a month later in Yorkshire – the resulting floods were the worst in two decades, ruining crops, killing large numbers of livestock and causing considerable damage to property. As the *York Courant* put it, there was a fear that the floods 'have done infinite damage' in every part of the country. The area for 'several miles' around Thorne was flooded, with several cows seeking refuge by climbing the stairs of dwelling houses while the many poor families were absolutely without food. Much of the winter wheat that had survived the extended freeze in low-lying areas was destroyed in the inundation.[11]

The price of wheat rose steadily from autumn 1794. This was marked in Sussex in the final months of the year by food riots, strikes amongst the agricultural labourers, incendiary attacks on farmers' corn stacks and threatening letters sent to millers, claiming that they and the farmers were 'all agreed to starve us poor'.[12] If late 1794 marked the start of the crisis and the famine-like conditions that gripped England until the bountiful harvest of 1796, the early spring of 1795 marked the start of a period of, as Wells put it, 'hypercrisis', when prices rose dramatically as supplies contracted and expectations of the coming harvest rapidly diminished.[13] Beyond rapid inflation, household earnings had been hit by the freezing weather of early 1795. Much agricultural and industrial work was thus not possible, which forced many individuals out of employ.[14] Real wages were thereby even further depressed, and the Cobham index figure of 86 (1790 = 100) does not fully represent the depth of desperation faced when work could not be obtained or when prices were at their highest.[15] Perhaps the best description of this shift came from an anonymous Lincolnshire pamphlet writer in 1796: 'fluctuations in the price of the necessaries of life, makes what was a good day's wage twenty years ago, a starving one now'.[16]

It was in this context that Sir Frederick Eden began his investigation into, as he put it, 'the state of the poor'. He began his survey in 1792 and completed it in 1796, prior to publication in 1797. Just over half of Eden's parish studies and labouring family budgets were compiled in 1795.[17] His motivation, as with David Davies' similar study that began in 1787 and for which most reports were collected in 1789 and 1790,[18] was to make sense of the labouring condition. In particular, the timing of the main period of data collection was spurred on by the 'difficulties' agricultural workers laboured under in 1794 and early 1795 in consequence of the 'high price of grain, and of provisions in general'.[19] While, as Craig Muldrew has asserted, Eden's budgets are likely to significantly underestimate the amount of food consumed by virtue of labouring families being unable to afford their usual levels of consumption,[20] what matters is the extent to which labouring families were – or were not – able to meet what Davies stated to be a level of 'tolerable comfort'. While Davies' definition of 'tolerable comfort' for a family with three small children included school costs and the necessary malt to brew 'small beer' and was therefore above the bodily subsistence line, even when these costs (at £4 5s. per annum) were excluded, the yearly necessary income of £26 to achieve the 'wheat bread' standard diet was beyond many families. As Gazeley and Verdon's analysis of Davies and Eden's labouring budgets has shown, even outside those months of hypercrisis, for much of the 1790s four out of five families primarily engaged in agriculture were unable to meet Davies' minimum standard.[21] Moreover, during periods of inflation, the ability to meet this standard was disproportionately impacted by family size, the cost per child increasing at a greater rate than that of the overall family expenditure.[22] Further, in the final years of the eighteenth century, women's earning capacity was diminishing, both in agriculture and in the 'putting out' industries, not least spinning in the home, an employment that was rapidly being supplanted by factory-based machine-spinning.[23] As Gazeley and Verdon have shown, using these models suggests that there were 'endemic levels of poverty across the country', but it necessarily follows that in the low-wage counties of the south and east, levels of absolute need were more pressing still. The function of the distance from a local industry was in part responsible for this geography: lower wages in the south and east were thus in part a function of the lack of alternative employments.[24] In short, even before the hypercrisis of 1795, plebeian families, especially those in the agrarian south and east, were finding it increasingly difficult not only to be 'tolerably comfortable' but even to meet a minimum subsistence level without support beyond wages.

Real wages for the majority of the population – agricultural labourers and the artisans of urban England alike – had been in a steady decline since the middle of the century. Whilst research on the standard of living for this period attests to this being an uneven pattern across space and time,[25] what is certain is that when confronted by spikes in prices of the things of subsistence, most plebeian families were simply unable to cope for long; what savings and credit were available (if any) were soon exhausted.[26] This was compounded by the fact that in the south, and not just in overwhelmingly agrarian communities, poor relief, as Keith Snell has noted, became relatively less 'generous, flexible, and humane'. This was itself a response to structural unemployment and rising poor rates.[27] The impact of unprecedentedly rapid population growth was inflationary too: the population rise from 5.7 million at mid-century to 8.7 million by the turn of the nineteenth century was not matched by the level of agricultural production.[28]

The impact of war spending (both on commodities and salaries), the measures necessary to fund the mobilisation in continental Europe (and at home), and the fiscal measures and the impact of government demand for credit on credit markets all affected a general inflation.[29] In particular, the effect of provisioning a huge standing army and navy also had a significant and, during the war, sustained inflationary effect on the price of foodstuffs. In industrial communities the impact of these pressures was particularly profound. Given that the war acted to freeze British producers out of most export markets, many skilled, industrial workers were structurally subject to un- or serious underemployment, though this was partly mitigated by the material and personnel demands of the war effort.[30] Thus downward, if uneven, pressure on industrial wages combined with the increasing cost of subsistence put huge pressure on many industrial communities in the towns and countryside alike.[31] Indeed, as Wells notes in his magisterial study of the crisis of the 1790s, it was the subsistence crisis itself that precipitated recession in the textile industries in Lancashire, north Somerset, Gloucestershire, Wiltshire and Yorkshire. The need to pay higher wages to workers, something in part enforced by (already) organised trade union activity as well as one-off actions elsewhere, acted to increase costs at the very same time that internal consumer demand declined. In turn, localised unemployment became a genuine problem in cloth-making areas.[32]

Debate surrounding the impact on predominantly agrarian communities has focused on the *relative* ease of access of rural workers to foodstuffs. As Andrew Charlesworth has suggested in relation to what he identified as a relative paucity of protest in the countryside compared to urban England in 1795, farmworkers had 'more direct access to food, either supplied by farmers at lower prices … or simply by taking grain without payment, either as a "perk" of the job or as simple pilferage' than urban workers.[33] Whatever the undoubted truth about relative ease of *access*, the rising tide of prosecutions for agrarian commodity and property crime in the 1790s attests to the fact that access was neither a given nor necessarily went unpunished.[34] The impacts of structural change and war also had a profound impact on real wages. Notwithstanding that, according to the Bowley–Wood index, average standardised weekly earnings for agricultural labourers increased from 57 in 1792 to 103 in 1814, when set against commodity prices, real wages, as Ian Gazeley and Nicola Verdon have noted, 'stagnated at best'. Drawing on a wage series at Cobham in Kent as first delineated by Gordon Mingay, for every year of the war real wages were below the level of 1790 – this, as chapter one detailed, a year of a mini-crisis in the agrarian south.[35]

Consumption politics

Such understandings necessarily rest on a set of assumptions as to how the poor spent their income and what they consumed. As Eden notes, while labourers and other workers in northern counties benefitted from a diverse diet encompassing various soups and pottages, porridges and puddings, barley and oat breads, peas and potatoes, the southern labourer subsisted on an 'unvarying meal of dry bread and cheese from week's end to week's end'.[36] Labouring families' diets were in part determined by economic reality and in part by habit, the consumption of brown bread in the south being frowned upon as both being 'purgative and relaxing' and as an affront against their right to purchase the finest white wheaten bread: the little bit of status and self-respect southern labourers could normally afford.[37] In the Midland parishes this aversion to anything other than pure white wheaten was not quite so absolute, though as a correspondent to Arthur Young's *Annals of Agriculture* related of Lincolnshire, 'People like to eat wheaten bread of the finest sort; though a great many, of all descriptions, use rye and barley bread.'[38] As Adrian Randall has noted, there was a steady shift in the second half of the eighteenth century, even in the north, to a diet based on fine wheaten bread and away from coarser and mixed breads.[39]

According to Davies' dietaries of five families – excluding one detailing the budget of a family for which the father had absconded – gathered in his home parish of Barkham in 1787, while there was some variation in the amount families spent on bread and flour relative to bacon, butter and other weekly sundries, it was far and away the biggest part of their expenditure. Including yeast and salt, the amount spent on the necessaries to make bread every week varied between 37 per cent and 73 per cent of the weekly spend. This excludes the amount spent on rent calculated as a yearly sum, the average being 59 per cent. Even these averages are at once too high and yet too low. As Muldrew notes, the consumption of beer was not a consistent presence in either Davies' or Eden's household budgets, which is both a reflection of the timing at which the budgets were collected – a period of rapidly rising provisions prices – and probably the result of a tendency for poor households to underestimate beer consumption when faced with the questions of moralising clergymen.[40] In the 1760s, Young had reckoned that southern labourers spent one-sixth of their wages on beer, this notwithstanding the fact that beer was often provided to labourers at work, though the amount no doubt decreased as cereal prices rose in the late 1780s and into the 1790s, while employment practices shifted to include beer only at harvest time rather than all year round. This gap, at least in part, makes up for the calorific deficit.[41] Thus the averages are slightly biased towards bread spending. Conversely, of the five families one spent far less on flour by virtue of being able to purchase very cheap pork from the farmer, and another kept a pig fed on barley, beans and peas which, when slaughtered, helped to feed the family for much of the year (see table 3.1). Either way, as Eden noted there was a 'remarkable difference' between the proportion of income spent on food between southern and northern labourers, the workers of the north spending far less of their income on basic bodily subsistence.[42]

All of this is to paint with a broad brush, offering a general overview rather than a granular analysis. While the returns to Eden's survey detail such divisions at large, they also reveal patterns of consumption varying at the level of the individual, household, community, parish and district according to, amongst other factors, wage differentials, access to commons and other resources allowed through both customary and illicit practice, pig keeping and allotment holding. Indeed, as recent studies by Williams, Shave and French

Table 3.1 Amount spent on making bread per week for five Barkham (Berkshire) families, 1787

	Man, wife & 5 children, infant–8	*Man, wife & 4 children, infant–6*	*Man, wife & 3 children, infant–5*	*Man, wife & 3 children, infant–6*	*Man, wife & 2 children, aged 4 and 7*
Bread (d)	79	64	31	48	53
Weekly (d)	108	92	84	92	84
%	73	70	37	52	63

Source: adapted from D. Davies, *The Case of Labourers in Husbandry Stated and Considered* (London: C.G. & J. Robinson, 1795), pp. 8–13, 146–7.

have all attested, there was no one experience of being poor, but instead a multitude of experiences due to variations in familial circumstances and their balancing of the 'economies of makeshifts'.[43] Either way, in all communities, but especially those of the south and east, non-structural exogenous shocks impacting upon the supply and the price of wheat would necessarily have a dramatic and, in relation to wages, disproportionate effect. And this came in the form of harvest (and market) failures.

Responding to hunger crises

One response to the subsistence crisis of 1795–6 was for the rulers of the parish and the nation to do nothing. Beyond a huge spike in acquisitive acts outside the law – whether simple theft or by the principles of redistribution that underpinned some food-rioting practices – the necessary outcome of such an extreme *laissez-faire* strategy would necessarily be famine. As detailed in chapter one, Roger Wells has claimed that famine *was* a feature of the crises of both 1795–6 and 1800–1. Using Oddy's typology of famine and drawing upon Malthus' commentary on rising levels of mortality in the 1790s, Wells asserted that while deaths from starvation were few in the period, both crises witnessed increased levels of mortality 'owing to hunger-related disease'.[44] Given both that stock levels were regionally and locally uneven due to the fragility of grain market supply mechanisms and that real income levels varied both locally and regionally and between trades, the geography of 'excess' levels of mortality was also variable, the south-west being especially vulnerable. In this way, the discourse of starvation was rooted in a very real, felt reality. Reduced calorific intake reduced bodily capacity to labour and to ward off disease and infection. Increased levels of morbidity in this context begat increased levels of mortality, not least in the young and old.[45]

Before we attempt to understand local expedients we need briefly to consider nation-level responses. Responses by Pitt's government to the 1795 crisis were, paradoxically, both slow and opportunist, guided more by the midsummer supply-related hypercrisis than issues of plebeian affordability in the early months of the year. Beyond the repressive measures taken to put down food rioting and political opposition, government intervention in relation to the subsistence crisis figured in regulation to encouraging and supporting the massive importation of corn (a policy that acted to depress the market and force prices back to more affordable levels in the spring of 1796), the marketing of bread and other foodstuffs, and otherwise providing encouragement to transform consumption habits. A meeting of the Privy Council – at which Pitt was present – in the spring of 1795 rejected a report from London aldermen to legislate to extend the setting of the Assize of Bread from the price of flour alone to both flour and wheat prices. Indeed, against a popular belief that the government intended 'to make Bread at a reduced price for the poor', ministers steadfastly refused any kind of direct intervention beyond circulating details of schemes to reduce wheat consumption and attempts to encourage London bakers to not make any bread finer than the Standard Wheaten loaf. This mirrored the ethos of the Bread Act of 1773 (13 Geo. III, c.62) which allowed for the retailing of bread coarser than the Standard Wheaten independently of the assize. This was implemented in several provincial jurisdictions and by midsummer gained government support. Pitt's ministers even eventually won the argument against sustained opposition that it should be adopted in London by way of example.[46]

Government attempts to encourage the adoption of the 1773 Act, a Privy Council pronouncement that councillors would personally eat nothing finer than the Standard Wheaten loaf – a pronouncement to be printed and distributed at midsummer quarter sessions – and, as Wells put it, the Home Office 'seiz[ing] every opportunity to recommend wheat substitutes', generated considerable goodwill from local magistrates and the nobility. There are countless examples of local adoption but ultimately such policies were impossible to meaningfully enforce.[47] Plebeian protests in the south and east against being forced to eat brown bread or, worse still, substitutes like rice and potatoes, no doubt tested local resolve. The Lewes press reported during the summer of 1795 that the 'mouths of farmers' men are full of murmurs about the use of brown bread', whilst in Hampshire it was related that '[o]ur labourers have refused to eat any bread but the finest … & throw the Standard Wheaten into riot'. The desires of poor consumers necessarily effected the actions of bakers: the attempt to enforce the 'brown bread' policy in Berkshire was abandoned on the representation of the Reading bakers, while in Dorchester bakers refused to bake mixed bread as no one would buy it.[48]

It was not until late 1795 – with ministers now accepting that the wheat harvest had been deficient, a Privy Council survey suggesting yields to be at best 75–80 per cent of usual levels – that the government first resolved to legislate: first, successfully passing a measure through Parliament in December that did little more than encourage the rich not to consume fine bread and to otherwise support the baking of mixed breads; second, in the form of introducing a Bill to repeal clauses covering the assize on loaves coarser than the Standard Wheaten loaf and on mixed breads. Copies of the new arrangements were sent out to all quarter sessions in time for the Epiphany sessions in 1796, where they were readily adopted. Lord Sheffield, speaking at the East Sussex Epiphany sessions, went further, stating his belief that parishes should supply their poor with the means of subsistence by planting potatoes, cabbages and beans.[49] These expedients, however, only exacerbated problems, fuelling class-driven disputes. The servants of an East Sussex farmer protested at his giving them barley bread. In an attempt to resolve the dispute, the farmer and his protesting labourers went before a sitting of the magistrates at Lewes, who ruled in favour of the farmer, as he also supplied his servants with good meat and broth as well as the obnoxious bread. Other problems with the new legislation were also apparent. By freeing mixed breads from assize regulation and instead leaving it to the millers and bakers to decide what was 'proper and reasonable' to put into the mix, Parliament had essentially created a charter for adulteration.[50] Ultimately, as Randall has put it, whatever government efforts and popular resentments may have been, 'hunger alone forced consumption towards other commodities', with market prices causing most consumers to alter their normal cereal consumption habits.[51]

Government responses to the crisis also took in other supply-side measures. One policy innovation, albeit not backed up with legislation, was that all wastes should be enclosed and brought under cultivation to expand the arable acreage. The Kent Agricultural Society readily supported this policy, recommending the move to members as being 'of the highest public utility'.[52] Interventions to support poor consumers, though, barely figured. Prime Minister Pitt's Poor Law Bill of 1796 was the only attempt by the government to introduce substantive legislation in response to the crisis, but the hotchpotch of Speenhamland-lite income support, legalising (and encouraging) work by children as young as five and repressive measures brought forth howls of opposition and was never actually debated in Parliament.[53] Note that Pitt's bill was first promised by the government in response to a bill introduced by Samuel Whitbread in December 1795 that attempted to set minimum wages; this was roundly defeated.[54]

Local responses to the crisis are necessarily harder to track: absences and silences in the archive not necessarily indicative of a lack of action. Poor law records, whether in the form of policy-recording vestry books or overseers' accounts, survive for only a small fraction of parishes for the late eighteenth century, and even when they do it is not always possible to infer intentions or read shifting policy regimes. Likewise, other sources, be it newspaper reports, diaries or correspondence, only occasionally and unsystematically record responses to crises. Indeed, the action of a benevolent factory master proactively increasing wage and piece rates was not likely to make the pages of the local press, and neither was a farmer partly paying his labourers in kind with wheat. Beyond the problem of the structuring effects of archival presences and absences,[55] what is abundantly clear is increased levels of mortality due to, as Wells put it, 'hunger-related disease', evidence of the inability in many locales of existing systems and structures to cope with the spike in prices and the contraction in supply of the necessities of life.[56] Simply put, in such periods of rapid inflation and temporary spikes in prices, vestries and overseers would need to increase expenditure even to meet existing obligations, or face complaints by the impoverished and contractors alike and orders from magistrates to issue relief. For instance, the Yorkshire parish of Howden, having agreed terms in December 1794 to 'farm' the management of the workhouse, revisited the terms of the contract on four occasions between 4 May 1795 and 7 January 1796, the language justifying the changed terms shifting from the 'high price', through 'very high price' to 'very exorbitant Price of every Necessary of Life' as the crisis deepened.[57] In the same way that the contractor of the Howden workhouse *requested* a change in contractual terms, so the agency of the poor was central to the ways in which direct relief costs increased without any shift in policy. This could be through the mechanism of simply applying for relief – or an increase in their existing 'weekly pay' – or, in the case of relief being refused, through applying to a magistrate. An extreme example of the latter tactic occurred on 7 March 1795 when 37 'paupers' travelled 10 miles en masse from their native Hurstpierpoint (Sussex) to complain to the Lewes bench that their parish officers had refused them relief.[58] As J.R. Poynter asserted, the mid-1790s represented the point at which the 'principal check on the autonomy of local units' in the form of magistrates ordering relief began to increase.[59] Indeed, in the context of Jacobin threats and widespread food rioting, judicial intervention in support of the claims of the impoverished was obviously politic.[60]

One way in which paternalistic support for the needs of the poor was performed was through raising subscriptions, making donations to subscriptions and offering charitable gifts to the poor. These were invariably decidedly *performed* and public acts. While public – and often highly gendered – performances of philanthropy on the part of the nobility and gentry were customary features of every Christmas and New Year in many rural and market-town parishes,[61] the severity of the weather combined with the hyperinflation in the cost of wheat engendered a palpably different response.[62] From late 1794, public subscriptions were set on foot throughout England. Closest to the customary mode of seasonal giving was a 'humanely raised subscription' at Great Malvern by which 1,200 lbs of beef were distributed to the indigent 'poor' at Christmas 1794 to help 'alleviate' their 'distresses'.[63] Typical of the market-town subscriptions was that raised at Maidstone at Christmas 1794 and which by 6 January had already assisted 900 families with free coal and subsidised flour. This example, perhaps in part due to the *Maidstone Journal* imploring that neighbouring parishes follow suit, was soon followed by virtually all the surrounding parishes as directed by Mrs Bouverie, including the especially hard-hit hop parishes where the freezing conditions curtailed labouring at a time of traditionally heavy demand for piece workers. In the spirit of government interventions, if atypical of subscriptions in 1795 – though widely practised in response to the crisis of 1800 – was the establishment of a soup kitchen at Lewes, whereby reportedly 'upwards of a thousand persons' partook of pea broth thanks to the generosity of a Mr Kemp.[64]

The rulers of the major population centres also entered into subscriptions. By the turn of 1795 a subscription at Birmingham had already raised £1,700. At Norwich, the bishops, magistrates and other 'principal inhabitants' led a subscription by way of 'soliciting the guardians of the poor' 'to add to the allowance of the out-door poor', as well as to 'alleviate the wants of the little shop and shop-keepers' who are now reduced from paying poor rates to become 'themselves real objects of charity'. Individual London parishes similarly raised subscriptions in early 1795 – including one organised by the vestry at St Mary-le-Bone – while the City of London gave £1,000 as a spur to a 'general subscription' for the relief of the poor.[65]

While the language of many reports of subscriptions emphasises the humane intentions of such schemes in relieving distress, the involvement of some vestries in organising and allocating subscriptions suggests that subscriptions were not always without stipulation or politics. The Oxford University and City subscription was, in distinction to the Norwich scheme, only for those 'not chargeable to their respective parishes', again evidence of collusion between poor law authorities and the instigators of the scheme. The vestry at Bromley (Kent), in response to a plea from the bakers later in the summer of 1795 that they could not afford to sell the standard wheaten loaf at less than 11d. per quarter loaf, agreed that if they sold such loaves to the poor at 9d. – reduced ten days later to 8d. – the difference would be paid by a 'voluntary fund'. Such a scheme, mirroring a similar arrangement at Wokingham (Berkshire) in January, necessarily meant either that bakers had to use their discretion in deciding who 'the poor' were – and as the Norwich case testifies, hyperinflation could reduce even ratepayers to a state of abject need – or were guided by lists compiled by overseers and vestries.[66]

More explicit were the schemas developed at Westminster St James, where it was noted that 'discretion be vested in the Committee in the distribution of these articles [bread, meat and coal]', and at Tynemouth, where a committee was formed to 'seek out the real objects'. Similarly, the first report in early January of subscriptions in Sussex detailed that the poor were to be provided with 'bread in proportion to earnings', evidently a progenitor of the Speenhamland scheme. The receipt of such forms of relief was not only tied to stipulations but had consequences too. The Frampton (Lincolnshire) vestry instigated a subscription in December 1795 to meet the 'difficulty' faced by the poor due to the 'very high' price of corn. It was designed to 'serve' 100 people for up to four months, allowing recipients half a stone of mixed wheat and barley flour or a half stone loaf per week per person at 9d. and 18d. respectively. Those considered eligible must have an income of less than £10 per year, an estate worth less than £5 a year, and an annual rental of less than £10. Further, if recipients were found to be selling on their flour and bread, they would lose all future benefit from the scheme.[67]

Relief, whatever the express intentions of subscriptions, was rarely given without stipulation – measuring income and bodily need bound with moral judgement and surveillance – or without consequences. If, as Thompson suggested, the performance of paternalism relied, hegemonically, on plebeian acceptance of patrician values and socio-cultural power, so the receipt of *all* forms of charity was necessarily rooted in reciprocity.[68] But in the context of the crisis of 1795, given the near universality of subscriptions, not only in the market towns and cities but in rural parishes too, charitable giving represented an attempt to buy popular passivity. Indeed, against the Jacobin threat and the ever-present possibility of food rioting, knowing the poor and attempting to bind them to passivity represented the ultimate Pittite dream.

Of course, support from subscriptions lasted only as long as the fund collected. While some donations to such schemes were generous, wartime inflation and much- increased fiscal pressure – including rocketing poor rates – on individual incomes meant that members of the middle class and lesser members of the gentry could not necessarily afford to be bountiful in their 'support' for the poor. As the editor of the liberal *Hull Advertiser* bemoaned, while subscriptions raised 'by the affluent' were 'laudable', what was needed was a regular reassessment of the poor rate 'so that the burden was equally borne'. Setting on foot subscriptions was a patrician sleight of hand. They continued:

> It is an ingenious thing for a person of great property, to set afloat a voluntary subscription, and give his guinea, or couple of guineas, where his assessment to the poors' rate for the emergency would be twenty.[69]

In some places, subscriptions were kept open, or funds raised in January and February proved sufficient to continue supporting into the spring those who met the terms of their scheme. At York, for instance, the 'distress committee' whose efforts started with 'distributing' coals in mid-December 1794 was in action until the beginning of March, and was again active from early July when, in response to the pre-harvest supply crisis, they secured several lots of imported grain from Hull and Scotland and sold it ground to 'the poor' at 2/6 per stone. In reporting the response to the midsummer hypercrisis in the city and beyond, the York press were quick to claim that subscriptions anew had been raised in 'every large town and corporation' in the country, and to assert that reports of riots in Birmingham and Warwickshire in late June and early July were 'greatly exaggerated'.[70] Yet the existence of any form of riot in English market towns and major urban centres in the summer and the need to raise further funds was evidence enough that earlier subscription schemes had failed to meet all needs, not least of those deemed not to be worthy or in sufficient want. When the funds ran out, necessarily all those hitherto supported were cast adrift. The inadequacy of subscriptions to meet all plebeian needs and the failure, at least locally, to address issues of manipulation in supply and marketing were best attested by the fact that the period from the start of 1795 and midsummer saw the most intense resort to both food rioting and radical politicking drawing explicitly on the starvation trope. In the south-east, food rioting in the winter of 1794 and 1795 was exclusively a feature of the countryside, including against export and on two occasions also accompanied by strikes of agricultural labourers. In one furious case of *taxation populaire* at Worth in rural north Sussex on 2 March, the soldiers refused to fire on the rioters as 'the people were right'. Tellingly, the wave of urban rioting occurred in the spring, i.e. between the two spurs to patrician action.[71]

Subscriptions, especially when handled by vestries and other local institutions, represented de facto forms of local policy response to the crisis. So too were ad hoc bodies formed to deal with the crisis, such as the committee of 'gentlemen' – composed of MPs, baronets, clergy and land-owners – formed in London who resolved not only to 'use all the means in their power' to put the laws against 'forestalling, jobbing, and the like' into action but also to encourage the rich to 'SUPPRESS all LUXURIOUS and UNNECESSARY SUPPLIES of the TABLE'.[72] Elsewhere there were attempts to organise more-than-parochial schemes to standardise relief given through subscriptions and other funds. In early 1795 an attempt was made to revive a system first used in Hertfordshire during an earlier subsistence crisis – the precise date is unclear, though it is likely to be 1790. An advert placed in the *Salisbury and Winchester Journal* espoused this systematised attempt to 'ascertain the exact quantities of bread' poor families consume a week, the mealmen and bakers they deal with, and their ability to pay for a quartern loaf. The difference between cost and income would then, 'during times of distress', be met in the form of a ticket issued by the 'vestry or else-where' to be exchanged with the mealmen and bakers, 'for the poor should be indulged as far as may be with the liberty of purchasing of their own tradesmen'.[73] This was, then, a de facto minimum-income policy focused on the price of bread, though not necessarily funded by the rates. Nor is there evidence that the advert had any effect.

Such actions were necessarily outside the operation of the poor law in that they relied on charitable giving, both of money and time, rather than the parish poor rates. Legion are the examples of parishes adopting similar resolutions to the subscriptions that offered subsidised bread and flour. The following examples from Sussex are indicative. At Beckley, near Hastings, 'certain poor families' were to receive subsidised flour for 'ready money only'. At nearby Icklesham only the 'industrious labourers' were eligible to purchase flour at a shilling a gallon. The Easter meeting of the Horsham vestry agreed to sell flour 'to their poor neighbours' at the subsidised price of 10d. per gallon 'for some time to come', while in late June the Eastbourne vestry agreed that subsidised flour should be provided directly from two millers to certain poor people 'as may appear proper objects to this Vestry'.[74] What unites the policy-making practices of vestries is, again, whatever the humane intentions that underpinned such schemes, a sense of the balance between determining and detailing worthiness (a moral judgement) and need (a bodily judgement). Indeed, some parishes even produced lists of those deemed worthy objects. For instance, the vestry of the Kentish parish of Brookland agreed to produce a 'detailed list of those eligible' for subsidised 'dressed meal' and meat.[75]

Beyond extending the net of relief, few other expedients were open to vestries. One that some parishes attempted was to make greater use of their poorhouse or workhouse. As detailed above, Howden vestry had negotiated to contract the running of their workhouse at the beginning of the crisis in December 1794, though at least some of the cost savings achieved by such a strategy were offset by having to increase the sums paid to the contractor to meet their increased costs.[76] An alternative strategy was to ignore rising costs and try to hold contractors to the agreed terms. The case of Dymchurch, a small but densely populated coastal parish in Romney Marsh (Kent), is instructive. In early 1791 the vestry voted to purchase a building to centrally house the poor, resolving later that year to enlarge it to accommodate all the parish poor. Completion of the works in late 1791 led to the withdrawal of the weekly payment to all the elderly, widows and illegitimate children, forcing them either to enter the house or seek alternative means of subsistence, a perfect exemplification of the so-called 'workhouse test' first codified in Knatchbull's Act of 1723. Subsequently the vestry contracted out the running of the house, but during the early months of 1795 the contractor, to cut the rising provisions bill, served up poor-quality food. The poor duly complained to the vestry that it was not fit to eat. But rather than improve the terms of the contract, the parish compelled the 'master' to resign and a new contractor was sought.[77] The case of Dymchurch is perhaps extreme, but plenty of parishes elsewhere reacted to rising relief costs during the crisis by resolving to establish workhouses – for instance, as agreed by the Heckington (Lincolnshire) vestry on 17 March – or to build bigger houses, as at Yalding (Kent), where in June the existing house was found inadequate to the crisis.[78]

Speenhamland

That it is not expedient for the Magistrates to grant that assistance by regulating the Wages of Day Labourers, according to the directions of the Statutes of the 5th Elizabeth and 1st James: But the Magistrates very earnestly recommend to the Farmers and others throughout the county, to increase the pay of their Labourers in proportion to the present price of provisions; and agreeable thereto, the Magistrates now present, have unanimously resolved that they will, in their several divisions, make the following calculations and allowances for relief of all poor and industrious men and their families, who to the satisfaction of the justices of their Parish, shall endeavour (as far as they can) for their own support and maintenance. That is to say, when the Gallon Loaf of Second Flour, Weighing 8lb. 11ozs. shall cost 1s. then every poor and industrious man shall have for his own support 3s. weekly, either produced by his own or his family's labour, or an allowance from the poor rates, and for the support of his wife and every other of his family, 1s. 6d. When the Gallon Loaf shall cost 1s. 4d., then every poor and industrious man shall have 4s. weekly for his own, and 1s. and 10d. for the support of every other of his family. And so in proportion, as the price of bread rise or falls (that is to say) 3d. to the man, and 1d. to every other of the family, on every 1d. which the loaf rise above 1s.

By order of the Meeting.
W. BUDD, Deputy Clerk of the Peace.[79]

So went the best known, and the most notorious, response to the crisis of 1795, that revised by the Berkshire magistrates meeting at an adjourned general sessions at the Pelican Inn in the Berkshire hamlet of Speenhamland on 6 May 1795. Whilst the story is now so well engrained in English social history that it hardly bears repeating, a few details are worth relating. First, the infamous scale adopted detailed a series of minimum incomes depending on family size and the price of a standard wheaten gallon loaf: if families' income fell below this threshold, the difference would be made good by the parish from the poor rates. Second, the scale asserted that a single labourer required the equivalent income to three gallon loaves a week with an extra loaf and a half per each extra family member; thus in the minds of the Berkshire magistrates the consumption of bread was not merely a useful proxy for the subsistence of the poor – wheaten bread *was* the subsistence of the poor. Third, the purpose of the magistrates' meeting had been advertised to consider labourers' wages and the price of corn.[80] The scale recommended at the meeting, as funded through the poor rates and delivered through the overseer and vestry, was no on-the-hoof policy decision.

Neuman has also shown that the practice of supplementing wages through the poor rates and offering allowances in times of unemployment was already engrained in some Berkshire parishes. While drawing upon the work of A.W. Ashby, E.M. Hampson and Beatrice and Sidney Webb in noting that some parishes made occasional allowances in aid of wages from the very start of the poor law in the early seventeenth century,[81] it was, reckoned Neuman, the impact of Gilbert's Act (1782) that led to 'allowances in aid, or place, of wages became extended and regularised.'[82] An enabling Act, when adopted it forbade the incarceration of able-bodied paupers in 'Houses of Industry' – the chosen euphemism for workhouse in Gilbert's Act – and thereby forced parishes to support such needy claimants with out-relief either in kind (a practice, as Snell notes, that was diminishing) or in cash as de facto wage supplements. Gilbert's unions – and individual parishes operating under the auspices of Gilbert's Act – were until recently little studied and even less understood. New studies by Samantha Shave and Graham Rawson, building on suggestive evidence presented by Wells, have shown both that such unions and individual parishes were far more common and widespread than we had hitherto thought, and, as Shave has shown, often found to be lodging able-bodied labourers in their Houses of Industry.[83] Therefore, the precise impact of the working of Gilbert's Act on the adoption of scales is, at best, ambiguous.

In 1787 Sir William Young, MP for the Buckinghamshire rotten borough of St Mawes, introduced a bill before the Houses of Parliament that, amongst other objects and clauses, would legally formalise the payment of one-third of a pre-agreed rate of wages out of the rates for those out of employ and sent 'round in rotation to the parishioners, proportionately as they pay to the Rates'. While the bill failed, Eden, in his review of the evolution of the poor laws, noted that the clause 'borrowed from a practice, which is very general in Buckinghamshire, and many of the midland counties'.[84] Indeed, Eden's own survey noted the operation of the practice in two parishes surveyed: at Winslow (Buckinghamshire) where up to 40 labourers at a time were so employed and invariably 'wholly employed by the rates'; and at Kibworth Beauchamp (Leicestershire) where roundsmen were employed during the winter the parish paying 4d of the 10d per day wage.[85] As Boyer has suggested, 'Parliament's actions in 1782 simply legitimised the policies of a large number of parishes' that had, in some cases, long since offered out-relief to able-bodied claimants. Thus legitimated, and with the need increasing as real wages declined and under- and unemployment increased, such payments became more widespread.[86]

In Neuman's Berkshire, such wage supplements took several forms but all related either to supporting those, as at Uffington (1783), 'out labour' and 'not imploid', or, as in the case of Jonathan Coxhead at Hungerford (1783), to offering relief 'more than his pay', 'presumably', notes Neuman, 'because the overseer calculated that his wages were insufficient'. Shinfield vestry even instigated a 'round' in 1780, predating the policy that became widespread in the cornlands after 1815, whereby those out of work were sent round the ratepayers and employed, usually, in proportion to the value of their assessment to the poor rates, the wage often either in part or full paid from the rates.[87] Further, having taken into 'Consideration the present dearness of every necessary Article of Life', a plan was devised at the Berkshire quarter sessions in July 1791 to 'determine to regulate their future Allowances to the Poor', setting out a scale of minimum incomes according to family size. While, as Neuman asserts, it is not absolutely clear that the policy was adopted – much less actually implemented – what is telling is that the magistrates were considering systematic income supplements, thus systematising, as C.R. Fay put it, 'a practice which, because it was becoming widespread [in Berkshire], needed to be conducted on some regular plan'.[88]

We also know that other minimum-income schemes had been devised and formally supported elsewhere before 1795. As noted above, Hertfordshire had devised a plan to assure the poor received minimum incomes as tied to the price of the quartern loaf. Better known was the resolution of the Dorset Michaelmas quarter sessions in 1792 that 'on the complaint of any industrious and peaceable poor person', the magistrate/s must order the overseer of the complainant's parish to 'relieve him or her with such sum as shall make up, together with the weekly earnings of him, her, and their family, a comfortable support for them'.[89] Predating the meeting of the Berkshire magistrates in 1795 were similar 'bread scales' agreed at the Buckinghamshire and Oxfordshire Epiphany sessions earlier that year. Similarly, at the same time as the Speenhamland scale was agreed, the magistrates at nearby Basingstoke (Hampshire) *implemented* a similar scale. They were followed by, amongst others, the magistrates at Kings Somborne.[90] The agreement at Basingstoke followed a resolution made at the Hampshire Epiphany sessions to inquire into the state and management of the poor. Each magistrates' bench was to form a 'sub-committee' and was to answer questions regarding poor rates; rents; population; manufactories; the 'rate of husbandry wages'; employment of women and children; the existence of poorhouses/houses of industry – and their effect on poor rates and the 'morals of the poor'; Sunday and charity schools; the price of wheat, bacon, flour, meat and other necessities; the amount of necessary subsistence 'to do justice to his Employer'; the practice of calculating on applications for relief 'necessary for subsistence'; the mode of living amongst the poor; and, finally, the existence of friendly societies. If the motivation was self-evident, we can only speculate as to the inspiration for such a wide-ranging survey.[91] The similarities to Eden's survey are striking, though given the first of his Hampshire parish surveys were not undertaken until October 1795 it is more likely that the subjects of analysis reflected the interests and expertise of the magistrates in attendance, and that the debate on the issue in part shaped Berkshire resident Eden's survey. Indeed, as Neuman and Wells have stated, the adoptions of scales did not come out of the blue. In Oxfordshire, many parishes as soon as the harvest was finished made 'all the Labourers Roundsmen' at 4s. a week for married men, an extra 6d. per week for their first two children, and a further shilling for the third child and above. According to Charles Dundas, a Berkshire MP and chair of the Berkshire bench, this expedient had failed as by November 1794 labourers were 'absolutely in a state of starvation'. Duly, the Oxfordshire Epiphany sessions raised the minimum amount to 6s., such wages to be 'made up by the Overseers exclusive of rent' if the 'utmost exertions of a family cannot produce' the minimum incomes. Similarly, at the Berkshire Epiphany sessions, Dundas made the case for permanent wage increases to meet the rise in subsistence costs, though this was rejected.[92]

There was no *one* scale that diffused outward from Speenhamland. Rather, as Shave has suggested, it makes more sense to write of Speenhamland-style scales, a range of different practices all united by the principle of systematically detailing minimum levels of subsistence and the principles of parish support.[93] What marks the Speenhamland scale, and the others detailed and given judicial force between 1790 and 1795, out is not that they represented the moment at which payments to the able-bodied 'poor' were first made but rather that they were the first attempts to systematise the measurement of need, juxtaposing corporeal capacity, the cost of bodily subsistence and income. From a humanitarian perspective, as James Huzel has noted, the influence of such scales was important to those families in desperate want. The edicts of magistrates acted, at least in some locales, to force parishes to be more generous in their support of those in need.[94]

Such edicts were, in practice, little more than recommendations. As Neuman has shown in his systematic analysis of Berkshire, few parishes in that county adopted the formal scale agreed at Speenhamland, notwithstanding the resolve of the justices to enforce it. A scale devised by the Malling

(Kent) bench in August 1795 of minimum incomes for different categories of the rural poor was, likewise, never compelled on parishes in the division. It would require a claimant to make a complaint before the magistrates compelled the vestry to take action. This interplay between bench and vestry was evidently understood by the Yalding vestry, a parish within the Malling Petty Sessional division, when five years later they decreed that no person resident outside of the parish was to be relieved without the order of a magistrate.[95] Elsewhere, the scale adopted by the Gloucestershire magistrates in late 1795 was, as Wells put it, 'quietly ignored'. Moreover, the Hampshire bench were quick to rescind the scale they had adopted. Their decree on 14 July 1795 asserted that as wages were on the increase the former measure was no longer necessary, though still allowed that for families with a large number of children parish officers would still need to make good any deficiency in their wages.[96]

Far more frequent, at least in the 1790s and early 1800s, were semi-formalised or ad hoc systems adopted by individual parishes. Evidence abounds in parishes in the cornlands of supplementary payments made to labouring families, whether listed as 'to make up the wages' or under various subterfuges such as child allowances. Peasmarsh (Sussex) in April 1795 devised a scale, seemingly unilaterally, that offered families for each child above three in number 1/6 a week, or for 'such children' to go into the workhouse. At Pulborough in mid Sussex, an ad hoc but fundamentally similar scale was developed: those poor families with more than two children were to be 'relieved' or the children, at the discretion of the master, would be taken into the workhouse. A frank admission of the soon entrenched nature of these schemes was made by Lord Sheffield in his plea to his resident parish of Fletching in the Sussex Weald at the start of the Grain Crisis of 1799–1801, that those 'whose earnings will not maintain their families' must be relieved with any consumable other than bread corn.[97]

More telling still was the wording of question nine asked by the survey instituted under the terms of the 1803 Poor Act (43 George III, c.144): 'What was the total amount of money earned by the labourer of the poor *towards their maintenance* in that year, and as such *accounted for* to your parish?' (emphasis added). This was both acknowledgement of the importance of keeping the poor under surveillance and knowing their earnings and circumstances, and a tacit recognition that for many poor families poor relief formed a vital part of their subsistence given the now endemic nature of Speenhlamd-type schemes in the cornlands.[98] What matters is that all such schemes were united by the same principles of measurement, surveillance and moral judgement, whether relief payments offered were dynamic in response to changing need or static 'weekly pays', or were prescribed by magistrates or devised by parish officers and vestry members. Moreover, they represented a shift away from the provision of casual relief and one-off subscription provision to systematic support, duly making workers objects of calculation and control.

Adoptions and perversions

In light of the increased costs of poor relief during the crisis many vestries subsequently introduced schemes to limit their costs. The vestry of the Dorset market town of Blandford Forum, having improved the terms with their contractor and levied a special poor rate to provide subsidised bread 'to the indigent poor' in 1795, noted in April 1797 a massive increase in the relief bill. They therefore decided to rigorously apply the workhouse test. The following year the vestry also resolved to establish a manufactory in the work-house to spin hemp and flax and entered into a contract with a man from Quidhampton (Hampshire) to instruct the poor in spinning and weaving and in managing the workhouse.[99] Quadring (Lincolnshire) decided in June 1796 to build a workhouse for the first time, while in the same county Holbeach vestry agreed in October 1797 to systematically bind the children of the poor as apprentices as soon as they reached sufficient age. Burton upon Stather (also Lincolnshire) adopted a policy in April 1798 that as soon as anyone applied for relief an inventory of their goods was to be made. If the applicant was judged to have 'more than necessary', their goods would be sold by the parish as the parish officers thought proper.[100] Increasing the amount spent on relief – and thus increasing the poor rates – was not a given, a return, in the south and east at least, to earlier, more generous relief regimes. Rather, it was a response, albeit geographically uneven, to crisis.

The impact of 1795 is also hard to quantify with any certainty, not least because the first systematic parish survey post-1795 occurred in 1803, i.e. after the equally calamitous subsistence crisis of late 1799–1801. Before considering the 1803 report, it is, therefore, worth delineating responses to the latter crisis. Wells has noted several features: restrictions to and removals of non-settled poor; unparalleled claims for charitable aid against increased aversion to 'repetitive rate and charity demands' and in particular a 'collapse' in support from the middling people; and, ultimately, the collapse of some relief schemes, especially in London.[101]

In short, there was no particular or peculiar response that altered the trajectory of poor relief practice. Some places instituted scales, seemingly for the first time during the subsistence crisis of 1799–1801: for instance the Kentish parishes of Ightham, Wittersham and Farningham and the Surrey parish of Godstone all introduced similar scales determining the amount and cost of subsidised flour the poor could purchase according to family size between November 1799 and February 1800.[102] There is also evidence that even in the *relative* comfort and prosperity of 1802 some parishes were still experimenting with ideas of minimum incomes: Wealden Horsmonden vestry decided to fix all labourers wages at 10s. a week, though what mechanism underpinned this pronouncement is unclear.[103]

More typical, though, were attempts to retreat from such Speenhamland-style support mechanisms. The tightening sinews of inflation and inflationary fiscal policy – including rising poor rates – combined with economic recession meant that defining and determining the minimum needed to bodily exist (and for those employed to be useful to employers) became more important than ever before as vestries balanced legal (and moral) responsibility with rising costs. As the Alfriston (Sussex) vestry agreed in April 1801, 'every person who receives a flour allowance and has children that go to work' was, as a condition of that relief, to give up half their child's earnings 'to be applied to the poor rate'.[104] Some places even explicitly minuted the retreat from systematic support: New Romney (Kent) resolved in May 1802 that due to the decrease in the 'price of every article necessary for life' that some 'paupers' would be 'taken off' 'weekly pays'; six years later the same vestry decided no longer to pay 'allowances' to any 'workmen or tradesmen' or any of their labourers employed by the parish.[105] If the latter resolution was telling in that it admitted the continued problem with rural unemployment during even the non-crisis years of the Napoleonic War, the former speaks to the fact that the logic of Speenhamland-style systems rested on an assertion of what the minimum necessary for labouring families to get by was. Indeed, the New Romney resolution made it absolutely explicit that, at least in some parishes, this equated to the most basic definition of subsistence: the articles necessary for life.

While snapshots are necessarily problematic due to the influence of one-off and atypical features – a parish paying off a debt, having a large surplus in hand from the previous year, responding to local and national crises – the data collected in 1803 usefully overcomes some of these limitations. First, by being a national survey, local variations in relief patterns are evened out: 'excess' expenditure in one parish is balanced by a 'deficit' of spending in another. Second, the data for 1803 runs from Easter 1802 to Easter 1803, and as such beyond the crisis of 1799–1801. If anything, 1802 was, in the context of the war years, atypical in terms of benefitting from two excellent harvests in a row, strong demand and tighter employment.[106] Thus by using the level of expenditure on the relief, management and administration of the poor – an imperfect proxy for *real* expense but better than the amount of rates levied – several trends are apparent.[107] The average increase in the cost of supporting the poor between 1776 and 1803 was 207 per cent. The largest increases in costs were not in the scale-adopting and predominantly agrarian counties of the south but instead in the west and north. Indeed, of the ten counties with increases in excess of 250 per cent, all were north of the line from the Wash to the Bristol Channel – the line poor law historians often refer to as marking the division between Speenhamland and non-Speenhamland zones – and included all four of the most northerly counties (Northumberland, Durham, Cumberland, Westmorland) and all of Yorkshire.[108]

This was, of course, in part a response to rising populations in northern industrialising communities and a function of extremely low – compared to southern and eastern counties – levels of poor law expenditure in the 1770s. As Margaret Hanley has shown, the amount spent on poor relief in the Lancashire parish Tottington increased sixfold from the 1760s to the 1790s, and this before the industrial growth of the ensuing decades.[109] Even in remote, agrarian parts of the Yorkshire Wolds costs had spiralled. In Goodmanham (population 149), the amount spent on the poor increased from £4.16.3 in 1776 to £32.10.10 in 1786 and to £96.10 in 1803; at Lund (population 310) poor law expenditure increased from £23.0–. in 1786 to £110.10.11. Using the 1801 census figures, this meant that Goodmanham spent £0.65 per head – above the national average of £0.53 (and only just below that spent on average in Dorset and Hampshire) – while Lund spent a nationally low but regionally high £0.30. Tellingly, Goodmanham had been enclosed in 1777 and Lund in 1795. The attendant loss of common and commonable rights no doubt impacted upon the ability of the local poor to eek out an existence without parish support.[110] Arguably more significant still were places like Spaldington, an arable parish in the flatlands of the Vale of York with a population of only 79 in 1801, where expenditure rose from a negligible £12.18.3 in 1776 to £183.11.8, or some £2.33 per head.[111] Thus in some northern locales, the cost of supporting the poor had not increased considerably in the 1790s and early 1800s – and any significant increase whatever the initial base would, after all, be felt by rate payers – but was not out of line with impoverished agrarian communities in the south and east.

The eight counties that spent in excess of £0.70 per head on supporting the poor were all were south of the same line – Kent (£0.70), Wiltshire, Northamptonshire, Berkshire, Essex, Buckinghamshire, Oxfordshire and Sussex (£1.17), in order of increasing expenditure – but, with the exception of Sussex (237 per cent), these had also been subject to below average increases in expenditure since 1776. It is important to note, however, that the midland counties of Leicestershire (£0.64) and Warwickshire (£0.59) were also significantly above the national average expenditure per head. In these southern counties the relief of the poor from the rates was not only traditionally more generous, but the practice of so supporting the poor was also culturally and politically ingrained in parish government.[112] Moreover, all were predominantly agrarian, though Kent had a large urban population and north-west Wiltshire still supported a large though declining cloth industry. In such places, not only had the cost of relief increased against inflation but it had also extended to support those placed into need by structural changes and the response to the effects of the Napoleonic Wars.

Beyond costs, the (admittedly sparse) qualitative commentary in the 1803 Report gives some indication of these shifts. In the Kentish parish of River, an 'allowance' was given to 'those with large families' at 1s. per head per week with occasional clothes in addition.[113] At Cheam (Surrey) the overseer had devised a scale relating to minimum incomes, if 'the earnings of each family did not supply these means, the Parish made up the deficiency'.[114] Elsewhere, the entrenched nature of parish subsides based on measurements of need was alluded to at Bullington (Hampshire) and Cornwell (Oxfordshire), where higher than usual wages kept rates low, the Cornwell overseer noting that the farmers had 'always made a Point of giving our Labourers good wages', and thus outside of 'particular cases' could support themselves without resort to the parish.[115] Where parishes had strictly applied the workhouse test, not only had relief costs fallen but the number of poor had also decreased, again indicative of the burden of supporting families whose income was insufficient to meet an agreed level of subsistence. For instance, at Marsham (Norfolk) when the new Buxton and Itteringham Union workhouse opened at Easter 1802 it led 'immediately' to a 'considerable Diminution' in the 'Number of paupers' and an attendant reduction in expenses.[116] Such cases are not necessarily representative in themselves, but do speak to wider trends and truths.

The map of relief in 1803 does not, however, neatly accord with Blaug's delineation of 'Speenhamland counties' (table 3.2), as defined by whether parish returns to the 1824 Select Committee on Labourers' Wages related the practice of paying wage supplements or not. As Blaug notes, though, 'With a system so heterogeneous, any generalization is bound to be subject to serious qualification'. Indeed, his delineation of the geography of relief practices was subject to the qualification that in some Speenhamland counties the payment of wage supplements was 'more prevalent' than in others, or, to be precise, that the system was 'pervasive in eight southern counties' but also 'fairly widespread in twelve others'.[117] Blaug's analysis, though, is predicated on his attempt to debunk the 'myth', as he saw it, of the architects of the New Poor Law that the payment of Speenhamland-style wage subsidies represented not only a perversion of the Elizabethan poor laws and local labour markets, but also tended to diminish agrarian capital, and were, in the words of Rev. Malthus, 'a direct, constant, and systemical encouragement to marriage'. Or, the more the system relieved the more it needed to relieve. As detailed above, while magistrates in some locales quickly retreated from scales formulated in 1795 on the understanding that they were no longer necessary, and while many parishes attempted to mitigate the effects of burgeoning relief costs by resorting to new restrictions, it was not until the deep agrarian depression that followed the end of the Napoleonic Wars that the discourse of 'abuse' really took hold.

In the public mind, poor relief was considered not only something 'that they might claim' but something 'they had every right to do so'.[118] In this way the right to poor relief was, by 1795, absolutely immersed in the (after Keith Wrightson) micropolitics of parish life. As I have noted elsewhere, claimants' mobilisation of a discourse of 'rights' became integral to the day-to-day operation of the poor law system.[119] The creation of scales and the systemising of wage supplements in the 1790s thereby acted to intensify existing dynamics. Evidence of this comes in the form not only of the mass application of 'paupers' from Hurstpierpoint to the Lewes bench in March 1795 complaining that they had been refused relief,[120] but also of subsequent similar examples and threats made to parish officers that claimants *would complain* to the magistrates. Indeed, the juxtaposition between wages and poor relief – often explicitly framed through the dual discourses of hunger and starvation – was the hallmark of the popular response to the

Table 3.2 Delineation of English counties according to payment of wage subsidies as detailed in the 1824 Select Committee on Labourers' Wages

Speenhamland counties (italic = 'system pervasive')			*Non-Speenhamland counties*		
Bedfordshire	Leicestershire	*Wiltshire*	Cheshire	Hertfordshire	Shropshire
Berkshire	*Norfolk*	Yorkshire, E.R.	Cornwall	Kent	Somerset
Buckinghamshire	Northamptonshire	Yorkshire, N.R.	Cumberland	Lancashire	Staffordshire
Cambridgeshire	Nottinghamshire		Derbyshire	Lincolnshire	Surrey
Devon	Oxfordshire		Durham	Middlesex	Westmorland
Dorset	*Suffolk*		Gloucestershire	Monmouth	Worcestershire
Essex	Sussex		Hampshire	Northumberland	Yorkshire, W.R.
Huntingdonshire	Warwickshire		Herefordshire	Rutland	

Source: M. Blaug, 'The myth of the old poor law and the making of the new', *Journal of Economic History*, 23:2 (1963), 178–9.

1799–1801 subsistence crisis. And the intervention of the bench therein was vital in settling claims. By way of example, in February 1800, 50 labourers gathered at Petworth to complain to the magistrates that in consequence of the high price of provisions their families were close to starvation. Sir Godfrey Webster, officiating, sent a summons to all parish officers to attend the next meeting of the bench, after which the men seemingly went home placated.[121] That summer, a 'number' of labourers went to the Ardingly parish officers warning that unless their wages were augmented – i.e. subject to a Speenhamland-style supplement – their families would become a burden on the parish: presumably a threat that their children would need to be institutionally cared for. The most dramatic example of this occurred on Valentine's Day 1801, when a '300' person coalition from the Wealden parishes of Chiddingly, East Hoathly, Framfield and Buxted descended on the Lewes bench to apply for relief.[122] In short, the entrenched discourse that poor relief represented an unalienable right combined with the pervasive discourses of hunger and starvation to help firmly embed Speenhamland-style payments throughout the cornlands.

Such practices can also usefully be understood an as extension of the principle of plebeian appeals to their patrician betters that underpinned, as Thompson put it, the moral economy, extending the principle from actions exclusively related to the marketing of food to actions that juxtaposed the affordability of food, wages and relief.[123] The two following examples drawn from the Wiltshire parish of Box perfectly elucidate this new dynamic. On 24 October 1806 'Wm Bausher threatened to go to the Justices meeting on Tuesday to complain of having too', thereby showing he understood not only how his 'right' to relief could be upheld but also the local workings of the law. Three years later James Bartlett similarly threatened that 'if the Parish would give him 2 shirts for his Children he would not proceed with applying to the Magistrates'. We need, therefore, to understand that relief was never a given but rather the outcome of a tripartite tussle between those in need, ratepayers and magistrates.[124]

The perverse logics of hunger

The logic of Speenhamland-style schemes and their embedded nature in the cornlands meant that there was a break in the foundational link between hunger – both as bodily felt and as a discourse – and food prices. The focus now shifted to poor relief. Indeed, beyond the agency and legal wherewithal of claimants, one of the critical reasons that the principles of Speenhamland-style payments became so ubiquitous is that they allowed agriculturalists to share the burden of the cost of supporting farmworkers with the wider ratepaying community. The logical extension of the parish 'making up' the wages of labourers earning less than the minimum dictated by scales was that farmers cut wages as low as possible, thereby spreading employment costs to all ratepayers. As long as demand was more or less equal to supply in local labour markets, farmers still needed to employ a regular coterie of workers. Moreover, they might even pay a premium to employ the most efficient and productive workers, or at least seek to employ the 'best' workers in the parish before their fellow vestrymen. But when farmers cut back their workforces post-1815, wage subsidies provided no protection against pauperisation and de facto unemployment. Those labourers who remained directly employed by the farmers were invariably married and with children, because, in the words of Rev. Pratt of Selscombe (Sussex), at 'full wages' they would still receive child allowances from the parish.[125] Speenhamland-style systems, without close magisterial surveillance or active, patrician involvement of members of the gentry and nobility on parish vestries, could act to subsidise farmers.

As Henry French, drawing upon the unusually full archive of the Essex parish of Terling, has argued, labouring families 'experienced a creeping "reliance" on relief, in the form of systematic "family allowances" – between 20 and 30% of income for many families for several months of the year.' Other families had to expend a greater proportion of their income on food, and were thus also more reliant on occasional, ad hoc payments to supplement wages and their subsistence needs. For the period between the autumn of 1815 and autumn 1817 (when the post-war depression was, with the exception of 1822, at its nadir, 'amplified significantly by the consequences of freak climatic conditions experienced in 1816') the reliance on the vestry increased to between 50 and 75 per cent of total income for half of the Terling families on relief. During this period, so French's analysis asserts, 'persistent unemployment', as he terms it, impacted upon 17 per cent of the population of Terling, or some 131 people out of a population of *c.* 759 souls.[126] Thus unemployment was not only widespread, but the wider downward impact upon wages, in turn, meant that all labourers were in some way drawn into the web of poor relief. Or as Snell has put it, 'free labour [had] to become pauperised to find employment'.[127]

If unemployment was a factor in the creation of scales in the 1790s, post-1815 it became *the* driving issue. In agrarian communities, the problem was simply one of excess supply of both food and labour. As Rev. Gleig of Waltham (Kent) put it, 'Multitudes of disbanded soldiers and sailors … [were] sent back to their parishes', thereby inverting the war years' dynamic from 'a competition among the farmers to find men' to a 'a competition among the men to find masters'. At first, farmers were reluctant to cut wages, presumably in part due to the fear of reprisals from labourers turned incendiarists. As food prices plummeted – in part due to declining demand from the British state to feed fighting forces and the oversupply effects of a succession of good harvests – and stayed low, the outcome was not, as would have been the case in the war years, a depoliticising of hunger. Rather, declining agriculturalists' incomes meant that farmers '[struck] off a certain number from their employ leading to numbers of young, healthy, and willing persons [who] no longer knew where to apply for a day's work'.[128] In manufacturing districts, this dynamic was further complicated by a reduction in state demand, which was compounded by the effects of opening British markets to foreign competition, and the reduction in demand from markets which British manufacturers had hitherto monopolised. The resultant reduction in demand was met by decreasing prices and inevitably a reduction in employ.[129]

Mass unemployment meant that, notwithstanding lower food prices, hunger remained a biting reality and perpetual fear for the rural and industrial poor alike. The response at first was slow, with parishes making a combination of ad hoc payments as well as making amendments to Speenhamland-style schemes – which had persisted in many locales[130] – to address chronic poverty in the new deflationary age. For instance, the vestry of the Hampshire parish of Amport resolved in January 1816 that: 'Mr Green offers Household bread at 1 3.5d pr Gallon, therefore the allowance of Head is to be 1s 10d – giving an advantage of 1/2 (half) to the poor (and the sixpence above is to be taken from the Household price in future).' As bread prices declined in the late autumn of that year, so the vestry resolved to reduce allowances and take money out of the allowance to help pay the poor's house rents.[131]

In most places, though, Speenhamland-style payments in support of wages had been abandoned but were revived post-1816. This took several forms. Some parishes simply adopted ad hoc make-work schemes: sending men to work on the roads or digging stone and gravel for the roads, or doing other menial work for the parish such as clearing out gutters and repairing paths. A variation on the theme of the vestry as both labour exchange *and* employer was the parish farm. The vestry leased farmland (sometimes a whole farm) on which men otherwise out of work were engaged in cultivating and harvesting, and the food was either sold to supplement the poor rates or used to provision parish workhouses.[132] More typical, apart from in the smallest parishes, were myriad variations on the roundsmen scheme – also known as the billet, especially in Berkshire; the yardland; the stem, especially in Hampshire and Wiltshire; or, the ticket – wherein the parish acted to arrange the employment of, and usually in part paid for, those out of work. Usually this was a response to male unemployment, but in some instances such schemes were used to employ both women and children. For instance at the aforementioned Amport in April 1820, 'all the girls' were 'taken to the different farms and employed 'till harvest in proportion to the different rents', and the same month at Bishops Waltham (Hampshire) 10 children were 'billeted' to the occupiers.[133] What unites such schemes was that the link between hunger and relief was broken; the link was now wages. This is not to say that hunger was not an issue – as chapter two demonstrates, the discourse of starvation arguably found new stridency post-1816 – but rather that the humane intentions of Speenhamland-style schemes in the 1790s as a way of alleviating hunger gave way to a grinding, utilitarian attempt to statutorily relieve the poor in the cheapest possible way.

The example of an early post-1815 depression 'billet' scheme from Quadring (Lincolnshire) is instructive. The policy stated that no labourer should have more than 1/6 a day and that the ratepayers should employ one out-of-work labourer for one day a week per £10 they were assessed to the rates; thus there was an active incentive for farmers to pay their standard labourers no more than 1/6 or even to dismiss such men safe in the knowledge that the whole community of ratepayers would have to make good the employment. Even more prone to obvious manipulation was the system at East Hendred (Berkshire), where the vestry in early 1816 agreed that the 'billet' men were to be paid 3/6 'and the rest to be made up out of the book', an obvious enticement to make all men unemployed.[134] In most cases, though, the reality of hiring habits was usually more complex, especially in parishes where farmers effectively comprised the whole vestry and thus had to pay for labouring families' support one way or another. As witness Thomas Brown of Luton (Bedfordshire) attested to the 1818 House of Lords Select Committee on the Poor Laws, farmers were also happy to pay differentially according to the man's skill and ability, while, apart from in disastrous years – such as 1816, 'the year with no summer' – the demands of the harvest employed all hands at advanced piece rates.[135] The effect of this was perhaps best illustrated in the answer of Richard Martin from the Sussex parish of Shipley to the 1828 Select Committee on the Employment or Relief of Able-bodied Persons from the Poor Rates: some 192 out of an estimated 240 labourers in the parish had received some form of relief in the previous year, with typically between 40 and 80 – and sometimes more – men employed by the parish, mostly on road contract work outside of the parish.[136]

The manipulation of local labour markets by vestry interventions in arranging and paying for work incensed many ratepayers who were not only forced to subsidise the wages of farmers' men, but under allocation schemes had also to engage labourers themselves. Rev. Wake, the rector and tithe-holder of Over Wallop in Hampshire, went as far as to publish a stinging attack on his fellow vestry men for their 'abuse of the poor rate'. According to Wake's solicitor: 'As to the stemming of men, I always told you there was no such law. If an overseer has paupers out of employ, and he cannot find any for them, the whole parish must contribute, by a just and equal rate, to support them. Pray do not be so imposed on.' Wake duly took his case to the 1819 Hampshire Lent quarter sessions.[137] Vestry-generated policy had no basis in statute law. Thus, notwithstanding the potential benefits of roundsmen-type schemes, legal challenges were likely to be upheld. Mindful of this potential pitfall, in February 1829 the Brenchley (Kent) vestry enquired of their local magistrates as to the legality of 'labour rates' (or the 'Oundle Plan'). The latter were supposedly first adopted in either the Northamptonshire parish of Oundle or the Oxfordshire parish of Cropredy *c.* 1820, and given extensive positive publicity thereafter as a way in which farmers were incentivised not to throw all their men on the parish. This scheme set a rate, levied against the poor rate assessment, which either had to be paid or the ratepayer had to 'discharge' the rate by employing 'surplus' labour (defined as the number of labourers left over after an allocation of labourers based on either the rates, rental or acreage) at a set wage against the rate.[138] The 1824 Select Committee on the Employment of Agricultural Labourers also noted the problem of enforceability and duly offered their support for a bill placed before Parliament that would give legal sanction to labour rates. This bill never reached the statute book, but labour rates were finally given legal force in 1832 by the Agricultural Labourers Act.[139] Another widely practised scheme, especially popular in the south-east, was the quota system whereby the farmers' rental, rateable value or acreage determined the total number of labouring parishioners employed. While such a policy was, in practice, impossible to enforce, it not being rooted in law, in theory it meant that farmers had to employ a minimum number of labourers and as such there was no incentive to make their men below the threshold unemployed.[140]

Against the issue of the enforceability of parish schemes, and given magistrates' role as the ultimate arbiter in determining relief and employment policy, the revival of bench-led scales represented an obvious solution. Indeed, given that parish employment schemes – of whatever colour and complexity – were in essence Speenhamland-style income-support schemes, the revivification of official scales was simply an extension and standardisation of existing practice in determining what labouring families needed to bodily subsist. What is striking is how quickly this approach was enacted, not least, as noted above, given that parishes were slow in 1815 to respond to the rapidly unfurling crisis. From the extant archive of south-eastern parishes for 1815, I have uncovered explicit evidence of the adoption of roundsman-style schemes only in the Hampshire parishes of Amport and Minstead.[141] Rapidly rising provision prices from April 1816 seem to have been a spur to wider adoption. But while the parallels with 1795 and 1800 are striking, the difference was widespread unemployment in both agrarian counties and industrial regions and far from systematic resort to subscriptions to support those in need.[142] The upturn in the resort to roundsman-style schemes was also matched by evidence that magistrates, at least in some locales, were responding to appeals for relief by making reference to scales. Several southern witnesses before the 1817 House of Lords committee infer such arrangements: John William, a magistrate at Burnham (Buckinghamshire) related that he allowed half a crown per extra child above two in number; Thomas Poole, a Somerset magistrate, also related that he allowed an extra shilling a week for labouring families with more than two children.[143] We also know that, at least in some places, such scales went beyond existing only in the heads of magistrates to actually exist on paper, papers being printed and duly circulated about parishes. The Hindon division of Wiltshire issued such a printed scale on 5 March 1817 (it was later presented before the aforementioned 1828 Select Committee) – the same year a scale was devised for the district of the Menabilly estate in southern Cornwall.[144]

Thereafter, such 'official' scales were frequently set throughout the south and east until a backlash in the late 1820s. As the authors of the report of the 1824 Select Committee on Labourers' Wages noted, scales were 'at present pursued in many counties',[145] and while their survey did not directly ask about the existence of scales they were explicitly detailed in responses from Bedfordshire, Berkshire, Devon, Dorset, Gloucestershire, Hertfordshire, Kent, Oxfordshire and Wiltshire.[146] We know that a scale operated in the Fawley Division of Hampshire in the early 1820s. The bench met at Winchester as the harvest drew to a close in the desperate year of 1822 to reduce already parsimonious 'allowances'. This was a response to declining prices of provisions and an attempt to prevent rural labourers working at higher harvest rates then claiming parish-supported allowances throughout the rest of the year.[147]

Limiting analyses only to explicit mentions of the use of scales necessarily under-represents the prevalence of such bench-sanctioned payments. For instance every division in Sussex reported paying systematic child allowances, which are de facto evidence of scales. It is also telling that while the paying of child allowances was not as prevalent in the west and north, only Cumberland, Northumberland and Somerset related that the practice of partly paying labourers' wages from the rates did not occur in their several divisions, and in the latter county the payment of child allowances was prevalent. Even supposedly avowedly anti-Speemhamland counties like Cheshire, Durham, Herefordshire, Lancashire, Monmouthshire, Shropshire and the West Riding of Yorkshire related that in some cases labourers' wages *were* made up. Districts like Witham (Essex) and Ellow (Lincolnshire) could also report that the practice had, respectively, 'nearly ceased' and had been 'abandoned', evidence that the practice had been even more widespread.[148] What is different about this revival is that the scales tended to be simpler than those adopted in the 1790s, related not to bread prices (ergo, a consideration of what a poor family needs to get by) but instead to bodily and moral judgements, as much arbitrary as measured: what the minimum amount of relief was that a parish could get away with paying labouring families.

By 1827 the Berkshire magistrates had realised the effect of their earlier policy, something that had been officially reinforced in the late 1810s and again reiterated in the early 1820s.[149] 'The reward of industry' had been reduced to bare subsistence; wages 'should best find their own level'. Justices were to 'use powers' to correct 'this abuse'.[150] The Berkshire experience in some ways mirrors the national picture. According to Boyer's calculations, between 1824 and 1832 the proportion of all parishes paying such allowances fell from 75 per cent to 50 per cent.[151] This followed a national ideological shift: the 1824 Select Committee asserted that allowances forced wages down, made the labourer think that relief was a right 'whether idle or industrious', and created 'dissatisfaction between the labourer and his employer'. The 1828 Select Committee on the Employment of Labourers from the Poor Rates went further: it should be made illegal to aid the wages of labourers from the poor rate, and the 'right to employment' was at odds with the law and the market mechanism.[152]

While the national average was 50 per cent of parishes paying allowances in 1828, this hid complex regional and local patterns. Some 82 per cent of (reporting) Sussex parishes paid allowances, with 74, 73 and 72 per cent of parishes in Hampshire, Berkshire and Wiltshire, respectively. Yet in Dorset, a county with notoriously low wages and in the stranglehold of active, interventionist Tory judicial control, only 44 per cent of reporting parishes paid allowances, a figure that went down to 19 per cent in Bedfordshire, a county with a history of magistrates actively engaged in poor law innovation.[153] The persistence of such schemes was not a function of vestrymen's ideological opposition to the principles of Smithian political economy; rather it reflected both local political and policy resolve and the reality of how the agricultural depression impacted upon southern and eastern labour markets. As Henry Boyce, the overseer of Walderslade (Kent), detailed, while he believed the theory that if wages were lower more labourers would be employed, the reality was that those currently not employing any labourers would still not be in any position to be employers, whilst those with the necessary capital would be 'over-burdened with labourers'. In the neighbouring parish of Ash, so Boyce relayed, every Thursday there was an auction for the unemployed labourers. Yet whilst a notional bid of a penny would secure the services of a labourer, often no bids were made.[154] Perhaps the best example of the sheer intractability of the issue comes from Speen, the very parish where the meeting of the Berkshire magistrates had taken place in 1795. Notwithstanding the 1827 quarter sessions judgement, the vestry, 'on account of the great mischief which has arisen to the labouring poor, from the late system of employing them in the gravel pit + on the roads', introduced a roundsmen scheme with an allied scale of wages according to family size, if not the price of bread.[155] With good reason, as Wells has put it, the system had become 'embedded in the principal cornlands'.[156]

Beyond the paradox of universality

If there is an occasional sense of both exasperation and mania in the responses of both magistrates and farmers, the making of universal relief in the form of Speenhamland-style minimum income policies – in whatever form, and whatever the initial intention – was never without stipulation or expectation. If the final decades of the old poor law resembled a welfare state in miniature, in practice, as several generations of poor law historians have stated, the principle of relief was rarely concerned with welfare as progressive politicians might understand it.[157] While this is not to say that the Elizabethan poor law was ever meant to be either generous or absolute,[158] the post-1815 system increasingly – and increasingly universally – had more in common with later neoliberal systems through shared emphases on means testing and a corresponding shift from entitlement. Herein lies a paradox. If the effect of the plethora of allowance systems as a response to mass unemployment was to drag all labouring families into pauperism, the logic of such payments – whether formally constituted as scales or not – rested on knowing the minimum needs, costs and income of relief recipients at the unit of the household. The commitments of such minute investigative demands, of knowing the parish population, on top of the administrative load of extending the envelope of relief, placed a huge burden on vestries and especially overseers, who, after all, were unpaid and also had their normal occupations to attend to. The same was true of magistrates, though a complaint of some respondents to parliamentary surveys and investigations was that magistrates acted in arbitrary and unilateral ways without fully investigating the circumstances of those who made appeals to them.[159]

The response of parishes, especially those with large populations, which developed complex social policy webs was fourfold: to overwhelm the overseer; to share the load by appointing additional overseers; for the vestry to assume further responsibilities for investigating claims and determining relief; or to professionalise and create dedicated committees and hire dedicated 'assistant' overseers. The latter approach was not a new strategy. Some populous parishes established sub- or 'select' committees prior to 1815 either as a temporary measure in response to crises – Framfield (Sussex) in response to a spike in demand due to the 'unexampled severity in all classes of society' in the spring of 1811 established a committee to examine poor relief costs – or to meet structural changes, as in the aforementioned example of the creation of a dedicated relief committee at Frampton (Lincolnshire) in April 1816. In some places such 'permanent' committees were given specific tasks: for instance in May 1798 the Wincanton (Somerset) vestry created a committee of nine men 'to examine into the Managemt. and expenditure of the Workhouse'.[160] Similarly, some parishes experimented with assistant overseers before they were legally formalised in 1819 (on which see below). Indeed, as with the establishment of committees and select vestries before 1818, the practice was reasonably widespread; the large but sparsely populated Somerset parish of Chew Magna appointed an assistant overseer as early as 1769.[161]

The turning point came with the passing of the so-called Sturges Bourne Acts in 1818 and 1819. Not only did these two enabling acts for the first time legally sanction the adoption of a select vestry and the appointment of an assistant overseer (both under the auspices of the 1819 Act), but the publicity surrounding their passing and the proselytising effect of the example of successful early adopters swelled the number of parishes that adopted either both or one of a select vestry and an assistant overseer. As Shave has shown, adoption of select vestries was rapid, if uneven: just over 11 per cent of all English parishes had adopted the provisions in the first year of operation, the figure peaking at just short of 16 per cent of all parishes operating a select vestry in 1825–6 (this of course masked the fact that many parishes adopted and abandoned select vestries between these years). In Shave's sample counties of Dorset, Hampshire, Somerset, West Sussex and Wiltshire, the figure in the first year of operation was closer to 14 per cent, thereafter being broadly equivalent to the national rate of adoption before declining more sharply from 1825–6 to just over 9 per cent in 1833–4. The figure for the adoption of assistant overseers was rather higher, and continued to increase after the mid-1820s, rising to some 25 per cent of parishes in Shave's sample counties – within which the counties ranged from only 15 per cent in Dorset to 33 per cent in Hampshire. By 1833–4, 20 per cent of all English parishes employed an assistant overseer.[162]

If some select vestries on their foundation drastically shifted relief policy – Steeple Ashton (Wiltshire) select vestry, meeting for the first time on 21 May 1833, instigated deep, blanket cuts to existing weekly pays – others instigated more subtle shifts aimed at better understanding the basis of claims for relief. For instance, at Fawley (Hampshire) it was agreed in September 1819 that in future all 'out paupers' except those on weekly pay would only be relieved at the select vestry, while the Hougham (Kent) select vestry demanded that 'all paupers' must in future produce a certificate detailing how many children they had and how much money the family earned per week. Such policies were often backed up by moral pronouncements and, presumably on the back of evidence regarding wages, policy relating to non-agricultural workers: Botley (Hampshire) select vestry on Christmas Eve 1822 asserted that 'Every man on the parish shall attend divine service or receive no pay' and four months later that 'no mechanic or handicraft' person be relieved when out of work except in the form of a loan.[163] While assistant overseers were often charged with running parish workhouses or administering and running employment schemes in addition to the usual duties of the overseer (collecting rates, issuing relief), many parishes explicitly detailed that their appointment was in line with the principles of Sturges Bourne's Acts to 'distinguish, in the Relief to be granted between the deserving, and the idle extravagant or profligate'.[164] Thus at Bishops Waltham (Hampshire) the assistant overseer, appointed in July 1819, was to 'enquire' into the 'character and condition' of all those applying for relief.[165]

Of course, the process of surveying the poor as to their situation, income and needs was not new: the various committees and sub-committees founded in 1795 to administer subscriptions and special parochial relief schemes did something broadly analogous. Rather, the investigations and the subsequent policy decisions of select vestries and assistant overseers were backed by law, supported by the wider public and parliamentary rhetoric of the need to reform the poor laws, and, in the case of select vestry decisions, the fact that it needed two magistrates to overturn a relief decision compared to only one magistrate for a decision from a general vestry.[166] But whatever the wider attempt by parishes that adopted the precepts of the Sturges Bourne acts to limit the amount spent on relief, where bench/devised scales existed select vestries had little choice but to apply the spirit of such scales. Further, against the context of mass un- and underemployment, parishes might use select vestries and assistant overseers to try to restrict payments and even limit who was eligible for support, but wages in the south and east were so low and the need to provide at least a minimum level of support to those out of work meant that in practice labouring families were still immersed in the web of relief.

It was precisely this dynamic, of being pauperised and yet subject to the stigma of unemployment schemes and the close, personal investigation of assistant overseers and select vestries, that meant that assistant overseers and overseers became demonised in the eyes of the parish poor. At Northiam (Sussex), three days after a select vestry meeting in November 1822 descended into a riot, for which three young men were indicted at the winter assizes, Rev. Lord had his haystacks set on fire.[167] In late 1824, John Wilson, the assistant overseer at Staplehurst (Kent), had three rockets fired at him whilst riding home from a vestry meeting. The rockets missed Wilson but startled his horse, throwing him to the ground and severely injuring him. More compelling still was the letter posted on the Mayfield vestry door in early January 1825 which warned overseer Day that 'Wee do Intend Washing Our Hands inn Your Blood'.[168] Moreover, during the Swing rising, the removal of assistant overseers from the parish by the poor – a version of the 'mock mayor' customs and an inversion of the rituals of justice – was a defining protest form in the Weald. Likewise, many overseers, assistant overseers and prominent vestry men were subject to both threats, assault and incendiary attacks against their property during the winter of 1830.[169]

It is also important to note that while investigations into circumstances allowed for a fine-tuning of the parish's relief responsibilities, or even totally absolving the parish officers of responsibility for an individual or family, it did not remove the fact that all such judgements were rooted in some understanding as to what was the minimum necessary for a family to get by. Or rather, what was the minimum income that a parish could get away with for rural workers and their families. Indeed, the appointment of assistant overseers, alongside policies such as contracting out the running of poorhouses and workhouses, represented a creeping professionalisation of the poor relief system: individuals developed specific expertise in the abstract about populations and policy efficacy and application, and applied it to both the level of the parish and the household. The following chapter explores these ideas in detail, specifically in the context of workhouse dietaries, the clearest expression of the making of the poor as biological subjects of scrutiny and investigation. If the most infamous manifestation of this came with the passing of the New Poor Law with its strict emphasis on the principles of less eligibility, the chapter also explores earlier antecedents as operated by separate parishes and pre-1834 poor law unions, before then going on to explore the implementation of workhouse dietaries in the new centrally controlled but still locally operated system.

Notes

1 S. Webb and B. Webb, *English Local Government. Volume 7. English Poor Law History. Part I: The Old Poor Law* (London: Longman, 1927); S. Webb and B. Webb, *English Local Government. Volume 8. English Poor Law History. Part II: The Last Hundred Years Old Poor Law* (London: Longman, 1929). The same framework still persists; see: A. Brundage, *The English Poor Laws, 1700–1930* (Basingstoke: Palgrave, 2002).

2 S. Hindle, *On the Parish?: The Micro-Politics of Poor Relief in Rural England c. 1550–1750* (Oxford: Oxford University Press, 2004); J. Healey, *The First Century of Welfare: Poverty and Poor Relief in Lancashire, 1620–1730* (Woodbridge: Boydell & Brewer, 2014); S. King, *Poverty and Welfare in England, 1700–1850* (Manchester: Manchester University Press, 2000); S. Shave, *Pauper Policies: Poor Law Practice in England, 1780–1850* (Manchester: Manchester University Press, 2017).

3 T. Malthus, *An Essay on the Principle of Population* (London: J.M. Dent and Sons, 1803, 2nd edition), p. 83; M. Blaug, 'The myth of the old poor law and the making of the new', *Journal of Economic History*, 23:2 (1963), 176; G. Boyer, 'Malthus was right after all: Poor relief and birth rates in south-eastern England', *Journal of Political Economy*, 97:1 (1989), 93; S. Williams, 'Malthus, marriage and poor law allowances revisited: A Bedfordshire case study, 1770–1834', *Agricultural History Review*, 52:1 (2004), 82.

4 K. Polyani, *The Great Transformation: The Political and Economic Origins of our Time*, ed. F. Block (Boston, MA: Beacon, 2001), ch. 7, p. 81; T. Rogan, *The Moral Economists: R.H. Tawney, Karl Polanyi, E.P. Thompson and the Critique of Capitalism* (Princeton, NJ: Princeton University Press, 2017), pp. 80–3.

5 F. Block and M. Somers, 'In the shadow of Speenhamland: Social policy and the old poor law', *Politics & Society*, 31:2 (2003), 283–323.

6 L. Hollen Lees, *The Solidarities of Strangers: The English Poor Laws and the People, 1700–1948* (Cambridge: Cambridge University Press, 1998); S. King, Poverty and Welfare in England; A. Kidd, *State, Society and the Poor in Nineteenth-Century England* (London: Macmillan, 1999).

7 M. Blaug, 'The myth of the old poor law'; D.A. Baugh, 'The cost of poor relief in south-east England, 1790–1834', *Economic History Review*, 28:1 (1975): 50–68; Boyer, 'Malthus was right after all'.

8 M. Neuman, *The Speenhamland County: Poverty and the Poor Laws in Berkshire, 1782–1834* (New York: Garland, 1982); R. Wells, *Wretched Faces: Famine in Wartime England, 1793–1803* (Stroud: Allan Sutton, 1988), chs 12–14.

9 *York Courant*, 22 and 29 July and 12 August; *Star*, 16 August; *Sun*, 20 September 1793.

10 *Sussex Weekly Advertiser*, 7 July 1794; Wells, *Wretched Faces*, pp. 36–7; *Maidstone Journal*, 18 November and 2 December 1794.

11 *Hull Advertiser*, 16 January and 20 February; *Sussex Weekly Advertiser*, 26 January and 2 February; *Kentish Gazette*, 30 January and 13 March; *Maidstone Journal*, 3 February; *York Courant*, 16 and 23 February 1795.

12 East Sussex County Record Office, Lewes (hereafter ESCRO), Q0/EW 32, East and West Sussex Quarter Sessions Order Book; West Sussex County Record Office, Chichester (hereafter WSCRO), QR/W608, f.58, West Sussex Epiphany Sessions Roll 1795; *Sussex Weekly Advertiser*, 24 November 1794 and 16 March; *London Gazette*, 17 January and 14 February 1795.

13 Wells, *Wretched Faces*, pp. 36–7.

14 For evidence of unemployment see, for example, a subscription raised at Birmingham in late December 1794 to support the 'distressed' and the 'unemployed labouring poor' and at Hythe (Kent) where local grandee William Deedes ordered that all the unemployed were to be supplied with 'all goods' at half price on his expense: *Northampton Mercury*, 3 January; *Kentish Gazette*, 23 January 1795.

15 G.E. Mingay, 'Agriculture', in Alan Armstrong (ed.), *The Economy of Kent, 1640–1914* (Woodbridge: Kent County Council, 1995), pp. 51–83. For a more nuanced and contextualised reading of real wages see: K. Snell, *Annals of the Labouring Poor: Social Change and Agrarian England, 1660–1900* (Cambridge University Press, 1985), esp. pp. 37–40.

16 Anon., *Essays on Agriculture: Occasioned by Reading Mr Stone's Report on the Present State of that Science in the County of Lincoln. By a Native of the County* (London: W. Richardson, 1796), p. 35.

17 F. Eden, *The State of the Poor: Or, An History of the Labouring Classes in England, from the Conquest to the Present Period*, vol. 1 (Cambridge: Cambridge University Press, 2011/1797), p. ii; I. Gazeley and N. Verdon, 'The first poverty line? Davies' and Eden's investigation of rural poverty in the late 18th-century England', *Explorations in Economic History*, 51 (2014), 97.

18 D. Davies, *The Case of Labourers in Husbandry Stated and Considered* (London: C.G. & J. Robinson, 1795).

19 Eden, *State of the Poor*, vol. 1, p. 1. Davies, the rector of the Berkshire parish of Barkham, detailed his motivation thus: 'These poor people, in assigning the cause of their misery, agreed in ascribing it to the high prices of the necessities of life. "Every thing (said they) is so dear, that we can hardly live." In order to assure myself, whether this was really the case, I enquired into the particulars of their earnings and expenses': *The Case of Labourers*, p. 6.

20 C. Muldrew, *Food, Energy and the Creation of Industriousness: Work and Material Culture in Agrarian England, 1550–1780* (Cambridge: Cambridge University Press, 2011), p. 156.

21 Gazeley and Verdon, 'The first poverty line?', 99–103.

22 Ibid., 99–101.

23 Ibid., 105–6; P. Sharpe, 'The female labour market in English agriculture during the Industrial Revolution: Expansion or contraction?', *Agricultural History Review*, 47:2 (1999), 161–81.

24 Gazeley and Verdon, 'The first poverty line?', 106–7.

25 See ibid.; G. Clark, 'Farm wages and living standards in the industrial revolution: England, 1670–1869', *Economic History Review*, 54:3 (2001), 477–505. Also see: E. Griffin, 'Diets, hunger and living standards during the British industrial revolution', *Past & Present*, 239 (2018), 71–111.

26 Wells, *Wretched Faces*, p. 1; Lees, *The Solidarities of Strangers*, p. 37.
27 Snell, *Annals of the Labouring Poor*, p. 108. Also see King, *Poverty and Welfare in England*, p. 155.
28 M. Overton, *Agricultural Revolution in England: The Transformation of the Agrarian Economy* (Cambridge: Cambridge University Press, 1996), p. 65.
29 Wells, *Wretched Faces*, p. 55.
30 N. Raven, "'A humbler, industrious class of female": women's employment and industry in the small towns of southern England, *c*. 1790–1840', in P. Lane, N. Raven and K.D.M. Snell (eds), *Women, Work, and Wages in England, 1600–1850* (Woodbridge: Boydell and Brewer, 2004), pp. 170–89. On the cloth industry see: A. Randall, *Before the Luddites: Custom, Community and Machinery in the English Woollen Industry, 1776–1809* (Cambridge: Cambridge University Press, 1991).
31 As Navickas notes of the Lancashire handloom weavers, the situation deteriorated more markedly in the following decade: K. Navickas, *Loyalism and Radicalism in Lancashire, 1798–1815* (Oxford: Oxford University Press, 2009), pp. 186, 223.
32 Wells, *Wretched Faces*, p. 57; A. Randall, 'The industrial moral economy of the Gloucestershire weavers in the eighteenth century', in J. Rice and J. Rule (eds), *British Trade Unionism, 1750–1850: The Formative Years* (London: Longman, 1988), p. 30.
33 A. Charlesworth, 'The development of the English rural proletariat and social protest, 1700–1850: A comment', in M. Reed and R. Wells (eds), *Class, Conflict and Protest in the English Countryside, 1700–1880* (London: Frank Cass, 1990), pp. 59–60.
34 R. Wells, 'Social conflict and protest in the English countryside in the early nineteenth century: A rejoinder', in Reed and Wells (eds), *Class, Conflict and Protest*, pp. 65–81; F. McLynn, *Crime and Punishment in Eighteenth Century England* (London: Routledge, 1989), p. 334.
35 Gazeley and Verdon, p. 97, citing A. Armstrong, *Farmworkers: A Social and Economic History, 1770–1980* (London: B.T. Batsford, 1988), p. 53.
36 Eden, *State of the Poor*, vol. 1, pp. 496, 497–533.
37 Ibid., p. 526; Wells, *Wretched Faces*, esp. ch. 13.
38 *Annals of Agriculture*, 24 (1795), 122, 127, 280.
39 A. Randall, *Riotous Assemblies: Popular Protest in Hanoverian England* (Oxford: Oxford University Press, 2006), p. 213.
40 Muldrew, *Food, Energy and the Creation of Industriousness*, p. 68; also see Gazeley and Verdon, 'The first poverty line?', 95.
41 A. Young, *A Six Weeks Tour, Through the Southern Counties of England and Wales* (London: Nicoll, 1769), p. 320; Muldrew, *Food, Energy and the Creation of Industriousness*, p. 229. As Gregory Clark notes, though, the proportion of wages given in kind as beer, while hard to calculate, was low and declining: Clark, 'Farm wages and living standards', 480.
42 Eden, *State of the Poor*, vol. I, pp. 496–7.
43 Eden, *State of the Poor, passim*; S. Williams, *Poverty, Gender and Life-cycle under the English Poor Law, 1760–1834* (Woodbridge: Boydell & Brewer, 2011);

S. Shave, 'The dependent poor? (Re)constructing the lives of individuals "on the parish" in rural Dorset, 1800–1832', *Rural History*, 20:1 (2009), 67–97; H. French, 'How dependent were the 'dependent poor'? Poor relief and the life-course in Terling, Essex, 1762–1834', *Continuity and Change*, 30:2 (2015), 193–222.

44 D.J. Oddy, 'Urban famine in nineteenth-century Britain: The effect of the Lancashire cotton famine on working-class diet and health', *Economic History Review*, 36:1 (1983), 68–86; Wells, *Wretched Faces*, pp. 8, 54.

45 Wells asserts that the two crises led to 'demographic disturbance': Wells, *Wretched Faces*, pp. 69–71. Conversely, Wrigley and Schofield assert that mortality rates in the 1790s were consistent with other contiguous decades: E.A. Wrigley and R.S. Schofield, *The Population History of England 1541–1871* (Cambridge: Cambridge University Press, 1989/1981), p. 136.

46 Wells, *Wretched Faces*, ch. 11 and pp. 202–3; Randall, *Riotous Assemblies*, pp. 213–14. This policy also continued into the autumn: for instance see Eden, *State of the Poor*, vol. 1, p. 533: Dr Irvine to the House of Commons Committee in 1774 regarding methods of making flour from wheat and subsequently reprinted by Parliament in November 1795.

47 Wells, *Wretched Faces*, pp. 203–8.

48 *Sussex Weekly Advertiser*, 20 July 1795; Wells, *Wretched Faces*, pp. 13, 207–8, 213 and 216; K. Bawn, 'Social protest, popular disturbances and public order in Dorset, 1790–1838' (PhD thesis, University of Reading, 1984), p. 22.

49 Wells, *Wretched Faces*, pp. 209–12; Randall, *Riotous Assemblies*, p. 213; *Kentish Gazette*, 5 and 8 January; *Sussex Weekly Advertiser*, 18 January 1796.

50 Wells, *Wretched Faces*, pp. 211–12; *Kentish Chronicle*, 12 January 1796.

51 Randall, *Riotous Assemblies*, p. 213; Wells, *Wretched Faces*, p. 213. See also J. Hammond and B. Hammond, *The Village Labourer, 1760–1832: A Study in the Government of England Before the Reform Bill*, ed. G.E. Mingay (London: Longman, 1978), pp. 80–6.

52 *Maidstone Journal*, 12 January; *Kentish Gazette*, 19 February 1796.

53 J.R. Poynter, *Society and Pauperism: English Ideas on Poor Relief, 1795–1834* (London: Routledge, 1969), pp. 62–76.

54 Williams, *Poverty, Gender and Life-cycle*, pp. 94–7.

55 On such structuring effects see C.J. Griffin, 'Knowable geographies? The reporting of incendiarism in the eighteenth- and early nineteenth-century English provincial press', *Journal of Historical Geography*, 32:1 (2006), 38–56.

56 Wells, *Wretched Faces*, p. 8.

57 East Yorkshire Record Office, Beverley (hereafter EYRO), PE121/63, Howden vestry minutes, 1774–1819, 19 December 1794, 4 May, 13 July and 10 November 1795, and 7 January 1796.

58 *Sussex Weekly Advertiser*, 9 March 1795.

59 Poynter, *Society and Pauperism*, p. 10.

60 M. Neuman, 'A suggestion regarding the origins of the Speenhamland plan', *English Historical Review*, 84:331 (1969), 317.

61 On this tradition see: J. Gerard, 'Lady Bountiful: Women of the landed classes and rural philanthropy', *Victorian Studies*, 30:2 (1987), 183–207. For a local

case study of these dynamics see: S. Thomas, 'Power, paternalism, patronage and philanthropy: The Wyndhams and the New Poor Law in Petworth', *Local Historian*, 32:2 (2002), 99–117.

62 For instance, it was widely reported that the high sheriff of Somerset, Mr Knatchbull, had 'caused five bullocks to be killed and distributed among the poor' of the parishes of Babington, Stratton and the neighbourhood. The report was even twice detailed in the *Oracle and Public Advertiser*, 5 and 10 January 1795.

63 *Oracle and Public Advertiser*, 30 December 1794.

64 *Sun*, 14 January 1795; *Maidstone Journal*, 30 December 1794, 6, 13 and 20 January 1795; D. Harvey, 'Aspects of agricultural and rural change in Kent 1800–1900' (PhD thesis, University of Cambridge, 1960), pp. 221–5.

65 *Oracle and Public Advertiser*, 7 and January; *Sun*, 2 January 1795.

66 CKS, Bromley Vestry Item 5, Bromley vestry minutes, 20 and 30 July; *Oracle and Public Advertiser*, 5 and 10 January 1795.

67 *Oracle and Public Advertiser*, 12 January; *General Evening Post*, 5 February; *Sussex Weekly Advertiser*, 12 January; Lincolnshire Record Office, Lincoln (hereafter LRO), FRAMPTON PAR/10/3, Frampton vestry minute, 3 December 1795.

68 E.P. Thompson, 'Patrician society, plebeian culture', *Journal of Social History*, 7:4 (1974), 382–405.

69 Wells, *Wretched Faces*, p. 141; *Hull Advertiser*, 7 November 1795.

70 *York Courant*, 16 March, 6, 13 and 20 July 1795.

71 On the geography and timing of south-eastern food rioting see: C. Griffin, 'As lated tongues bespoke: Popular protest in south-east England, 1790–1840' (PhD thesis, University of Bristol, 2002), pp. 145, 148–9. On the Worth riot see: *Sussex Weekly Advertiser*, 9 March 1795.

72 *Oracle and Public Advertiser*, 29 May 1795.

73 *Salisbury and Winchester Journal*, 23 February 1795.

74 ESCRO, PAR 237/12/2, Beckley vestry minute, 19 January; ESCRO, PAR 401/12/1 Icklesham vestry minute, 23 January; *Courier and Evening Gazette*, 21 April; ESCRO DE/A1/3, Eastbourne vestry minute, 28 June 1795.

75 CKS, P49/8/3, Brookland vestry minute, 31 July 1795.

76 *Sussex Weekly Advertiser*, 9 March 1795.

77 CKS P125/8/1, Dymchurch vestry minutes, 27 February, 31 May, 24 June and 1 November 1791, and 18 April 1795.

78 LRO, Heckington PAR/10/1, Heckington vestry meeting, 17 March. By early 1796 the Yalding vestry abandoned the plan in an attempt to join the newly formed Gilbert's Union centred around nearby Coxheath: CKS P408/8/1, Yalding vestry minutes, 17 June 1795, 28 February and 6 March 1796.

79 *Reading Mercury*, 6 May 1795.

80 Ibid.

81 A.W. Ashby, *One Hundred Years of Poor Law Administration in a Warwickshire Village* (Oxford: Oxford University Press, 1912), p. 155; E.M. Hampson, *The Treatment of Poverty in Cambridgeshire 1597–1834* (Cambridge: Cambridge University Press, 1934), p. 37; Webb and Webb, *The Old Poor Law*, p. 172.

82 Neuman, 'A suggestion regarding the origins', 318.
83 Shave, *Pauper Policies*, ch. 2 and pp. 268–78; G. Rawson, 'Economies and strategies of the northern rural poor: The mitigation of poverty in a West Riding township in the nineteenth century', *Rural History*, 28:1 (2017), 69–92. For a contextual but now superseded article see: A.W. Coats, 'Economic thought and poor law policy in the eighteenth century', *Economic History Review*, 2nd series, 13:1 (1960–1), 46.
84 R. Thorne, 'Young, Sir William, 2nd Bt (1749–1815), of Delaford Park, Bucks.', in R. Thorne (ed.), *The History of Parliament: the House of Commons 1790–1820*, vol. 5, www.historyofparliamentonline.org/volume/1790-1820/member/young-sir-william-1749-1815 (accessed 13 September 2018); Eden, *State of the Poor*, vol. 1, pp. 395–7, note 1.
85 Eden, *State of the Poor*, vol. 2, pp. 29–30 and 384.
86 G. Boyer, *An Economic History of the English Poor Law, 1750–1850* (Cambridge: Cambridge University Press, 1990), p. 24.
87 Neuman, 'A suggestion regarding the origins', 318; Neuman, *Speenhamland County*, p. 185.
88 Neuman, 'A suggestion regarding the origins', 319–20; C.R. Fay, *The Corn Laws and Social England* (Cambridge: Cambridge University Press, 1950/1932), p. 339.
89 S. and B. Webb, *The Parish and the County* (London: Longman, 1906), pp. 546–7, note i; Neuman, 'A suggestion regarding the origins', 317.
90 Wells, *Wretched Faces*, ch. 17; R. Wells, 'Social protest, class, conflict and consciousness, in the English countryside, 1700–1880', in M. Reed and R. Wells (eds), *Class, Conflict and Protest in the English Countryside, 1700–1880* (London: Frank Cass, 1990), pp. 135–8; Webb and Webb, *The Old Poor Law*, p. 177; Hammond and Hammond, *The Village Labourer*, p. 163; *Reading Mercury*, 4 and 11 May; *Hampshire Chronicle*, 17 October 1795.
91 *Reading Mercury*, 15 and 22 January; *Sussex Weekly Journal*, 23 February 1795.
92 Eden, *State of the Poor*, vol. 2, pp. 218–66; Neuman, *Speenhamland County*, pp. 75–80; Wells, *Wretched Faces*, pp. 293–4.
93 Shave, *Pauper Policies*, pp. 5, 29.
94 See J. Huzel, 'The labourer and the poor law, 1750–1850', in G. Mingay (ed.), *The Agrarian History of England and Wales, Vol. 6, 1750–1850* (Cambridge: Cambridge University Press, 1989), p. 775.
95 CKS, PS/Ma/4, Malling Petty Sessions Minute, 3 August 1795; CKS, P408/8/2, Yalding vestry minute, 1 November 1800. For an examination of the dynamics of out-parish relief see: S. King, '"It is impossible for our vestry to judge his case into perfection from here": Managing the distance dimensions of poor relief, 1800–40', *Rural History* 16:2 (2005), 161–189.
96 Wells, *Wretched Faces*, ch. 17 esp. pp. 296–300; Wells, 'Social protest', pp. 135–8; Neuman, *Speenhamland County*, p. 165.
97 ESCRO, PAR 440/12/1, Peasmarsh vestry minute, 27 April; WSCRO, PAR 153/12/1, Pulborough vestry minute, 10 May 1795; *Sussex Weekly Advertiser*, 2 December 1799; Griffin, 'As lated tongues', pp. 142–5, 147–8, 154–5 and 160–1; Wells, 'Social protest', pp. 135–6.

98 British Parliamentary Papers (hereafter BPP), 1803–4 (175), vol. 8, 'Abstract of the answers and returns made pursuant to an act, passed in the 43d year of His Majesty King George III. Intitled, "An act for procuring returns relative to the expense and maintenance of the poor in England"' (hereafter '1803 Returns'), p. iii.

99 Dorset County Record Office, Dorchester (hereafter DCRO), PE/BF/VE 1/1, 13 April and 7 July 1795, and VE 1/3, 24 April 1797, 10 May and 26 October 1798.

100 LRO, Quadring PAR/10/3, Quadring vestry minute, 3 June 1796; LRO, HD/65/1/5, Holbeach vestry minute, 3 October 1797; LRO, Burton upon Stather PAR/10/1, Burton vestry minute, 9 April 1798.

101 Wells, *Wretched Faces*, pp. 310–17.

102 CKS, P202/8/1, Ightham vestry minute, 2 November 1799; P399/12/8, Wittersham vestry minute, 9 December 1799; P145/8/1, Farningham vestry minute, 16 February 1800; Surrey History Centre, Woking, P25/3/1, Godstone vestry minute, 2 December 1799.

103 CKS, P192/8/2, Horsmonden vestry minute, 31 October 1802.

104 ESCRO, AMS/5567/1, Alfriston vestry minute, 6 April 1801.

105 CKS, P309/8/7, New Romney vestry minutes, 6 May 1802 and 7 May 1808.

106 E.L. Jones, *Seasons and Prices: The Role of the Weather in English Agricultural History* (London: Allen and Unwin, 1963), pp. 156–7.

107 Imperfect in that it does not include monies spent by surveyors of the highways on employing those out of work, and does not take account of income generated from employment of the poor in parish and union workhouses.

108 BPP, '1803 returns', pp. 713–16.

109 M. Hanley, 'Being poor in nineteenth-century Lancashire', in A. Gestrich, S. King and L. Raphael (eds), *Being Poor in Modern Europe: Historical Perspectives 1800–1940* (Bern: Verlag Peter Lang, 2006), pp. 79–81.

110 EYRO, zDDX131/1/6, Copy of Enclosure Award and plan relating to Goodmanham, 1777, and AP/3/24, Goodmanham Enclosure Act, 1775; EYRO, PC56/1, Lund Enclosure act, 1794; IA/101, Lund Enclosure Map, 1795.

111 BPP, '1803 returns', pp. 588, 590.

112 On which see King, *Poverty and Welfare in England*, esp. chs 1 and 6.

113 BPP, '1803 returns', p. 218.

114 Ibid., p. 508.

115 Ibid., pp. 400, 428.

116 Ibid., p. 324.

117 Blaug, 'The myth of the old poor law', 157, 158, 159.

118 S. Hindle, 'Dependency, shame and belonging: Badging the deserving poor, c. 1550–1750', *Cultural and Social History*, 1:1 (2004), 15–16; S. Hindle, 'Civility, honesty and the identification of the deserving poor in seventeenth-century England', in H. French and J. Barry (eds), *Identity and Agency in England, 1650–1800* (Basingstoke: Palgrave, 2004), pp. 38–59.

119 K. Wrightson, 'The politics of the parish in early modern England', in A. Fox, P. Griffiths and S. Hindle (eds), *The Experience of Authority in Early*

Modern England (Basingstoke: Palgrave, 1996), pp. 10–46. Griffin, *The Rural War*, pp. 32–3.

120 *Sussex Weekly Advertiser*, 9 March 1795.

121 *Sussex Weekly Advertiser*, 24 February 1800.

122 *Sussex Weekly Advertiser*, 24 February and 21 April 1801; Wells, *Wretched Faces*, p. 426; R. Wells, 'The moral economy of the English countryside', in A. Randall and A. Charlesworth (eds), *Moral Economy and Popular Protest: Crowds, Conflict and Authority* (Basingstoke: Macmillan, 2000), p. 230; TNA, HO 42/61, fos 156–8, Richmond, Goodwood, 16 February, to Portland, enclosing H. Shadwell, Ringmer to Richmond, 15 February 1801.

123 Thompson, 'Moral economy'; P. Jones, 'Swing, Speenhamland and rural social relations: The "moral economy" of the English crowd in the nineteenth century', *Social History*, 32:3 (2007), 271–90.

124 Wiltshire and Swindon Record Office, Chippenham [herein WSRO], 1719/6, Box vestry minutes, 24 October 1806 and 17 November 1809. On this dynamic see: Wells, 'Social protest', p. 158. On the triangulation of rural social relations see: P. King, 'Edward Thompson's contribution to eighteenth-century studies: The patrician-plebeian model re-examined', *Social History*, 21:2 (1996), 215–28.

125 BPP. Commons, 1824 (392), vol. 6, 'Report from the select committee on labourers wages' (hereafter '1824 Report'), evidence of Rev. John Pratt, Selscombe, Sussex, 12 April 1824.

126 H. French, 'An irrevocable shift: Detailing the dynamics of rural poverty in southern England, 1762–1834: A case study', *Economic History Review*, 68:3 (2015), 769–805, esp. 780–2; French, 'How dependent were the "dependent poor"?', 215–16.

127 Snell, *Annals of the Labouring Poor*, p. 27.

128 A. Armstrong, *Farmworkers: A Social and Economic History 1770–1980* (London: Batsford, 1988), p. 64; G. Gleig, *The Chronicles of Waltham* (London: R. Bentley, 1835), pp. 80–1.

129 J. Burnett, *Idle Hands: The Experience of Unemployment, 1790–1990* (London: Routledge, 2002), ch. 3.

130 The overseers' accounts books of Berkshire parishes in 1815 are littered with references to 'bread money' or 'bread allowances', evidence of the persistence of the principles and practices of Speenhamland before the post-war depression. For instance see: Berkshire Record Office, Reading (hereafter BRO), D/P124/12/3, Sulhampstead Abbots, Overseers Accounts, 1800–1831; BRO, D/P22/12/4, Bradfield Overseers Accounts, 1808–1818; BRO, D/P48/12/2, Drayton, Overseers Accounts, 1794–1821; BRO, D/P92/12/2, Peasemore Overseers Accounts, 1810–1830 (where the practice was abandoned in 1816).

131 HCRO, 43M67/PV1, Amport vestry minutes, 17 January and 6 November 1816.

132 C.J. Griffin, 'Parish farms and the poor law: A response to unemployment in rural southern England, c. 1815–35', *Agricultural History Review*, 59:2 (2011), 176–198.

133 HCRO, 43M67 PV1, Amport vestry minute, 21 April; HCRO 30M77 PV1, Bishops Waltham vestry minute, 28 April 1820.

134 LCRO, Quadring PAR/10/3, Quadring vestry minute, 1 April; BRO, D/P 66/8/1, East Hendred vestry minute, n.d. (but *c*. 1 March 1816).

135 BPP, 1818 (400) vol. 19, 'Report from the House of Lords Select Committee on the Poor Laws', pp. 72, 89–90, 200.

136 BPP, 1828 (494) vol. 4, 'Report from the Select Committee on that part of the Poor Laws relating to the employment or relief of able-bodied persons from the poor rate' (hereafter 1828 Report), p. 25.

137 HCRO, 15M84/Z3/61, Rev. Henry Wake, *Abuse of the Poor-Rate!! A Statement of Facts* (Andover, self-published, 1818); *Hampshire Chronicle*, 26 April 1819.

138 Neuman, *Speenhamland County*, p. 168; CKS, P88/8/1, Chevening vestry minutes, 14 February and 14 March; CKS, P/347/8/1, Staplehurst vestry minute, 1 May 1822; HCRO, 6M77 PV1, Eversley vestry minutes, 17 and 29 November 1822.

139 1824 Report, p. 8; WSRO, 1551/48, Poulshot vestry minute, 3 January 1827; CKS, P45/8/2, Brenchley vestry minute, 9 February 1829.

140 Griffin, *The Rural War*, pp. 36, 278.

141 HCRO, 43M67/PV1 and 90M71 PV1, Amport vestry minute, 22 September and Minstead vestry minute, 8 December 1815.

142 Though note the example of Spalding, where a 'large subscription' was raised in the winter of 1816 from which subsidised bread, meat, potatoes and coals were sold to the poor. The consequence was a much-reduced poor rate: BPP, 1819 (529) vol. 2, 'Select Committee to consider Poor Laws: Report, minutes of evidence', p. 112.

143 BPP, 1817 (462) vol. 6, 'Select Committee to consider Poor Laws: Report, minutes of evidence, appendix', pp. 97–8, 172.

144 HCRO, 44M69/J30/1, Printed scale for regulating parochial relief by the price of standard wheaten bread adopted in the Hindon (Wiltshire) division 5 March 1817; PP, 1828, p. 62; Cornwall Record Office, Truro, R/5145, Scale for regulating poor relief, 1817.

145 1824 Report, p. 7.

146 1824 Report: Stalbridge (Dorset, mistakenly recorded as Tolbridge), Bedford (Bedfordshire), Guildford (Surrey), pp. 32, 35–6, 38, 47–8; 1825 Abstract: Abingdon (Berkshire), Cullumpton Division (Devon), Dudstone and Kings Barton (Gloucestershire), Dacorum (Hertfordshire), South Aylesford (Kent), Bullingdon, Thame and Dorchester (Oxfordshire), and Chippenham and Calne, Heytesbury, and Marlborough (Wiltshire), pp. 2, 10, 16, 22, 24, 36, 46.

147 *Hampshire Chronicle*, 9 September; *Cobbett's Weekly Political Register*, 21 September 1822. The Fawley bench were presumably unperturbed by a case heard at the Hampshire assizes the previous month in which a labourer of Bramshaw parish – close to Fawley – was acquitted on the charge of having sent a letter to the Bramshaw guardian of the poor threatening to burn his premises. The alleged motivation? Having only paid him sixpence a day for working on the parish roads: *Hampshire Telegraph*, 15 and 22 July 1822.

148 BPP, 1825 (334) vol. 4, 'Select Committee on Poor Rate Returns: Report, appendix (1824)' (hereafter 1825 Poor Rate Returns), Abstract: Somerset (but widespread child allowances), Durham 'in a few cases' in Chester East Division (p. 12), Grimsworth 'very rarely' and paying of house rents when over two children at Radlow (North East) Hundred (Herefordshire, p. 20), Lancaster Hundred 'in part' (Lancashire, p. 26), Elloe (Lincolnshire) abandoned (p. 30), Usk Upper Division (Monmouthshire) house rents in some cases (p. 30), Newport Division (Shropshire) 'in very few instances' (p. 38). Witham (Essex) has all but ceased (p. 14).

149 For instance see: BRO, D/EX 1457/4/30, Scales of bread allowances, Sonning, 1819; Neuman, *Speenhamland County*, esp. p. 122.

150 *Reading Mercury*, 15 January 1827.

151 Baugh, 'The cost of poor relief', 60–4; Boyer, 'Malthus was right after all', 96.

152 1824 Report, p. 7; 1828 Report, p. 4.

153 E. Hobsbawm and G. Rudé, *Captain Swing* (London: Lawrence and Wishart, 1969), p. 75. On Dorset see: C.J. Griffin, 'The culture of combination: Solidarities and collective action before Tolpuddle', *Historical Journal*, 58:2 (2015), 443–80; C. Beardmore, 'Landowner, tenant and agent on the Marquis of Anglesey's Dorset and Somerset estate, 1814–44', *Rural History*, 26:2 (2015), 181–99; Shave, 'The dependent poor?'. On Bedfordshire see: Williams, *Poverty, Gender and Life-cycle*.

154 1828 Report, pp. 20–5 (Evidence of Henry Boyce, overseer, Walderslade, 10 June 1828).

155 BRO, D/P116/8/5, Speen vestry minute, 9 October 1830.

156 R. Wells, 'Historical trajectories: English welfare systems, rural riots, popular politics, agrarian trade unions, and allotment provision, 1793–1896', *Southern History*, 25 (2003), 89.

157 On the idea of a welfare state in miniature see: M. Blaug, 'The poor law report reexamined', *Journal of Economic History*, 24:2 (1964), 229.

158 On the role of negotiation versus entitlement in the early years of the Elizabethan Poor Law see: Hindle, *On the Parish?*, esp. pp. 164–70.

159 For instance see: 1825 Poor Rate Returns, pp. 19–23.

160 ESCRO, PAR343/12/1, Framfield vestry minute, 10 May 1811; LCRO, Frampton vestry minute, 12 April 1816; Shave, *Pauper Policies*, p. 114. As David Green has noted, the adoption of such provisions was the standard across London parishes: D.R. Green, *Pauper Capital: London and the Poor Law, 1790–1870* (Farnham: Ashgate, 2009), pp. 89–91.

161 Shave, *Pauper Policies*, p. 115. Neuman noted that seven Berkshire parishes nade such appointments before 1819, the earliest being Hungerford in 1786: Neuman, *Speenhamland County*, p. 181.

162 S. Shave, 'The impact of Sturges Bourne's poor law reforms in rural England', *Historical Journal*, 56:2 (2013), 409.

163 WSCRO, 1489/9, Steeple Ashton vestry minute, 8 April, and select vestry minute, 21 May 1833; HCRO, 25M60 PV1, Fawley select vestry minute, 1 September; Canterbury Cathedral Archives, U3/49/8/1, Hougham select

vestry minute, 30 November 1819; HCRO, 40M75 A PV2, Botley select vestry minute, 24 December 1822 and 29 April 1823.

164 Shave, *Pauper Policies*, p. 114.

165 HCRO, 30M77 PV1, Bishops Waltham vestry minute, 9 July 1819.

166 Snell, *Annals of the Labouring Poor*, p. 117.

167 *Sussex Advertiser*, 11, 18 and 25 November, 23 and 30 December 1822; TNA, HO 64/1, fos 46–7 and 310–13, Charles Jenkin, Northiam, E.J. Curteis, Battle, both to Peel, 13 November; TNA, Assi 94/1856, indictments of John Carter, David Saunter and William Saunter for riotous assembly, Charles Weston and George Eastwood for arson, 'Complaint' against John Morgan for spreading fire, Sussex winter assizes 1822.

168 *Kent Herald*, 11 November 1824; *Sussex Advertiser*, 10 January 1825.

169 Griffin, *The Rural War*, see esp. pp. 95–7, 113, 116, 134, 143–4, 149, 169, 174–5, 181–5, 221–2, 284.

4

Dietaries and the less eligibility workhouse: or, the making of the poor as biological subjects

Much of the second 'book' of the first volume of Frederick Eden's *State of the Poor* was given over to a musing – analysis is too strong a word, too certain a process for the mix of history, reportage and opinion – on the diet and dietary customs and habits of 'the poor' throughout England, though the commentary frequently travelled elsewhere in the British Isles and overseas too.[1] As Eden put it, '*The prices of provisions* and of *labour* are so intimately connected with the circumstances of the Poor, that no writer has ever thought of dissociating them.' To make sense of this equation, without which 'it is hardly possible to form any accurate judgment of the condition of the labouring classes', it was necessary for Eden to determine not only the incomes of the poor and the prices of what they spent their money on but also precisely what it was that the poor ate and how much of it was necessary to sustain them.[2] Indeed, the dietary of the poor was at the centre not only of Eden's study but also that by David Davies whose *Case of Labourers* similarly detailed collected budgets and dietaries of poor households.[3]

As considered in the previous chapter, the household dietaries, and Eden's broader survey of consumption habits, revealed the decisive preference for pure white wheaten bread as the staple of the southern labouring diet. While white bread was supplemented by cheese and beer, and – when it could be afforded – meat and tea, the consumption of the finest, purest bread was a critical marker of the culture of the labourer and held as central in their right to self-determination. In the north and the west, other cereals – notably barley in the west and oats in the northern counties – complemented and even altogether replaced wheat in the labouring diet, though potatoes were also increasingly assuming prominence in many locales. This greater variety, as Davies and Eden saw it, not only increased the dietary choice open to such northern and western labouring families but also left them less exposed to price volatility, the demand – and hence price – for wheat being non-elastic. As bacon and most other non-wheaten bread foodstuffs became luxuries as opposed to staples, so labouring budgets increasingly allowed the purchase of just bread, some cheese and tea, beer, occasional clothes and rent.[4]

In this way, calculating what a poor family needed, or rather what the bodies of poor labouring men, women and their children needed, became absolutely defined by how much bread a labouring body needed to survive each day and how much it cost. There are elements of this bodily calculation in Davies' and Eden's budgets. They, of course, were humanely motivated by their personal experience of administering poverty to improve the condition of the poor rather than attempting to work out what the minimum labouring families need to get by. Likewise there is a suggestion of calculation in Knatchbull's Act. The 'workhouse test' of less eligibility – that conditions inside the workhouse should be worse than those outside of the poorest labourer living outside the house – was rooted in an understanding of the worst conditions, but this is relational rather than absolute.[5] But in Speenhamland-style scales, and in the context of the crises of the 1790s and early 1800s, we see an absolute reducing of the labouring body to what was needed to get by, a crude calculation of the mechanics of getting by through the function of bread.

If this did not take the form of the precise calculation of calories (Nicolas Clément coined the term and invented the concept in 1824[6]) it at least rested on a rudimentary understanding of food energy. If there was disagreement between Eden and Davies as to the precise nature of the perfect dietary – Eden espoused the nutritional efficiency and substitutionary efficacy of soups; Davies instead saw them as leading to the 'waste' of 'vast quantities of flesh-meat', meat itself being an inefficient use of some 'the richest lands of the country' – both were agreed that it was economically, socially and politically desirable that the labourers of the south and east had more diverse diets. This was also, as Eden saw it, a moral issue. 'A labouring man in the county of Cumberland', so Eden reckoned, 'can, and does' earn as much as a labourer from Hertfordshire but his 'expenditure (more especially in the articles of diet and apparel) is comparatively insignificant'. As such, the notional Cumberland labourer – for which Eden wishes us to read the northern labourer – used 'superior economical skill and care in culinary contrivances' and can 'indulge himself in many savoury dishes … which the labourer of the South can scarcely ever afford.'[7] Beyond stating his admiration for the frugality and culinary versatility of the northern labourer, Eden shied away from explicitly detailing solutions ('I have, purposely, and almost wholly, abstained from drawing conclusions from the facts here presented').[8] Davies, by way of contrast, offered a seven-point plan. In addition to the need to affect 'a reduction of the prices of certain necessary articles' (point 2), the plan also detailed the desirability of '[c]orrecting the improvidence of the lower people, and encouraging frugality amongst them' (point 4). Reworking the dietary of the southern labourer was vital in 'solving' pauperism.[9]

Eden and Davies also differed in their respective opinions as to the efficacy of workhouses. Drawing on data from his parish of Barkham, Davies noted that the poor rate was lower than in surrounding parishes and yet there was no workhouse. Further, he asserted that notwithstanding the high cost, as he saw it, of relieving the poor in workhouses, the 'little work … done in these houses' was 'so ill-executed, that the goods are scarcely saleable', while as the 'Tracts of Messrs Zouch, Townsend, Howlett, and McFarlan' proved that workhouses had 'ill effects of the health and morals of their inhabitants'. Thus 'after a little time', workhouses 'almost always become mere receptacles of idle and vicious persons; many of whom live better there at the public expense, than some honest people can do, who work hard to keep their families from the parish'.[10] If for Davies workhouses were invariably inefficient, ill disciplined and offered too great a comfort to those who ill deserved it, Eden was more positive, if not without criticism, noting for instance that the workhouse at Aldersgate (London) did not continue 'long in a thriving state'.[11]

One feature of the supposedly well-regulated and governed workhouse that came in for particular praise was the standardised pauper dietary, which even in the south comprised a diet far more diverse than the standard wheaten loaf and cheese. Getting at the precise motivations of most of the workhouse dietaries collected by Eden is impossible, though some general observations are possible while in some cases impulses were explicitly related. In the case of the Epsom (Surrey) workhouse dietary – though admittedly this was not the most diverse dietary of southern workhouses – portions were both 'plentiful' and 'in general, wholsome and good'. That at nearby Esher was likewise 'not stinted to any particular quantity', while the dinner of meat and potatoes – this a shift from bread since the start of the 'present scarcity' – of those in the Sutton Colefield (Warwickshire) workhouse was likewise 'not stinted to a limited quantity'.[12] That at Norwich in 1784 had been in the practice of giving inmates a daily serving of cooked beef which equated to 19½ oz per man, woman and child. When this was replaced by a cheap soup of oatmeal, pease, bread crusts and 'cheeks', combined with buying in rather than brewing beer, a saving of £6,000 was achieved over three years.[13]

We should be careful, however, in reading too much into such qualitative comments. They do not necessarily reflect the universal picture in the 1790s, nor do they absolutely relate a diet that was adequate to the bodily needs of inmates (who were likely to be engaged in less calorie-intensive work than those outside the house) let alone labourers engaged in agricultural work. Indeed, Eden's calculation of a possible dietary for a workhouse of size 1 to 400 individuals equated to, according to Carole Shammas' calculation, 'a little less' than 2,900 calories – significantly below the 3,500 minimum calories necessary to sustain an adult working man.[14] Further, Eden's model workhouse diet included meat, suet, milk, cheese, butter, peas, rice, bread, flour and beer (see table 4.1). This was not only more diverse than most of the parish and union workhouse dietaries he detailed but also a significant

Table 4.1 Eden's model workhouse dietary, per inmate per week

Flesh	Milk	Rice	Pork	Pease	Flour	Suet	Cheese	Butter	Bread	Beer
1 meal	1 meal	1 meal		1 meal	1 meal			Whole week	Whole week	
10 oz	1 pint	2 oz	2 oz	1/3 pint	7½ oz	2 oz	3 oz	1 oz	4 lb 14 oz	1½ gallons

Source: F. Eden, *The State of the Poor: Or, An History of the Labouring Classes in England, from the Conquest to the Present Period*, vol. 1 (Cambridge: Cambridge University Press, 2011/1797), vol. 3, p. 356.

dietary advance over the diet of most southern and eastern labourers living outside of workhouses. It is also important to note that the table was taken from William Bailey's 1758 treatise *The Manifold Causes of the Increase of the Poor*. Eden copied this four-decade-old dietary in the appendices to volume 3 of *The State of the Poor* as 'likely to be useful' and as a 'much to be desired' guide in workhouse management and regulation.[15]

There is evidence to suggest that the dietaries reported (and those designed) by Eden represented a long-term decline in calorific value compared to those from the earliest years of the poor law; the decline that took place, according to Shammas, was evident by the first quarter of the eighteenth century. While her sample of early dietaries is necessarily small, it is apparent that this decline was a function of diminishing amounts of milk and cheese and a greater reliance on butter (which contains almost no calcium or protein), and a greater reliance on grains relative to meat.[16]

Those dietaries detailed in the first and second editions (published in 1725 and 1732 respectively by the Society for the Promotion of Christian Knowledge) of the influential *An Account of Several Work-houses for Employing and Maintaining the Poor* tended to be more generous in terms of quantity and quality and more diverse in the fare offered than most of the dietaries detailed in Eden's report. That at Wisbech (Cambridgeshire) comprised 'good Beef, Broth, Dumplins, Pease Porridge, Milk Porridge, Bread and Cheese', the 'Quantity according to every one's Stomach at Noon; at Morning and Night not so much, given out by the Mistress of the Kitchen'. Inmates of the Strood (Kent) workhouse established in 1722 – the rector Rev. Caleb Parfect having 'with great Application visited several places in Kent and Essex, to be inform'd of the best Methods for employing the poor' – had meat in several forms on six days of the week, butter or cheese every day, and regular milk-based dishes, broth or porridges.[17]

The workhouse run by the Quakers at Clerkenwell was relatively generous, offering bread, cheese, butter and beer for breakfast and supper – with broth instead of cheese and butter twice a week), with a different meat-based dish four days a week for dinner and three different hot dinners on the other nights.[18] There were exceptions to this rule, though. For instance, Hanslope (Buckinghamshire) parish was run on a slight deviation from the 'workhouse test' system. Claimants were offered either a tokenistic amount in out-relief or a place in the workhouse. The house therefore existed both as a net and as a deterrent. The diet much more sparse than most others detailed in the 1725 *Account*, meat only being offered twice weekly and on the other days 'their Diet is only a piece of wheaten Houshold Bread, small Beer, and sometimes a Pudding', with either porridge or – 'after the Flesh days' – broth.[19] Hanslope is some six miles distant from Olney, the parish where Matthew Marryott established his career as a workhouse manager, contractor and poor law entrepreneur. The workhouse at Olney operated under the principles of less eligibility, outdoor relief having been all but withdrawn. The workhouse test applied, and the workhouse regime was based on strict discipline and a meagre diet. As Tim Hitchcock has detailed, Marryott went on to found a small poor law empire, helping to establish workhouses – possibly including that at Hanslope – and taking on contracts to run existing workhouses throughout the Home Counties and London, installing assistants to do his work. Marryott's example and direct influence was also, so Hitchcock suggests, fundamental to the framing and passing of Knatchbull's 'Workhouse Test' Act of 1723. 'Marryott' workhouses, though, were subject to particular criticism. The 1731 pamphlet *The Workhouse Cruelty: Workhouses Turn'd Gaols and Gaolers Executioners* reproved Marryott and his employees and associates for starving the poor, the withholding of food – sometimes in conjunction with confinement in 'Dark Holes' – leading in some cases to death, whether by absolute starvation or conditions aggravated by being starved.[20]

Adequacy and inadequacy

It is now well established thanks to the work of Shammas and Muldrew, amongst others, that such dietaries were absolutely inadequate to the minimum necessary nutritional demands of labourers.[21]

As noted above, there is a danger in drawing universal conclusions from the calorific value of workhouse dietaries given that the energy demands of those resident in workhouses were likely to be significantly lower than those labouring in the fields for twelve hours a day. But against that qualification, at least in times of crisis, the perception that those working people who resided in workhouses during this period had a better diet than those who did not probably held true. Indeed, the dietaries gathered by Eden at the height of the subsistence crisis of 1795 probably tend to over- represent the institutional use of potatoes and rice in southern and eastern workhouses, while underestimating the consumption of wheat, though not necessarily the net calorific value of workhouse fare to inmates. Further, the workhouse dietaries detailed by Eden for southern and eastern parishes suggest a more varied diet than working people outside the workhouse might regularly eat, with the January 1795 report from Ashford relating that while the consumption of meat in 'most parts of Kent' was a daily occurrence 'ten years ago ... they now seldom taste it in winter, except [if] they reside in a poor-house'. Similarly, those resident in the Gressingham workhouse of 50 united parishes in Norfolk had an unusually diverse and full diet with portions reportedly 'abundantly sufficient' and vegetables from the garden served in 'great plenty' during the season.[22] By way of contrast, 'those on the outside had a problem' and suffered from, as Shammas has put it, 'nutritional famine'.[23]

The persistence of the discourse that workhouses and parish poorhouses were too soft and too generous in feeding their inmates, and, further, that the principles of the 'Workhouse Test' were rarely enforced, was central to critiques of the old poor law.[24] Of course, the reality was more complex and contingent – even in the case of Gilbert's Act's 'Houses of Industry' with their statutory emphasis on the 'comfort' and 'humane' treatment of their institutionalised poor. For instance, breakfast at the Gilbert's workhouse at Reigate (also serving the Surrey parishes of Buckland, Headley, Morley and Nutfield) was the nutritionally thin 'water-gruel, with pottage' or 'broth and bread'.[25] The consumption of meat in most southern workhouses was still infrequent – at Blandford (Dorset) twice a week, at Stony Stratford (Buckinghamshire) three times a week – and cheese and bread still formed the dominant part of most southern workhouse diets.[26] Diets of northern workhouses were little different, though, as the example of Howden (East Riding of Yorkshire) as set out with a new agreement with a contractor in 1792 details, the provision of alternatives to wheaten bread as a staple was more common (see figure 4.1).[27] The Gilbert's house built exclusively built for the parish of Alverstoke (Hampshire) between 1799 and 1801 was an early adopter of some of the principles set out in Bentham's 1796 tract (on which see below). The rooms of the master, matron and committee assumed a surveillance position in the centre of a cross placed within a larger square. The architecture of the house was clearly designed not just for efficiency but also as a visual symbol of a regime that, while using the language of care central to Gilbert's Act, still expected children, the elderly and infirm – unless 'past labour' – to labour in the house while subsisting on the calorifically deficient dietary inspired by the workhouses at Alton (Hampshire) and Farnham (Surrey).[28]

Moreover, we know from protests by workhouse inmates in the 1790s and early 1800s that workhouses were not always comfortable and humane. While the archive no doubt under-represents such complaints, those over the dietary at Dymchurch (1795, Kent), the conduct of the master at Battle (1802, Sussex) and the running of the Coulsdon workhouse (1805, Surrey) were probably indicative of the experience of being an inmate in many such institutions.[29] Threats against workhouses also provided a critical narrative of the Swing quasi-insurrection in the south-east, while that at Birchington (Isle of Thanet, Kent) was set on fire, though little damage was done, and those at Selborne and Headley (Hampshire) were all but demolished by Swing protestors.[30] As Swing activist Timothy Willcocks at Ash-next-Sandwich (Kent) put it, 'he would as soon be hung as go to the Workhouse'.[31] Such popular fears and loathing notwithstanding, workhouse dietaries were used as a way of getting poor workers outside the house to change their consumption in the subsistence crises of the 1790s and early 1800s – Great Chart vestry in January 1800 directed their overseers to procure a copy of the dietary of the nearby Ashford workhouse, 'the same to be fixed in a public place', in their attempt to reduce the consumption of wheat in the parish – and were subject to criticism by poor law reformers.[32]

Let us not be under any misapprehension as to why workhouses were established under the old poor laws: economy; a desire to manage the poor more efficiently and thereby reduce the 'burden' on the poor rates. In the North Riding of Yorkshire, a 'second phase' of workhouse building in the final years of the eighteenth century was a response to, as R.P. Hastings put, it increasing poor rates, and this in a 'county lacking serious poor law problems'.[33] As the Shinfield (Berkshire) vestry put it when resolving in December 1768 to erect a workhouse:

> Whereas the Poors Rates ... have of late years greatly increased to such a Degree as at this Time to become an enormous and insupportable Burthern to the Inhabitants of the said Parish, and it being apprehended that if a Workhouse was erected for the Habitation and Employment of the Poor (the want of which is imagined to be one great Cause of the present great expence) the Burthern of the Inhabitants would be thereby greatly alleviated.[34]

That 'at the same time the poor would be better and more happily provided for' was evidently a secondary consideration at best, and quite possibly a moralistic post hoc rationalisation for institutionalising the parish poor.[35]

In this way, the number of workhouses – and the number of parishes combining as part of Gilbert's or Local Act unions – grew, so that by 1776–7 1,951 workhouses were in operation in England and by 1803 3,709 parishes relieved all or part of their poor in workhouses, some 27.4 per cent of all reporting parishes. The proportion of parishes using workhouses by 1803 was highly variable, from only 6.49 per cent of Westmorland and 6.71 per cent of Monmouthshire parishes to 87.98 per cent of Middlesex (including the City of London) and 70.78 per cent of Suffolk parishes. As a rule, the further west and north the county, the lower the proportion of parishes with workhouses. The rapidly industrialising and urbanising Lancashire and West Riding of Yorkshire (at 35.4 per cent and 23.45 per cent of parishes respectively) were the exceptions to this rule, and even this is in part a reflection on the large number of parishes combined into Gilbert's Unions.[36] Part of the increase in the number of parishes using workhouses between 1776 and 1803 can be attributed to parishes establishing workhouses unilaterally – as in the case of Howden (East Riding) in December 1790 or Quadring (Lincolnshire) in June 1796[37] – or in Gilbert's Unions – in Hampshire alone

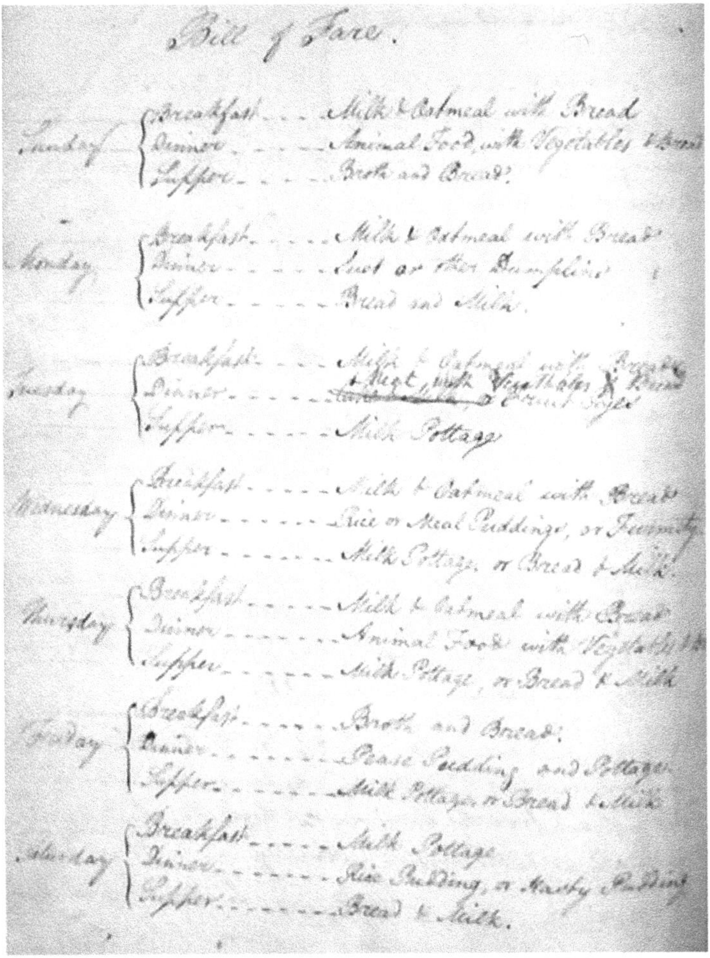

Bill of Fare.

Sunday	Breakfast	Milk & Oatmeal with Bread
	Dinner	Animal Food, with Vegetables & Bread
	Supper	Broth and Bread.
Monday	Breakfast	Milk & Oatmeal with Bread
	Dinner	Suet or other Dumplings
	Supper	Bread and Milk.
Tuesday	Breakfast	Milk & Oatmeal with Bread
	Dinner	Meat, with Vegetables & Bread
	Supper	Milk Pottage
Wednesday	Breakfast	Milk & Oatmeal with Bread
	Dinner	Rice or Meal Puddings, or Frumity
	Supper	Milk Pottage, or Bread & Milk.
Thursday	Breakfast	Milk & Oatmeal with Bread
	Dinner	Animal Food with Vegetables [illegible]
	Supper	Milk Pottage, or Bread & Milk
Friday	Breakfast	Broth and Bread;
	Dinner	Pease Pudding and Pottage
	Supper	Milk Pottage, or Bread & Milk
Saturday	Breakfast	Milk Pottage
	Dinner	Rice Pudding, or Hasty Pudding
	Supper	Bread & Milk.

Figure 4.1 Howden workhouse dietary, 1792

in addition to the aforementioned Alverstoke, unions were formed that centred on Farnborough (1794) and Headley (1795)[38] – in response to the subsistence crises of the 1790s. And, as the previous chapter detailed, as the cost of poor relief soared after 1815, so another wave of parishes adopted workhouses for the first time or, more commonly, tightened the regulation and management of their existing ones. The collision of 'economy' with a desire to reform the 'morality' of the poor often informed such shifts in policy. The decision to establish a workhouse at Bishops Waltham (Hampshire) in April 1818 was a result of a desire to 'regulate the poor'.

Likewise the Mayfield (Sussex) vestry resolved in March 1826 to bring 'all single women with bastards' into the workhouse and remodel the dietary so that it was 'no better than that of labourers out of the house'.[39] But against such attempts to restrict and limit the cost of running workhouses (of which provisioning was by far the greatest expense), and against accusations of cruelty and starving the poor (which became a common claim from the late 1820s and a defining discourse of the liberal and radical press from the mid-1830s[40]) claims of inefficiency, moral corruption and dietaries in excess of the quantity and quality those living outside the workhouse could afford were legion. The next section explores these critiques in relation to the making of the New Poor Law.

Diet and the making of the New Poor Law: Early antecedents

The nature and scope of critiques of the old poor laws were as complex and multifaceted as initial Acts of Elizabeth themselves. Indeed, from the very implementation of the Elizabethan poor laws of 1598 and 1601 – the system was not meaningfully established or near universal until the 1630s – there were critiques and suggestions for revision and reform, including those that led to the Settlement Law of 1662.[41] While it is possible to find elements of the Act of 1834 in earlier revisions, based on earlier critiques and innovative practices, there is no sense that these teleologically led to the New Poor Law. For until the publication of Malthus' *Essay*, critiques called for a revision rather than wholesale reworking of the law.[42] Rather, as J.R. Poynter has asserted, the reforms of 1834 had their 'roots' in debates first given the oxygen of publicity in eighteenth-century pamphlet litera-ture, of which there was a steady drip in the early 1700s, a stream from the 1790s and a flood after 1816.[43] Mostly written by MPs, farmers, ratepayers, the clergy and others 'closely associated' with administering the poor laws, such pamphlets invariably reported recently implemented local reforms, or detailed 'abuses' in the administration of the poor laws and offered pos-sible policy remedies.[44] Some pamphlets generated considerable influence, though this was often a function either of their being written by powerful and influential individuals – MP Thomas Gilbert's two poor law pamphlets of 1764 and 1775 predated his successful poor law union-facilitating Act of 1772, while Bentham's 1796 tract on 'Pauper Management' influenced both pre- and post-1834 'model' workhouses – or the schemes detailed therein subsequently being held up as exemplars by powerful poor law reformers and the 1832 Poor Law Commissioners.[45] As Marshall and more recently Shave have noted, George Nicholls, the author of a series of pamphlets detailing the 'anti-pauper' experiment at the Bentham-influenced Southwell (Nottinghamshire) workhouse, discussed his ideas with the authors of the 1832 Report, and through the influence of Robert Peel was subsequently appointed by Nassau Senior to the Poor Law Commission.[46] In turn, as Mandler has shown, Nicholls had been directly influenced by Eden's *State of the Poor* and Edmund Burke's *Thoughts and Details on Scarcity* (1795), Burke's open letter to Prime Minister Pitt.[47]

What is remarkable about this substantial – if not in itself coherent – body of reformist literature is that even though a key tenet of the Elizabethan poor law was the idea that those in need and able to labour should be set to work 'to get their bread by' (as the Report of the 1817 Select Committee on the Poor Laws put it), debates were rarely framed around relief and bodily need.[48] Indeed, even in response to the subsistence crisis of 1766–7 pamphlets regarding the poor laws framed their arguments in relation to morality, complexity and cost, not in terms of diet and subsistence.[49]

This emphasis on the principles of supporting the poor rather than the materiality and everyday practices of relief meant that, in essence, considerations of bodily being were subsumed in a wider discourse about support, or rather about being deserving or undeserving of ratepayer support. The same understanding is writ through Gilbert's pamphlets. In his 1781 pamphlet Gilbert had argued that despite spending on the poor laws now exceeding £2 million every year, and that 'exclusive of all the Public and Private Charities, which are immense', the poor were still 'distressed, begging, and starving, in most parts of the Kingdom'. Thereafter issues of subsistence and diet are barely featured.[50] Indeed, beyond his noting that the regulation of 'Houses of Industry' needed to 'guard against every Imposition and unnecessary Expense' and that only where 'Impositions have crept in' did existing workhouses not answer the problem, diet was mentioned only in relation to punishing those who refused to labour.[51]

The exceptions were those pamphlets that explicitly detailed existing relief regimes or proposed new ones. But here matters of diet and subsistence were considered not by way of critique of the profligacy of poor law practice, or the poor themselves, but instead by describing the ways in which diet was used a policy tool. For instance, the parish of St Giles in the Field (London) recommended to the governor of the workhouse 'those who have been ancient Housekeepers, and lived well, and are reduced by Misfortunes, from the other Poor, who are become so by Vice or Idleness … and in such manner with respect to their Lodging, Cloathing, Diet or otherwise'. The sick were also allowed a different dietary from that set out in the 'bill of fare', while other workhouse regulations were in part framed around consumption.[52] The children used 'to be kept in poor Families' at Strood (Kent) 'and kept up in the grossest Idleness and Vice!', but the foundation of the workhouse in 1720 meant they were now 'inur'd to Labour, and help to maintain themselves earning at least their Diet'.[53] At the Limehouse workhouse in Stepney (London), the master having been a 'Sea-Faring Person, feeds them after the Method used on Ship-board' of 'messes' of boiled meat, with roots when in season, amongst other meals.[54] More explicit still was the justification detailed in an anonymously authored 1729 pamphlet, *The Case of the Poor*

Considered. 'A main advantage' from workhouses – or as the author saw it 'publick manufactor[ies], for maintaining and employing the poor' – was that bulk buying and provisioning led to 'the cheapness of joint maintenance'.[55]

If the above examples detail the ways in which food was a lever of wider policy goals and ideologies – rewarding industry and punishing idleness and immorality; something that had to be worked for rather than a right; a quasi-science, something learnt and evolved – the opening lines of the SPCK's (Society for Promoting Christian Knowledge) 'Prayer to be Used in Workhouses' suggests something deeper: 'O Gracious Lord God, who hast opened thy Hand, and satisfied us with Good; who hast cloathed the Naked, filled the Hungry, and gathered the Poor, who were scattered and solitary, into one House.'[56] This goes beyond policy and practicality and instead hints at the idea that the function of the workhouse, and by extension the poor law at large, could be reduced to meeting bodily need, clothing the naked body and filling the empty stomach of the worthy. Yet as Mandler has asserted, the workhouse test was rarely ever truly implemented, and even when it was used as a device to single 'out the morally corrupt who did not want to work at all' parishes tended to be 'outflanked' by resistance from magistrates and labourers.[57]

To be outflanked, though, does not mean that no attempts were being made to theorise the point of minimum bodily need. In 1783 Rev. Porteus of Glasgow wrote an open letter to the citizens of that city on the then hottest local political topic: the rising cost of maintaining the poor. That Scotland's Kirk-based system was already relatively more parsimonious and gave the poor fewer entitlements is by the by,[58] for what matters here is the abstract theorisation of how to support human body function but no more. It is also important to note that Porteous was not advocating keeping the poor in a state of only just bodily being, but rather that to know that state was to be able to keep them just above it. As Porteous noted:

> [A]s it is a difficult matter to ascertain precisely what is necessary to preserve life, so it would be disagreeable to recite the history of sailors on short allowances, and other histories of a similar nature, from which alone the information could be got; wherever the starving point lies, the managers of charity funds should endeavour to be above it.[59]

Fifty years later Porteus' theorisation was cited by Charles Mott, then working as an Assistant Poor Law Commissioner under the auspices of the New Poor Law. If Mott was quick to deny that his enquiries as to dietaries were not 'recurring to the starving point', Mott's reference to Porteous and his protestation speak to both the political potency of the idea of starvation and the persistence of attempts to understand the point at which the pauper body could not be sustained.[60] Indeed, as we will see later in this chapter, the very idea of basic biological adequacy – or in Mott's language, the boundary between 'sufficient' and 'insufficient' – was necessarily premised on understanding the point of inadequacy, the starvation point.[61] Certainly the poor subjected to dietaries based on these principles saw it as an attempt to only just keep them alive. Thus in language prescient of that used to protest New Poor Law dietaries, a remarkably lucid letter from 'A Member of the West Suffolk Friendly Society' to the *Bury and Norwich Post* in April 1830 complained that scales 'decreed that the labourer should no longer be considered as a free agent, but as a slave or domestic animal; fed, not according to his value, but his necessities'.[62] The 'starving point' was never written into law but the principle had powerful effects.

Diet and the making of the New Poor Law: Lessons on scarcity

1795 proved to be the turning point in placing a greater emphasis on the issue of subsistence and food. The most obvious evidence of this shift was no less than Eden's survey, motivated, as detailed in the previous chapter, by the inability of the poor to support themselves in the crisis of 1795 despite rising poor rates.[63] Malthus' famous essay, while not directly inspired by the crisis, did, in its second edition, draw upon 'lessons' from the period. But the attempt to make sense of the scarcity, and the ensuing crisis, brought about a range of other reactions that combined the workings of the grain market and the operation of the poor law. Further, responses to Whitbread's and Pitt's poor law bills – introduced to parliament on 9 December 1795 and 22 December 1796 respectively – provoked the production of yet more pamphlets, while, as Poynter has asserted, 'growing dissatisfaction' with subsidising the food costs of labouring families as the 'emergency dragged on' also fanned the flames of public opinion.[64] Beyond those pamphlets that primarily engaged with the cause and solution to scarcity outside of considerations of the poor laws – for which the 'answer' was that the poor needed to eat less bread, or that more land needed to be cultivated – food was placed at the centre of considerations. Thus for Burke's *Thoughts on Scarcity* – itself generative of a mini-industry of pamphlet production – the scarcity was real enough but the impacts were exaggerated, for no one, as he saw it, had died from famine. The solution was neither to regulate wages, as in Whitbread's failed bill, nor to increase relief to the poor through the rates, but rather for those in genuine need to rely on charity.[65]

If Whitbread believed that wages needed to be regulated so that the poor could be supported without the rates, Pitt, whose politicking was fundamental in the failure of Whitbread's bill, believed that the poor should be made to labour – either inside or outside of 'Schools of Industry' – or forced to support themselves. Another aspect of the Bill was what became known as 'cow money', a form of de facto relief that would allow labourers to rent three acres on which to keep a cow and, so the idea went, keep themselves off the poor rates. While Pitt's bill failed – it was withdrawn on 28 February 1797, having been subject to near universal criticism, including from Bentham who saw the 'cow money' as an assault on capital – the idea that the poor should be supported to help themselves gained wider currency.[66] Arthur Young, through his *Annals of Agriculture*, detailed a scheme to allot the poor sufficient land for a potato garden and grazing for a cow, though ultimately despite the extensive self-publicity and support of the Earl of Winchilsea the idea did not gain traction, let alone someone willing to introduce a bill to Parliament.[67] The idea of the poor finding their own subsistence was also writ through suggestions that in the face of a decline in real wages and rising food prices the poor needed to find solace not in poor relief but, if worthy of support, from private charity. The duty of their social betters was to 'determine' what their 'proper subsistence' was.

Post-1815, the connection between the poor laws and the subsistence of the poor remained, at first, a peripheral discourse in debates about poor law reform. The focus tended to fall instead on the supposedly morally and economically deleterious effects of Speenhamland-style 'making up' of labourers' wages.[68] For instance, the 1828 Select Committee on the relief of 'able-bodied persons' from the rates concluded that such payments militated against 'the laws of nature' by encouraging the materially comfortable single man – who could previously 'afford many humble luxuries' – to marry and rear children.[69] The 1817 Report from the Select Committee on the Poor Laws was different. Outwardly Benthamite in its application of the principles of political economy to social policy and Malthusian in its language of 'natural states', the report followed a revival of poor law pamphleteering after 1815.[70] Severe distress in all sectors of the economy and in all regions placed spiralling poor relief costs under an unprecedented level of scrutiny. As the previous chapter detailed, the response of agrarian parishes followed the paradoxical path of extending the net of welfare to all labouring families while at the same time devising schemes to limit relief and thus poor rates. Public debate given voice in pamphlets, the press and Parliament thus moved between two different poles: the total reworking of the existing system and the defence of the principles of poor relief. The abolitionist position on the efficacy of workhouses was muddled, though. By way of example, Middleton in the second edition of his *General View of the Agriculture of Middlesex* – the county with by far the highest proportion of parishes relieving all or part of their poor institutionally – lamented that the 'lodging and diet in the workhouses, in every instance, are superior to what the industrious labourer can provide for his family'. And yet, despite Malthus' support for the effective operation of the workhouse test, Middleton still explicitly referenced Malthus in support of the idea that workhouses represented a support to the 'vicious and idle' and increased the price of provisions by virtue of decreasing the quantity of food 'that would otherwise fall to the share of the labourers'.[71]

If many reformist and abolitionist writings focused on the supposed effects of the allowance system, others began to remake the case for, as William Clarkson put it, the 'deterrent workhouse'.[72] Beyond the case made for the success of closely regulated parish workhouses, with strict dietaries and disciplinary regimes, and supported variations on the workhouse test, the 1817 Report offered a clear, radical, national model based on a system of parochial or pan-parochial 'working schools'. Noting that many workhouses had been subject to criticism as being 'rather in truth, in many instances, houses of idleness and vice', in other parishes 'such establishments seem to be indispensible'.[73] On this basis, in the attempt to 'encourage frugal habits' and to prevent wages from 'squandered away', children below the age of 14 supported in idleness 'very scantily' on bread and water would be forced to attend the working schools, their labour at which would pay for the bread contract and the other running costs of the school.[74] This would, so the logic goes, act to reform the morals of the poor, while the withdrawal of allowances would also help to undo the 'extensive system of pauperism' and return the poor to their 'natural states'.[75] Indeed, in questioning the witnesses called, the committee consistently probed the idea of 'subsistence': those involved in running workhouses were specifically questioned as to 'diet rolls' and 'the way of estimating' the amount of food given.[76]

While the 1817 Committee stopped short of recommending a national system of workhouses, the emphasis on strict regulation and regulation of dietary (as both cost control measure and a way of enforcing the principles of less eligibility) mirrored Jeremy Bentham's 1796 'pauper management' scheme. Bentham envisaged 250 huge workhouses nationwide in which 2,000 inmates would be fed on a spartan diet, existing institutional diets being both 'excessive' and too expensive due to their reliance on bread – when other meal would be cheaper – and meat.[77] The most infamous attempt to impose Bentham's vision was, as noted above, the Southwell workhouse, the publicity around which proved so influential to Senior and Chadwick, but this was not constructed until 1824.[78] Before that date, while the principle of what would become known as less eligibility – or rather, as W. Clark put it in his 1815 *Thoughts and Management and Relief of the Poor Etc.* (1815), 'that parish relief should never place its objects in a better situation than those who support themselves' – was given voice it remained, as Poynter notes, an 'abstract exhortation until embodied in some method of application'.[79] For many parishes struggling with the realities of fraught social relations in the context of the post-war depression, just administering a version of the poor law that struck a balance between affordability for ratepayers and the demands and resistances of labourers and magistrates was all but impossible. The costs of establishing a workhouse on Bentham's model and forbidding out-relief were a step beyond even that: a practical and political impossibility.

As noted, the Alverstoke workhouse adopted some of the architectural principles of Bentham's scheme but being a Gilbert's parish it was forbidden, apart from in cases of absolute destitution, from offering anything other than out-relief to the able-bodied.[80] Other parishes met with the approval of the authors of the Poor Law Report 1834 for adopting some of the principles of less eligibility, if outwith the full operation of the workhouse test. At the Berkshire parish of Cookham, under the close control and scrutiny of the vicar Rev. Thomas Whateley, relief was regulated by a select vestry who set all able-bodied labourers applying for relief to 'hard work [trenching] at low wages by the piece'. By earning wages lower than the market rate, the labourer found, in the words of Whateley, that 'the parish is the hardest taskmaster and the worst paymaster he can find, and [this] thus induce[s] him to make his application to the parish his last and not his first resource'. Otherwise, the workhouse, constructed before 1777, operated under a version of the principles of the workhouse test. Of the two 'classes' of inmates, the 'old, infirm and impotent' were allowed 'an ample supply of butcher's meat and other suitable food', while the 'idle, improvident and vicious' were kept on 'nothing but bread and cheese'. Before this 'experiment', the cost of relief in the parish, as the *Report* had it, was 13,300 peck loaves per annum; thereafter it was only 5,400 loaves, evidence not only of the 'success' of the scheme as the Commissioners had it but also that the poor were thought of not only in terms of monetary cost but also the nutritional and biological cost of their subsistence. In the eyes of the Commissioners, Cookham provided an exemplar of how best to run a parish within the limits of the existing laws.[81]

What united these schemes, at least in principle, was the idea that the 'condition of the independent labourer' was 'taken as a standard' – however debased and pitiful that might be – against which the applicant for relief should expect less, either in or out of the workhouse. Further, as the respondents for the parishes saw it and the Commissioners took at face value, 'these objects seem to have been effected with little real severity in any point, and least of all in that of food.'[82] But there were limitations. Attempts to impose the principles of less eligibility without the workhouse were referred to as the so-called 'outdoor labour test'. Yet despite the approbation of the positive effects of schemes such as those of Cookham and Welwyn by the Commission, they were still deemed imperfect. Indeed, despite the fact that some of the examples detailed in the Report were parishes run by men of considerable influence – Whately had been recommended as one of the Commissioners by assistant commissioner and future chair of the Poor Law Board C.P. Villiers; Henry Russell of Swallowfield (Berkshire) was a friend of Chadwick – the economist and Stroud MP Poulett Scrope's attempt to include a clause maintaining the principle of outdoor relief in the Poor Law Amendment Act on the very terms of these schemes was voted down.[83]

The limitation came in the case of workhouse regimes where although '[i]n some instances a low diet was prescribed *in terrorem* ... there appears to have been scarcely ever a rigid enforcement of the rule', and therefore 'the paupers within the work-house enjoyed a diet profuse compared with that of the independent labourers of the same district.'[84] Indeed, while some workhouse regimes were praised by Nassau Senior and Edwin Chadwick – Southwell being the cause célèbre – most were slated. '[In] by far the greater number of cases', they asserted, 'the whole body of inmates subsisted on food far exceeding both in kind and in amount, not merely the diet of the independent labourer, but that of the majority of the persons who contribute to their support.' Indeed, Poulett Scrope claimed that the Commission's own evidence detailed only four successful examples of the application of the pure principles of the workhouse test: Southwell, Bingham (both Nottinghamshire), Uley (Gloucestershire) and Llangaddoch.[85]

The Poor Law Commission and the model dietaries

Despite the Commission's unchecked assertion of the effectiveness of the workhouse test – and here Tawney's famous summary of the report as a 'brilliant, influential, and wildly unhistorical document' is especially apt – workhouse dietaries did not take centre stage in either the Report or the copious appendices.[86] Only once in the actual Report (that is to say the proscription and justification, excluding the copious appendices) are dietaries detailed, and this in relation to the Lambeth workhouse.[87] A little more is made of diet by way of ideals. But even this hints at uncertainty in application. Thus:

> The standard, therefore, to which reference must be made in fixing the condition of those who are to be maintained by the public, is the condition of those who are maintained by their own exertions. But the evidence shows how loosely and imperfectly the situation of the independent labourer has been inquired into, and how little is really known of it by those who award or distribute relief. It shows also that so little has their situation been made a standard for the supply of commodities, that the diet of the workhouse almost always exceeds that of the cottage … It shows also, that this standard has been so little referred to in the exaction of labour, that commonly the work required from the pauper is inferior to that performed by the labourers and servants of those who have prescribed it: So much and so generally inferior as to create a prevalent notion among the agricultural paupers that they have a right to be exempted from the amount of work which is performed and indeed sought for by the independent labourer.[88]

But if this was, as yet, largely unknown, the 'standard' of diet by way of 'the exaction of labour' was knowable, hinting at a science of pauper physiology. So, as the *Report* put it:

> It might be conceived, à priori, that the standard of comparison, i.e., the condition of the lowest class of independent labourers, is indefinite; but when examined, it is found sufficiently definite for the purpose: their hours of labour in any neighbourhood are sufficiently uniform: the average of piecework which able-bodied labourers will perform may be correctly ascertained, and so may the diet on which they actually sustain health.[89]

This ability to scientifically know what was necessary to 'sustain health' was also necessary in combatting claims that the new system might lead to a rise in 'mendicity and vagrancy'. Thus, 'the able-bodied claimant should be entitled to immediate relief on the terms prescribed ... and should be received without objection or inquiry'. Their – though the *Report* tellingly uses the gendered 'his' – 'compliance' with this 'prescribed discipline' thereby 'constitut[ed] his title to a sufficient, though simple diet.' Rejecting this 'simple diet' would be a priori evidence that 'he' was 'undeserving'. And whilst initially, as had been the case in 'dispauperised parishes', 'popular opinion' might be that every mendicant was the product of absolute rejection of their demands for relief, this would soon change as the sufficiency of diet in the new system was known.[90] Indeed, drawing on reports of the Uley and Southwell workhouses, the recommendations of the *Report* were seemingly paradoxical. Workhouse regimes should be 'irksome' and 'intolerable' to the indolent and disorderly by virtue of making those unaccustomed to labour work, 'strict discipline' should be imposed, and 'acknowledged luxuries, such as fermented liquors and tobacco' restricted. And yet, food would be 'more ample in quantity and better in quality than that of which the labourer's family partakes'.[91]

As to the point of distinctions in diet between different classes of inmate, there was some contradiction, at least in spirit, between the idea that the old should be allowed certain indulgencies while at the same time claiming that:

> If you give to particular people an extra allowance on special grounds, all the rest will exclaim, 'Why should not we have it as well as they?' and too often they get it. That which was only intended to be the comfort of the few, and as an exception, at last, one by one being added to the list, becomes the general rule; and, when once established, there are few annual officers who will interfere to abridge the accustomed allowance.[92]

As to universality, so the Commissioners argued, 'we think conclusively ... that all local discretionary power as to relief should be withdrawn'. Drawing on the evidence of Charles Mott, an old poor law entrepreneur running the Newington and Lambeth workhouses and Peckham House Asylum and soon to be an Assistant Poor Law Commissioner, it was believed that local discretion as to 'modifying the dietaries' was a bad thing. 'I am decidedly of opinion', proclaimed Mott, 'that no such authority can be beneficially exercised, even by the local manager and superintendent of any place', for 'deviation[s]' and 'extra indulgence' had 'a tendency to extend and perpetuate itself which cannot be resisted'. In this way, a 'uniformity of excess' would be produced, and all 'equalised to the profuse standard'.[93] 'Uniformity in the administration of relief' was therefore essential in preventing comparison between relief regimes and discontent due to dietary differences; 'bringing the management, which consists in details, more closely within the public control' was the solution. Yet again, there was some inconsistency in the geographical and nutritional application of this principle and an acknowledgement as to how achievable it might be in practice anyway:

> We deem uniformity essential; but in the first instance it is only an approximation to uniformity that can be expected ... And although uniformity in amount of relief may be requisite, it may be requisite that the relief should be invariably the same in kind. In Cumberland, and some other of the northern counties, milk is generally used where beer is use in the southern counties. The requisite equality in diet would probably be obtainable without forcing any class of the inmates of the workhouses in the northern counties to take beer, or those in the southern counties to take milk.[94]

These ambiguities found their way into the text of the Poor Law Amendment Act itself. As Johnston has noted, the Act 'contained little mention of the practical organisation of the system'.[95] In relation to pauper diet, the Act merely detailed (in section 21) that regarding new or altered workhouses:

> [T]he dieting, clothing, employing, and governing of such Poor... and all Powers of regulating and conducting all other Workhouses whatsoever, and of governing, providing for, and employing the Poor therein, and all Powers auxiliary to any of the Powers aforesaid, or in any way relating to the Relief of the Poor, shall in future be exercised by the Persons authorised by Law to exercise the same, under the Control, and subject to the Rules, Orders, and Regulations of the said Commissioners; and the said Commissioners and Assistant Commissioners respectively...[96]

Further, according to the diktats of the Commissioners, occasionally outdoor relief might be given, including relief in kind as food.[97] Even beyond the parliamentary interventions relating to outdoor relief, the drafting and passing of the bill generated very little in the way of critical commentary in relation to matters of subsistence. This was probably a reflection on the fact that the bill contained no prescriptions relating to diet and the limited, essentially unorganised nature of opposition to the bill per se.[98] Even Cobbett, by then the MP for Oldham, who characteristically did not pull his punches in his parliamentary and written critiques of the bill, made no explicit reference to workhouse dietaries. Indeed, his only reference to diet came in relation to the poor laws in Scotland, specifically that this system with which the Commissioners were so enamoured had forced the poor onto 'the cheapest of diets' and had failed to relieve the starving in the crisis of 1819.[99]

The Act – the third reading took place on 1 July, and Royal Assent was granted on 14 August 1834 – gave Commissioners Frankland Lewis, George Nicholls and J. Shaw-Lefevre, and secretary Chadwick, absolute control to determine, dictate and regulate all matters relating to pauper diet, both institutionally and in terms of (occasional) out-relief. In practice, this meant that the principles of the *Report* were put into practice, with, as Johnston notes, only 'some deviations'.[100] First meeting on 23 August, in the ensuing weeks the Poor Law Commission (PLC), or rather Chadwick, issued circulars and copies of the statute to all English and Welsh parishes and established bureaucratic protocol and procedures. From late October, the process of appointing assistant commissioners – those 'comets, the travelling prodigies' as *The Times* put it – began. They were to be responsible for the onerous job of putting the policies of the Commission into operation on the ground, not least in shaping and creating the new poor law unions and in acting as the link between the Commission and parishes and the nascent unions.[101] The job of the assistants was made even harder by virtue of the fact that the Commission did not always set unambiguous and consistent policy, for instance in relation to the size of union workhouses. Further, in relation to workhouse regulations, attempts to rigidly impose Commission policy by the assistants often met opposition, in the face of which the Commission often yielded, leaving the assistants 'unsupported'.[102]

This lack of policy detail also pertained to workhouse dietaries and pauper diet. Initial circulars from Chadwick on behalf of the Commission attempted to gather information about the existing facilities, policies and depth of pauperism from parish overseers, detailed the provisions of the Act or attempted – often unsuccessfully – to assert that until unions were formed, the old laws still pertained in the relief of the poor. The first formal advice relating to diet was issued in the circular of 8 November 1834 which recommended that parishes move towards 'the gradual substitution of relief in kind, i.e. in bread, and other necessaries, for relief in money'.[103] Or as Chadwick put it in response to a letter from the Udimore (Sussex) assistant overseer concerning the existing 'allowance system', the PLC disapproved of any 'arbitrary scale' and instructed that relief in proportion to need should be given in foodstuffs.[104]

In the light of this significant yet ambiguously worded 'order', the assistant commissioners (initially operating only in the south and Midlands) had to attempt to encourage enforcement while meeting with the opposition of parish vestries, magistrates and the poor themselves. The insistence of William Hawley, the Assistant Poor Law Commissioner for Sussex, that Battle's parish officers should 'ensure that claimants had legitimately expended all their peak harvest earnings before receiving unemployment benefit' prompted a 'street protest' by claimants and a formal protest from the vestry to the PLC.[105] Elsewhere in East Sussex, a 'peaceful' gathering of the 'labouring classes' on Ringmer Green discussed wages – the circular coincided with near universal wage cuts – and poor relief, while 100 labourers from several different parishes, including 20 from Chailey, in mid-November adopted the by now traditional tactic of descending upon the Lewes bench to request work and relief. Hawley attended and reportedly assiduously took notes of proceedings.[106] Wage cuts and attempts to withhold relief led to widespread labourers' strikes in the west of the county. By mid-December it was reported that most parishes had struck work at some point in the preceding six weeks.

The similarity to the Swing protests of 1830 was appropriately mimetical considering that the New Poor Law was a direct response to Swing.[107]

The first acts of coordinated open opposition to the operation of the newly formed poor law unions were engendered by attempts to enforce giving relief in the form of tickets to be exchanged for food with local shopkeepers in the Milton and Faversham unions of East Kent. Protests between 1 and 8 May targeted relieving officers, overseers and Guardians alike for their role in enforcing the new regulations, something the local poor believed was an entirely local situation, insisting 'that if it was the law it would extend to West as well as East Kent + indeed all over England'; no unions had by then been formed in the west of the county. The protests also inverted the earlier protest discourse of 'Bread or Blood': the chant at the siege of Doddington workhouse (the former parish workhouse now called into temporary service of the Faversham Union) on 3 May was 'no tickets, no bread'. The word 'Kill' was also chalked on the workhouse door. If the Doddington protest won some slight concessions – the relieving officer offered additional relief to those with large families on application, and a promise he would raise their complaints before the Board at their meeting on Friday – it exposed not only the complexity of the politics of food in the new system but also the tensions between locality and centre, and between assistant commissioners and Westminster.[108] Rev. Poore, chairman of the Sittingbourne bench and active in suppressing Swing in the locality, was a vocal critic of the New Poor Law. Assistant Poor Law Commissioner for Kent Sir Francis Head attempted to keep Poore quiet by arranging his becoming chair of the Milton Union on its creation on 25 March; this failed, and in the fallout Poore resigned his position. Head claimed that Poore had acceded to the crowds' demands and had been duly cheered on by the protestors, and that, further, his call for military support at Sittingbourne was 'unnecessary', prompting Poore to protest at Head's 'irregular' intervention into judicial matters, accusing Head of 'gross and scandalous libel' in claiming that Poore had yielded to intimidation. The disagreements between Poore and Head degenerated into a public slanging match, even drawing in Home Secretary Lord John Russell.[109]

It was not without justification then that the *First Report* stated that 'the discontinuance of out-door relief, or relief in aid of wages, was found to be impracticable, or only practicable with an extent of trouble, and an expenditure of labour'. Alert to the political opportunity though, the PLC asserted that only the speedy implementation of the workhouse system offered a solution.[110] Indeed, in the words of the *First Report*, '[i]mmediately after our arrangements respecting the preparative alterations of the out-door relief were completed, the provision of workhouse accommodation was presented for our consideration.' Beyond considerations as to whether the new unions would need to construct a new workhouse or whether existing buildings would suffice, the PLC 'found it necessary [for which read, they were ideologically committed] to prescribe for those unions possessing workhouses regulations comprehending what appeared to us to be the essentials of workhouse management and classification'.[111] Even though the Commission did not think it 'expedient to promulgate these regulations as general rules and regulations', instead 'appl[ying] them in particular cases, with local modifications suggested by local inquiries', there was very little regarding the regulation of diet: rule 19 blandly stated that 'The diet of the paupers shall be so regulated as in no case to exceed, in quantity and quality of food, the ordinary diet of the ablebodied labourers living within the same district.'[112] Beyond this, rule 27 stated that those guilty of breaking workhouse rules would be 'deemed to be refractory' and punished by either 'such confinement and alteration of diet as the board of guardians shall direct'.[113] Indeed, it is evident from the text of the *First Report* that while the classification and segregation of paupers in workhouses and the migration of 'surplus' labourers to northern industrial district and the Americas had much exercised the Commission, the issue of diet had not. Beyond the regulations, matters dietary appear in the *First Report* only in relation to some little comment on the cost savings from contracting for food and goods, it being noted that in Kent unions had even collaborated in issuing even larger contracts to effect yet higher savings, and in Head's report on Kent wherein he related the 'alteration I have made in the dietary of the paupers (which, compared with that of the labourer of this county, has now ceased to be attractive)' which was 'freely' supported by the Guardians of the eleven unions of East Kent.[114]

As Ian Miller notes, initially 'nutritional well-being was not a prime goal of the New Poor Law; it was instead subordinated to driving principles of discipline and deterrence, and closely intertwined with the behavioral policing and governing of paupers'.[115] And this emphasis generated popular opposition. Indeed, even in the early months when the system was still being formed, the imposition of new workhouse dietaries in Head's Kent generated controversy. At Deal workhouse in May 1835 – Deal did not join the Eastry Union until April 1836 – the inmates 'objected' to the new dietary. Several 'daring and determined characters' assaulted one of the Guardians and the visitor to the union, leading to their being arrested.[116] Prominent East Kent farmer Edward Hughes, of Smeeth in the East Ashford Union, a vocal critic of the Poor Law Amendment Act, having previously believed that the new workhouse dietary was inadequate, took it upon himself to try the diet himself. After a month of the trial, Hughes, so he informed Head, had only eaten five-sevenths of the food provided, though one can assume that Hughes was in a better bodily state to exist on a limited diet than most workhouse inmates.[117]

In other places pressure from Assistant Poor Law Commissioners was not the stimulus to experiment with new parsimonious dietaries. For instance, at West Hampnett Union, chaired and run as if a personal fiefdom by Sussex grandee and owner of the most of the lands that comprised the union the Duke of Richmond, four new dietaries were developed: one for those from one to three years old; one for those between three and ten; one for the infirm; and another for everybody else. While dietaries were, of course, not novel, the complexity of the system and the strict measurements of each foodstuff for each meal were. Moreover, the emphasis on gruel – served with bread every breakfast – was a radical break with southern labouring diets. Further, the regular meals of meat previously served now became only occasional: the butchery tools of the Westhampnett workhouse from its previous incarnation as the parish workhouse were now put up for public sale. 'So low' was the dietary of the Westhampnett Union that the radical *Brighton Patriot* reported two months later that the master of the workhouse intended to resign his position because he was 'ashamed of it'. In the face of this opposition, Richmond further revised the dietaries in the mode of that long since practised at the St George's workhouse in Hanover Square (London), which had recently been publicised in a timely pamphlet published by John Leslie, the 'Governor and Director of the Poor' of that establishment, which in part acted to fill the void of PLC directions.[118]

The paucity of provision and the economy of the initial Westhampnett and Hanover Square dietaries acted to spur popular opposition, which was further fanned by statements regarding the cost of keeping paupers in 'properly' regulated workhouses by assistant commissioners attempting to win over ratepayers. Thus at a meeting of 'deputy Poor Law Commissioners' – presumably Hawley but who else is unclear – with 'gentlemen, farmers, and others' of the new Chailey Union it was related, so the respondent of the *Brighton Patriot* asserted, that in a new workhouse the poor could be kept at 1/9 a week, or less than a penny a meal. 'What they will be fed upon we know not', went the report, 'but certainly not on the beef, and pork, and bacon, and wheaten bread, to which the people are entitled'.[119] The editor of the *Suffolk Chronicle* likewise was incensed with reports of a 'supposed regulation of the Poor Law Commissioners' to keep the poor at 1/3 a week, their rival local newspapers the *Bury & Norwich Post* retorting that according to Leslie's account of the Hanover Square workhouse it was quite possible to provision workhouses not to make them 'a place of attraction to the idle and debased' but instead 'to keep the bodies of the inmates in health' and slash costs. So much was also the rhetoric of assistant commissioner Dr Kay in his meetings with ratepayers and poor law officials in Suffolk. The old workhouses of the county, so ran his totalising claim, had been overly generous. The commissioners of 1833 had found, as he related when in Ipswich to 'develop the principles' of the New Poor Law, that the wages of 'independent labourers' would only procure 121 ounces of solid food a week for each family member (Kay did not detail the size of the family) yet the dietary in the Framlingham workhouse provided 256 ounces. Besides, the dietary he now suggested was 'not greatly different from that of the army, though somewhat lower', and – in an extraordinary use of evidence – had been more than sufficient to sustain farmer Hughes of Kent and convert him from critic to supporter of the New Poor Law.[120] Thus against the initial quiet from the PLC in public communications on the matter of diet, it was absolutely central to the discourses and ploys of assistant commissioners in attempting to win over poor law laodiceans.

In short, in the first year of the New Poor Law, the discretion in matters of diet vested by the Act in the PLC was, in turn, vested by the PLC in assisstant commissioners and individual unions. That changed when on 4 December 1835 the PLC issued six model dietaries, so as to cater for different regional cullinary customs. As Johnston has noted, bread was the staple of each dietary, but most also contained gruel, broth, potatoes, cheese and, occassionally, meat.[121] According to the *Second Report*, the genesis of the dietaries – each intended for the able-bodied but with variations for the young (under 9) and old (over 60), with discretion left to medical officers for the diet of the sick – was as follows. Having 'always been sensible of the importance of establishing a fixed dietary in the several workhouses', as detailed in the *Second Report*, the PLC worked from the principle that:

> the details of such dietary ought not to be uniform throughout the country, but rather that they should be governed by the ordinary mode of living in the district in which each particular workhouse might happen to be situated; adopting, as a principle, that the workhouse dietary should in no case be superior to the ordinary mode of living of the labouring classes in the neighbourhood.[122]

A range of 'sufficient' dietaries were duly 'obtained' through the Assistant Commissioners, and six 'of a character sufficiently varied to meet almost every variety of circumstances' were selected and 'circulated … among the Unions' with guidance 'which should govern the Guardians in their selection of that particular dietary most suitable to the circumstances of their Union'.[123]

Yet none of this relates how what was 'sufficient' was known and measured. We do know, however, that Chadwick also engaged in reearch into the diet of 'independent' labourers. As Peter Gurney has put it, workouse dietaries were '[o]ne of Chadwick's pet subjects', although he was ideologically predisposed towards the creation of a standard dietary rather than any attempt to address local variations in diet and culture.[124] But Chadwick's research uncovered the unpalatable truth that the diet of many labourers living outside of the workhouse was so poor that any attempt, in the name of less eligibility, to offer still smaller institutional rations would likely provoke unrest.[125] Or as Blaug put it, 'The Commissioners of 1834 found out to their surprise that the cost of maintaining workhouse inmates at a minimum diet sometimes exceeded the wages of agricultural workers in surrounding district.'[126]

Arguably more useful in explaining the genesis and form of the dietaries was Mott's report published in the *Second Report*. 'One of the most important subjects connected with the relief of the poor', claimed Mott, 'is the regulation of the dietaries of workhouses, respecting which misconceptions exist, arising from a want of information as to the, quantities of food necessary for the support of human life, or from the properties of food not being sufficiently known.' This being the case, Mott duly 'devoted more time to the inquiry than many have thought it worth while', drawing on accounts from farmers, the diets of 'ordinary labourers', as well as those engaged in more physically exacting labour – and even the diet of soon-to-be Assistant Poor Law Commissioner Sir Edward Parry on his Polar expedition.

Starting with the premise that '[u]niformity of diet as to quality can hardly be attained, nor indeed is it absolutely necessary. Provincial habits are difficult to conquer. The labourers of Norfolk and Suffolk would hardly be prevailed upon to forego their dumplings, or the Cornish men their pies', Mott found his enquiry checked by the limited knowledge of 'the chemical properties of food generally'. Indeed, if the calorie, as a concept and unit of measurement, had been invented in France in the previous decade, understandings of nutrition still tended to be limited to the weight of food. Protein was not described and named until 1838.[127] Within these limitations, Mott's analysis focused instead on discerning the point at which health is sustained, not 'starvation points', he was at pains to assert, and what labourers and others engaged in physical work got bodily by on. Having gathered 'and selected with care' returns from southern labourers, Mott discerned that the average consumption for a labouing family for which the labourer was engaged at 2 shillings a day was 122 ounces for week, or 140 ounces (134 of bread and 6 of meat) per male labourer, allowing 'that the man consumes [a higher] proportion'. Of this, bread contained four-fifths nutritive matter, while meat was only one-third nutritive matter. Urban mechanics and those working in factories consumed rather more food, and relatively more meat, but no more nutritive matter. Extending his study to 'the quantities of food consumed by men using extreme bodily exertion, as mowers or sawyers, and prize-fighters when training', he found that they required a 'proportionate increase of sustenance' of 'from 27 to 30 ounces per day, equal to from 20 to 23 ounces of nutritive substance'. The same amounts were broadly representative of that necessary to sustain Parry and his men on their expedition to the North Pole. Mott admitted that there was no absolute standard that met all bodily needs: amongst the sick there was no commonality of need, while amongst those in good health '[m]uch, I admit, depends upon constitution, and the nature of their employment'. Notwithstanding these qualifications, Mott asserted that it would be 'perhaps impossible, to establish any given daily quantity of food to suit the capabilities of every stomach … as to form a tolerably correct rule for the whole'. To generalise, though Mott acknowledged that this was not infallible, persons of moderate health but engaging in little exercise and exertion required between 12 and 18 ounces of food per day (or 10 ounces of nutritive matter). Those in good health and used to moderate labour – such as agricultural labourers or mechanics – needed between 18 and 24 ounces (or 16 ounces of nutritive matter), while those engaged in 'hard labour' or 'violent exertion' needed 24 to 30 ounces (22 ounces of nutritive matter). By way of comparison, the most modest of the six model dietaries (dietary number 1) offered 133 ounces of food per week (19 ounces per day), the most generous (dietary 4) 182 ounces (26 per day). If PLC dietary one was a little light of a normal labouring diet, all the others were more than adequate. As such, Mott concluded, that those 'condemn them [the PLC dietaries] as insufficient are totally unacquainted with the subject upon which they so loudly declaim'.[128]

Given the guiding principle of less eligibility, it could be argued that five of the six diets containing, supposedly, greater nutritive matter than the diet of Mott's independent labourer represented a contradiction. The PLC attempted to bypass the paradox of sufficient yet less eligible – this a necessary product of serving two competing masters, humane and economic – by publicly passing the buck to individual unions. The instruction in the circular detailing the six dietaries stated that in choosing which dietary to adopt, 'especial reference must be had to the usual mode of living of the independent labourers of the district in which the Union is situated'. Adjustments then should be made to make sure that 'on no account must the dietary of the workhouse be superior or equal to the ordinary mode of subsistence of the labouring classes of the neighbourhood'. This then had to be communicated to Somerset House, who, in turn, would 'issue the same under seal, and thus render its observance imperative'.[129]

Issuing their sanction 'under seal' meant little if the PLC could not enforce dietaries. Indeed, whatever Mott's analysis and notwithstanding the ways in which the PLC's propaganda machine effectively propagated evidence to support their claim as to the claimed adequacy of the model dietaries, ultimately the PLC lacked the necessary powers of coercion to absolutely enforce their wish. Moreover, as Johnston has shown, for a variety of different reasons, after being trialled, PLC-sanctioned dietaries were often found not to work for a particular union and were replaced by dietaries of their own making.[130] The complexity of the situation was furthered by the fact that beyond the guidance offered by assistant commissioners on the ground and the orders issued by Somerset House, individual Boards of Guardians often cooperated in sharing information and policy ideas including concerning dietaries.[131] Nor did the official dietary policy of the PLC prevent unions from offering poor-quality foodstuffs – something fostered by the legal obligation to issue contracts to the lowest-priced tenders[132] – with lower nutritional value. Nor did it prevent union officials and employees from abusing their positions of power and trust in withholding – for whatever reason – the food that inmates should expect. Combined, these dynamics produced a system that for all the PLC's claims of fairness and sufficiency meant that the experience of inmates was decidedly uneven, with the policy emphasis on deterrence and economy structurally producing dietary regimes that tended towards the either barely adequate or the inadequate. The next section considers the ways in which critique and scandal helped to further shape the system.

Bare lives: Protesting pauper dietaries

And here we have the workhouse, but not just the workhouse – for, after all, this was hardly a new device for relieving and reforming the poor – but also the ward (divided by gender, by wellness), the dining room, the kitchen, the workroom, the Guardian's committee room and the 'blackhole' in which recalcitrant paupers were confined. Cumulatively these sites constituted the workhouse as a biopolitical space, each room configured to achieve a particular end in disciplining and shaping the pauper body.[133] In turn, the workhouse existed at the centre of the web of parishes that comprised the union, and the union part of the wider constellation that orbited around the Poor Law Commission in Somerset House. The tools and rules of governing the workhouse – stretching from the London heart through the assistant commissioner veins to the local capillaries in the form of the Guardians and the workhouse master – were ultimately an attempt to render the pauper as, after Giorgio Agamben, bare life, the pauper body given enough (shelter, comfort, food) to get by according to biological understandings of the population.[134] Opposition to the New Poor Law was framed in these terms: a policy, a set of devices, with which to, at best, oppress the poor, or at worse to murder them. As the anti-New Poor Law propaganda piece *The Book of Murder* – a satire on Malthus and the New Poor Law and written, some believed, by a Commissioner – saw it, poor families should be limited to three heads and all subsequent children should be gassed at birth in dedicated hospitals, or 'child death factories'. First published in Huddersfield in 1833 by radical Joshua Hobson, later to be the publisher of the Chartist newspaper the *Northern Star*, the first edition sold 5,000 copies. A second edition soon appeared, and then in 1839 was reissued by London printer John Hill.[135]

The popularity of the ghoulish satire attests that the theme struck a chord with the public both before and after the implementation of the New Poor Law, helping at first to inform popular sentiment and then later reflecting opinion. Indeed, the 1839 publication came after the serialisation of Charles Dickens' *Oliver Twist* (from 1837, published in novel format in 1839), 'a pathetic and saleable narrative' that, in the elliptical words of the Commission, had to 'a considerable extent, enlisted [public opinion] on the side of error'.[136] It also followed a dismal satire in the Tory *Blackwood Magazine* which suggested that the flesh of the poor who died during the awful winter of 1837–8 should be used to make a nourishing soup for their loved ones left behind, their bones used to make spoons and forks – this a reference to fact that in the early New Poor Law workhouse there was no cutlery – to eat it with.[137]

Such satires could only gain popular and political traction if they reflected a broader public perception that the new system was institutionally cruel and operationally vituperative. The reality, as mirrored in subsequent debates amongst poor law historians, was nuanced. But evidence of small kindnesses did not make for lively copy for the press nor was it

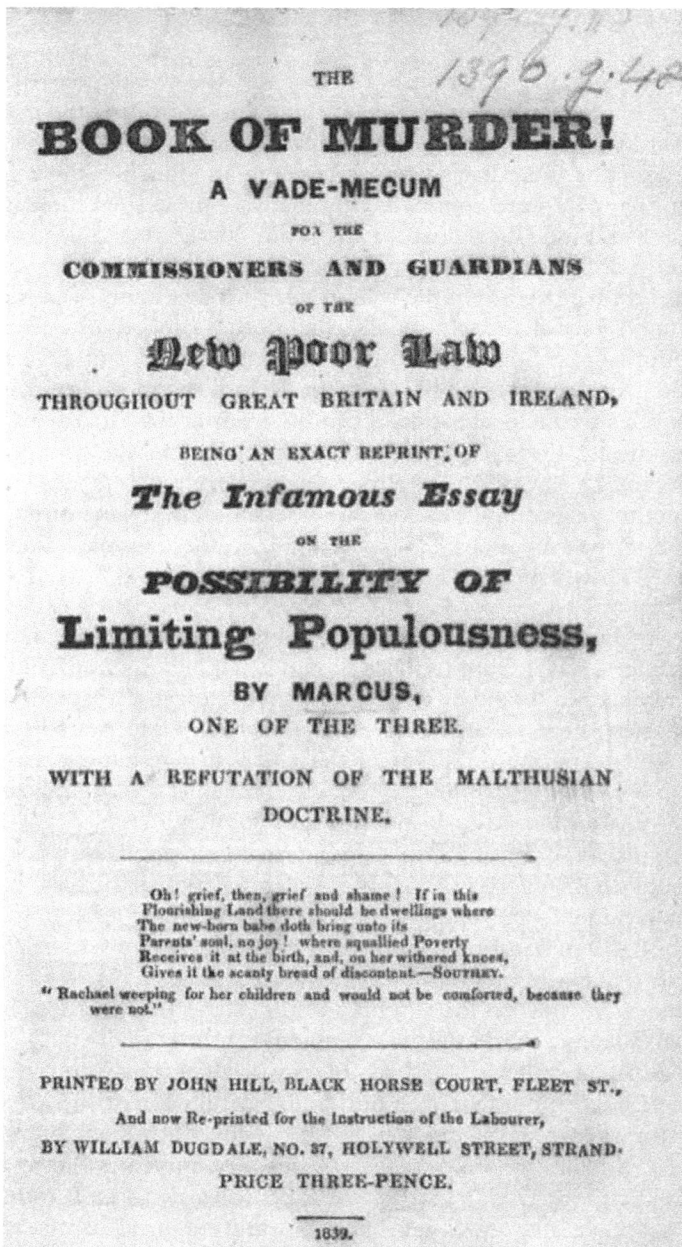

Figure 4.2 Front cover of Marcus's *The Book of Murder*, 1839

enough to stimulate the epistolary classes into outraged action. Ultimately, public opinion was informed by a torrent of reports and pamphlets about abuses in and outside of the workhouse.[138] While the Commissioners were not monsters who wilfully and explicitly encouraged starvation and violence, much popular sentiment disagreed. When unions were first created in the south and east – the regions for which the Poor Law Amendment Act was ultimately created – stories quickly circulated of the system being an attempt to starve the poor.[139] And such stories had terrible effects. At Seaford (Sussex) an old woman committed suicide rather than go to the workhouse at Eastbourne – the 'barracks' as she saw it – while at Andover when the new workhouse was opened on 25 March 1837, one man in a 'most afflicted state' decided to take his own life rather than submit to starvation.[140] At Chesham (Buckinghamshire) in the new Amersham Union, on the order being given to move the old men into the workhouse at Amersham, a riot broke out to prevent their removal, a rumour having spread that the men would never be seen alive again. Likewise in and around the South Molton Union in north Devon, the poor were, as the *Second Report* of the Poor Law Commission put it, 'acting under the grossest deception' that the bread distributed as relief-in-kind was poisoned, such relief only being given by way of 'destroying the paupers'. Even the slightest touch of the adulterated bread would result in instant death.[141]

Such popular fears were informed by, and helped to revivify, the discourse of starvation, something that proved remarkably persistent in the early decades of the nineteenth century but was notably prevalent during and immediately after Swing. In the context of the imposition of the New Poor Law, it found both popular voice – as in the banner carried by Swing protestors at Lenham proclaiming 'Starving at 1s. 6d. a week' – and was deliberately deployed in radical politicking – as in the handbill circulated in the countryside in January 1831 entitled 'Starvation of the Poor'.[142] Indeed, claims that popular opposition to the New Poor Law were predicated on the two lines of the stoppage of out-relief and the breaking up of families are wide of the mark.[143] While both elicited significant popular opprobrium, both in the south and east and subsequently in the Midlands and north, the most sustained and powerful way in which popular and radical opposition was figured was located precisely in the starvation discourse. As Assistant Commissioner Hawley put it in the Commission's *Second Report*: 'The objections which were raised against the dietary tables, submitted to the Boards of Guardians, created if possible, a still stronger sensation than the question of separation.'[144] Guardians and workhouse staff (and many local ratepayers) were viewed as unfeeling Gradgrindians happy to see the poor starve if it meant the 'problem' disappeared (and their rates fell). The Commission (and law-makers) were likewise, to extrapolate from popular feeling, believed to be engaged in an abstract exercise in which the poor were at once a disaggregated surface on which power could be imposed (and novel tools of rule experimented with) and something to be legislated out of bodily being.

As is well established, John Walter, the proprietor of *The Times* and until the general election of 1837 one of the County Members for Berkshire, used every opportunity to attack the principles and operation of the New Poor Law, turning the pages of his newspaper over to coverage of poor law cruelties and to exposing of scandals. The idea, as Ian Anstruther put it, was to 'sink the commission' with a constant stream of 'propaganda'.[145] Reporting in *The Times*, whilst undoubtedly biased, was not misleading. Rather, Walter was able to draw on a steady stream of reports from wherever poor law unions had been established, or where the sprit of the law had been applied to the management of existing but pre-unionised workhouses. And given the policy preeminence of the principles of less eligibility, and the desire to make paupers 'work' for their food, finding evidence of inadequate institutional diets and the limiting effects of insufficient nutrients was not difficult. Nor was finding evidence of popular opposition: the operation of the first unions to be created – the first, Abingdon (Berkshire), was formed on 1 January 1835 – generated a reliable flow of reports of plebeian protests, first in the south, then later in the north and Midlands.[146]

Walter also found support – and a ready source of reports to reprint or plagiarise – in the form of the many, especially Tory, provincial newspapers that similarly considered the centralising principles of the New Poor Law anathema to their values. In the south-east, for instance, the Canterbury-published *Kent Herald* proved a persistent side in the thorn of local Boards of Guardians and to successive Assistant Poor Law Commissioners. By way of example, in late 1835 and early 1836 reports included accounts of relieving officers having absconded, of relieving officers' property being the targets of campaigns of malicious damage, of inadequacies in dietaries and medical care, the degradation of the powers of parish overseers due to the 'arbitrary and dictatorial power' of the Commissioners and Boards of Guardians who acted like 'petty magistrates', a riot in the Blean Union workhouse, and an attack on the Guardians and workhouse visitor at Deal workhouse.[147] It is important to note that such opposition did not immediately extend to northern Tory or radical newspapers. The *Leeds Times* declared in April 1834 that it was 'calculated to eradicate abominations which have long deserved the abhorrence of the people', and the Tory *Bolton Chronicle* related that the Bill (as it then was) must recommend itself 'to every person who had paid the least attention to the practical working of the poor law'. This was an attempt to right the abuses of the agrarian south and east, a southern bill that would also aid sound administration in the industrial north. The realisation of the practical consequences of the Poor Law Amendment Act, though, soon transmogrified initial support into outward opposition.[148]

After initial resistance to the temporary measure of offering relief-in-kind and to the shock of the separation of children, women and men in workhouses, what ultimately persisted were reports of the absolute inadequacy of workhouse dietaries and the related issue of pauper ill health and derisory medical care. If the most obvious manifestation of this was the Andover Scandal in the mid-1840s that ultimately proved to be the Poor Law Commission's undoing (on which more below), *The Times* and the many other 'anti' national and provincial newspapers were not short on copy detailing inadequate dietaries. It was arguably in the avowedly radical press, and, ergo, in the radical reform movement more broadly, though, that the cruelties of the law and the venality of the Commissioners, Guardians, relieving officers and workhouse staff were most unrestrainedly exposed. Further, unlike *The Times*, the radical press rooted their opposition to the New Poor Law not in the abstract terms of values or being un-English but in clear class terms. If, as William Cobbett initially put it, the New Poor Law was the the 'Poor Man's Robbery Bill', an attempt to deny the poor their ancient rights, it soon became the 'Accursed Starvation Bill', a deliberate attempt to try to eliminate the poor rather than to abolish poverty.[149]

That the New Poor Law had been passed by the 'reformed' Parliament acted to fuel the politicisation of the new poor relief system. As Cobbett had proclaimed at his 'Chopsticks' Festival' – held symbolically at the Swing centre of Sutton Scotney in July 1832 to mark the passing of the Reform Bill; Chopsticks was the name he gave to rural workers – the Bill would be 'a bundle of waste paper' unless a reformed Commons listened to '*what measures ought to be adopted*'.[150] Reform, so the line went, failed, for it begat the New Poor Law. Thus the first issue of the radical *Brighton Patriot* newspaper, published on 24 February 1835 just as poor law unions were being formed in Sussex, declared that it was to be devoted to securing a further reform of parliament and the abolition of the Corn Laws, amongst other established radical demands. At first they did not explicitly demand the repeal of the New Poor Law – after all, its effects were as yet not known – but did devote much of the opening editorial letter to it. The Act was symptomatic of a landed elite who were 'willing to wound, but afraid to strike', unwilling to pay the costs of assisted emigration of 'surplus hands' and now also unwilling to either pay sufficient wages or relief. The New Poor Law 'compell[ed] the labourers to rest content with just such wages as their employers choose to give them, though inadequate to the support of a boy.'[151]

The *Brighton Patriot* proved persistent in its exposing of the effects of less eligibility dietaries. During the first winter of the operation of the new southern unions the 'English labourer' had been exposed 'by a system of law the most horrible ever introduced into a civilised country' to 'misery, starvation, and ABSOLUTE DEATH'. 'This was', the report continued, 'no vain assertion … but the grave silently closes over thousands of victims'. One such case related was that of a labourer set to 'work' on the treadmill in the Henfield workhouse. On his refusing due to having 'insufficient' food, he complained before the Guardians that while he was prepared to work he would only do so 'if you will allow me a sufficiency of food'. He was duly sentenced before the Steyning bench to three weeks' imprisonment, a sentence he did not see out before he died in the gaol. Such was the 'Malthusian Poor Law Bill'.[152] The introduction of the Commission's model dietaries generated further opprobrium. Reports included those of the matron of the old poor house at East Grinstead who had complained that the 'dietary of the Poor Law Commissioners' had caused 'universal complaint' as it was 'insufficient to sustain life': she was duly replaced by a former member of the London police. At Hellingly workhouse the male inmates upon the introduction of the new dietary placed their ration of bread on sticks and paraded about, one man walking about the streets asking those who passed whether it was enough bread to live upon. The following morning the inmates were given both bread and broth, but proceeded to break the basins and then smashed several windows and destroyed their beds.[153]

It was the aforementioned case of the Westhampnett Union in West Sussex that arguably proved to be the short-lived *Patriot*'s most dogged campaign. As noted, the Duke of Richmond's union was an earlier adopter of less eligibility dietaries. This was a source of constant comment in the paper, even subject to a 12-verse doggerel:

A Sussex-bred Peer, who resides in the county,
And famed for his piety – not for his bounty,
Compels a poor widow, 'gainst her inclination,
By fasting and prayer, to work out her salvation,

He has urged this poor widow, but cannot prevail,
To feast in the workhouse on Richmond's grand scale;
On the Scottish, Malthusian, Whig dietree [dietary],
On Lennox's Nectar [water] and skilligalee [a thin oatmeal broth].

In the light of reports that Richmond spent £19,000 a year running his foxhounds, the feeble workhouse dietary was bound to provoke particularly vitriolic comment. Higher than usual mortality rates in the summer of 1837 were quickly attributed by the press to the inadequacy of the dietary, while a public meeting held in Chichester the previous spring petitioned for the repeal of the Poor Law Amendment Act as, amongst other things, a system based on dietaries that were 'absolutely insufficient for the maintenance of health', with 'starving families' compelled to become thieves 'for the supply of their immediate wants'.[154] Westhampnett Union also proved an avatar of awful aheadness through the adoption of bone-crushing as a form of workhouse employ. The disciplining 'success' of this encouraged Assistant Commissioner Hawley to recommend the practice to other unions in his charge, including, fatefully, Andover.[155]

Opposition, it is important to note, was not confined to the press nor framed only in terms of radical discourses. When the impoverished and ailing Barnett family of Mundham, an agrarian parish south of Chichester, were forced to turn to the Westhampnett Union for support as labourer Charles was out of work in early 1841, they were offered the chance to enter the house. And with no option beyond starving, stealing or begging, they accepted. Charles and his wife Hannah and two girls were duly separated. Charles never saw his wife again. On 28 February Hannah died; the following day three-year-old Ann also died. Charles and his surviving daughter left the workhouse to bury his wife and infant daughter, a circumstance so affecting that a subscription was entered into to erect a headstone to mark the grave. Tragically, this was not uncommon. What was remarkable was that the stone was used to make a permanent memorial to the cruelty and human corruption of the New Poor Law in the form of a biblical quotation: 'The bread of the needy is his life; he that defraudeth him thereof is a man of blood.'[156]

Such cases not only fed the anti-New Poor Law press in the south and London but also fired the emergent anti-Poor Law movement in the north. As Nicholas Edsall has noted, almost every issue of the *Northern Star* and at almost every anti-Poor Law meeting in Lancashire 'horrific stories of starvation and cruelty in workhouses' were related.[157] Indeed, the Poor Law Commission had wished not to begin forming northern parishes into unions until the commercial slump had improved, but the need to implement the Registration Act – which placed responsibility for registering births, marriages and deaths and was due to come into force on 30 June 1837 and thus provided an enforced impetus – and early southern scandals fed the nascent protest movement.[158] As noted, much of the northern press was at first supportive of the Act, but the fact that many thought the Act was a response to the problems of the south helped to generate a widespread belief that the New Poor Law should not apply to them and their well-run parishes. This and the belief that the provisions would prove expensive whilst the law represented a perversion of local parochial and patriarchal responsibilities to the poor further engendered opposition amongst ratepayers and industrialists, while the established traditions of both plebeian and middle-class radicalism widened the phalanx of resistance. As Knott has noted, while the Assistant Commissioners were happy to meet with 'the better sorts of person' and listen to their concerns, working men and women were excluded from such meetings. Instead, popular opposition found initial voice and form through pre-existing plebeian organisational forms and bodies: the militant Linen Weavers' Union and the Radical Association at Barnsley and Oldham respectively provided both the organisation and the leadership of anti-New Poor Law campaigning. Outwardly, opposition in the north, in distinction to southern resistance, was both organised and coordinated: a network of Anti-Poor Law Committees was quickly established in the West Riding of Yorkshire. It also appeared quite different from southern opposition, drawing, at first, on the radical tropes of the yoke of new forms of bureaucracy and the concretising of class rule rather than the fear of starvation. But the publicity of southern scandals soon shifted the focus, even though northern New Poor Law workhouses were yet to be meaningfully in operation (Cheshire being the only northern county already formed into unions by the end of

1836). Thus soon-to-be editor of the *Northern Star* and New Jerusalem Church minister William Hill proclaimed at a meeting in Huddersfield on 2 February 1837 that the Act was 'unconstitutional, and denied the right of the poor to live'. A speaker at a meeting in Newcastle in June 1838 went further still: 'They immured the needy, the old and the helpless in bastilles, and poisoned them in their dungeons with water gruel; and what other name could he give it but ... murder'.[159]

Anti-Poor Law campaigning in the north might have drawn upon protest discourses that transcended regional and occupational difference but ultimately the techniques and forms were very different: rallies (including anti-Poor Law counter-Coronation demonstrations in June 1838), pamphleting and the use of the press. In short, the techniques that had defined radical organisation in the industrial districts earlier in the 1830s and would later define the non-violent Chartist campaign were also central to the anti-Poor Law movement. And as Knott has shown, a prevalent popular understanding was that the only way to repeal the Poor Law Amendment Act was for working men first to obtain the right to vote.[160] The ends necessarily collided too: only a truly enfranchised parliament would repeal the Poor Law Amendment Act, while campaigning against the New Poor Law was a way in which Chartism could be grounded in material realities of everyday life for working men and women. Claims that Chartists did not campaign against the New Poor Law are thus wide of the mark; rather the anti-Poor Law movement in the north bled into and informed the emergence of Chartism. As Sheffield radical Samuel Roberts saw it, the New Poor Law was 'the parents of the Chartists'.[161] Leading Chartist Feargus O'Connor was at once an early northern critic of the New Poor Law and the Leeds representative of the proto-Chartist London Working Men's Association. His *Northern Star* was an anti-Poor Law mouthpiece before the People's Charter was published. He was not alone. Of the 20 northern delegates to the 1838 Chartist Convention, 14 had already been actively campaigning against the New Poor Law. To Engels it was the 'one voice among the workers – the voice of hatred against the [New Poor] Law ... it is that this new Poor Law has contributed so greatly to accelerate the labour movement, and especially to spread Chartism ... it facilitates the development of the proletarian movement which is arising in the agricultural districts.'[162]

While this is not to say that opposition to the New Poor Law became interchangeable with Chartism, there was some truth in the claims of the Poor Law Commission made in 1839 that the petitions, 'riots' and writings against the New Poor Law were the work of agitators who were as ready to speak for the Chartists or the Anti–Corn Law League.[163] For instance in Sussex, Charles Brooker, a tanner, Minister in the Countess of Huntingdon Connection and one-time Alfriston overseer, tried to get elected to the Eastbourne Union Board of Guardians to oppose the workings of the New Poor Law from within. Unsuccessful, Brooker adopted the tactics of the northern resistance, writing pamphlets – including *The Murder Den, and Its*

Means of Destruction; Or, Some Account of the Working of the New Poor Law (1842) – and press articles and organising meetings. He also became an active Chartist, twice unsuccessfully standing for election to Parliament in Brighton as the Chartist candidate and using this platform to continue his campaign against the New Poor Law. He died, suddenly, and appropriately, 'in a fit of apoplexy' in January 1843.[164]

Ultimately opposition to the New Poor Law and Chartism were both, to co-opt the words of Rev. Joseph Rayner Stephens, 'a knife and fork question'. Universal manhood suffrage was necessary to throw off class oppression and ultimately starvation. As Peter Gurney has put it, Chartists 'talked incessantly about the problem of scarcity', 'hunger and consumption' being 'overtly politicised' in the 'gothic melodramatic tropes' which were so prevalent in popular culture in the 'Hungry Forties'.[165]

Central to these tropes was the idea that the poor, through hunger, were being reduced by the New Poor Law to eating whatever they could get their hands on: grass, dead dogs, human flesh. In many ways it was the potent combination of the poor being reduced to a state of starvation – this being already established by manifold cases of abuse and maltreatment – and the suggestion of cannibalism that turned the case of the inmates of the Andover workhouse gnawing on bones in 1845 into a scandal. If remarkably little studied, the case is well known and while it needs little introduction some points are worth making. Opened in March 1837, Andover workhouse – and the wider union – soon became a notoriously grinding place for the poor. During the bitterly cold winter of 1837–8 the Andover Guardians refused to give outdoor relief. A subscription was raised in the town to help fend off starvation for those who did not enter the house. As chairman of the Board of Guardians Rev. Dobson had put it to the Commission the previous winter, 'I hear from all quarters that the current of private charity never ran so clear'. An application that winter to the Commission by the only guardian sympathetic to the plight of the poor to grant the Andover inmates Christmas dinner was refused on the basis that it was a deviation from the principles of less eligibility. Such was the unyielding operation of the union. The workhouse master and matron – Waterloo veteran Colin McDougal and his wife Mary Ann – were spiteful and vindictive, and systematically diverted provisions from the paupers to themselves, including 'extras' ordered by medical doctors.[166]

As detailed above, the practice of bone-crushing had been adopted in the union on the recommendation of Assistant Commissioner Hawley, the dust being sold as bone meal fertiliser. Not only was the work of crushing bones physically demanding and dangerous – flying splinters scarred the face – but for those existing on a dietary inadequate to the maintenance of life the putrefying flesh and bone marrow represented potential sustenance. Most were butchers' bones, but some were human bones from graveyards that had been cleared. It is highly improbable that any paupers gnawed on such old bones for no nutrition could be so gained, but the proximity between fetid food and human remains was political dynamite. The idea that in the Andover workhouse the distinction between the living and the dead was infinitely mutable, a line not so much crossed as indistinct, was further reinforced in the public mind by the fact that some of the inmates had placed a human lower jaw on a nail in the bone-crushing room. Here humanity did not exist.[167] Such reports helped to reinforce the prevalent idea that the New Poor Law was an attempt not only to starve the poor but also to make dead pauper bodies useful. Assistant Commissioner for Kent Edward Tufnell related to the Commission in 1839 that a story had circulated in the county that 'the children in the workhouse were killed to make pies with, while the old when dead were employed to manure the guardians' fields'.[168]

After being exposed in Parliament and in pages of *The Times*, home secretary Sir James Graham ordered an enquiry under Assistant Commissioner Parker. The abuses at Andover were duly highlighted, and covered in detail by *The Times* and other London papers. Parker's witless and uncaring response to witnesses and his attempts to defend the dietary, the McDougalls and the Board proved his undoing. But other than Parker's sacking nothing happened. The enquiry thus having failed to quell public outrage – the Andover outrages being mobilised by Anti-Poor Law activists in the north, including the Rochdale Guardians prosecuted by the Commission for refusing to implement the Poor Law Amendment Act – a Select Committee was eventually called and sat in the summer of 1846. There were it concluded, no mitigating circumstances: all was cruel and corrupt. The balanced testimony of the Andover inmates was juxtaposed with Commissioner Chadwick's staunch defence of the dietary against the wretched evidence before him. Outwardly, the scandal appeared to be the straw that broke the camel's back: the Poor Law Commission was not renewed by Parliament in 1847 – it had previously been extended in 1842 – and was duly replaced by the Poor Law Board. But beyond the fact that the two senior Board members now sat in Parliament so that they could be held to public account, nothing in policy terms or in relation to the everyday lives of workhouse inmates really changed beyond a slight loosening of the dietary. Indeed, as Shave has shown in relation to other New Poor Law scandals, popular opposition acted to uncover abuse but ultimately the Commission showed little care or contrition, making slight changes to practice and local personnel but never allowing the system to be changed.[169]

To claim that 'what actually happened in workhouses was largely irrelevant' – the quote is Lynn Hollen Lees' – is unhelpful, though. For while abuses and scandals most obviously and dramatically helped to shape public opinion, the hard everyday realities of workhouse inmates acted to ground and make all-too-believable the endemic culture of abuse that pervaded the system. *The Book of Murder* might be a satire because it spoke truths to the abuses of power that constituted the operation of the New Poor Law. *Oliver Twist* might be a novel but its Poor Law Commission-aggravating popularity was precisely because it spoke to the making of bare life.[170] Whatever the limited successes of such popular opposition in forcing the abandonment of less eligibility workhouse dietaries, let alone the whole of New Poor Law apparatus, these struggle matter in that they were writ not in Tory, patrician terms but rather in the language of emergent humanitarianism, the active support for the innate value of human life. As Gurney has suggested, the scandal at Andover – and to this we must add the litany of other scandals and abuses that made it to the pages of the press – was a defining moment in the making of middle-class humanitarianism, and 'nascent humanitarians' were part of the wider 'clamour' against the workings of the New Poor Law.[171] Indeed, from the very beginning of the workings of New Poor Law opposition was expressed using the language of 'humanity' and 'humane'. A report in July 1835 of the removal of an elderly couple from St Davids in Exeter to Tiverton workhouse despite the fact that they only needed four shillings a week to supplement the man's wages prompted the local press to bemoan that:

> Upon what principle this was recommended to the Poor Law Commissioners and adopted by the Legislature it is impossible to conceive, unless as an experiment on the refinement of cruelty … Economy could have had nothing to do with it, except our modern Economists have adopted the retrograde rule of 'penny wise, and pound foolish.' It is certainly to be regretted that the poor have been taken entirely out of the hands of the Magistrates, on the absurd and disgraceful plea that they were 'too humane.'[172]

Chancellor Lord Brougham, the report concluded, might wish to recall all printed copies of his speech in support of the Poor Law Amendment Bill, 'for we believe it will not add to his Lordship's present of future fame, or to his popularity, as the able supporter of humane and enlightened opinions.'[173] Or to return to Rochdale, guardian Livesey was met with loud cheers when he proclaimed that 'the revelations … of the system carried on in the Andover Union were such as to make every one with a spark of humanity shudder'.[174] Here we see both calls to show humanity to the poor and the casting of aspersions on the humanity of those who managed the New Poor Law. The latter point was arguably the only criticism that ever prickled the Poor Law Commission. As Assistant Commissioner Alfred Power put it in the *Second Report*:

> I cannot conclude this report without adverting to the unscrupulous reflections which have been cast on the humanity of those immediately engaged in the administration of the new law … In the whole of this there is not one Union in which your authority to regulate the dispensation of relief has been carried further than the issue of the five following regulations, to which, mild and salutary as their operation has been found in practice, I think it would be difficult to find even a theoretical ground of objection.[175]

Poor Law Commission protestations as to the humanity of their New Poor Law received short shrift, though, from critics of the policy against the tsunami of evidence of institutional cruelty. Occasionally even other branches of government would act (inadvertently) to highlight how hollow the Commission's claims were. In 1839, as a one-off, the Register General's Office included the category 'starvation' as a cause of death in their annual report. The report, authored by Chadwick appointee physician William Farr, showed that 63 of the 148,000 deaths reported in the previous year had been from starvation. This was a direct and official rebuttal of Chadwick's claim that the New Poor Law had made it impossible to die of starvation in England and Wales.[176]

Much anti-New Poor Law campaigning needs to be read as part of a wider emergent humanitarian sensibility. Popular opposition might have lacked obvious moral visionaries,[177] but it should be considered alongside the campaigns for the abolition of slavery and the so-called Factory Movement culminating with the Ten Hour Act of 1847. Humanitarianism can also be read in the broader mission of Chartism, conceived as a movement for the dignity and right to life of working people.[178] As Alan Lester and Fae Dussart have asserted, this new sensibility was also witnessed in a variety of colonial settings, notably from the 1830s, with '[t]he proliferation of new encounters between emigrant Britons and indigenous peoples… [giving] rise to novel social problems on an unprecedented geographical scale'.[179] And given that, as will be considered in chapter five, the English poor were increasingly being thought of as just as distant and different as the aboriginal people of Empire, this matters. Visual depictions showed the dehumanised pauper: only-just-living cadavers, or brute creations, variously simian or creatures of the Neolithic.[180] Emergent humanitarian sensibilities, by extending the hand of human kindness, acted to place the poor at a distance, othering them as debased creatures worthy of pity. And as we will see in chapter six, this dynamic was also at play in conceptualising and responding to the hunger of distant, racialised others during the Great Famine of Ireland.

Notes

1 F. Eden, *The State of the Poor: Or, An History of the Labouring Classes in England, from the Conquest to the Present Period*, vol. 2 (Cambridge: Cambridge University Press, 2011/1797).

2 Eden, *State of the Poor*, vol. 1, p. vii.

3 D. Davies, *The Case of Labourers in Husbandry Stated and Considered* (London: C.G. & J. Robinson, 1795).

4 *State of the Poor, passim*; Davies, *The Case of Labourers, passim*.

5 On Knatchbull's Act see T. Hitchcock, 'Paupers and preachers: The SPCK and the parochial workhouse movement', in L. Davison, T. Hitchcock, T. Keirn and R. Shoemaker (eds), *Stilling the Grumbling Hive: The Response to Social*

and Economic Problems in England, 1689–1750 (Stroud: Alan Sutton, 1992), pp. 145–66; J. Broad, 'Parish economies of welfare, 1650–1834', *Historical Journal*, 42:4 (1999), 985–1006.

6 J. Hargrove, 'History of the calorie in nutrition', *Journal of Nutrition*, 136:12 (2006), 2957–61.

7 Davies, *The Case of Labourers*, p. 48; Eden, *State of the Poor*, vol. 1, p. 4.

8 Ibid., p. xxiix.

9 Davies, *The Case of Labourers*, p. 73.

10 Ibid., pp. 26, 63, 83.

11 Eden, *State of the Poor*, vol. 1, p. 213.

12 Eden, *State of the Poor*, vol. 2, pp. 697, 713, 747–8.

13 P. Higginbotham, *The Workhouse Cookbook* (Stroud: History Press, 2008), p. 35.

14 C. Shammas, *The Pre-industrial Consumer in England and America* (Oxford: Oxford University Press, 1990), p. 140.

15 Eden, *State of the Poor*, vol. 1, pp. 330–3.

16 Shammas, *The Pre-Industrial Consumer*, pp. 141–3.

17 Anon., *An Account of The Several Work-Houses for Employing and Maintaining the Poor; Setting Forth the Rules by Which They are Governed, Their Great Usefulness to the Publick, and in Particular to the Parishes Where They are Erected* (hereafter *An Account of the Several Workhouses*), 1st ed. (London: J. Downing, 1725), pp. 89, 36, 57.

18 Anon., *An Account of the Several Work-Houses*, 2nd ed. (London: J. Downing, 1732), p. 53.

19 Anon., *An Account of the Several Work-Houses*, 1st ed., p. 78.

20 Hitchcock, 'Paupers and preachers'; Anon., *The Workhouse Cruelty: Workhouses Turn'd Gaols and Gaolers Executioners* (London: Printed for Charity Love-poor, 1731).

21 Shammas, *The Pre-Industrial Consumer*; C. Muldrew, *Food, Energy and the Creation of Industriousness: Work and Material Culture in Agrarian England, 1550–1780* (Cambridge: Cambridge University Press, 2011), esp. ch. 3.

22 Eden, *State of the Poor*, vol. 2, pp. 280, 458–9.

23 Shammas, *The Pre-Industrial Consumer*, p. 140.

24 On this point see the following section.

25 Eden, *State of the Poor*, vol. 3, p. 722.

26 Ibid., pp. 147, 29.

27 East Yorkshire Record Office, Beverley (hereafter EYRO), PE121/63, Howden vestry minute, 14 June 1792.

28 S. Shave, 'The welfare of the vulnerable in the late 18th and early 19th centuries: Gilbert's Act of 1782', *History in Focus*, 14, www.history.ac.uk/ihr/Focus/welfare/articles/shaves.html (accessed 15 September 2018). For the Farnham dietary see: Eden, *State of the Poor*, vol. 3, p. 716.

29 Centre for Kentish Studies, Maidstone (hereafter CKS), P125/8/1, Dymchurch vestry minutes, 18 April 1795; Surrey History Centre, Woking, 6672/2/1, Coulsdon vestry minute, 23 February 1805, East Sussex County Record Office, Lewes (hereafter ESCRO), PAR 236/12/1/2, Battle vestry

minute, 20 November 1802. For an analysis of workhouse protests under the New Poor Law in London see: D. Green, 'Pauper protests: Power and resistance in early nineteenth-century London workhouses', *Social History*, 31:2 (2006), 137–59.

30 Birchington fire: *Kentish Gazette*, 8 November; *Kent Herald*, 11 November. Threats were made against workhouses at Andover (Finkley), Elham and Margate: *Hampshire Chronicle*, 29 November; The National Archives, London (hereafter TNA), HO 44/21, fos 241–2, 'A Kentish Farmer', South Kent, to Home Office, 13 September; TNA, HO 52/8, fos 77–8, John Boys, Margate to Phillips, 26 November 1830. For the destruction of workhouses in Hampshire see C. Griffin, *The Rural War: Captain Swing and the Politics of Protest* (Manchester: Manchester University Press, 2012), pp. 108–10.

31 TNA, TS 11/943, Prosecution brief prepared by the Treasury solicitor against Timothy Willocks (but not brought to trial), November 1830.

32 CKS, P81/8/1, Great Chart vestry minute, 15 January 1800.

33 R.P. Hastings, *Poverty and the Poor Law in the North Riding of Yorkshire: 1780–1837*, Borthwick Publications 61 (York: Borthwick Institute, 1982), pp. 21, 22.

34 Berkshire Record Office, Reading (hereafter BRO), D/P110/8/1, Shinfield vestry minutes, 28 December 1768.

35 Tenders for the construction of the house were not put out until February 1770, as an attempt to secure a grant of land on Lee Common from the squire proved more problematic than initially envisaged: BRO, D/P110/8/1, Shinfield vestry minutes, 28 December 1768 and 12 February 1770.

36 British Parliamentary Papers (hereafter BPP), 1803–4 (175), vol. 8, 'Abstract of the answers and returns made pursuant to an act, passed in the 43d year of His Majesty King George III. Intitled, "An act for procuring returns relative to the expense and maintenance of the poor in England"' (hereafter '1803 Returns'), p. 716. On the use of Gilbert's Unions in the West Riding see: G. Rawson, 'Economies and strategies of the northern rural poor: The mitigation of poverty in a West Riding township in the nineteenth century', *Rural History*, 28:1 (2017), 69–92.

37 EYRO, PE121/63, Howden vestry minute, 15 December 1790; Lincolnshire County Record Office, Quadring PAR/10/3, Quadring vestry minute, 3 June 1796.

38 Hampshire County Record Office, Winchester (hereafter HCRO), 57M75/PO16, 'An Account of Money expended in the House of Industry belonging to the united parishes of Bramshott, Headley & Kingsley', Headley Account Book 1795–1852; HCRO, PL2/2/2, Farnborough Workhouse Account Book, 1794–1822.

39 HCRO, 30M77 PV1, Bishops Waltham vestry minute, 26 April 1818; ESCRO, PAR422/12/1, Mayfield vestry minute, 27 March 1826.

40 On this point see H. Barker, *Newspapers and English Society 1695–1855* (London: Routledge, 2014), pp. 197–201.

41 S. Hindle, *On the Parish?: The Micro-Politics of Poor Relief in Rural England c. 1550–1750* (Oxford: Oxford University Press, 2004); J. Healey, *The*

First Century of Welfare: Poverty and Poor Relief in Lancashire, 1620–1730 (Woodbridge: Boydell & Brewer, 2014). For the best study of the impact and use of the 1662 revision see: K.D.M. Snell, *Parish and Belonging: Community, Identity and Welfare in England and Wales, 1700–1950* (Cambridge: Cambridge University Press, 2006), ch. 6.

42 T. Malthus, *An Essay on the Principle of Population* (London: J.M. Dent and Sons, 1803, 2nd edition).

43 J.R. Poynter, *Society and Pauperism: English Ideas on Poor Relief, 1795–1834* (London: Routledge, 1969), p. 21.

44 K.D.M. Snell, *Annals of the Labouring Poor: Social Change and Agrarian England, 1660–1900* (Cambridge University Press, 1985), p. 110; S. Shave, *Pauper Policies: Poor Law Practice in England, 1780–1850* (Manchester: Manchester University Press, 2017), pp. 162–3, 257.

45 T. Gilbert, *A Scheme for the Better Relief and Employment of the Poor* (London, 1764); T. Gilbert, *Observations upon the Orders and Resolutions of the House of Commons, with Respect to the Poor, Vagrants, and Houses of Correction* (London, 1775); J. Bentham, *Pauper Management Improved: Particularly by Means of an Application of the Panopticon Principle of Construction: Anno 1797, First Published in Young's Annals of Agriculture: Now First Published Separately* (London: R. Baldwin & J. Ridgway, 1797); P. Mandler, 'The making of the new poor law redivivus', *Past & Present*, 117 (1987), 131–57, esp. 148–50.

46 D. Marshall, 'The Nottinghamshire reformers and their contribution to the New Poor Law', *Economic History Review*, 13:3 (1961), 396; Shave, *Pauper Policies*, pp. 28–9.

47 Mandler, 'The making', 142.

48 BPP, 1817 (106) vol. 84, 'Report from the Select Committee of the House of Commons on the Poor Laws', p. 15.

49 For instance see: Anon., *A Digest of the Poor Laws, in Order To Their Being Reduced Into One Act* (London: P. Uriel, 1768) which only mentions food and diet in relation to regulations in the Assize of Bread; and, H. Zouch, *Remarks upon the late Resolutions of the House of Commons Respecting the Proposed Change of the Poor Laws* (Leeds: G. Wright, 1766), which makes only one reference to 'need' and none to matters of subsistence in any context.

50 T. Gilbert, *Plan for the Better Relief and Employment of the Poor; for Enforcing and Amending the Laws Respecting Houses of Correction, and Vagrants; and for Improving the Police of this Country. Together with Bills Intended to be Offered to Parliament for those Purposes* (London: Wilkie, 1781), p. 1.

51 Ibid., pp. 2–3, 87.

52 *An Account of the Several Workhouses*, 1st ed., pp. 33, 43.

53 Ibid., p. 131.

54 Ibid., pp. 68–9.

55 Anon., *The Case of the Poor Consider'd; or the Great Advantages of Erecting a Publick Manufactory, for Maintaining and Employing the Poor* (Edinburgh: J. Maclaurin, 1729).

56 *An Account of the Several Workhouses*, 2nd ed., p. 185.

57 Mandler, 'The making', 134.

58 On poor relief systems and policies in Scotland see: R. Mitchison, *The Old Poor Law in Scotland: The Experience of Poverty, 1574–1845* (Edinburgh: Edinburgh University Press, 2000).

59 D. Porteous, *A Letter to the Citizens of Glasgow* (Glasgow: Robert Chapman, 1783), p. 12.

60 Poor Law Commissioners, *Second Annual Report of the Poor Law Commissioners for England and Wales* (hereafter *Second Report*) (London: Charles Knight, 1836), p. 385.

61 Ibid., p. 385. On this point see Shammas, *The Pre-Industrial Consumer*; Muldrew, *Food, Energy and the Creation of Industriousness*; the figures in V. Johnston, *Diet in Workhouses and Prisons, 1835–1895* (New York: Garland, 1985), p. 131; and the table of calories in Higginbotham, *The Workhouse Cookbook*, p. 57.

62 *Bury and Norwich Post*, 21 April 1830.

63 Eden, *State of the Poor*, vols 1–3.

64 Poynter, Society and Pauperism, p. 47.

65 E. Burke, *Thoughts and Details on Scarcity, Originally Presented to the Right Hon. William Pitt, in the Month of November 1795* (London: F.C. Rivington, 1800); Mander, 'The making of the new poor law', 142; Poynter, *Society and Pauperism*, pp. 52–5.

66 G. Stedman-Jones, *An End to Poverty? A Historical Debate* (New York: Columbia University Press, 2005), pp. 77–8. On Malthus' impact on Pitt's poor law thinking see: J. Huzel, 'Malthus, the poor law, and population in early nineteenth-century England', *Economic History Review*, 22:3 (1969), 437, n.2.

67 On Young's advocacy for potato plots and the wider cultivation of the tuber see: R. Hoyle, 'The poor man's wants, the rich man's luxury' (draft paper, 2017). My thanks to Professor Hoyle for sharing this with me. Also see Poynter, *Society and Pauperism*, pp. 98–105.

68 The 1818 House of Lords report on the poor laws considered the 'making up' of wages from the rates but did not relate that such Speenhamland-style schemes were often related to the price of bread. The 1819 Report from the Committee on the Poor Laws made much of the idea that allowances represented a perversion of the principles of the Acts of Elizabeth – drawing on evidence from Eden to make the claim – but made no reference to food and subsistence and very little to the use of workhouses: BPP, 1818 (400), vol. 5, 'Select Committee of House of Lords to Consider Poor Laws', Appendix: p. 9; BPP, 1819 (529), vol. 2, 'Select Committee to consider Poor Laws', pp. 3–10. On this dynamic see chapter five and S. Williams, *Poverty, Gender and Life-cycle under the English Poor Law, 1760–1834* (Woodbridge: Boydell & Brewer, 2011), ch. 5.

69 BPP, 1828 (494), vol. 4, 'Report from the Select Committee on that part of the Poor Laws relating to the employment or relief of able-bodied persons from the poor rate', p. 7.

70 While relatively few poor law pamphlets were published in the early years of the nineteenth century, a feature of those published was attacks on workhouses: variably as expensive, as shown by the returns of 1802–3, and as

a deviation from the principles of the Acts of Elizabeth: Poynter, *Society and Pauperism*, p. 192.

71 J. Middleton, *General View of the Agriculture of Middlesex*, 2nd edition (London: G. and W. Nicol, 1807), p. 75; C. Drysdale, *Life and Writings of Malthus*, 2nd edition (London: G Standring, 1892), pp. 76–7.

72 W. Clarkson, *An Inquiry into the Cause of the Increase of Pauperism and Poor Rates* (London: s.n., 1816).

73 BPP, 1817 (462), vol. 6, 'Select Committee to consider Poor Laws: Report, minutes of evidence, appendix', p. 20.

74 Ibid., pp. 12, 16.

75 Ibid., pp. 9, 10, 14–15.

76 Ibid., pp. 31–2, 37, 99–100.

77 J. Bentham, 'Tracts on poor laws and pauper management: Outline of a work entitled Pauper Management Improved', *The Works of Jeremy Bentham* (Edinburgh: W. Tait, 1843), vol. 8, p. 387.

78 J. Becher, *The Anti-Pauper System* (London: W. Simkin and R. Marshall, 1828), p. 15.

79 W. Clark, *Thoughts and Management and Relief of the Poor* (London: R. Cruttwell, 1815); Poynter, *Society and Pauperism*, p. 283.

80 Shave, 'The welfare of the vulnerable'. This point was widely flouted by Gilbert's 'Houses of Industry': Shave, *Pauper Policies*, ch. 2.

81 BPP, 1834 (44), 'Report from His Majesty's commissioners for inquiring into the administration and practical operation of the Poor Laws Poor Law Report' (hereafter Poor Law Report), section II.I.13 and II.II.41, appendix c, p. 56.

82 Poor Law Report, p. 130 ('Remedial measures').

83 A. Brundage, *The English Poor Laws, 1700–1930* (Basingstoke: Palgrave, 2002), pp. 60–4.

84 Poor Law Report, II.1.24.

85 Hansard, 3rd ser. (1834), cols 1320–34 (26 May).

86 R.H. Tawney, *Religion and the Rise of Capitalism* (London, 1926), p. 272; Poor Law Report, p. 35.

87 Poor Law Report, II.2.90.

88 Poor Law Report, II.1.9.

89 Poor Law Report, II.1.97.

90 Poor Law Report, II.2.32 and 33.

91 Poor Law Report, II.1.20.

92 Poor Law Report, I pp. 176–7; II.2.44.

93 Poor Law Report, II.2.44 and 45.

94 Poor Law Report, pp. 165–6, cited in Johnston, *Diet in Workhouses and Prisons*, p. 14.

95 Johnston, *Diet in Workhouses and Prisons*, p. 15.

96 'An Act for the Amendment and better Administration of the Laws relating to the Poor in England and Wales', c.86 (Geo. IV) 1834, s.21.

97 Ibid., s.52.

98 Brundage, *The English Poor Laws*, pp. 57–66.

99 *Cobbett's Weekly Political Register*, 21 June 1834. On Cobbett's opposition see: *Cobbett's Weekly Political Register*, esp. 15 March, 3 May, 7, 14 and 21 June 1834; I. Dyck, *William Cobbett and Rural Popular Culture* (Cambridge: Cambridge University Press, 1992), pp. 205–9. On the crisis in Scotland in 1819 see: B. Gordon, *Political Economy in Parliament 1819–1823* (London: Macmillan, 1976), pp. 67–8. Note: the newly elected MP for Renfrewshire, John Maxwell, related in the House of Commons that the strict applications of the principles of political economy were the cause of the crisis rather than the solution.
100 Johnston, *Diet in Workhouses and Prisons*, p. 15.
101 *Times*, 13 November 1834; Brundage, *The English Poor Laws*, ch. 4.
102 Brundage, *The English Poor Laws*, p. 95.
103 Poor Law Commissioners, *First Annual Report of the Poor Law Commissioners for England and Wales* (hereafter *First Report*) (London: Charles Knight, 1835), appendix A, sections 1–6, p. 7.
104 For the Commission's phrases see: TNA, MH 12/13076/3, Henry Freeman, Assistant Overseer for Udimore near Rye, to the Poor Law Commission, with the Commission's annotations, 11 February 1835.
105 R. Wells, 'Resistance to the New Poor Law in the rural south', in J. Rule and R. Wells (eds), *Crime, Protest and Popular Politics in Southern England, 1740–1850* (London: Hambledon, 1997), p. 95.
106 *Brighton Herald*, 22 and 29 November 1834.
107 *Kent Herald*, 12 November; *Brighton Herald*, 29 November and 6 December 1834.
108 See C. Griffin, 'As lated tongues bespoke: Popular protest in south-east England, 1790–1840' (PhD thesis, University of Bristol, 2002), pp. 232–5; D. Hopker, *Money or Blood: The 1835 Riots in the Swale Villages* (Broadstairs: s.n., 1988).
109 TNA, HO 52/26, fos131–3, 135–7 and 158–163, 41/12, pp. 205–7, Poore, Murston, to Russell, 5 and 6 May, Francis Head, Canterbury, to Rt. Hon. J. Frankland, Lewes, 10 May; Phillips, to Poore, 8 May 1835.
110 *First Report*, p. 9.
111 Ibid., pp. 28, 31.
112 Ibid., p. 31; 'Orders and Regulations to be observed in the Workhouse', proforma, p. 98, rule XIX.
113 *First Report*, p. 100.
114 Ibid., pp. 50–2, 168.
115 I. Miller, 'Feeding in the workhouse: The institutional and ideological functions of food in Britain, ca. 1834–70', *Journal of British Studies* 52:1 (2013), 3.
116 *Kent Herald*, 21 May 1835.
117 *Rochester Gazette*, 25 August 1835. According to assistant commissioner Tufnell in the *Second Report*, all eleven Kent unions formed by that point determined on adopting the same dietary (what became the PLC's dietary number two and was subsequently adopted by all 26 Kent unions), 'and [it] has now been observed for more than a year in East Kent without complaint'. But on its introduction, many of the Guardians thinking it 'too low',

Tufnell, 'recommended the complainants to test it, by trying it … always with the result of satisfying the most incredulous of its sufficiency'. *Second Report*, p. 208.

118 *Cobbett's Weekly Political Register*, 13 June; *Brighton Patriot*, 25 August and 17 November 1835.

119 *Brighton Patriot*, 14 April 1835.

120 *Suffolk Chronicle*, 31 October; *Bury & Norwich Post*, 30 September, 11 November and 23 December 1835. Kay repeatedly used the discourse of 'indulgence' and 'abundance' in his reports relating to the old workhouse systems of Norfolk and Suffolk: *Second Report*, pp. 156–8.

121 Johnston, *Diet in Workhouses and Prisons*, p. 18; *Second Report*, pp. 56–9.

122 *Second Report*, pp. 28–9.

123 *Second Report*, p. 29.

124 P. Gurney, *Wanting and Having: Popular politics and Liberal Consumerism in England, 1830–70* (Manchester: Manchester University Press, 2015), p. 73.

125 S.E. Finer, *The Life and Times of Sir Edwin Chadwick* (London: Methuen, 1952), pp. 117–19.

126 M. Blaug, 'The myth of the old poor law and the making of the new', *Journal of Economic History*, 23:2 (1963), 162.

127 H. Harold, 'Origin of the word 'protein''', *Nature*, 168: 4267 (1951), 244.

128 *Second Report*, pp. 334–40.

129 *Second Report*, pp. 63–4 (circular).

130 Brundage, *The English Poor Laws*, p. 97; Johnston, *Diet in Workhouses and Prisons*, p. 130.

131 Shave, *Pauper Policies*, ch. 4.

132 On the development of the contracting system see: D. Brown, 'Pauperism and profit: Financial management, business practices and the new poor law in England in Wales' (PhD thesis, King's College London, 2014).

133 On this point see: F. Driver, *Power and Pauperism: The Workhouse System, 1834–1884* (Cambridge: Cambridge University Press, 1992), pp. 11–13.

134 G. Agamben, *Homo Sacer: Sovereign Power and Bare Life*, trans. D. Heller-Roazen (Stanford, CA: Stanford University Press, 1998).

135 Anon. ('Marcus, One of the Three'), *The Book of Murder! A Vade-mecum for the Commissioners and Guardians of the New Poor Law … Being an Exact Reprint of the Infamous Essay On the Possibility of Limiting Populousness, With a Refutation of the Malthusian Doctrine*, 2nd ed., with a preface (London: John Hill, 1839). On the reception and circulation of *The Book of Murder* see: J. McDonagh, *Child Murder and British Culture, 1720–1900* (Cambridge: Cambridge University Press, 2003), pp. 101–12.

136 C. Dickens, *Oliver Twist, or, the Parish Boy's Progress* (London: Bentley, 1839); Poor Law Commission, *Report of the Poor Law Commissioners to the Most Noble the Marquis of Normanby, Her Majesty's Principal Secretary of State for the Home Department, on the Continuance of the Poor Law Commission* (hereafter *1840 Continuance Report*) (London: Her Majesty's Stationery Office, 1840), pp. 31, 30.

137 I. Anstruther, *The Scandal of the Andover Workhouse* (London: Bles, 1973), p. 105.
138 D. Roberts, 'How cruel was the Victorian poor law?', *Historical Journal*, 6:1 (1963), 97–107; U. Henriques, 'How cruel was the Victorian poor law?', *Historical Journal*, 11:2 (1968), 365–71; Shave, *Pauper Policies*, ch. 5.
139 N.C. Edsall, *The Anti-Poor Law Movement, 1834–44* (Manchester: Manchester University Press, 1971), p. 32.
140 *Brighton Patriot*, 28 April 1835; Anstruther, *Scandal*, p. 97.
141 Anstruther, *Scandal*, p. 28; *Second Report*, p. 353.
142 *Kentish Gazette*, 29 October 1830; *Times*, 19 January 1831; *Sussex Advertiser*, 31 January 1831.
143 Anstruther, *Scandal*, p. 28. As Knott asserted, middle-class opposition was also motivated by the centralisation of social policy and the rising costs of supporting a growing bureaucracy: J. Knott, *Popular Opposition to the 1834 Poor Law* (London: Taylor & Francis, 1986), p. 269.
144 *Second Report*, p. 216.
145 Anstruther, *Scandal*, p. 102.
146 *Times*, 30 April and 1 May (opposition to separation of men and women in the Eastbourne workhouse, including a meeting of 500 labourers at Jevington Holt); 14 May (various reports of rioting against the implementation of the New Poor Law in Kent and Sussex); 4 and 5 June (trial of the Doddington rioters); 6 June 1835 (strike of labourers at Ringmer, West Firle Union, in opposition to giving relief-in-kind).
147 *Kent Herald*, 17 December 1835; 14, 21 and 28 January 1836.
148 *Leeds Times*, 26 April; *Bolton Chronicle*, 26 April 1834, cited in Knott, *Popular Opposition*, p. 93.
149 *Cobbett's Weekly Political Register*, 30 June 1832; *Brighton Patriot*, 5 April 1836.
150 *Hampshire Telegraph*, 2 July; *Cobbett's Weekly Political Register*, 30 June 1832. On the festival see: Dyck, *William Cobbett and Rural Popular Culture*, pp. 198–9.
151 *Brighton Patriot*, 24 February 1835.
152 *Brighton Patriot*, 5 January 1836.
153 *Brighton Patriot*, 9 February and 29 March 1836.
154 *Brighton Patriot*, 11 and 25 August, 6 October, 17 November 1835, 3 May 1836; *Times*, 14 July 1837.
155 TNA, MH 32/39, 9 September 1837, cited in Anstruther, *Scandal*, p. 118.
156 *Morning Post*, 29 May 1841. The quote is from Ecclesiasticus, 34:21.
157 Edsall, *Anti-Poor Law Movement*, p. 124.
158 Knott, *Popular Opposition*, p. 92; L. Goldman, 'Statistics and the science of society in early Victorian Britain: An intellectual context for the General Register Office', *Social History of Medicine*, 4:3 (1991), 415–34.
159 K. Navickas, *Protest and the Politics of Space and Place, 1789–1848* (Manchester: Manchester University Press, 2015), pp. 135–41, 159–63; Knott, *Popular Opposition*, pp. 100–4; *Northern Liberator*, 30 June 1838.
160 Knott, *Popular Opposition*, p. 132.
161 S. Roberts, *Chartism and its Causes and Cure: Addressed to the Clergy and Others of Sheffield and Eccleshall* (Sheffield: Whittaker and Co., 1839), p. 3.

162 Knott, *Popular Opposition*, p. 136; F. Engels, *The Condition of the Working Class in England in 1844*, trans F. Kelley Wischnewetzky (Cambridge: Cambridge University Press 2010/1892), p. 292.

163 *1840 Continuance Report*, pp. 28–9. On this point see: Edsall, *Anti-Poor Law Movement*, ch. 8; C.P. Griffin, 'Chartism and opposition to the New Poor Law in Nottinghamshire: The Basford Union workhouse affair of 1844', *Midland History*, 2:4 (1974), 244–9.

164 R. Wells, 'Popular protest and social crime: The evidence of criminal gangs in rural southern England, 1790–1860', in B. Stapleton (ed.), *Conflict and Community in Southern England: Essays in the Social History of Rural and Urban Labour from Medieval to Modern Times* (Stroud: Alan Sutton, 1992), pp. 147–9; M. Chase, *Chartism: A New History* (Manchester: Manchester University Press, 2007), p. 180; C. Brooker, *The Murder Den, and Its Means of Destruction; Or, Some Account of the Working of the New Poor Law...* (Brighton: William Woodward, 1842). For Brooker's obituary see: *Spectator*, 21 January 1843.

165 The quote is from Stephen's speech at the huge Kersal Moor, Manchester, Chartist demonstration on 24 September 1838: *Northern Star*, 29 September 1838; Gurney, *Wanting and Having*, pp. 30, 31.

166 TNA, MH 32/39, Hawley to Poor Law Commission, 31 March 1838; MH 12/10661, PLC to guardian Hugh Mundy, Andover, 22 December 1837; *Berkshire Chronicle*, 31 December 1836; Anstruther, *Scandal*, pp. 112, 125.

167 Anstruther, *Scandal*, pp. 117–18; Gurney, *Wanting and Having*, p. 88. The practice of bone-crushing was widespread in southern unions: by 1844 53 Wessex unions had adopted the practice, whilst 15 and 18 unions in the south-west and south-east respectively also used bone-crushing to employ the workhouse poor: Shave, *Pauper Policies*, p. 174.

168 TNA, MH32/70, Edward Tufnell to PLC, 10 January, 1839, cited in Crowther, *Workhouse*, p. 31.

169 Gurney, *Wanting and Having*, pp. 83–95; *Times*, 16 September 1845; Shave, *Pauper Policies*, p. 42, ch. 5.

170 L. Hollen Lees, *The Solidarities of Strangers: The English Poor Laws and the People, 1700–1948* (Cambridge: Cambridge University Press, 1998), p. 150; Anon., *Book of Murder*; Dickens, *Oliver Twist*.

171 Gurney, *Wanting and Having*, pp. 95, 81.

172 *Woolmer's Exeter and Plymouth Gazette*, 11 July 1835.

173 Ibid.

174 *Times*, 16 September 1845.

175 *Second Report*, p. 271.

176 J. Vernon, *Hunger: A Modern History* (Cambridge, MA: Harvard University Press, 2007), pp. 81–2 and 305, notes 1 and 2.

177 On moral visionaries see: M. Barnett, *Empire of Humanity: A History of Humanitarianism* (Ithaca, NY: Cornell University Press, 2011), p. 9.

178 F.J. Klingberg, *The Anti-Slavery Movement in England: A Study in English Humanitarianism* (New Haven, CT: Yale University Press, 1926); R.G. Cowherd and A.H. Cole, *The Humanitarians and the Ten Hour Movement in England* (Cambridge, MA: Baker Library, Harvard Graduate School of

Business Administration, 1956). The point about Chartism remains to be systematically told, but see: M. Sanders, *The Poetry of Chartism: Aesthetics, Politics, History* (Cambridge: Cambridge University Press, 2009), p. 169, n.12.

179 A. Lester and F. Dussart, *Colonization and the Origins of Humanitarian Governance: Protecting Aborigines Across the Nineteenth-century British Empire* (Cambridge: Cambridge University Press, 2014), p. 23.

180 On this point see chapter five below.

Part III

Theorising hunger

5

The biopolitics of hunger: Malthus, Hodge and the racialisation of the poor

To say that power took possession of life in the nineteenth century, or to say that power at least takes life under its care in the nineteenth century, is to say that it has, thanks to the play of technologies of discipline on the one hand and technologies of regulation on the other, succeeded in covering the whole surface that lies between the organic and the biological, between body and population. We are, then, in a power that has taken control of both the body and life or that has, if you like, taken control of life in general – with the body as one pole and the population as the other (Foucault, *Society Must Be Defended*).[1]

The universal implementation of workhouse dietaries – based on an understanding of the minimum the human body needed to sustain itself – and other disciplining techniques and technologies implemented by the New Poor Law placed the abstract pauper *body* rather than the pauper at the centre of social policy. This shift can be usefully be understood as a form of what Michael Foucault has labelled biopolitics, a profound change in the nineteenth century from sovereign power, or the rule of the sword, which rested on the right to take life or to let live, to the state now being invested with a new right to make live and to let die.[2] As David Nally has put it, this did 'not mean that the "power of death" [was] completely abandoned, but rather that violence must [now] be rationalised by appealing to future improvements: the pauper will be converted into a sturdy labourer; the prisoner will be rehabilitated; savage populations will be civilised; and wastelands will be transformed into productive environments'.[3] Put differently, there was a shift in the basis of rule from determining who lives or dies (through the exercise of military and judicial power) to the regulation of the very basis of life itself, the state determining the conditions on which the right to life should be granted – and taken away.[4] This new way of governing manifested itself in multiple ways: first discursively, then latterly through policy (both 'from the bottom up' and as legislated for) and ultimately in the form of new institutions, writ in documents, committees, even architecturally.[5] Then, as much as today, being useful, having some civic function, came before simply being allowed to be human.

These new techniques of governing constituted a shift to a biopolitics, or perhaps more correctly 'biospolitics', a conflation of the Greek *bios* (life) and politics (the practices and technologies of governing a territory). While in the classical sense politics denoted action and decision-making relating to all, it was concerned not with populations but the *populus* (the people), a (conceptually) homogenous group that comes before and without knowledge of itself and its condition of being. In this understanding life is simply given. It is assumed to be stable, unchanging and, as Thomas Lemke puts it, 'a stable ontological and normative point of reference', neither transformable nor in the purview of the state as something subject to transformation.[6] Biopolitics thus represented a profound shift in terms of an understanding that life itself is transformable and controllable. And when these transformations were placed at the core of politics, life now became the object of administration and regulation at the level of populations.

This shift was not concerned with the *individual* body per se. Rather, individual bodies were, so the understanding goes, measured so that the idealised body (and therefore subject) could be defined in relation to observed averages and state-set standards.[7] To know populations, though, required the advent of new political knowledges and the birth of new disciplines and methods: the mass population survey and the attendant rise of statistics and demography.[8] These combined with the advent of human biology led to the emergence of epidemiology and human nutrition allied to the rise of chemistry.[9] In this way, populations en masse and individual bodies – which in themselves were not important – could be understood as points on the 'whole surface' that stretched from the organic to the biological. This is a spatial conception of the shifting biological contours of power, not only at the level of Foucault's metaphors, but also in terms of operation. Power was now enacted against, literally, the surface of the body, which was then placed on the 'normal curve', compared 'on the same conceptual space to the entire population'.[10] In this, hunger was determined and measured: when is the body in a state of minimum biological being, profoundly hungry but not literally starving?

Beyond knowing the biological, biopolitics related to the ways in which bodies were acted on, made to yield, in making the idealised, normalised population. The surface of life itself was thus 'covered' by the twin technologies of discipline and regulation. These techniques of governing – collectively Foucault's tools of governmentality – extended to 'correction, exclusion, normalization, disciplining, therapeutics, and optimization'.[11] Of course, none of these techniques came prefigured, predetermined, but were, in the late eighteenth and early nineteenth centuries, made and figured, in a process of becoming. This was necessarily dependent on experimentation in turning belief and ideology into practice – the practices of biopolitics did not come prefigured – and was also, again, defiantly placed in the making of new spaces of discipline and control. As in Foucault's early work, the critical emphasis is in the ways in which this took material form in new sites of discipline. The New Poor Law workhouse was one such site.

History and biopolitics

If the concept of biopolitics is rooted in a distinctly Foucauldian archaeology of knowledge, a particular telling of the past that speaks to the present, the application of the concept has been overwhelmingly focused on the here and now. In some ways this it is not surprising. Given that the logic of biopolitical power ('biopower') is dependent on the very idea (or representation) of life, it follows that the concept is of the present, its concerns anchored in the moment of life. Political geographer Andrew Baldwin goes further. To him biopolitics is a politics of futurity, a concern for how the 'future is rendered knowable through specific practices' that intervene on the present.[12] And as Foucault himself noted, there is a conceptual issue in attempting to write histories of biopolitics, for before the early nineteenth century there was no biology as the science of life 'for life did not exist. All that existed was living things.'[13]

But to claim that historians and historical geographers have altogether left biopolitical analyses to social scientists is to paint with too broad a brush, for the concept has figured strongly in histories of colonialism and post-colonialism. Indeed, as Scott Morgensen notes of settler colonialism, the practice can be considered to be 'exemplary of the processes of biopower'. And as Nally has delineated in his analysis of the ways in which corporate agribusiness is reconditioning life (human, animal, bacterial) 'to quicken the reproduction of capital', a biopolitics of food provisioning can be understood as emerging as part of the rise of political liberalism and laissez-faire economics in the nineteenth century.[14] This, he goes on, was not figured only as a reworking, or rather a dismantling, of the moral economy, but rather as something that was globally manifest, in the development of colonial plantations and in other forms of what David Harvey has called 'accumulation by dispossession'.[15]

Nally's paper forms part of a broader project examining the politics of 'food security' and colonial authority as expressed in relation to large-scale subsistence crises.[16] Central to this is his groundbreaking rethinking of Ireland's Great Famine. To Nally, drawing on David Keen's earlier analysis of famine in south-west Sudan, the Irish famine had functions as well as causes.[17] In this analysis, famine is shown to be a 'biopolitical regime of governance', scarcity being mobilised, manipulated and even made a tool by which populations could be managed.[18] The onset of potato blight represented, so Nally argues, an opportunity to 'regenerate' Irish society; thus the discourses that 'aid' and 'improvement' represented mirrored the language often used to justify acts of colonial dispossession elsewhere: humanitarian and progressive.[19]

To justify the acts of making live and (especially) letting die that comprised aspects of the response of the British state (see the following chapter for a more nuanced reading of British popular responses), it was first necessary to make the Irish, for which read the poor, landless Irish, as subjects *and* things to subject. The dispossessed Irish poor were already written as existing in a state beyond human need, as a different sort of colonial being. Indeed, in many pre-famine writings we see the Irish poor, invariably rural and defiantly wretched, already told and understood in racial terms. As a *Times* editorial put it in 1799, the Act of Union would act to 'humanise' the 'barbarous' Irish by virtue of 'observing civilised manners'. If, as Michael De Nie has claimed, the roots of such racial 'othering' can be found as early as the Norman invasion of the twelfth century, by the early nineteenth century 'new trends in ethnology and anthropology' could be used to justify existing prejudices in scientific terms. The justification of the Irish Poor Law of 1838 – itself based on the principles and form of the English and Welsh New Poor Law – was based squarely on the supposed moral and physical degeneracy of the Irish people. The analysis of the need and the prescription for the remedy were framed precisely in the emergent Victorian discourse of racial profiling and classification.[20] The workhouse and hard labour were not a racial cure but rather an attempt to yoke, to make yield, to civilise. Thus whatever the suffering of the Great Irish Famine, the Scottish social critic Thomas Carlyle on his tours of Ireland in 1846 and 1849 could use his 'observations' of the Irish people to formulate, as Nally puts it, 'a racial politics based on a *hierarchy of human worth*', often drawing on equine metaphors, beasts of burden. Such observation and analysis were, then, a justification for the use of the tools of biopolitics and the exercise of biopower.[21] The language of race, and thus the attendant acts of making race, were a way of placing social groups at particular places on the biopolitical curve and thus justifying their being subject to acts of exceptionalism.

If the rule of colonial power, even in the context of the Union of 1799, relied upon biopolitics which, in turn, relied upon human exceptionalism, it is another act of intellectual exceptionalism to think that colonial rule was the only context in which making difference was writ in racial terms and put into practice through the tools of biopolitics. Thus, while Thomas Babington Macaulay in his famous *History of England* could write that the 'Aboriginal Irish' were perceived 'not to belong to our branch of the great human family … They were distinguished from us by more than moral and intellectual peculiarity', his book was infused with the language of ethnography in writing of 'native' and 'dominant' races in relation to the metropole.[22]

In *Society Must Be Defended*, Foucault directly connects the advent of biopolitics with state-sponsored, or at least state-encouraged, inscriptions of racial othering. Writing race, with the attendant co-constitution of bodily 'knowledges', allowed the state to engage in 'fragmenting the field of the biological that power controls'. To Foucault the making of race was:

[A] way of separating out the groups that exist within a population ... a way of establishing a biological-type caesura within a population that appears to be a biological domain. This will allow power to treat that population as a mixture of races, or to be more accurate, to treat the species, to subdivide the species it controls, into the subspecies known, precisely, as races.[23]

As Catherine Mills has suggested, race, therefore, provided a biological legitimisation for allowing one group – for which read race – to (ideally) die to allow another to flourish.[24] Race begat a biopolitical racism.

While we need to be mindful of Stuart Hall's claim that there is no general theory of racism, only historically specific racisms,[25] the making of race – and hence racism – in Ireland and England, whilst different, were contextually united. Besides, so many Irish migrant workers in England settled and became part of – especially urban – working communities, so that in some contexts the everyday fortunes of the English and Irish poor were all but the same.[26] It is, therefore, a further act of exceptionalism to think that social commentators, law-makers, and policy innovators and enforcers did not also use the same languages and methods of ethnographic enquiry to make sense of the English rural worker. This was not the simple writing of the English labourer as a Macaulian 'dominant' race in comparison to colonial subjects, but rather something more complex and nuanced, rooted in precisely the same early ethnographic animalistic tropes: an internal subaltern, the internal colonial subject. The argument here is not that this was a necessary precondition for the advent of biopolitics in Britain, but rather that it informed and shaped its emergence, that this making figured the conditions for the New Poor Law and the workhouse. To make the rural worker as a biopolitical subject they first had to be rendered as 'other', not just in terms of status, occupation, even class, but in terms of their bodily being different. The pauper body had to be made before it was classified and governed. This process had a deeper history – the practice of badging the poor was supported in law from 1697, but the discourse of badging or marking the poor by way of deterrent had roots in the sixteenth century[27] – but ultimately found consistent voice in the very debates on the old poor laws and the condition of the labourer of which the New Poor Law and the biopolitical institution of the New Poor Law workhouse were the policy precipitates.

Malthus and the biopolitical population

In moving for a second reading of the Poor Law Amendment Bill on 21 July 1834, Lord Chancellor Henry Brougham systematically addressed the arguments of those who defended the old poor laws. Having considered, and dismissed, the case that the system protected the character of the labourer and prevented them from becoming 'a mere beggar of alms', Brougham moved to consider the case, as he saw it, that the laws of Elizabeth offered the only means of 'effectually checking or preventing an increase of population':

> I verily think, that the history of human errors can produce no parallel to the mistake into which these learned and ingenious persons have fallen. If you had to seek out the most efficacious means of removing every prudential check to population – nay, if you wished to accelerate its march by a wilful, I might almost say, a wicked, encouragement to heedless and imprudent marriages, and by a premium for numbers of children – you could not devise any more perfect than are afforded by the Poor-laws, as administered in this country. What is the language they speak to the peasant? – 'Here is a fund at your command – you have only to marry – only to get children – and here is a fund for the support of yourselves and your children, to be doled out in proportion to their numbers.'[28]

The evidence for this was provided by 'the collection of a mass of evidence, the largest, the most comprehensive, the most important, and the most interesting, that perhaps was ever collected upon any subject', but the philosophical case was made by Rev. Malthus. Effusive in his praise, Brougham implored that

> When I mention talent, learning, humanity – the strongest sense of public duty, the most amiable feelings in private life, the tenderest and most humane disposition which ever man was adorned with – when I speak of one the ornament of the society in which he moves, the delight of his own family, and not less the admiration of those men of letters and of science amongst whom he shines the first and brightest – when I speak of one of the most enlightened, learned, and pious ministers whom the Church of England ever numbered amongst her sons – I am sure every one will apprehend that I cannot but refer to Mr Malthus.

Malthus' *Essay on the Principle of Population* was, Brougham went on, 'one of the greatest additions to political philosophy'.[29] If those who drafted the Elizabethan Poor Law 'were not adepts in political science' – 'they could not foresee that a Malthus would arise to enlighten mankind upon that important, but as yet ill-understood, branch of science' – they were guilty of separating labour and the reward of labour.[30] The poor laws, as they stood, provided a disincentive to labour which duly ruined the character of the labourer, and through Speenhamland-like allowances provided an encouragement to procreate without regard for the consequences.

> 'Take no trouble of providing for your child' – to the child, 'Undertake not the load of supporting your parent – throw away none of your money on your unfortunate brother or sister – all these duties the public will take on

itself.' It is, in truth, one of the most painful and disgusting features of this law, that it has so far altered the nature of men.[31]

As Brougham and others saw it, Malthus was right. While his arguments are so well known that it is not necessary to sketch them in detail, some points are worth iterating. First, Malthus was not the first prophet to proclaim the dangers of exponential population growth. Fellow clergyman Joseph Townsend's 1786 *Dissertation on the Poor Laws* made the connection between poor relief and population growth explicit:

> When industry and frugality keep pace with population, or rather when population is *only* the consequence of these, the strength and riches of a nation will bear proportion to the number of citisens: but when the increase is *unnatural and forced*, when it arises only from a community of goods, it tends to poverty and weakness [emphasis added].[32]

The focus of Townsend's ire was Gilbert's Act of 1782, which was supposedly overly generous in its treatment of the poor in new 'humane' workhouses. Under such a system, the poor were provided, as Townsend saw it, with food when they would otherwise be unable to procure it. The result would inevitably be population growth, for as 'long as food is plenty, they will continue to increase and multiply'.[33] He went on:

> Hunger will tame the fiercest animals, it will teach decency and civility, obedience and subjection, to the most perverse. In general it is only hunger which can spur and goad them [the poor] on to labour; yet our laws have said they shall never hunger.[34]

This went beyond metaphor. The poor, in Townsend's conception, were actually beasts.[35]

Second, while one of the spurs for Malthus to take up his pen was the debates on the poor laws in the 1790s (on which see below), the direct spur to action was the recently published essays by William Godwin and the Marquis de Condorcet, both of whom had advanced utopian theories on the subject of human progress.[36] Third, there is very little in the first edition of the *Essay* that deals explicitly with the poor laws. As Mark Blaug put it, on the subject of Malthus' objection to the old poor law '[i]t is simply that not much can be said'.[37] Subsequent generations of poor law historians have focused, one might almost say obsessively, on Malthus' claim that Speenhamland-style payments 'afford[ed] a direct, constant and systematical encouragement to marriage, by removing from each individual that heavy responsibility ... for bringing beings into the world which he could not support', variably finding evidence to support or to rebut his theory.[38]

Fourth, whatever the specific genealogy, influence and precise nature of Malthus' contributions, what ultimately matters is the way in which his ideas became enmeshed in the fabric of the debate about the future of poor relief in England and Wales. The 'popularization of Malthus', as James Huzel puts it, was not just a function of his ideas being taken up by political economists, Benthamists and other poor law reformers, but also a product of the way in which Malthusianism assumed a totemic and toxic status amongst radical politicians.[39] While this is not the place to offer a detailed consideration of the ways in which Malthus' ideas were consumed and critiqued by Cobbett and other radicals, it is important to note that such radical and popular interest rested on Malthus' placing of the pauper body at the centre of his prescription. The 'check-population parson', to use Cobbett's tag, did not see the individual human body, indeed in true biopolitical style was not concerned with the individual body, but instead sought to act on all pauper bodies to effect a regulation of the population. Discouraged from marriage and denied the means to populate, the poor were governed not as individuals, families and communities but rendered as the abstract body, or rather its *surface*, disciplined and regulated. To Cobbett this was an act 'of greater cruelty than any recorded in the history of the massacre of St Bartholomew'; to tell the 'destitute working-man [sic], that "he hath no claim upon the community for even the smallest portion of food"' made Malthus 'brutal'.[40]

If the parliamentary debates over the future of the poor laws in 1834 represented the highpoint of Malthusian thinking in public life, the post-Napoleonic Wars period was, as Peter Dunkley has it, the 'heyday of Malthusian, abolitionist sentiment'.[41] The sharply rising population in the 1810s and 1820s (rising in England from 9,538,827 in 1811 to 11,261,427 in 1821 and then again to 12,992,297 in 1831) combined with the post-war agrarian depression and dramatic increase in the national cost of poor relief to stir both reformist and abolitionist rhetoric, with Malthus providing the intellectual rationale. Of course there were other influences, not least in the form of the ideas of Bentham and more broadly in the market 'logics' of political economy.[42] Nor should we forget that the *Essay* was widely reviled – and not just by radical politicians but by many across the political spectrum and from opposing walks of life. In the words of James Bonar, 'for thirty years it rained refutations'.[43] The precise influence of Malthus on the abolition of the old poor laws and the making of the new remains a subject of conjecture,[44] but it is beyond doubt that the Malthusian case that Speenhamland-style payments 'afford[ed] a direct, constant and systematical encouragement to marriage, by removing from each individual that heavy responsibility ... for bringing beings into the world', had powerful support in parliament and beyond.[45]

If one has to look very hard in the Poor Law Commissioners' *Report* (and appendices) of 1834 to find explicit mention of Malthus – the Reverend was mentioned six times, and not once by the Commissioners in the report proper but rather in the appendices by virtue of responses from those parish worthies surveyed[46] – the influence of Malthus' *Essay* permeated the analysis offered therein. As is well known, the position established in the first edition of the *Essay* published in 1798 was abolitionist: only the repeal of the poor laws would 'give liberty and freedom of action to the peasantry of England'.[47] In place would be a network of county 'deterrent workhouse' where 'the fare should be hard', although Malthus later backtracked even on this idea due to the potential impact on the availability and price of food for the 'independent' poor.[48] Yet as Anne Digby has detailed, Malthus softened his prescription in subsequent decades, both shifting his position on the settlement laws – they should be retained due to concerns that an increased supply of cottages might act as an encouragement to marriage – and by the late 1820s even in relation to maintaining statutory relief to the aged, infirm and children.[49] It is a combination of the 'principles of population' and the policy pronouncements of late period Malthus – he died on 29 December 1834, days before the first New Poor Law union came into being – then that underpin the Commissioners' analysis.

As considered in other contexts in chapter four, in some ways we should not see the *Report* as establishing a new intellectual orthodoxy but rather as part of an existing genealogy. The influence of poor law debates on Malthus' thinking can be seen during the subsistence crisis of 1795–6. It was, after all, the publication of Prime Minister Pitt's 'Poor Bill', which would have given statutory relief 'as a matter of right and honour' to families with three or more children if it had been successful, which provided one of the spurs for Malthus to write the first edition of his famous *Essay*.[50] Samuel Whitbread, the major advocate of poor law reform in the Napoleonic period, having seen his minimum income bills fail in 1795 and again in 1800, proposed a further bill in 1807 that extended a complex system of rewards to 'encourage industry' and criminal penalties to the indigent, as well as a system of national education. This was no Malthusian abolition: indeed, if enacted Whitbread's bill would have represented an extension of the web of the poor relief system. Rather, in introducing his bill, Whitbread drew extensively on Malthus' writing, balancing generous praise of his theory ('I am desirous of doing the most ample justice to his patient and profound research … and to the soundness of the principles on which he proceeds. I believe them to be incontrovertible') with a critique of his policy prescriptions.[51] Malthus duly put pen to paper – this was his only pamphlet on the poor laws per se – in returning the critique and defending himself from the 'imputation of hardness of heart'.[52] Although there were aspects of Whitbread's bill that Malthus approved of, the idea that parishes should be permitted to use the rates to build cottages (or poor houses) in which the poor would be housed was subject to particular ire, this being a measure, as the parson saw it, that would act to encourage marriage and thus promote population growth.[53]

The first genuinely Malthusian attempt to reform the poor laws came in the form of the William Sturges Bourne-chaired 1817 Select Committee on the Poor Laws. Sturges Bourne was an abolitionist in the mode of Malthus. The *Report* did not make explicit reference to the *Essay* but was infused with

Malthusian thought. In debunking a system of statutory relief, the report asserted:

> [S]uch a compulsory contribution for the indigent, from the funds ori-ginally accumulated from the labour and industry of others, could not fail in process of time, with the increase of population which it is calculated to foster, to produce the unfortunate effect of abating those exertions of the labouring classes, on which, according to the nature of things, the happiness and welfare of mankind has been made to rest.

Ergo, the poor laws, as they stood, represented an affront to the real 'nature of things'. This reads as if from the pen of the parson himself.[54] If the result of the Select Committee represented reform rather than abolition, the main provisions of the two resulting Acts (in 1818 and 1819) represented a signifi-cant attempt not only to reduce the burden of relief but also to challenge the idea of universality through the appointment of Assistant Overseers and the election of select vestries.[55] Further, if the 1824 and 1828 select committees on the poor laws – these were more narrowly framed investigations of labourers' wages and the employment of able-bodied labourers from the poor rates respectively – made no reference to Malthus, the idea of 'surplus population' permeated both. The denunciation of roundsmen-type employment schemes made in the 1824 Report was in part justified by the Malthusian understanding that such schemes encouraged a 'surplus population' as labourers only had to marry to increase 'their pittance'. Indeed, such Malthusian language was writ large in the minutes of southern agrarian vestries. Those out of work were not only jobless but also surplus or supernumerary. The first use of such lan-guage in a vestry minute that I have uncovered occurred at Mere (Wiltshire), where those out of employ in November 1819 were considered to be 'super-fluous'. The first use of the derogatory 'surplus' occurred at Ninfield (East Sussex) in May 1821, from which time many other parishes, notably in the Weald where the problem of unemployment was most acute, began to use this loaded language.[56]

Of course, to claim that the New Poor Law was just a work of Malthusian thought is to deny the manifold other influences that informed both the debate and the Poor Law Amendment Act itself. But undoubtedly the Act is underpinned by Malthusian intent: the removal of all Speenhamland-type payments (including child allowances), the principle of less eligibility, the aim to withdraw out-relief, separate wards for men and women (thus liter-ally preventing paupers from procreating) and the implementation of 'bare life' workhouse dietaries. If controlling the level of the population was a sec-ondary concern, the New Poor Law was concerned with the biopolitical regulation of the population.

Cobbett's objection to Malthus and his fellow population 'feelosophers' ultimately rested on the unwritten but implicit claim in the *Essay* that the poor were somehow different from other members of the population, feckless individuals with no regard for their wellbeing or future who married and populated according only to when and how much the vestry was prepared to dole out, little more than hungry and carnal automatons. To Cobbett, labouring people had a domestic predilection for large families. This notion was supported both by scripture (which demanded procreation) and nature through 'the very first and most imperative laws' of sexual instinct.[57] To legislate against this way of being was, to quote Ian Dyck, a 'wholesale denial of the labourer's right to sexual expression'. As Cobbett saw it this was 'another conspiracy against labouring people', and something that rural workers needed to understand.[58] And through the medium of his influential and widely read *Political Register* – where Malthus' ideas were reviled and regularly refuted – and his 1820 satirical play 'Surplus Population', Cobbett did his best to make sure that his audience understood. Whether Malthus was regularly a subject of conversation in rural taprooms is perhaps a moot point, but Cobbett evidenced some effect of his mission. As a correspondent to the *Register* put it in June 1831:

> Those who have been in the habit of calling us (the poor people) the '*swinish multitude*', take it for granted that our propensities to procreation are precisely the same sort of those of pigs, and that of course, allowing us to indulge in the gratification of those propensities would be the means of overstocking this country with paupers; which are creatures of a far more offensive description to the '*feelosofers*' than even swine are. You have shown us how we became a 'swinish multitude', how we became paupers in your Protestant Reformation; and now you have beautifully shown us that the '*data*' of these feelosofers have been assumed in gross ignorance...[59]

Thus if the written Malthus provided the philosophical basis for the biopolitical policies and spaces of the New Poor Law, the attendant need to also make biopolitical subjects made it necessary to render the poor rural worker as other, not just in terms of status, occupation or even class, but in terms of their bodily being different. It is precisely this that Cobbett – and others – objected to in their between-the-lines reading of Malthus (and not enough between the lines in Townsend's earlier interjections), because these claims and discourse informed and coloured the debate about poor law reform. Whether the 'LABOURER' who wrote the above missive to Cobbett really was a labourer or not – the eloquence of the letter is no reason to deny the attribution – what ultimately matters is that Cobbett highlighted a critical *becoming* ('You have shown us how we became a "swinish multitude"') that allowed for the poor to be kept in a state of bodily functioning but no more.[60]

This state of becoming was writ using the same devices – albeit in a different register – as the telling and making of enslaved peoples and other early colonial subjects. When the rural worker was made a biopolitical subject they became internal colonial subjects: the subaltern closest in, a distinct and decidedly bestial race. Indeed, the making as different, as a race, was necessary as a precondition under the New Poor Law to grant the moral consent to control pauper bodies and, therefore, to experiment with forms of bodily control and the biopolitical negation of individual agency.

The labourer reduced

By the middle of the nineteenth century agricultural workers remained the largest – and dominant – occupational group, a situation only decisively overturned by 1871.[61] England at mid-century was still a nation dominated by agriculture, a nation of landowning parliamentarians and agricultural workers. Indeed, even after the occupational and economic balance shifted and England had truly become an industrial nation there was, as Barry Sloan has put it, a paradox in that English national identity 'remained inseparably associated with the countryside and with ideals of rural life'.[62] A deeper paradox still is the fact that such representations – bucolic, idyllic tellings of the countryside – were at odds with popular representations of rural workers. The point is complex and riven with contradiction. For much of the eighteenth century rural labourers had been depicted as comic, idiotic figures, content and comfortable, objects and subjects of humour. From the end of the eighteenth century, and especially from the outbreak of the Napoleonic Wars, loyalist tellings of rural workers shifted from comedic to heroic, the labourer a subject of admiration as the productive backbone of the nation, the symbol of British identity and values. The countryside, so the point goes, was full of loyal and free John Bulls, their lives the polar opposite of their oppressed, shackled French cousins. This discourse mirrored a broader shift in representational practice rooted in a concern that the actuality of rural life should be depicted in poetry and painting, itself a reflection of a desire to assert British progress, productivity and harmony. As John Barrell notes, at the turn of the nineteenth century 'the image of wage-labourers, of a rural proletariat, selflessly and irremissively engaged in the back-breaking work of the fields was everywhere hinted at in paintings of farmworkers, but was very hard to represent' given that the actuality was hungry, haggard and dirty men (and women and children, though in this conception they are quite consciously written out). Thus the solution was to place the working body at a distance where it was tiny and powerless.[63]

The process of pictorially placing out of view mirrored the parallel process of the changing ways in which rural workers were thought of. Agricultural labourers – and their families – in the period beyond 1815 were increasingly seen as a problem: poor, workless, pauperised, poorly housed, dirty, uneducated and (ultimately) degenerate. As Alun Howkins has asserted, by the 1820s the labourer was no longer a subject of national pride, the sturdy, independent backbone of the nation, but instead subject to both derision and moralising pity. The fieldworker had become 'Hodge', 'a cross between hedge (where he spent much of his time…) and clod (the substance on his boots and in his brain)', as Jan Marsh has put it. As Mark Freeman has suggested, the 'Hodge' stereotype might never have been universal but it was the dominant representation of the labourer in the mid-nineteenth century, a conception shared not just by urban dwellers but also by the rulers of rural England and even some farmers too.[64]

Central to this discourse was the idea that 'know[ing] literally nothing', the 'clodhopper' might feel injustice but was unable to theorise it or do anything to alleviate it. As John Dent, Liberal MP and agriculturalist, put it, the labourer was not only 'unimaginative, ill-clothed, ill-educated, ill-paid, [and] ignorant of all that is taking place beyond his own village' – note the gendered language here – but also 'dissatisfied with his position and yet without energy or effort to improve it'.[65] Hodge was not originally an insult: the cognomen for agricultural workers dated back at least to Chaucer, who used it as a diminutive of the common countryman 'name' Roger. It was not until the mid-eighteenth century that it was used as a term of derision.[66] The shift to becoming a label of abuse was a function of the long-term decline in the fortunes of agricultural workers in the agrarian south and east, a trend evident from the 1780s but accelerating post-1815. As Snell notes, Hodge was a figure of the agrarian south, 'impoverished and stolidly comic', the latter a return to earlier depictions and best expressed in William Gardiner's comic verse *The Adventure of Hodge and the Monkey* (1852) wherein 'Hodge' and 'the clown' are synonyms.[67] The derisive use of the term was a representation not just of declining fortunes, the ragged, haggard state of agricultural workers placing them yet further culturally and bodily from their social betters, but also of a belief (in part a function of the former dynamic) that working rural men were only interested in wages and beer. Indeed, there was some truth in that wages had by the turn of the nineteenth century assumed primacy in determining the living standards of the rural poor.[68] Moreover, as waves of protest from 1800 through 1816 and 1822 to the Swing rising of 1830 attest, wages had also become the key driver of protest in the rural south and east.[69] But whatever the importance of wages, it was the creeping belief that, as Townsend put it in his 1786 *Dissertation*: 'The poor know little of the motives which stimulate the higher ranks to action – pride, honour, and ambition. In general it is only hunger which can spur and goad them on to labour.'[70] For the importance of wages read hunger, and for hunger read the reflexive workings of an inferior, an animal.

Hodge's home – beyond the hedge – was the English south and the counties of East Anglia, those places where industry was either decayed or decaying (or had never existed) and wages were depressed by the paucity of other employment opportunities beyond the agrarian at a time when agricultural fortunes were in long-term decline. In the northern counties, while housing was often just as wretched, wages were higher, a function of further employment opportunities in mining and industry, which in turn increased access to education.[71] Of course such broad regional generalisations hide a variety of local variations, but it is telling that Hodge was placed in the south and in particular in 'Wessex', where wages were lowest and conditions the most desperate. According to Thomas Hardy in his essay 'The Dorsetshire labourer', it was Dorset 'where Hodge in his most unmitigated form is supposed to reside'.[72] Hardy was not alone in such a reading. The many writings on Hodge invariably place him in the south and especially in the south-west; the northern labourer in comparison is written as a happy soul belonging to a noble group. Indeed, Richard Heath in his *The English Peasant* (1870) asserted that Sussex labourers were locked in 'superstition, ignorance, immorality, and poverty', the labourers of Devon locked in 'depression and hopelessness ... miserably housed and under-fed'. By contrast, those of Northumberland had better opportunities but were also happy due their being 'of a race which has dwelt for generations on the battle-field of English history'.[73]

Heath's study was one of several such investigations into the state of the rural poor from the 1870s through to 1914. Some were a response to the rise in agricultural unionism in the form of Joseph Arch's National Agricultural Labourer's Union, but in the main they were driven by a deepening sense of middle-class despair about, and disconnection from, rural workers. This was allied to the rise of social investigation, which found form in numerous publications on the plight and travails of Hodge. Some, such as Gardiner's *The Adventure of Hodge and the Monkey*, were mocking, even comedic. Some were deeply sympathetic but ultimately lacked real empathy, something Snell notes of both Hardy's novels and his journalistic writings: 'The Dorsetshire labourer' perpetuates the telling of the labourer as having an 'animal indifference' to his situation and the contempt of farmers and others.[74] Others made little attempt at empathy, starting from the perspective that the agricultural labourer was unknowable. Their prescriptions were based on what George Sturt labelled the 'objective' method, viewing the labourer with biologists' eyes 'as though they were animals'.[75]

For Richard Jefferies writing in 1880, Hodge – the eponymous figure of Jefferies' book *Hodge and His Masters* – was:

> utterly indifferent ... he makes no inquiry to understand about this or that, and shows no desire to understand ... Something in his attitude – in the immobility, the almost animal repose of limb, something in the expression of his features, the self-contained oblivion, so to say, suggests an Oriental absence of aspiration....

Or as the *Morning Chronicle*'s correspondent for the rural districts put it, the labourer's manner when accosted was 'timid and shrinking' and the distance 'greater than should separate any two classes of men'. Perhaps Jefferies' manner of putting on a Wiltshire dialect and labouring drag was deeply disconcerting for his putative subjects, though.[76]

In earlier writings we hear similar claims but the frame of reference is different. To the clerical reformer of rural hiring fairs Rev. John Eddowes, vicar of Garton-upon-the-Wolds in the East Riding of Yorkshire, the labourer was 'utterly neglected':

> Philanthropists have pleaded for the negro in chains ... legislators have emancipated the slave ... But scarce a voice has been raised in behalf of the country labourer ... His cry for help – for release from a slavery as real, if not as bitter, as the negro's ... has been deep, not loud, and therefore has not been listened to.[77]

The labourers' lot was carried silently, or vented in acts of drunkenness in the village alehouse or – though quite what evidence Eddowes had of this is unclear – in incest.

> His work is in the fields or farm yard all day long: it is laborious, and performed often in solitude and silence. He is not educated: he cannot enjoy the most interesting book, of even the newspaper: village politics are the only politics he cares to discuss: of the great questions which agitate the nation, he knows literally nothing.[78]

The implication is plain enough. The labourer had been reduced – adapted even, in a Darwinian sense – to become something of only reflexive response, rooted in the fields and farmyards, *lex loci*, a tribe. For Eddowes and other reformers, whatever their intentions, labourers had become, in the words of Richard Jefferies writing in the *Morning Chronicle* in January 1850, 'A physical scandal, a moral enigma, an intellectual cataleptic'.[79]

The brute creation

Whatever the differences, the discourses delineated in the works of early writers on the condition of (southern) agricultural labourers reflected generally held opinions among labourers' social betters. Their tone and language were no different from newspaper reporters and letter writers, or witnesses to parliamentary committees. Indeed, by the time of Heath, Sturt and Hardy this was a well-established discourse. As the editor of *Keene's Bath Journal* put it in relation to the state of the labouring poor during the winter of 1828–9, it was not so much the experience of unemployment that generated resentments but the fact that labourers were 'obliged to work harder by far than the worse treated slaves in the West Indies, for parish pay'.[80] Poor rural workers knew this too, and used the same language. The 'petition' of the poor of the parish to the 'Gentlemen of Burwash' (Sussex) sent during Swing related that:

> Sometimes If a Man any ways affronted [assistant overseer] Freeman he would send a man from one side or an End of the parish to the other to be revenged of him & then Laugh at him for his Slavery.[81]

If, as E.P. Thompson claimed in *The Making of the English Working Class*, being of a class was not available to the cognitive system of rural workers in the decades of the nineteenth century,[82] they *were* cognisant not only of their degradation but also their becoming racial subjects. This might in part be a function of Cobbett's oft-made allusion to the relative conditions of English labourers and enslaved peoples in the West Indies – the repeated line being that 'the slave in the West Indies was in a better condition'[83] – but also reflected the experience of everyday life. As a petition penned by the labourers of the dockland community of Queenborough on the Isle of Sheppey in August 1829 put it: 'We can work, we wish to work, we will work, but we cannot work as slaves hired by the Man.'[84]

As Cobbett believed, ratepayers viewed labourers 'not as men ... but merely as animals made for their service and sport'.[85] Labourers and their families were just another form of what we might understand as 'lively capital'. They existed somewhere on the same spectrum as livestock, working animals and slaves as things to be applied and controlled – and certainly at a lower point than expensive draught horses which, as Cobbett noted, often had better living conditions and diets than labourers (a variation on his 'slaves' trope).[86] The idea that labourers were a form of living capital, living labouring machines, was perhaps best attested by the scheme practised in some Sussex parishes in the period before Swing of harnessing workless labourers to wagons to draw stone on the roads. As the Sussex grandee the Duke of Richmond admitted, speaking in the House of Lords on 25 February 1830, 'the once happy peasantry of England' had through such schemes had been 'degraded to the state of the brute creation'.[87]

It is no surprise, then, that the same discourses and language can be found throughout the report and appendices of the so-called Poor Law Report of 1834. Edwin Chadwick and Nassau Senior's notoriously ideological perversion of the evidence of the 1832 'Rural queries' was used to smooth the passage of the New Poor Law. Here we have the writing of the labourer not only as a slave – both as a critique of the old poor law and in other unreflexive ways – but as belonging to a distinct race. Thus, as assistant commissioner Captain Chapman noted of parish apprentices, '[they] may be said to be a slave attached to the soil ... in some instances they are treated worse than slaves. They almost universally prove worthless, depraved and abandoned characters'; and Senior and Chadwick could coldly remark that labourers had 'a slave's security for subsistence without his liability for punishment'.[88] Claims to racial classification were made in a variety of contexts. Oxfordshire magistrate and Dorset landowner D.O.P. Okeden noted in his report that 'the illegal perversion of the Poor Laws' had created 'the present race', while the parish of Potterne (Wiltshire) was 'filled with a very discontented and turbulent race'.[89] The report of C.H. Cameron and John Wrottesley wrote of the superior 'race' of the 'Northumbrian peasant' in comparison to the 'English peasant of the southern counties, and the Irish peasant' who readily gave way to carnal pleasures, a reference to Malthus' critique of the poor laws as a 'systematic encouragement' to earlier marriage.[90] J.J. Richardson similarly remarked of Kettering (Northamptonshire) that 'a race of regular paupers has sprung up, insolent and idle to the last degree'.[91] Those who lived on the London fringe and subsisted in the marshland communities were a 'race lower than any yet known'. As the Lambeth correspondent relayed literally without recourse to metaphor, 'If you will have marshes and stagnant waters, you will there have suitable animals; and the only way of getting rid of them is by draining the marshes.' Reform the territory, transform the population. Most tellingly, the tag in the margin against this 'evidence' read: 'No conceivable degradation to which the species might not be reduced by giving facilities for a degraded breed.'[92]

None of this is to say that there was a universal belief that improvement was no longer possible; indeed most such writings in the 1840s and 1850s were treatises on the improvement of, as Wiltshire agriculturalist Henry Tucker put it in 1854, the human 'implement'.[93] But in detailing how improvement was possible it was necessary to assert the base level to which the labourer had sunk. As a report on the 'intellectual and moral condition' of the southern and western labourer published in the *Farmers' Magazine* in October 1850 put it:

> Taking the adult class of agricultural laborers, it is almost impossible to exaggerate the ignorance in which they live, and move, and have their being. As they work in the fields, the external world has some hold upon them, through the medium of their sense; but to all the higher exercises of intellect they are perfect strangers. You cannot address one of them without being at once painfully struck with the intellectual darkness which enshrouds him. There is, in general, neither speculation in his eyes, nor intelligence in his countenance; the whole expression is more that of an animal, than of a man … These are the traits which I can affirm them to possess, as a class, after having come in contact with many hundreds of Farm Laborers.[94]

The language here is not of class, indeed the writer (in a sentence later picked up by Jefferies) notes that there is a greater distance between himself and the labourers 'than *should* separate any two classes of men'. Class here is used reflexively, and what meaning it holds relates not to collective self-consciousness – for that ability is denied – but to ancient ideas of orders. As Tucker put it, 'He seems to belong to an inferior class of beings, when compared with the factory operative, the worker in the mines, the fishermen, the artisan, or the stable boy … [T]hey are aliens to shame, and strangers to the common decencies of life.'[95] Given to incest, intermarrying and witchcraft, the labourer is set apart from the true working classes and instead inscribed in exactly the same way and in exactly the same terms as colonial others. The labourer is the internal subaltern told biologically, intellectually and morally as racial other.

Race and rural England

By the 1830s the use of race as a popular idiom and discourse was firmly established. The constant references to race and racial signifiers in William Howitt's quasi-ethnographic *The Rural Life of England*, first published in 1838 and a hugely popular and influential text in determining prevalent attitudes and representations of rural England, was testament to the pervasiveness and popularity of racialised thinking.[96] Some of the wider influences are obvious. Early nineteenth-century rural elites were, of course, alive to debates on slave ownership and abolitionism. Self-interest concerning the colonial, slave-produced origins of so much wealth in rural England combined with ideas of race and practices of racism. Such debates also played on popular confusion over the status of enslaved, black peoples – whether present in the metropole, or placed, and imagined, in the colonies. Were they the same sort of humans and thus deserving of the same rights, or were they a different sort of human with different capabilities and functioning, not deserving or needing of the same rights and powers? But while race was in part understood – and given popular form – through reference to these varying scales of colonial circuits, there was a tension between the imperial trope of white, European superiority and the traditional Christian monogenist position that all races were as one, whatever differences in appearance there might be.[97]

Indeed, race was understood in reference to the need to make sense not only of colonial subjects at a distance but also those in the metropole. The language of race was permeated by a far deeper history of co-presence. The Christian concept of the 'Great Chain of Being' allowed for all things to be related, but provided a justification for racial difference: the 'Negro' was thus related to Europeans but existed in the chain of being closer to apes. Thus, when Africans were significantly present again in Britain from the sixteenth century – large numbers of black slaves had earlier been brought to Britain by the Romans – they were subject to racisms, with African people being mythologised as brutish, satanic and bestially concupiscent.[98] The lack of scientific evidence to support the idea that the 'Negro' was the link between apes and White Europeans provided a driver in the early nineteenth century of the rise of comparative anatomy, notably regarding cranial size, and the associated shift from monogenist thought to polygenism, or – put differently – from thinking about human difference as social to constructing difference biologically within a hierarchy of races.[99] The shift to polygenist thinking in the early nineteenth century – James Prichard's *Researches into the Physical History of Man* (1813) was the last major monogenist text[100] – was also fed by anxieties in the metropole as to who the British were. The need to position Britons as different – and better – than the Napoleonic French, than the poor Irish, than the subjects to be found in other colonies, was manifest in both the polygenist positioning of non-Britons (especially if they were black) as other and claims to an entirely specious ancient ancestry for the peoples of

Britain. They were Anglo-Saxons, imposed on by the Norman yoke, who by birth and the ancient lineage of dwelling on the island were the true natives of the land. And the sciences of comparative anatomy and phrenology (and from the late nineteenth century eugenics) and anthropology provided the tools, languages and 'proof' not only of racial difference but also that there was a hierarchy of races, a hierarchy of bodily worth.[101]

This intellectual and philosophical funk can be seen in the treatment of gypsies, who were at best rendered as picturesque subjects but more typically classified as apart from settled 'natives', a different breed and race. If such discourses pervade Hazlitt's *The Rural Life of England*, then Hazlitt's influence on Emily Brontë's *Wuthering Heights*' ambiguous take on race is no less profound. The protagonist Heathcliff is positioned as a liminal, uncertain and unsettling figure, deliberately racially indeterminate. Race was deliberately used as a linguistic device, a disruptive trope, something that challenged and at the same time spoke to the classificatory impulses of late Hanoverian Britain. This works for the reason that it played on readers' own uncertainties and spoke to the cultural politics of the day.[102] Indeed, as Laura Tabili has shown, colonised peoples – and this can be extended to all groups made subaltern by colonising forces – became visible, and hence a problem, when they challenged their position. Ergo, discourses of racial inferiority became necessary tools developed 'as ideological justifications for European domination and privilege'.[103]

Being at home with the Empire – to borrow from the title of Catherine Hall and Sonja Rose's book – represented the latest in an infinitely long line of encountering (and making) difference. As Tabili notes, 'British culture was never homogenous', nor was it 'consensually formed', being 'crosscut by class, gender, region, religion, sexuality and other power relations'.[104] Indeed, the peoples of Britain were – and are – a fusion of multiple waves of conquerors, invaders and migrants, all, in time, forgotten until such moment of crisis that difference was asserted (and manufactured). At such moments of crisis, where one 'people' was not so much singled out as made as different, race was made and racisms violently asserted. Thus the practice of making difference and the languages of racially declaring difference were deep-rooted. The point of difference from the early nineteenth century onward was that the effects of Empire meant that co-presence became not only more obviously discernible – in skin colour, language, accent, dress, religion, habits and customs – but also increasingly economically manifest.

The large numbers of Irish migrant workers seeking work and a better life away from the brutalising effects of imperial rule in Ireland meant that settled workers and migrants were thrown into competition. This was less obviously manifested in the rapidly industrialising towns of the Midlands and North, where growth accommodated modulated antagonism, but was violently realised in rural England where gangs of migrant Irish harvest workers undercut the already pitiable wages of local rural workers and were repeatedly subject to threats and attacks.[105] As Ryan Hanley has recently shown, what little we understand of, as he puts it, 'working-class racism' in early nineteenth-century Britain has tended to be polarised between, on the one hand, the romanticised radical position that working solidarities negotiated difference in a cosmopolitan 'Black Atlantic' and, on the other hand, a deeply entrenched nascent white working-class supremacy. The reality was more nuanced. As Hanley has shown, English radicalism was writ through with a functional racism that was predicated on an attempt to defend the British worker. Campaigns against slavery were a material and political diversion from relieving the suffering of the indigent poor. What started, then, as not being against emancipation became virulently racist, questioning 'the very humanity of enslaved and free Africans in the same pages that their plans for a politically and socially reformed Britain took shape'.[106] Such working-class racisms burgeoned in the 1830s and 1840s precisely because of, as Satnam Virdee has suggested, 'a growing antagonism between the English and the minority worker'.[107] If to assume that all labouring families perceived overseas migrants as fundamentally different from themselves is a fallacy, it is an important conclusion that race was not just made by elites but also fanned by radical thinkers and the experience of poverty, that – after Edward Said – inferiorisation was not just practised by the nobs but also by the plebs.[108]

And herein another spatiality was at play. As Nancy Stepan notes, the making of European empires was also tied up with the intensification of industrialisation and urbanisation in the metropole: hence brown and black non-industrial peoples tied to the soil were literally positioned as being backward.[109] It does not require a huge leap of imagination to apply such thinking to the emergent urban–rural divide in England (and Britain more widely). Those who toiled on the land, in the woods and in the mines were not only literally but also figuratively placed apart. Indeed, the places of the labourer were also often told as places apart, as beyond comprehension, as being terra incognita and terra nullius all at once.

Race was, in sum, increasingly a live issue in rural England. The turning of the imperial gaze back from the colonies onto England, with all the attendant tools of making racial difference through claims and representations of immorality and 'hygienic deficiency',[110] meant that race was also 'found' in the anthropological sense – that is to say made, conceived, represented, measured, defined – in the metropole. Meanwhile, to draw on Christine Kinealy's work on the colonised Irish, the theories of Charles Darwin (and others) would go on to give depictions of racial difference 'the patina of scientific legitimacy', and the depictions of popular and political writers like Dickens and Engels all accepted and 'perpetuated racialised tellings of the Irish as culturally inferior'.[111] The same, in a different register but using the exactly the same tropes, devices and claims, was true of the English labourer.

Nally, in his analysis of the ways in which English commentators racialised the Irish poor, notes comparisons with colonial others, comments on appearance and habits, lack of learning, morality and the state of their dwelling.[112] All such claims, as we have seen, were also made of the English rural labourer. Moreover, we also see the same prescriptions: emigration, institutionalisation, bodily control, attempts to reduce birth rates and, for those left, elementary education. The making of the English labourer as a racial subject was rooted in, after the anthropologist Nicholas Thomas' conception of racism, the 'apprehension of types, distinctions, criteria or assessing proximity and distance, and in its technical applications – in, for instance, notions stipulating that certain forms of labour are appropriate to one race but not another'.[113] And one might add hunger to this list of apprehensions. As Lord Stanhope put it in a letter to the *Morning Chronicle* in December 1849, 'it is physically impossible to convert an agricultural labourer into a mechanic, or *vice versa*'.[114] In all of this hunger was at once a ploy, a necessary condition of the racialised population that needed to be controlled and remade, and also a biopolitical device in that very act of remaking.

By conceiving of the poor as a separate race, New Poor Law administrators and others were given moral consent to control the bodies of claimants, to experiment with forms of bodily control and the negation of individual agency in the making of new subjects. By conceiving of labouring families as not only different in class terms but also different in terms of bodies, intellect, ambition and morals, it legitimated – in exactly the same way that slaves had been created as distinct subjects, and as forms of colonial governance legitimised rule over colonised peoples – and gave moral consent to experiment in the making of new subjects of state rule. The state-led social experiments from the mid-1830s were attempts to make a better race of labourers and to put those who refused to yield into a space beyond life.

These intentions were only in part achieved, and that in large part through state-sponsored attempts to 'shovel out paupers' to the Americas. For many, the New Poor Law had removed hope altogether, acting when work was especially scarce to further erode relations between labourers and farmers, as evidenced through a huge upturn in the use of the weapons of rural terror from the late 1830s through to the late 1840s. But if labourers remained, in the eyes of their social betters, sullen, insolent and bestial, this was further fuel for reformers, evidence that more needed to be done. As William Hicke put it in his 1855 treatise on how to reform the 'moral, intellectual and physical conditions' of the labourer, having left education at a tender age as 'an animal machine' the labourer pursues life with no guidance beyond 'strong animal instincts and propensities'. The lack of education and animal-like living conditions precluded the labourer being anything other than born to be 'beasts that perish'. Hicke hoped that labourers learning 'habits of cleanliness and a systematic mode of living' would be the 'commencement of a better race of men'.[115]

Notes

1 M. Foucault, *Society Must Be Defended: Lectures at the Collège de France, 1975–76*, trans. D. Macey (New York: Picador, 2003), pp. 252–3.

2 On sovereign power see: M. Foucault, *The History of Sexuality: Volume I*, trans. R. Hurley (London: Penguin, 1981), esp. parts 4 and 5.

3 D. Nally, 'The biopolitics of food provisioning', *Transactions of the Institute of British Geographers*, 36:1 (2011), 38.

4 Foucault, *Society Must Be Defended*, p. 241.

5 C. Mills, *Biopolitics* (Chichester: Wiley, 2018), pp. 18, 25–8.

6 T. Lemke, M. Casper and L.J. Moore, *Biopolitics: An Advanced Introduction* (New York: NYU Press, 2011), p. 4.

7 Note that the idea of the idealised body remained, perversely, an abstract notion, rooted as much in surfaces (clean, keen, strong, deferent) or in antithesis as in measurement.

8 See for instance K. Levitan, *A Cultural History of the British Census: Envisioning the Multitude in the Nineteenth Century* (Basingstoke: Palgrave, 2011); T. McCormick, 'Political arithmetic and sacred history: Population thought in the English Enlightenment, 1660–1750', *Journal of British Studies*, 52:4 (2013), 829–57; M. Bulmer, K. Bales and K. Kish Sklah (eds), *The Social Survey in Historical Perspective, 1880–1940* (Cambridge: Cambridge University Press, 1991).

9 A.M. Lilienfeld, *Times, Places, and Persons: Aspects of the History of Epidemiology* (Baltimore, MD: Johns Hopkins University Press, 1980); E.V. McCollum, *A History of Nutrition: The Sequence of Ideas in Nutrition Investigations* (Boston, MA: Houghton Mifflin, 1957).

10 Foucault, *Society Must be Defended*, p. 252. Also see S. Ball, *Foucault, Power, and Education* (London: Routledge, 2013), p. 60.

11 Lemke et al., *Biopolitics*, p. 5.

12 A. Baldwin, 'Whiteness and futurity: Towards a research agenda', *Progress in Human Geography*, 36:2 (2012), 173.

13 M. Foucault, *The Order of Things: An Archaeology of the Human Sciences*, trans. A. Sheridan (*New York: Vintage*, 1973), p. 139.

14 Nally, 'The biopolitics of food provisioning', 37.

15 Ibid.; S.L. Morgensen, 'The biopolitics of settler colonialism: Right here, right now', *Settler Colonial Studies*, 1:1 (2011), 52; D. Harvey, 'The "new imperialism": Accumulation by dispossession', *Actuel Marx*, 1 (2004), 71–90.

16 D. Nally, 'Governing precarious lives: Land grabs, geopolitics, and food security', *Geographical Journal*, 181 (2015), 340–9; D. Nally and S. Taylor, 'The politics of self-help: The Rockefeller Foundation, philanthropy and the "long" Green Revolution', *Political Geography*, 49:1 (2015), 51–63; D. Nally, *Human Encumbrances: Political Violence and the Great Irish Famine* (Notre Dame, IN: University of Notre Dame Press, 2011); D. Nally, '"That coming storm": The Irish poor law, colonial biopolitics, and the great famine', *Annals of the Association of American Geographers*, 98:3 (2008), 714–41.

17 Nally, '"That coming storm"'; D. Keen, *The Benefits of Famine: a Political Economy of Famine and Relief in Southwestern Sudan, 1983–1989* (Princeton, NJ: Princeton University Press, 1994), p. 77.
18 Nally, '"That coming storm"', 716.
19 A. Lester and F. Dussart, *Colonization and the Origins of Humanitarian Governance: Protecting Aborigines Across the Nineteenth-century British Empire* (Cambridge: Cambridge University Press, 2014); S. Reid-Henry, *The Political Origins of Inequality: Why a More Equal World is Better for Us All* (Chicago, IL: Chicago University Press, 2015).
20 On the making of the Irish Poor Law, see: P. Gray, *The Making of the Irish Poor Law, 1815–43* (Manchester: Manchester University Press, 2009).
21 M. de Nie, *The Eternal Paddy: Irish Identity and the British Press, 1798–1882* (Madison, WI: University of Wisconsin Press, 2004), pp. 5–6; R.C. Shipkey, *Robert Peel's Irish Policy: 1812–1846* (New York: Garland, 1987), pp. 472–7; D. Nally, '"Eternity's commissioner": Thomas Carlyle, the Great Irish Famine and the geopolitics of travel', *Journal of Historical Geography*, 32:2 (2006), 319.
22 Elsewhere in the same volume Macaulay used stronger language still: 'They never worked till they felt the sting of hunger. They were content with accommodation inferior to that which, in happier countries, was provided for domestic cattle … Even within a few miles of Dublin, the traveller, on a soil the richest and most verdant in the world, saw with disgust the miserable burrows out of which squalid and half naked barbarians stared wildly at him as he passed': T.B. Macaulay, *The History of England from the Accession of James the Second* (London: Longman, 1849), vol. 2, pp. 100–1, 106, 332.
23 Foucault, *Society Must Be Defended*, pp. 254–5.
24 Mills, *Biopolitics*, p. 17.
25 S. Hall, 'Race, articulation, and societies structured in dominance', in H.A. Baker Jr, M. Diawara and R.H. Lindeborg (eds), *Black British Cultural Studies: A Reader* (Chicago, IL: Chicago University Press, 1996), pp. 16–60.
26 S. Virdee, *Racism, Class and the Racialised Outsider* (Basingstoke: Palgrave, 2014), pp. 14–15.
27 S. Hindle, 'Dependency, shame and belonging: Badging the deserving poor, c. 1550–1750', *Cultural and Social History*, 1:1 (2004), 6–35.
28 *Hansard*, 3rd ser. (1834), cols 223, 224 (21 July).
29 Ibid., 225; T. Malthus, *An Essay on the Principle of Population* (London: J.M. Dent and Sons, 1803, 2nd edition).
30 *Hansard*, 3rd ser. (1834), col. 230 (21 July).
31 Ibid., 229.
32 J. Townsend, *A Dissertation on the Poor Laws: By a Well-wisher to Mankind*, ed. Ashley Montagu (Berkeley, CA: University of California Press, 1971), p. 42.
33 Ibid., p. 38.
34 Ibid., p. 23.
35 On Townsend see R.G. Cowherd, *Political Economists and the Poor Law: A Historical Study of the Influence of Classical Economists on the Formation of Social Welfare Policy* (Athens, OH: Ohio University Press, 1977).

36 On these influences see R. Mayhew, *The Life and Legacies of an Untimely Prophet* (Cambridge, MA: The Belknap Press of Harvard University Press, 2014), ch. 2.

37 M. Blaug, 'The myth of the old poor law and the making of the new', *Journal of Economic History*, 23:2 (1963), 73.

38 Malthus, *Essay*, iv.v.9. For the latest instalment in social history's longest-running saga – and for a useful summary of the debate – see: S. Williams, *Poverty, Gender and Life-cycle under the English Poor Law, 1760–1834* (Woodbridge: Boydell & Brewer, 2011), esp. pp. 1–20.

39 J.P. Huzel, *The Popularization of Malthus in Early Nineteenth-Century England: Martineau, Cobbett and the Pauper Press* (Farnham: Ashgate, 2006), esp. chs 3 and 4.

40 Cited in ibid., ch. 3, notes 1 and 15.

41 P. Dunkley, 'Whigs and paupers: The reform of the English poor laws, 1830–1834', *Journal of British Studies*, 20:2 (1981), 130.

42 A. Brundage, *The Making of the New Poor Law: The Politics of Inquiry, Enactment, and Implementation, 1832–1839* (New Brunswick, NJ: Rutgers University Press, 1978), ch. 5.

43 J. Bonar, *Malthus and His Work* (London: Macmillan, 1885), p. 2.

44 See Huzel, *The Popularization of Malthus*; Mayhew, *Malthus*, esp. chs 3 and 4.

45 Malthus, *Essay*, iv.v.9; Brundage, *The Making of the New Poor Law*, p. 8.

46 BPP, 1834 (44), 'Report from His Majesty's commissioners for inquiring into the administration and practical operation of the Poor Laws Poor Law Report' (hereafter *Poor Law Report*), Appendix A, p. 50: Report of Capt. Chapman, Frome; Appendix B2, 172: reply of Thomas Hammond, vestry clerk, St. Andrew Holborn; Appendix C, 68–69c and 132c; Appendix D pp. 195–6: M. Gunston, Westbury. Also see Appendix C, 68–69c (regarding 'Home Colonies': tenants first employed might do well, but their children would 'greatly aggravate' the evil trying to be remedied and there would be much greater redundancy of population than before) and Appendix C, 132c (should prohibit marriage of minors by denying all recourse to the poor laws of such individuals, thus applying the principles that Malthus applies to all marriages).

47 Malthus, *Essay*, 1st edition, pp. 95–6.

48 A. Digby, 'Malthus and reform of the English Poor Law', in M. Turner (ed.), *Malthus and His Time* (London: Palgrave Macmillan, 1986), pp. 164–5.

49 Ibid., pp. 159, 164.

50 We know that Malthus did not publicly speak out against the Bill at the time, for no mention of it is made in what survives of his unpublished 1796 'pamphlet': The Crisis: *A View of the Present State of Great Britain, by a Friend to the Constitution* (London, 1796) and Bonar, *Malthus*, p. 30. On *The Crisis* see: D. Winch, *Riches and Poverty: An Intellectual History of Political Economy in Britain, 1750–1834* (Cambridge: Cambridge University Press, 1996), p. 253. On Pitt's Bill see J.R. Poynter, *Society and Pauperism: English Ideas on Poor Relief, 1795–1834* (London: Routledge, 1969), ch. 5.

51 Poynter, *Society and Pauperism*, pp. 62–76; Williams, *Poverty, Gender and Life-cycle*, pp. 94–5; House of Commons Debates, 19 February 1807, vol. 8, cc870.
52 T. Malthus, *A Letter to Samuel Whitbread, Esq. MP, on his Proposed Bill for the Amendment of the Poor Laws* (London: J. Johnson, 1807), p. 10.
53 Ibid., p. 10. On the ongoing debate and the failure of Whitbread's bill see Williams, *Poverty, Gender and Life-cycle*, p. 97.
54 BPP, 1817 (106), vol. 84, 'Report from the Select Committee of the House of Commons on the Poor Laws', p. 4.
55 On the operation of the 'Sturges Bourne' Acts see: S. Shave, *Pauper Policies: Poor Law Practice in England, 1780–1850* (Manchester: Manchester University Press, 2017), ch. 3.
56 BPP, Commons, 1824 (392), vol. 6, 'Report from the Select Committee on Labourers Wages', p. 4; Wiltshire and Swindon Record Office, 2944/78, Mere vestry minute, 1 November 1819; East Sussex County Record Office, PAR430/12/1, Ninfield vestry minute, 10 May 1821.
57 I. Dyck, *William Cobbett and Rural Popular Culture* (Cambridge: Cambridge University Press, 1992), pp. 102–3, note 118.
58 Ibid., p. 103.
59 *Cobbett's Weekly Political Register*, 11 June 1831.
60 Ibid.
61 BPP (1851), vol. 43, 'Census of Great Britain, 1851, Tables of the population and houses in the divisions, registration counties, and districts of England and Wales; in the counties, cities, and burghs of Scotland; and in the islands in the British seas', passim.
62 B. Sloan, 'An anxious discourse: English rural life and labour and the periodical press between the 1860s and the 1880s', Southampton Centre for Nineteenth-Century Research, Working Paper, November 2013, p. 1.
63 J. Barrell, 'Sportive labour: The farmworker in eighteenth century poetry and painting', in B. Short (ed.), *The English Rural Community: Image and Analysis* (Cambridge: Cambridge University Press, 1992), pp. 106–7, 126, 131.
64 J. Marsh, *Back to the Land: The Pastoral Impulse in Britain From 1880 to 1914* (London: Quartet Books, 1982), p. 60; M. Freeman, 'The agricultural labourer and the 'Hodge' stereotype, *c.* 1850–1914', *Agricultural History Review*, 49:2 (2001), 172–86. See also: A. Howkins, 'From Hodge to Lob: Reconstructing the English farm labourer, 1870–1914', in M. Chase and I. Dyck (eds), *Living and Learning: Essays in Honour of J.F.C. Harrison* (Aldershot: Ashgate: 1996), pp. 218–35; K.D.M. Snell, *Annals of the Labouring Poor: Social Change and Agrarian England, 1660–1900* (Cambridge: Cambridge University Press, 1985), pp. 5–14, 381–91.
65 J. Dent, 'The present condition of the English agricultural labourer', *Journal of the Royal Agricultural Society,* 2nd series, 7 (1871), 343–4, cited in Freeman, 'The agricultural labourer', 173–4.
66 Howkins, 'From Hodge to Lob', p. 218.
67 Snell, *Annals of the Labouring Poor*, p. 1; W. Gardiner, *The Adventure of Hodge and the Monkey: A Comic Tale* (London: T. Nonmus, 1852).

68 Snell, *Annals of the Labouring Poor*, p. 5; E. Fox Genovese, 'The many faces of the moral economy: A contribution to a debate', *Past & Present*, 58 (1973), 161–8.

69 C. Griffin, *Protest, Politics and Work in Rural England, 1700–1850* (Basingstoke: Palgrave, 2014), chs 5 and 6.

70 Townsend, *A Dissertation on the Poor Laws*, p. 15.

71 Freeman, 'The agricultural labourer', p. 174.

72 T. Hardy, 'The Dorsetshire labourer', *Longmans Magazine*, 2 (1883), 252.

73 R. Heath, *The English Peasant: Studies Historical, Local and Biographic* (Cambridge: Cambridge University Press, 2011/1893), pp. 191, 82, 86.

74 Snell, *Annals*, pp. 381, 388.

75 G. Sturt, *The Journals of George Sturt, 1890–1927*, vol. 2, ed. E.D. Mackerness (Cambridge: Cambridge University Press, 1967), p. 540; M. Freeman (ed.), *The English Rural Poor 1850–1914*, vol. 1 (London: Pickering and Chatto, 2005), p. 63.

76 R. Jefferies, *Hodge and His Masters* (London: Smith, Elder, 1890), p. 78; *Morning Chronicle*, 1 December 1849.

77 J. Eddowes, *The Agricultural Labourer as He Really is; or Village Morals in 1854* (Driffield: s.n., 1854), pp. 17–18. The conceptual parallels to the practice of lip-sewing are striking. For instance see Banu Bargu's recent paper on the practice in the context of the 'jungle' refugee camp in Calais, where lip-sewing has been used to symbolically highlight being deprived of a voice, when words spoken meet an audience with no ears: B. Bargu, 'The silent exception: Hunger striking and lip-sewing', *Law, Culture and the Humanities* (2017), 1–28.

78 Eddowes, *The Agricultural Labourer*, p. 13.

79 *Morning Chronicle*, 18 January 1850.

80 *Keene's Bath Journal*, 2 March 1829.

81 ESCRO, AMS 5995/3/12, Gentleman of Burwash to H.B. Curteis, Beckley, plus enclosure, 9 November 1830.

82 E.P. Thompson, *The Making of the English Working Class* (Harmondsworth: Penguin, 1968), p. 17.

83 *Cobbett's Weekly Political Register*, 9 May 1835.

84 TNA, HO 40/24, fo. 18, Petition forwarded to the Home Office from Queenborough, 8 August 1829.

85 Dyck, *William Cobbett*, p. 153.

86 W. Cobbett, *Rural Rides*, ed. I. Dyck (London: Penguin, 2001), pp. 214–15.

87 *Cobbett's Weekly Political Register*, 6 March 1830.

88 *Poor Law Report*, pp. 32, 432.

89 Ibid., pp. 281, 287.

90 Ibid., p. 428.

91 Ibid., p. 680.

92 Ibid., p. 1637 (Appendix A, Evidence of Lambeth).

93 H. Tucker, *An Address Upon the Condition of the Agricultural Labourer* (London: Longman, 1854), p. 5.

94 *Farmer's Magazine*, October 1850.

95 Tucker, *An Address*, pp. 8, 11.

96 W. Howitt, *The Rural Life of England* (London: Longman, 1838).
97 C. Hall, N. Draper, K. McClelland, K. Donington and R. Lang, *Legacies of British Slave-ownership: Colonial Slavery and the Formation of Victorian Britain* (Cambridge: Cambridge University Press, 2014); K. McKenzie, '"My voice is sold, & I must be a slave": Abolition rhetoric, British liberty and the Yorkshire elections of 1806 and 1807', *History Workshop Journal*, 64 (2007), 48–73. Here the influence of the Great Chain of Being, so central to centuries of Christian theorising on race, was central, on which see: A. Lovejoy, *The Great Chain of Being: A Study of the History of an Idea* (London: Routledge, 2009/1936), esp. chs 7–9.
98 C. Bressey, 'Cultural archaeology and historical geographies of the black presence in rural England', *Journal of Rural Studies*, 25:4 (2009), 386–95; I. Duffield, 'Skilled workers or marginalised poor? The African population of the UK 1812–1852', *Immigrants and Minorities* 12:3 (1993), 49–87; N. Stepan, *The Idea of Race in Science: Great Britain, 1800–1960* (Basingstoke: Macmillan, 1982), p. 8.
99 Stepan, *The Idea of Race in Science*, pp. 9–11.
100 J. Prichard, *Researches into the Physical History of Man*, ed. G. Stocking (Chicago, IL: Chicago University Press, 1973).
101 On the influence of eugenic thought in Britain see: M. Thomson, *The Problem of Mental Deficiency: Eugenics, Democracy, and Social Policy in Britain, c. 1870–1959* (Oxford: Oxford University Press, 1998).
102 Hazlitt, *Rural Life*, vol. 1, part 3, ch. 1, E. Brontë, *Wuthering Heights* (London: Thomas Cautley Newby, 1847); C. Heywood, 'Yorkshire slavery in Wuthering Heights', *Review of English Studies*, 38:150 (1987), 184–98.
103 L. Tabili, 'A homogenous society? Britain's internal 'others', 1800–present', in C. Hall and S.O. Rose (eds), *At Home with the Empire: Metropolitan Culture and the Imperial World* (Cambridge: Cambridge University Press, 2006), p. 59.
104 Ibid., p. 54.
105 D. MacRaild, *The Irish Diaspora in Britain, 1750–1939*, 2nd edition (Basingstoke: Palgrave, 2010), esp. chs 1 and 2. For attacks on Irish harvest workers see: Griffin, *Protest, Politics and Work*, pp. 33, 155.
106 R. Hanley, 'Slavery and the birth of working-class racism in England, 1814–1833', *Transactions of the Royal Historical Society*, 26 (2016), 123. For the classic reading of the 'progressive' position see: P. Linebaugh and M. Rediker, *The Many-Headed Hydra: The Hidden History of the Revolutionary Atlantic* (Cambridge: Cambridge University Press, 2000). One can think of a similar dynamic at play in John Murdoch's deliberate positioning of 'Highlanders' as a separate race: this was at once a response to inferiorisation and his making of a new form of radical Gaelic Highland nationalism against the homogenszing discourses and dispossessing practices of British nationalism in the late nineteenth century. J. Hunter, *The Making of the Crofting Community* (Edinburgh: John Donald, 1976), pp. 129–30.
107 Virdee, *Racism, Class and the Racialised Outsider*, p. 26.
108 On inferiorisation see: E. Said, *Orientalism: Western Representations of the Orient* (New York: Pantheon, 1978).

109 Stepan, *The Idea of Race*, pp. 4–5.
110 Tabili, 'A homogenous society?', p. 55.
111 C. Kinealy, 'At home with the Empire: The example of Ireland', in Hall and Rose (eds), *At Home with the Empire*, p. 92.
112 Nally, *Human Encumbrances*, pp. 82–90.
113 N. Thomas, *Colonialism's Culture: Anthropology, Travel and Government* (Princeton, NJ: Princeton University Press, 1994), p. 79.
114 *Morning Chronicle*, 4 December 1849.
115 W. Hicke, *The Agricultural Labourer Viewed in His Moral, Intellectual, and Physical Conditions* (London: Groombridge and Sons, 1855), pp. 18–19, 36, 55.

6

Telling the hunger of 'distant' others

Hunger, as the previous chapters have shown, was not only bodily experienced but also asserted, affective, made and theorised. This chapter considers the way in which hunger was also understood – and thus experienced at arm's length – as relational. Hunger, it suggests, was not just something experienced and mobilised through direct experience and control but also something understood and mediated through the plight of distant others. Coinciding with public horror over the scandalous plight of those left to the mercy of the bare-life-making, pauper-starving New Poor Law, as well as the aftermath of the (partial) 1833 Slavery Abolition Act,[1] the Great Famine of Ireland provided a test for the limits to popular empathy and what might be considered as the emergence of humanitarian concerns in the period. Further, the chapter also considers the ways in which the hunger of distant others helped to shape the political understandings of hunger in a colonial age. It does not explore the central governmental response to these famines – though this provides a critical context – but instead examines popular responses to the hunger of others in the 1840s. Distance here is conceived in relation not only to those subjects of Empire in Ireland (and beyond), but also the responses of those in metropolitan and southern England to the sufferings of the Scottish rural poor during the concurrent Highland Potato Famine and, relatedly, to the privations of industrial workers in the north of England during what later became labelled as the 'Hungry Forties'. The primary focus here, however, is on Great Famine of Ireland, as both the devastating context that most obviously exercised the public mind in England and as the defining event in shaping new understandings of hunger in imperial Britain.

This chapter examines both the discourses of response (and how these helped to shape understandings of hunger) and schemes to relieve famine and the distant hungry. It is argued that against the ideologically driven official governmental response to these different famines, those who were only one act of misfortune away from being incarcerated in the workhouse and only one or two generations away from experiencing absolute hunger were quick to respond by setting up collections and relief schemes. We see in such responses, the chapter goes on to argue, an extension of the protest discourses of hunger explored in chapter two, the popular cultural potency of the fear of hunger reinvigorated by 'bare-life' workhouse regimes. The chapter also asserts that such relief schemes also mirrored the political critiques of domestic and imperial food policy issued by Chartist thinkers. Hunger was therefore increasingly expressed as relational, as something mediated not just by individual experience but also through the experiences of real and imagined communities that spanned parish, regional and national boundaries. Hunger was also mediated through competing political languages made policy. This is not to deny the absolute privations and sufferings that were all too real to many English workers in the 1840s. Rather it is to acknowledge that the popular politics of hunger were not bound by the body or borders but were rooted in the uneven contours of solidarity and reciprocity. Nor is it to claim that this was something universal. It was not. 'Shared' experiences underpinned empathy for some people in some places, but did not absolutely break down an entrenched working culture of xenophobia – attacks on Irish migrant workers continued into the late 1840s. It did, however, help to generate a new culture of labouring cosmopolitanism that would later be central to trade union internationalism. Invariably, this chapter is not about the understandings of the English poor per se in relation to hunger elsewhere, for their unmediated voice is impossible to recover: for instance, the working-class narratives detailed in Emma Griffin's *Liberty's Dawn* make no reference to popular readings of the Irish Famine.[2] Rather, it draws upon a deeper popular, and often defiantly radical and plebeian, response, something which spoke not to the sentiments of the rulers of England but instead to the views of the people.

Critical contexts

The Great Famine casts a shadow over the culture and politics of Ireland and its peoples so totally that it belongs to small group of events in global history that can truly be claimed as marking a profound fissure in time and space.[3] As has been well rehearsed, if not absolutely without controversy, between 1846 and 1852 scarcity-made-famine robbed Ireland of one million of its sons and daughters through starvation and conditions associated with chronic malnourishment, and ultimately led to two million others fleeing destitution (and possible death) by seeking a life overseas.[4] The shadow of this disgraceful episode is, unsurprisingly, also cast on the telling of Ireland's 'national story', taking a central part in both general survey histories and in famine historiography's dominant position in Irish social and political history and historical geography. While this has not always been the case – it was not until the 1990s that famine memorials increased in number from a 'small handful' to more than 100,[5] while likewise it was not until the 1990s that the famine assumed a vital place in the teaching of Irish history in schools and universities – the politics of hunger assume a central part in the story of Ireland in a way that is simply untrue of England.[6]

From the late 1980s, the historiography of the Great Famine has also witnessed an unprecedented flowering. From the pioneering acts of post-revisionist synthesis of, amongst others, Margaret Crawford, Peter Gray, and Christine Kinealy, through the more quantitative, economic history approaches of Joel Mokyr and Cormac O'Grada, to more recent culturally and politically sophisticated studies by Tim Pat Coogan, Emily Mark-Fitzgerald and David Nally, as well as John Crowley, William J. Smyth and Mike Murphy's *Atlas*, the famine has truly assumed a dominant centrality in Irish history.[7] One aspect of post-revisionist accounts that is truly novel – in comparison to both pre-1930s historiography and later revisionist accounts – is the emphasis placed on relief schemes, highlighting the ways in which the giving of 'relief' was constitutive of turning scarcity into a devastating famine. Conversely, this post-revisionist literature has also shown how humanitarian impulses acted to check further devastation. Indeed, the giving of relief in both the form of formal, statutory poor relief through the Irish Poor Law of 1838 and through public donations has become a critical theme in post-revisionist accounts, perhaps best reflected in Kinealy's 2013 monograph *Charity and the Great Hunger in Ireland: the Kindness of Strangers*.[8] Moreover, as James Donnelly notes, 'ever since the Great Famine people have debated the culpability of the British government in the mass deaths which marked and defined that horrendous social catastrophe.'[9] The response of the governments of Sir Robert Peel and Lord John Russell has been subjected to intense critical scrutiny. What has not figured in such studies, though, is the British public's reaction to the famine. The one exception is Donnelly's examination of British public opinion of the June 1847 Poor Law Amendment Act, and this was exclusively through the lens of the anti-relief *Times* and the *Illustrated London News*. Similarly, Kinealy's recent study of relief practices and giving has analysed in detail the workings of the British Relief Association of Extreme Distress in the Remote Parishes of Ireland and Scotland (BRA). It is important to note though that the BRA was established in January 1847 at the behest of Prime Minister Lord John Russell and assistant secretary to the British Treasury Sir Charles Trevelyan, and publicly backed in two letters of support by Queen Victoria. This was no spontaneous public outpouring of sympathy and support. While many working- and middle-class communities and individuals did generously the support the BRA, in relation to the British public reaction Kinealy's account focuses more on the actions of prominent individuals and businesses and groups supporting the mission of the BRA.[10]

This chapter builds upon these critical studies in asking what the British public response and reaction to the famine was before the founding of the BRA. In so doing, it widens Donnelly's study of British public opinion to encompass a broader range of sources of public record, considers the responses of the Anti–Corn Law League (ACLL) and the Chartist movement, and asks whether non-state sanctioned public subscriptions were raised before the 'official' call.[11] It does so, initially, by placing into perspective British official and state-sanctioned relief efforts and responses. Before that it is necessary to place the making of the famine into Ireland's wider colonial and geo-pathogenic context.

Crop failures do not themselves make famines

The potato harvest of 1845 promised to be prodigious. As the *Banner of Ulster* put it at the beginning of August, 'this crop – the staple of Ireland – is more abundant this season than it has been for several years past'.[12] Plants were healthy and there was 'scarcely' any blight 'in the North'. So bountiful would be the crop – the heaviest in years even – that prices were expected to fall.[13] A month later and in the full swing of harvest, the Belfast press was not only reporting a better than expected grain harvest in Antrim but also that the late unseasonal showers had in no way damaged the potatoes.[14] The *Dublin Evening Post* went further: '[T]here never, perhaps, was a finer growth of Potatoes, which are selling at about half the price of this time last year.'[15] The blessing of Divine Providence, so reckoned the *Limerick Chronicle*, had protected the crops and allowed a glut of new potatoes to be sold cheaply at Limerick market in late August.[16]

Reports from elsewhere in north-western Europe were in stark contrast. In early August a strange phenomenon was witnessed in the potato fields around Nijmegen and Heusden in the south Netherlands: potatoes dying in the course of one night.[17] Once infected, all potato plants in the field withered and dried up in a few hours. Similar reports were soon also being made in Belgium, northern France and around the Rhine. More or less concurrently, reports of an unusual blight also issued from the Weald of Kent and Sussex in England.[18] In late July, a localised 'partial blight' had been noticed, but by 12 August it had spread through East Sussex and Kent, leading to predictions that there would be a 'failure, to a great extent' in the crop.[19] 'Complaints' of potatoes having turned black and found to be of no use whatsoever were now 'very general.'[20] A week later the spread was said to be rapid, with cases confirmed on the east coast in Essex and Suffolk and westwards into Hampshire and Surrey.[21] By the end of August reports now confirmed that the blight had spread as far west as the area around Truro and Redruth in Cornwall. So extensive was the damage – and so all-consuming was critical commentary in the provincial and horticultural press – that speculation started as to the cause of the blight (variably the poor weather of the 'season' was to blame, murrain had spread from cattle or a pathogen was spread in the air) and as to ways in which the 'rot' could be cured.[22]

In Ireland these reports were noted with, as Kinealy puts it, 'curiosity rather than alarm'.[23] On 29 August the *Cork Examiner*, reporting on the 'most serious apprehensions' in southern England, could still reassure its readers that the north of England was as yet free from the blight and there was 'not the least symptom of its approach' anywhere in Ireland.[24] This was not strictly true, for in late August the blight had been observed at the Botanical Gardens in Glasnevin, Dublin.[25] While this was not initially made public, and similar observations were not published 'lest after all the suspected visitation should only prove imaginary',[26] on 6 September both the *Dublin Evening Post* and the *Waterford Freeman* announced that Irish potatoes had now been killed by the blight.[27] As the editor of the latter publication grimly reported, the spread of the blight was already 'considerable' and the likely consequences 'very serious'. Or as the *Cork Examiner* put it four days later, 'our worst fears are likely to be realised'; and soon, notwithstanding that markets continued to be plentifully supplied and prices low, it and other newspapers were warning of the likelihood of famine.[28]

While subject to revision and counter-revision, an effect of the potato blight – the water- and air-borne pathogen *Phytophthora infestans*, as it was later identified – was a famine with a mortality rate, according to Amartya Sen, higher than for any other recorded famine in human history, with only the Ukrainian famine of the 1930s comparable in the history of modern Europe.[29] Between 1846 (there were no famine deaths in 1845) and 1852 one million people perished, with some two million others leaving Ireland, many of these individuals also dying on their journeys or soon after arriving in America, Canada and England.[30] But, as historians of the famine have noted, crop failures do not themselves make famines: social, cultural, legal and political systems do. In the context of 1840s Ireland, it was arguably the interplay between three interrelated colonial systems that turned scarcity into famine.

First, the landowning system meant that the vast majority of the land was owned by a small group of largely absentee landlords who through land law and customary practices enjoyed almost total power over their tenants. Most tenants were landless labourers, holding one-year contracts with no incentive to invest in their small plots, while at the same time needing to maximise the return from their rental for the short term only, invariably in the form of the prolific potato. British acknowledgements that the system was essentially unfair and, given recent rapid population growth (from 6.5 million in 1841 to a probable 8 million in 1845), fears for the sustainability of agricultural subdivision led to the Devon Commission being established by Peel in 1843 to investigate the occupation of land. Reporting in early 1845, the Commission's investigations were neither as extensive as hoped for, nor its recommendations for land reform as wide reaching.[31]

Second, British mercantile policy was in a state of both ideological flux and geopolitical confusion. By the time the potato blight started to wreak its havoc in the fields of Ireland, political debate in the metropole was dominated by the clamour to repeal the Corn Laws and as such much thinking about the emergent crisis in Ireland was informed by mercantile theorising.[32] Indeed, in early public 'concern' in England over the potential impacts of the potato blight, we see the influence of Anti–Corn Law League discourses and even activists. Thus at a public meeting at Liverpool on 28 November 1845 to 'address Sir Robert Peel on the threatened scarcity of food in Ireland' it was suggested that rather than a 'private subscription', the most effective solution would be 'at once and for ever annihilating' all protective duties. The meeting concluded with three cheers for 'Mr Cobden', physically absent from the meeting but evidently present in other ways.[33] The position of the repeal lobbies in relation to Ireland – at once part of the union and yet commercially subject to different values and rules – was messy, provisional and decidedly partial. When, seemingly against the parliamentary odds, repeal passed through the Houses of Commons and Lords on 12 May 1846, it was applied in relation to Ireland in decidedly doctrinaire ways.[34]

Relatedly, and finally, Ireland's status as a colonial 'problem' while also part of the union was reflected in confused and often contradictory policy impulses and prescriptions. As noted, the issue of land reform never achieved wholehearted support from either Whigs or Tories, both often finding their governments reliant on support from Irish landowning MPs. Even the early evidence of famine conditions in late 1845 and early 1846 proved no spur to shift from the characteristic hesitancy to actually 'meddle' with Irish land policy. As Robert Shipkey has put it, Peel's 1841–6 administration initially followed the by now customary 'do nothing' policy in relation to Ireland. From 1843 the position of Peel's government shifted from policy inactivity to 'conciliation': this was evidenced in the setting up of the Devon Commission and Peel's unequivocal public support for Catholic education in the form of significantly increasing the grant to the Maynooth seminary in 1845.[35]

It is possible to overplay conciliation, though, for neither policy met Irish demands nor worked politically for Peel, a situation reminiscent of the political aftermath of his Irish 'concession' in the form of Catholic Emancipation in 1828–9. For the majority of British (elected) politicians, Ireland remained a problem. One hundred years of scarcity and famine and seemingly endemic agrarian protest against hard-nosed absentee landlords and their capitalist grazier tenants, producing grain, dairy and meat for the British market, had left successive Westminster governments frustrated at their inability to control the unruly island. Not even the bitter repression of the United Irishmen between 1798 and 1803 and the concurrent dissolution of the Irish parliament and the passing of the Act of Union between Great Britain and Ireland acted to check the perception that Ireland remained not only a problem but *apart*. The resurgence of Irish nationalism in the early 1840s through the Young Ireland 'movement' (arguably the most coherent, non-sectarian assertion of Ireland's right to self-government against British colonial self-interest), under the charismatic direction of John Blake Dillon and Thomas Davis, also represented a major nationalist threat to the future of the Union.

Contra the form of Irish nationalism peddled by Daniel O'Connell, it also represented a threat to the interests of landowners.[36]

There were also limits to empathy for the Irish rural poor amongst the British public. By the 1840s big British industrial cities – and parts of London – were synonymous with Irish migration, with mill towns like Glasgow, Manchester and Liverpool all having large settled Irish communities. Invariably employed at lower rates and housed in slum districts – Engels notoriously bemoaned the fact that the Irish in Manchester 'insinuate themselves everywhere' with 'all their brutal habits'[37] – Irish workers unsurprisingly were treated with suspicion and even contempt. Where the demand for labour was strong English and Irish workers coexisted reasonably peaceably, working together and forming close associations and families.[38] The same was not true of most places, though: Irish workers were more often transitory presences rather than settled. In the English countryside the employment of migrant Irish labourers in the harvest was a long-term source of contention. In the agrarian hinterlands of London, the employment of Irish harvest workers led to indigent labourers striking from work at Dartford in north Kent and over the Thames Estuary in Essex in 1736, and in Middlesex in 1774.[39] Anti-Irish feeling strengthened though after the end of the Napoleonic Wars when it became easier to seek work in England during the summer (before returning home to Ireland at the end of the harvest) and when un- and under-employment became chronic amongst English agricultural workers. Reports in the provincial press often referred to the roads of southern England 'swarming with Irishmen with wives and children in search of harvest work', while the hop harvest in the Kentish and Sussex Weald met with the creation of 'extensive encampments' of Irish workers.[40] Competition for work – and the ready flow of alcohol that accompanied the harvest – led to brawls between English and Irish workers, and – notably in the wretched years of 1829, 1830 and 1831 – the deliberate violent targeting of Irish workers and malicious attacks on the property of those who employed migrant Irish workers.[41]

Initial responses

Whatever British political and popular ambivalence, the British state had not given up on Ireland. Social reform, political control and the cultural embrace with the union remained the Holy Grail; the solution to the 'Irish problem' was (always) one piece of legislation away. As Gray has noted, '[t]he transformation of Irish society was to follow directly from Corn Law repeal', the latest in a long series of attempts to engineer colonial cohesion.[42] Nally has recently suggested that not only was the British state complicit in trying to reform Ireland, to bring it under *its* control, but that it also actively used Ireland as a test bed for new techniques of governing, new forms of governmentality. By positioning Ireland as both a form of property and a problem, it was also possible to assert the authority to regulate and classify the Irish body politic and the bodies of Irish men and women. The population was disaggregated according to their use, 'conduct and perceived threat to social order'.[43] The primary object of political strategy of this new approach then was biopolitics writ large: the regulation of 'the basic biological features of the human species' and under its prescriptions scarcity and famine made permissible as the possible means to provoke desired political and social outcomes.[44] As Nally, drawing on the work of David Keen, puts it, 'famines now ha[d] functions as well as causes'.[45]

The immediate reaction of the Westminster government to the sign of extensive potato blight in Ireland was to do nothing. Initially the policy was not without *some* justification, for home secretary Sir James Graham was correct in his assessment that while blighted, the crop was abundant.[46] Past shortages had not led to famines, hence there was hope – however naïve and misplaced – that Irish cottiers would be able to survive the winter without government intervention. Peel was also deeply sceptical of Irish communications in the early months after the identification of the blight, believing that, as in the past as he saw it, Irish magistrates were 'calling wolf'.[47] Pleas by the Lord Lieutenant of Ireland, Lord Heytesbury, on 27 October that to 'tranquilise the public mind and diminish the panic' the government ought to offer some, as Shipkey has put it, 'show of action' were ignored. The revived Mansion House Committee (formed in Dublin in 1821 to raise subscriptions to assist distressed areas) also made a plea to Peel through Heytesbury that exports should be banned, distilleries prohibited from using gran, public granaries founded and a programme of public works set up to employ those out of work. This too received short shrift. Missives from similar organisations in Belfast, Cork and Londonderry were likewise passed off.[48]

In short, the initial response was predicated on a combination of past prejudices and experiences: Peel's ideological adherence to the self-righting powers of political economy combined with what he perceived to be a lack of decisive evidence. Two factors are critical. Governmental refusal to ban exports was founded on two understandings. First, that if merchants could find an overseas market for diseased potatoes then they should be allowed to export them and bring cash into the economy, which, in turn, would be used to import nutritious foodstuffs. Second, food exports were normally limited to the main cash crop, wheat ('corn'), dairy products and livestock. While potatoes dominated the diet of the vast majority of the population – Irish labouring families did not just eat potatoes out of necessity but also supposedly preferred them to other foodstuffs – the acreage devoted to wheat far exceeded that given to potatoes. Wheat was a cash crop, a cash crop that supported Irish landlords, merchants and British bread-dependent consumers. Hence allowing wheat exports, especially after what had been a fine harvest, would be of no consequence.[49] Or so the theory went. This would later have public consequences as the theories of political economy were more doggedly and ideologically followed by Russell's Whig administration than Peel's Tories. By 1849, as George Bernstein has put it, 'the British were sick of the whole business and were reluctant to spend any more of their money on a people who would not help themselves.'[50] Non-interventionism was 'justified' by the political-economy policy prescription of laissez-faire and was supported by the 'famine mythology' that nothing could be done, that the deaths were acts of God.

In an effort to gather evidence as to the actuality of scarcity and the severity of the blight, in October 1845 Peel instituted a Scientific Commission and sent two scientific advisors to Dublin. Their reading of the evidence was eventually proved wrong: the claim that five-sixths of the crop would be lost was thankfully unduly pessimistic. Their claim was, however, at least in part responsible for a shift in policy.[51] When the potential severity of the situation was realised, in November 1845 it was agreed that a new approach was to be implemented from the following spring, when, so it was thought, food supplies would in all probability become perilously short. Mirroring government responses to the 1816 crisis and building upon relief offered by the 118 operable poor law workhouses, Peel instituted a programme of public works to employ those out of work, the secret purchase of £100,000 of Indian corn (maize) from the US and the creation of a Relief Commission.[52] The impact of these policies is hard to discern precisely, but it is worth noting that the 100 or so local relief committees (mostly based in the south-west) had to apply to the Dublin-based Relief Commission for Indian corn, and, if successful, were to *sell* it at market prices, later changed to cost price and in cases of extreme distress gratis. The Relief Commission was also slow to act: something not helped by the constant and resented interference of Trevelyan, the permanent secretary to the Treasury under both Peel and Russell's governments. Slowness as a result of monitoring was also a problem that afflicted the special relief department of the Board of Public Works administering public work programmes.[53] Furthermore, food depots supplying the local committees were not to open until May, notwithstanding the fact that localised shortages were felt from March. Food riots followed in Carrick-on-Suir, Clonmel and Tipperary, targeting merchants and forestallers charging 'famine' prices for wheat. Although the riots were put down by the military and provoked strong condemnation in Parliament, they did lead to some depots being opened earlier than had otherwise been planned.[54] The local committees also had some success in generating financial support through local subscriptions: the £98,000 so raised was supplemented by a grant of £65,914 from the Lord Lieutenant.[55] While the importation of Indian corn was not meant as a direct substitute for potatoes – Peel's intention was that it would help to keep the price of food down and deter hoarding by speculators – it did act as a substitute, albeit one popularly loathed, as evidenced in the popular satirical name given to maize, 'Peel's Brimstone'.[56]

Together, such measures (notwithstanding the myriad problems including administrative frauds on the public works that were widely publicised in the British press) were effective in preventing famine deaths, though badly stored and prepared Indian corn did lead to widespread illness. Against this 'success', it has been claimed that a consensus emerged in British public and political opinion. The efforts and expenses of the Westminster government had allowed, so the argument went, Irish landlords to shirk their duty. Peel's package was therefore just another sticking plaster against the pressing need to reform Ireland. Moreover, the giving of relief had supposedly acted to depress local stimuli to action.[57]

The blight reappeared in July 1846 and by mid-September the whole country was affected. Coinciding with a British political crisis and the fall of Peel's government in the fallout of the passing of the Importation Act on 16 May that repealed the Corn Laws, relief policy initially remained unaltered. Besides, Peel's policy of importing Indian corn was scheduled to end on 15 August and as a temporary expedient was never intended to continue after that date. The government now acted only as the supplier of last resort. Indeed, only a handful of depots remained open, and these in the worst affected areas of the west.[58] Yet against mounting evidence of likely chronic scarcity, the policy adopted by Russell's incoming (minority) Whig administration proved even more doctrinaire and inflexible than Peel's government. Considerable power now rested in the hands of Trevelyan and Charles Wood at the Treasury. Working from a belief that Irish taxpayers as opposed to the Treasury should be liable for relief costs, Russell's government not only decided *not* to renew the import of Indian corn but also determined that public works should now be funded through Poor Law taxation. Wages on public works were also now to be set below market rates, though such were the delays created by Treasury-imposed checks before works could start, and so late were payments often made, that the few potential positive effects of the scheme were further checked.[59]

Despite this, and the fact that in some places individuals refused to work on the schemes, such were the pay and the conditions of work – the Treasury in such cases decreed that the particular project would stop until all 'outrages' had stopped – the demand for public work exceeded supply in the exceptionally harsh winter. By January 1847 570,000 men were so employed, a figure that rose to 734,000 in March; thus at its peak one in three men and roughly two million people were supported by the public works programme.[60] But against this level of support, in January 1847 the British government resolved to end the programme of public works and by the autumn to make the poor law responsible for the maintenance of all individuals. A system of public soup kitchens was to meet needs in the interim. To this end, a 20 per cent reduction in public works was imposed on 20 March, with a sliding scale of further cuts following, this notwithstanding the fact that public soup kitchens in many places were not yet operative. In this way, so Russell's government desired, ultimately the needs of the suffering Irish would be met by Irish taxpayers. The market for foodstuffs would be left to operate without state intervention, and Irish society and the economy would be transformed. That winter, with the ports continuing to export huge amounts of corn and livestock to Britain and even America, the Irish constabulary estimated that 400,000 individuals died through want of food.[61] As the Irish radical newspaper the *Nation* put it, the abandonment of public works was a 'murderous absurdity', evidence of the British government's 'utter apathy to the tremendous responsibility with which they are trifling'.[62]

Alongside the slow withdrawal of the *direct* relief efforts of the British state, charity was not only encouraged but also directly supported by Russell's government. As noted, the landlord-dominated local relief committees had by August 1846 raised £98,000 in donations, but this represented a fraction of what was being spent, let alone what was needed to prevent a humanitarian disaster.[63] Moreover, in Britain, so Peel had believed, there would be little private sympathy, and thus no efforts were made to stimulate charity. If the Whigs too were slow to recognise the possibilities of harnessing charitable support, this soon changed. Through the influence of the Indian Relief Fund – which raised funds for Ireland in India and Ceylon – and pleas from Anglican clergy in Ireland, Trevelyan began to conceive that charity could provide an important safety net, which would allow the government to, as Gray puts it, 'adhere rigidly to its relief rules'.[64] Evangelical morality could thus save political economy. Providing that Irish landowners set the example, all would follow out of a sense of brotherly and sisterly compassion.

The British Association for the Relief of Extreme Distress in the Remote Parishes of Ireland and Scotland was founded in the City of London in January 1847. The Association was under the immediate lead of chair Thomas Baring, of the self-named bank that had earlier purchased the Indian corn on behalf of Peel's government, but had been founded at Trevelyan and Russell's instigation.[65] The (publicly stated) aim was to aid the poor 'who are beyond the reach of government' with food, clothes and fuel.[66] Advice was also taken as to the best means to proceed in Ireland from the most important pre-existing relief organisation, the Central Relief Committee, itself founded in Dublin in November 1846 by the Society of Friends and active in raising money from their members in both Ireland and England.[67] In support of this new British charitable initiative, the Queen issued an official letter in January 1847 calling for collections in every parish in the land, a measure supported by sermons in parish churches. The effect, as has been well documented, was immediate and emphatic. Personal donations from Queen Victoria of £2,000 – her support doubled due to the inclusion of Scotland in the scheme – and her ministers (Russell gave £300) made giving to Irish charity both an act of public and pious duty *and* fashionable.[68] By the time the BRA finished its activities in the summer of 1848 it had raised £470,041 1s. 2d., of which £391,700 17s. 8d. was expended in Ireland.[69] More than 15,000 donations had been made, including from British corporations, universities and the British army, as well as from overseas, mostly from British colonies.[70] Relief, it was resolved, was to be given in food rather money, though in some areas this rule could not be adhered to as no food was available to purchase. In the spring of 1847 seed oats were also distributed in the west, in a further departure from stated policy. Local committees were created, food depots founded, and agents and even the Royal Navy engaged to help determine need and distribute relief. Most of its money was expended that spring and summer of 1847; thereafter, on the introduction of the Poor Law Extension Act that August, its activities were confined to the most distressed unions, continuing until July 1848 when its funds were finally exhausted.[71]

Popular opinion in the metropole

Given the ravages of *Phytophthora infestans* in England and Scotland, initial commentary in the British press about the effects of the blight in Ireland was quick to draw parallels but also to forewarn of singularly devastating consequences given the reliance of Irish cottiers on the potato. As a letter to the *Cambridge Independent Press* suggested, the ongoing public scandal over the fact that inmates of the Andover Union workhouse in Hampshire had been reduced to supplementing their potato-heavy diet by gnawing green bones was a ready warning of the reliance on the potato. England might be 'far removed at present from the horrors of … the depopulation of famine', but this served as a warning.[72] More directly, as the *Wiltshire Independent* reported, 'Ireland is threatened with famine, not merely that periodical dearth between the potato-crops every year which puts a third part of the people into a state of destitution, but a failure of the potato-crop itself.'[73] Detailing cases of crop failure throughout Ireland, the piece concluded by predicting that as '[t]he consequences of such a failure of the staple food in Ireland are terrible to contemplate … Government will of course take some steps'.[74]

   With the notable exception of the Chartist press – of which more below – anti-Tory newspapers invariably suggested that the solution to the likely crisis was to repeal the Corn Laws and throw open the ports. Even some parts of the provincial and agrarian Tory press suggested that some limited, targeted opening of the Irish ports to allow relief for the sufferers of Ireland was laudable. As the editor of the *Ipswich Journal* put it: '[I]mportation made under the proper regulations … will excite no regret, or cause complaints from the agricultural interest.'[75] The temporary repeal of the Corn Laws would however offer *no* 'relief' to the Irish poor. The paper of the Hampshire landowners likewise believed it was 'an absurdity' opening the Irish ports for the import of corn because those in need 'cannot afford to purchase it'.[76] Instead, relief would come from 'the [charitable] benevolence of the people of England'.[77] The English public, so this line of thinking went, had a moral duty to support their famished neighbours – rather than English landowners and agriculturalists through public policy.

   The loudest voices, though, were those clamouring to open the ports as a prelude to (or part of an immediate) Corn Law repeal. Cobden was quick in the autumn of 1845 to offer free trade as the solution to the failure of the potato crop, with 'starvation staring in the face' of the people of the 'unhappy sister island'.[78] Such commentaries, not least his speech given at the Great League Meeting at Manchester on 28 October, were widely publicised and Cobden's argument and language were adopted in the editorials and published letters of the pro-Corn Law repeal press. A speaker at a 'great free trade meeting' at Taunton in late December even went as far as to claim that campaigning for the repeal of the Corn Laws was a 'noble struggle' for the good it would be in opening up the Irish ports to avoid 'all their horrors'.[79] Speakers at a further Manchester meeting in December again spoke in emotive terms about the likely sufferings of the Irish poor and (tellingly) the negative impact the blight had made on Manchester–Irish trade.[80] A £50,000 subscription was duly raised – not to relieve the Irish but to support the ACLL's campaign. Similarly at a public meeting in Sheffield to consider the repeal of the Corn Laws, in the main speech Alderman Dunn played on the emotional solidarities of the largely working-class audience by proclaiming, when mentioning the state of the poor in Ireland, that 'he could never do so without feelings that he could scarcely describe'.[81] While the first speech of a public meeting at Leeds on 3 December – postponed from noon to 7pm so as to enable the 'working classes' to attend – opened by making reference to the state of the hungry in Ireland and England, it asserted that the poor in both countries were the victims of 'class' legislation.[82] This belief was 'confirmed' by comments made by the Dukes of Richmond and Norfolk at a meeting of Sussex agriculturalists at Steyning, near Brighton, in early December. Richmond, improbably, suggested that labourers should 'uphold the flags of Nelson and Wellington' and import their own potatoes from Portugal, while Norfolk, explosively, recommended that the Irish eat their diseased potatoes with curry powder. Norfolk's comments quickly gained notoriety throughout Britain and Ireland, giving further credence to the emergent popular belief that the landed classes of both islands little understood or cared for the hungry working poor. The situation was especially pressing given that, as the Exeter press saw it, Ireland was 'bordering upon a state of absolute famine' with the 'same evil' also threatening England.[83]

Blight in Ireland was thus read as a warning for England's domestic situation – note that commentary on the possible effects of the blight in Scotland figured little in the initial English commentary – and mobilised as evidential ammunition in the increasingly vituperative battle between those for and against the repeal of the Corn Laws.[84] No less vitriol-laden was the relationship between the ACLL and the Chartist leadership, a dynamic which can be read as having impacted upon Chartist responses to the blight and emergent famine in Ireland.[85] While the ACLL swiftly and decisively attached themselves to the issue, prominent Chartists were more equivocal. Chartism had a loose grip on Ireland, only flourishing in Dublin (and then in partnership with the Irish Universal Suffrage Association) between 1841 and 1844. Thereafter, the most obvious connection was through Irish migrants in Britain subscribing to the Charter and assuming positions of power in the movement, notably founder and editor of the Leeds-based mouthpiece of the movement the *Northern Star* Feargus O'Connor, and advocate of the Chartist Land Plan Bronterre O'Brien. Moreover, in matters Irish there was considerable division between prominent Chartists, with dissent over O'Connor's prominent use of the *Northern Star* to espouse the repeal of the Union.[86]

The *Northern Star* first reported the existence of the blight in the Channel Islands and south and west England on 30 August 1845, but it was not until 1 November that the paper first alluded to the possibility of a famine in Ireland *and* England.[87] This, and subsequent reporting, were used to attack both the ACLL – accused of using the 'crisis' to advance the interests of 'capital' against those of 'labour' – and Peel's mercantile and colonial policy. O'Connor also used the opportunity of a speech in London on 5 November – his first in Britain that autumn – to mobilise the blight as evidence of the need for land reform and support for the Chartist Land Plan.[88] Beyond opportunism to push particular agendas, the early Chartist response was best summed up in an open letter from O'Connor to 'the Imperial Chartists' published in the *Northern Star*: 'the excitement of free trade, the militia, war, famine, and the Queen's speech, instead of diverting your attention from that all-important subject [land reform], will rather lead you to a consideration of it as the means of making you independent of all casualties, whims, caprices, and class legislation.'[89] Even as late as the May Day Chartist rally of 1847, when the full enormity of the effects of famine in Ireland were evident, the response of O'Connor and other prominent Chartists was to espouse the critical importance of the Land Plan as a solution to the Malthusian check.[90]

This is not to say that ACLL and Chartist commentary, speechifying and reporting were devoid of genuine sympathy towards the Irish poor. Indeed, what united pro– and anti–Corn Law repealers and Chartists alike was an apparent genuine fear for the human consequences of blight and government inaction. From early 1846, almost without exception each issue of the *Northern Star* made some reference to the effects of the blight (both in Ireland and elsewhere) and the actual and likely effects on the Irish poor. Yet outside of reprinting news from the Irish press, such reports were invariably used to make a broader political point. Thus on 14 February 1846, a report on the appearance in 'many districts' of 'pestilence' ('ever the attendant of famine') juxtaposed 'the assaults of the hungry' with 'sleek and fat horses ... a bloated police force, a gorged soldiery, bursting war horses'.[91] At the same time Peel was accused by O'Connor of a similar opportunism in using the pretext of the social dislocations of scarcity and the rise in agrarian protest to introduce to Parliament in May 1846 the Irish Coercion Bill. Ultimately the bill failed and with it brought down Peel's government.[92]

Nor were other public journals entirely without feeling in their reporting, but, as with Chartist commentary, at least before October 1846 reports on the state of rural Ireland were often used to offer a wider critique of British mercantile, agrarian and colonial policy. Thus the Church and State Toryism of the *Salisbury Journal* berated Peel for the state of Ireland:

> If any thing were wanting to demonstrate Sir Robert Peel's incompetence to carry on her Majesty's Government in Ireland, it might be found in the present state of that kingdom. [With] rampant and furious ... Orangemen in Ulster, and O'Connell and his followers ... howl[ing] for repeal of the Union in the south, Ireland was out of control. Against this, [f]amine, with all its attendant horrors, glares at them [Peel's cabinet].[93]

The solution, however, was not 'English charity, Saxon benevolence', as in the past, but instead the Irish Poor Law and the 'proprietors of the soil ... exposed to the indignation and disgust of the British public', who themselves had grown rich 'by exactions from these poor creatures'.[94] From a different political perspective, Peel was also subject to the scorn of the *Fife Herald* in late October for only having sent the two scientific commissioners to Ireland to investigate the 'disease' in the potato crop.[95] Less obviously racked by ideological feeling was a commentary in the *Leeds Times* on 8 November bemoaning that in the face of famine – 'already a pressing and palpable thing' – the poor were suffering as 'Ireland is being drained of her best food to supply the wants of England and Scotland'.[96] At the same time, Scottish potatoes were also still being exported to the Nordic countries and Baltic states. Through such trading England was again averting famine, but Ireland was still subject to the structured 'perennial famine' which kept a third of its population in a state of constant hunger and starvation and Scotland likely subject to comparable disaster.[97] Or as the *Cambridge Independent Press* put it, 'it is an extraordinary fact, that while the people of the south of Ireland are threatened with famine, the quays of Limerick and Waterford are crowded with vessels taking grain and other provisions for England.'[98] As Peter Gurney has suggested, in such ways the 'politics of provisions' remained at the centre of the British political stage in late 1845, the example of Ireland serving as a warning to England.[99]

Such early reports betray a degree of confusion as to the actual and likely impact of the blight on the people of Ireland and as to the best prescription to aid the problem. This was not even divided on political (or Corn Law repeal) lines. For every Tory press assertion that this was Ireland's problem came commentaries, such as that in the Tory *Hampshire Advertiser*, that the people of England had a charitable duty to help.[100] The only explicit *call* to raise subscriptions to aid those suffering from the early effects of the blight I have uncovered, though, related not to the Irish poor but instead the hungry of the Scottish Highlands.[101]

During the winter of 1845–6 this might have been a function of reports suggesting that the initial fears as to the universality and severity of the blight had not been realised acting to reduce the humanitarian impulse. This and the eventual government relief policies evidently impacted upon public willingness to collect money to support Ireland. Nor should we under-estimate the potential impact of the ACLL campaign to raise £250,000 through subscriptions, not least given that this campaigning was strongest in those places with the large migrant Irish communities and thus also where metropole–colony solidarities were strongest.[102] In the first half of 1846 other dynamics militated against the raising of public subscriptions. The reporting of abuses of state-funded public work schemes was, as noted, widespread, as were reports of agrarian protest and landlord evictions. Collectively such reports were taken by much of the press as evidence of purblind landlords and violent mendicant peasants, of a country beyond the help of further charitable giving.[103] This was best exemplified by Home Secretary Graham placing before Parliament on 8 June 1846 a bill by the name of 'Protection of Life (Ireland)' that was concerned not with famine relief measures but instead the means to put down 'agrarian insurrection'.[104] And this followed parliamentary utterances to the tune that past English subscriptions had simply found their way directly into the pockets of Irish landlords, their exported corn being purchased in England by subscriptions and shipped back to Ireland. As Peel had stated in the House of Commons after the Easter recess: 'I affirm that the responsibility rests rather upon those who are resident on the spot, and upon those who, not being resident, have a still moral obligation to transmit their subscriptions through their resident brethren.'[105] The duty was resolutely not that of the British people.

The depth of feeling on the issue was best summed up by an editorial of the independent, politically liberal *Bristol Mercury* in April 1846. The British government, it noted, had intervened in providing Indian corn but could not, so it had professed, undertake to feed the Irish people, this after all being the duty of Irish landlords. What stores it had left were being held for it foresaw 'a far worse time coming', and this retention was thus, as the paper asserted, the 'humane course'.[106] Irish landlords, by way of contrast, had only raised a 'few paltry hundreds' through subscriptions, even though the mechanisms to collect funds were in place via Daniel O'Connell's Union 'repeal rent' fund.[107] England, it thundered, was 'looked [to] for everything – and blamed for everything'.[108]

Beyond the emotive rhetoric and the misinformation regarding indigenous relief-raising, the fact that such reports even appeared in the politically liberal press powerfully acted to undermine British public action. This was explicitly, if sheepishly, acknowledged in reports of the 'munificent contribution' from India for the relief of the Irish poor.[109] As the *Morning Post* related:

> Whatever distrust may have been entertained at home at the representation made by the 'Mansion-House Committee' on the subject of Irish distress, there can be no second opinion as to the noble generosity which has prompted the remittance of no less a sum than three thousand pounds for its relief.[110]

A 'respectable meeting' had been held in Calcutta on 2 January, a general committee formed and various members of the Irish – note, not British – nobility, clergy and academy invited to become trustees of the 'Bengal

Subscription' and responsible for the distribution of the funds.[111] By 21 January, the subscription amounted to 39,000 rupees, with a further subscription started in Madras with hopes of the like happening in Bombay. As Kinealy notes, subscribers were supposed to be limited to British and Irish settlers, though some Indians also offered their support, with the Calcutta Committee (aka the Irish Relief Fund and the Indian Relief Fund) stating that even the smallest donations were welcome.[112] At a distance, it not at home, the British *did* raise relief funds by subscription before the prompt of the government-backed scheme.

The tenor of British public reactions changed markedly in late summer when, on the potato crop being dug, it was found to be an almost total failure. 'The people of this country', warned the editorial in the London *Standard* on 3 September, 'must prepare for exertions to save millions of our fellow subjects'.[113] While stopping short of advocating public subscriptions – though the subscription of 1822 had been a 'glorious monument to British generosity' – the columns of the paper in the ensuing days marked a notable shift in tone.[114] By the beginning of October the absolute certainty of a humanitarian disaster prompted a shift in British popular opinion and action. Well-attended public meetings to consider what means to adopt to alleviate the suffering of the Irish poor were held in London and entered into subscriptions.[115] Concurrently, the National Club (founded in London the previous June with the aim of upholding 'the Protestant Principles of the Constitution, and for Raising the Moral and Social Condition of the People' in Britain and Ireland) acted unilaterally. It resolved in 'this frightful emergency' to act on 'the impulse of their own feelings and on the suggestions of many' to open a general subscription to support both the Irish and the poor in the Scottish Highlands.[116] A large committee of noblemen and MPs was duly formed to determine upon the distribution of subscribed funds, and to provide against 'imposition' from claimants. This news prompted the *Standard* to change its line on subscriptions: 'they who feel and rejoice in "the blessedness of giving", may now indulge in their glorious disposition with a full assurance that they can do nothing but good.'[117] By mid-November the National Club had already raised over £900.[118]

This and the aforementioned other early October London subscriptions were by no means the only such funds raised before the foundation of the BRA in January 1847. While London was to remain the central focus for British relief efforts – something acknowledged by a deputation from the Cork Relief Committee being dispatched to London in November to solicit subscriptions – other local subscriptions were also launched.[119] While the archive is no doubt defective in recording such ad hoc, localised collections, it is striking that those schemes reported figured heavily in Lancashire and Yorkshire, counties with large migrant Irish populations and strong cultural and trade links with Ireland. Bristol, another large maritime city with a growing Irish population and a strong Irish trade, followed suit in raising a subscription in early January 1847.[120] Concurrently, in December the

Quakers also entered into a national subscription in Britain to aid the Central Committee in Dublin in establishing soup kitchens. By mid-December it was reported that £20,000 had been raised, of which £1,000 alone came from the 'good givers' of Leeds.[121]

The plight of distant kin

In many ways initial British public reactions to the famine mirrored those of Peel's Tory administration and those of the wider Imperial Parliament. Blight, and its likely attendant effects, were at once a domestic *and* a colonial issue. It was something that united Britain and Ireland for the *fear* of famine was not something confined to Ireland but something sensed in England and absolutely felt in the Scottish Highlands. The demotic experience of the 'Hungry Forties' in Britain mediated the understanding of the plight of more distant kin.[122] But while shared, lived experiences and an emergent labouring cosmopolitanism (as given expression in much Chartist writing) underpinned empathy for the hungry Irish in some places, it is important to note that there continued to be an entrenched culture of xenophobia.[123] Attacks on Irish migrant workers, for instance, remained an important part of working culture into the 1840s.[124]

In the case of the major centres of Irish migrant populations – the west coast towns, the mill towns, Clydeside – the experience of Irish hunger was not shared at a distance but something shared immediately and in place. Indeed, Famine-period migration to Britain followed established routes and concentrated on already established diasporic settlements. This only changed to a wider dispersal in the 1850s.[125] Against this Unionist interpretation, the wider political rhetoric was not that this was a British problem, a problem of the united countries of the Union. Rather, it was represented as a colonial problem, a consequence of the structural problems with the Irish economy and society. Together these dynamics meant that the undoubted deep human feeling for the sufferings of the Irish poor evident in the public response was tempered by the belief that, at best, this was another false alarm or, at worst, this was something the Irish had brought upon themselves, a belief later given scriptural frame in the 'providential' reading of famine deaths. Typified by the responses of both the ACLL and Chartist campaigners, the problem was therefore, as Gray and Nally amongst others have suggested, an opportunity to restructure Ireland – to change Ireland from a problem colony to an effective and profitable part of Britain.[126] This reading is given further depth by the fact that whereas before the autumn of 1846 popular subscriptions for the relief of the hungry Irish were not raised in Britain, they were raised in other British colonies. Such were the bonds of solidarity.

In addition, it is important to underline that beyond hardened positions, when the evidential realities of 'pestilence and famine' in Ireland became irrefutable, the response was unequivocal. Against the brutality of the policy response of Russell's government – and before the Treasury-sanctioned launch of the BRA campaign – subscriptions for the relief of the famine Irish *were* raised in Britain. Beyond the coordinated activities of the National Club, though, it is impossible to get at the depth of this subscription movement by virtue of its ad hoc, uncoordinated nature, and we will in all probability never know how universal or important it was.[127] Yet the existence alone of such pre-BRA local subscriptions is telling. It speaks directly to the existence of a humanitarian concern motivated not by government, royal speeches, popular political movements, religious foundations or even charities, but by a sense of colonial responsibility and human solidarity. It is important to note, though, that this corrective assertion of empathy does not act to diminish the importance of the popular fervour manipulated by the BRA subscription. Critically, nor does it reduce the human impact of the 'compassion fatigue' that followed the BRA: the discourse of the British press and political debate shifted from sympathy to asserting that resurgent Irish Nationalism and rural rebellion was evidence of 'monstrous ingratitude'.[128] Rather, it reminds us that there was not one British response but many, changing both over time, and between different places and groups.

As noted, the literature on this devastating, politically-framed famine, has since the early 1990s developed at pace, addressing gaps in our knowledge, asking new questions of the archive, and showing a more nuanced, sophisticated understanding of the catastrophe. Historical geographers in particular have contributed massively to these new understandings, visualising the effects of the famine and placing the events of 1845–9 into a wider theoretical and international context.[129]

Yet, as this chapter shows, we not only need to understand how the Famine was conceived and made as a colonial problem *and* solution, but also that it was popularly understood – at least in part – as being not being exclusively a problem of Ireland. Rather, as British (and more-than-British) relief efforts show, the hunger of the Irish poor had effects and ultimately affects beyond the island of Ireland. The possibility of famine striking the shores of England may have receded as a genuine threat, but its colonial co-presence meant that it was ever present in the minds of the English public. Further, the hunger of distant others, of those who would never be known but who were imagined through reading newspaper reports and listening to speeches and sermons, was felt: it engendered a response. The imagined geography and sociality of hungry others had transformative effects. It meant that hunger was no longer something only understood in relation to one's own body, one's kith and kin, one's community, but was conceived of relationally.

The affective power of hungry others was also heightened by the influence of the trope of hunger and starvation in Victorian fiction. As the work of Lesa Scholl and Tara Moore has shown, both tropes were persistent features of many Victorian novels, something heightened in Christmas fiction, which often spoke directly to public fears of famine. The rhetoric of benevolence that can be seen in work like Dickens' *Christmas Carol* stretched from the pulpit to the page and from the public house to the public meeting. Thus a figure like Scrooge's 'transformation in terms of sating his own social and physical hunger' serves to illustrate, as Scholl puts it, 'the tensions between liberalism, capitalism, masochistic self-sacrifice, and altruism that inevitably contribute[d] to dialogues between the needs of the individual and the broader needs of the community'.[130] In the same way that biopolitical strategies and devices made and reformed hunger at the level of the population – the hungry body was idealised and made abstract – so the suffering of distant others played upon the public mind, building on the persistence of popular fears of hunger and famine and the centrality of hunger politics in Victorian fiction, and served to transform popular understandings of hunger.

We must not forget though that a significant part of the affective horror of the Irish famine of the 1840s was its subsequent mobilisation popularly, politically and intellectually. If monumentalising the famine only assumed significant status in the 1990s, and this as part of a veritable famine industry, it is important to note that in the decade after the famine a glut of travel books and guides to Ireland was written. As Spurgeon Thompson has suggested, this was part of an attempt to 'culturally order the catastrophe'. With more people touring Ireland in the 1850s than ever before or would again until the 1970s,[131] the inevitable effect was to quickly marginalise folk memories and knowledges and put in place official narratives and accounts.[132] But outside of Ireland the now-swollen diaspora was not so directly subject to the disciplining logics of official memory. Rather, drawing on experience, second- (and third-) hand accounts, representations and polemics, a very different 'international narrative repertoire' of the Irish hunger developed. As Niall O'Ciosáin has asserted, from this mélange a different popular memory emerged 'consisting of a stylised repertoire of images, motifs, short narratives and supernatural legends'. As opposed to a silent hunger at home, the international Ireland gave voice to the persistence of hunger, a more than spectral presence everywhere.[133]

Notes

1 Slavery Abolition Act (1833), 3 & 4 Will. IV c.73.
2 E. Griffin, *Liberty's Dawn: A People's History of the Industrial Revolution* (New Haven, CT: Yale University Press, 2013).
3 For an important recent study of the memorialisation of the famine see: E. Mark-Fitzgerald, *Commemorating the Irish Famine: Memory and the Monument* (Liverpool: Liverpool University Press, 2013).
4 For a recent geographical analysis of the impact of the Great Famine on Irish demographics see: A.S. Fotheringham, M. Kelly, and M. Charlton, 'The demographic impacts of the Irish famine: Towards a greater geographical understanding', *Transactions of the Institute of British Geographers*, 38:2 (2013), 221–37.
5 Mark-Fitzgerald, *Commemorating the Irish Famine*, p. 2.

6 C. Kinealy, *This Great Calamity: The Irish Famine 1845–52* (Dublin: Gill & Macmillan, 2006), pp. xviii–xix.
7 M. Crawford, *Famine: The Irish Experience, 900–1900* (Edinburgh: John Donald, 1989); P. Gray, *The Irish Famine* (London: Thames and Hudson, 1995); P. Gray, *Famine, Land and Politics: British Government and Irish Society 1843–1850* (Dublin: Irish Academic Press, 1999); C. Kinealy, *Death-Dealing Famine: The Great Hunger in Ireland* (London: Pluto Press, 1997); C. Kinealy, *The Great Famine in Ireland: Impact, Ideology and Rebellion* (Basingstoke: Palgrave, 2002); C. Kinealy, *This Great Calamity: Charity and the Great Hunger in Ireland: The Kindness of Strangers* (London: Bloomsbury, 2013); J. Mokyr, *Why Ireland Starved: A Quantitative and Analytical History of the Irish Economy, 1800–1850*, 2nd ed. (London: Routledge, 2005); C. Ó Gráda, *The Great Irish Famine* (Cambridge: Cambridge University Press, 1995); C. Ó Gráda, *Black '47 and Beyond* (Princeton, NJ: Princeton University Press, 1999); T.P. Coogan, *The Famine Plot: England's Role in Ireland's Greatest Tragedy* (Basingstoke: Palgrave, 2013); Mark-Fitzgerald, Commemorating the Irish Famine; D. Nally, *Human Encumbrances: Political Violence and the Great Irish Famine* (Notre Dame, IN: University of Notre Dame Press, 2010); J. Crowley, J. Smyth and M. Murphy (eds), *Atlas of the Great Irish Famine* (Cork: Cork University Press, 2012).
8 Kinealy, *Charity and the Great Hunger in Ireland*.
9 J. Donnelly, '"Irish property must pay for Irish poverty": British public opinion and the Great Irish Famine', in C. Morash and R. Hayes (eds), *"Fearful Realities": New Perspectives on the Famine* (Dublin: Irish Academic Press, 1996), pp. 60–76.
10 Donnelly, '"Irish property"'; Kinealy, *Charity and the Great Hunger in Ireland*, chs 8 and 9. Also of note is David Nally's study of Thomas Carlyle's writings on his travels through Ireland from September 1846, though this is not a study of public reactions per se: '"Eternity's commissioner": Thomas Carlyle, the Great Irish Famine and the geopolitics of travel', *Journal of Historical Geography* 32:3 (2006), 313–35.
11 Donnelly, '"Irish property"'.
12 Report from the *Banner of Ulster* reprinted in *Freeman's Journal*, 6 August 1845.
13 *Leeds Times*, 9 August 1845.
14 *Belfast News-Letter*, 2 September 1845.
15 *Dublin Evening Post*; quoted in *Belfast News-Letter*, 2 September 1845.
16 *Limerick Chronicle*; quoted in *Belfast News-Letter*, 2 September 1845.
17 *Cork Examiner*, 20 August 1845.
18 *Sussex Advertiser*, 12 August 1845.
19 *Morning Post*, 15 August 1845, including report from *Kentish Observer*.
20 *London Standard*, 19 August 1845, including report from *Dover Chronicle*. Some 'failures' of the potato harvest had been noticed in Devon in late July, though whether this was due to the same blight seems improbable: *Sherborne Mercury*, 2 August 1845.
21 *Sussex Advertiser*, 19 August 1845; *Morning Chronicle*, 20 August 1845; *Cork Examiner*, 22 August 1845 (including letter to the editor from Body and Co., Mark Lane, London).

22 *Cork Examiner*, 27 August 1845; including report from the *Gardener's Chronicle*; *Royal Cornwall Gazette*, 29 August; *Sherborne Mercury*, 30 August 1845.
23 Kinealy, *This Great Calamity*, p. 31.
24 *Cork Examiner*, 29 August 1845.
25 E. Charles Nelson, *The Cause of the Calamity: Potato Blight in Ireland 1845–7, and the Role of the National Botanic Gardens, Glasnevin* (Dublin: Stationery Office, 1995), p. 5. As Nuala Johnson notes, under the lead of head gardener David Moore, Glasnevin became a major centre of study into the blight, though the various experiments into prevention and cures ultimately had no positive effect: *Nature Displaced, Nature Displayed: Order and Beauty in Botanical Gardens* (London: I.B. Tauris, 2011), pp. 60–3.
26 *Cork Examiner*, 10 September 1845.
27 *Dublin Evening Post*, 6 September 1845, quoted in A. Bourke, 'The use of the potato crop in pre-famine Ireland', *Journal of the Statistical and Social Inquiry Society of Ireland*, 21 (1968), 72; *Waterford Freeman*, 6 September 1845, quoted in *Cork Examiner*, 10 September 1845.
28 *Cork Examiner*, 10 September 1845; *Cork Examiner*, 15 September 1845; *Freeman's Journal*, 17 September 1845. See also: Bourke, 'The use of the potato crop'. It was not until the harvest of 1846 that the potato crop failed in the Highlands of Scotland due to the blight: T. Devine, *The Great Highland Famine; Hunger, Emigration and the Scottish Highlands in the Nineteenth Century* (Edinburgh: Birlinn, 1988).
29 For references on revision and counter-revision, see note 7 above. A. Sen, *Poverty and Famines: An Essay on Entitlement and Deprivation* (Oxford: Oxford University Press, 1990/1981).
30 5,000 famine refugees alone were buried at Grosse-Île in Quebec in 1847, this being the largest famine gravesite outside of Ireland: G. Tucker, 'The famine immigration to Canada, 1847', *American Historical Review*, 36:3 (1931), 533–49. For an excellent study of the public health implications of the arrival of the 'famine Irish' in Liverpool see: G. Kearns and P. Laxton, 'Ethnic groups as public health hazards: The famine Irish in Liverpool and Lazaretto politics', in E. Rodríguez-Ocaña (ed.), *The Politics of the Healthy Life: An International Perspective* (Sheffield, United Kingdom: EAHMH, 2003), pp. 13–40.
31 On the structure of Irish landholding and its agricultural and social effects see: R.C. Shipkey, *Robert Peel's Irish Policy: 1812–1846* (New York: Garland, 1987), pp. 472–7; Gray, *Famine, Land and Politics*.
32 P.A. Pickering and A. Tyrrell, *The People's Bread: A History of the Anti-Corn Law League* (Leicester: Leicester University Press, 2000).
33 *Freeman's Journal and Daily Commercial Advertiser*, 3 December 1845. On Cobden and the wider influence of the Anti–Corn Law League see: Pickering and Tyrrell, *The People's Bread*.
34 I. McLean and C. Bustani, 'Irish potatoes and British politics: Interests, ideology, heresthetic and the repeal of the Corn Laws', *Political Studies*, 47:5 (1999), 817–36.

35 Shipkey, *Robert Peel's Irish Policy*, pp. 468, 361.
36 On the aftermath of the United Irishmen's 1798 rebellion see J. Patterson's excellent *In The Wake of the Great Rebellion: Republicanism, Agrarianism and Banditry in Ireland after 1798* (Manchester: Manchester University Press, 2008). For the Young Ireland 'movement' see: R. Davis, *The Young Ireland Movement* (Dublin: Gill and Macmillan, 1988); G. Kearns, 'Time and some citizenship: nationalism and Thomas Davis', *Bullán: An Irish Studies Review*, 5:2 (2001), 23–54.
37 F. Engels, *The Condition of the Working Class in England*, ed. David McLellan (Oxford: Oxford University Press, 1999), pp. 101–5.
38 D. MacRaild, *The Irish Diaspora in Britain, 1750–1939* (Basingstoke: Palgrave, 2011), ch. 2, esp. pp. 41–8.
39 C.R. Dobson, *Masters and Journeymen: A Prehistory of Industrial Relations, 1717–1800* (London: Taylor & Francis, 1980), pp. 21, 154–65.
40 *Kent Herald*, 28 July 1825; Sussex Advertiser, 8 September 1828.
41 C. Griffin, *The Rural War: Captain Swing and the Politics of Protest* (Manchester: Manchester University Press, 2012), pp. 104–5, 108–10 and 113–14.
42 Gray, *Famine, Land and Politics*, p. 119.
43 D. Nally, 'The biopolitics of food provisioning', *Transactions of the Institute of British Geographers*, 36:1 (2011), 40.
44 M. Foucault, *Security, Territory, Population: Lectures at the Collège de France 1977–1978*, trans. A. Davidson, ed. G. Burchell (New York: Palgrave Macmillan, 2007), p. 1.
45 Nally, 'The biopolitics of food provisioning', 40. For David Keen's conception: *The Benefits of Famine: A Political Economy of Famine and Relief in Southwesern Sudan, 1983–1989* (Princeton, NJ: Princeton University Press, 1994).
46 British Library, Add Mss. 40451, fo. 286, Sir James Graham to Sir Robert Peel, 18 September 1845.
47 Shipkey, *Peel's Irish Policy*, pp. 468–9.
48 Ibid., p. 470; Kinealy, *A Death-Dealing Famine*, p. 56.
49 McLean and Bustani, 'Irish potatoes', 817–39; Kinealy, *A Death-Dealing Famine*, pp. 49, 60.
50 G. Bernstein, 'Liberals, the Irish Famine and the role of the state', *Irish Historical Studies*, 29:116 (1995), 536.
51 Kinealy, *A Death-Dealing Famine*, pp. 53–6. A further survey was carried out by the Irish constabulary in March 1846. The blight was found to have had the worst impact in Armagh, Clare, Kilkenny, Louth, Monaghan and Waterford, where losses were in excess of two-fifths of the crop.
52 Ibid., pp. 56–7; Kinealy, *Charity and the Great Hunger in Ireland*, pp. 18–23. On the state of the Irish Poor Law see: P. Gray, *The Making of the Irish Poor Law, 1815–43* (Manchester: Manchester University Press, 2009). It is important to note that *initially* import duties on Indian corn were not respited, for, in the words of Home Secretary Graham, 'if we opened the ports to maize duty-free, most popular and irresistible arguments present themselves why flour

and oatmeal, the staple of the food of man, should not be restricted in its supply by artificial means, while Heaven has withheld from an entire people its accustomed sustenance [...]. Can these duties, once remitted by Act of Parliament, be ever again reimposed?': Graham to Peel, 13 October 1845, quoted in C.S. Parker (ed.), *Life and Letters of Sir James Graham, Second Baronet of Netherby* (London: John Murray, 1907), p. 115.

53 The best study of the administration of the public works during the famine remains Arthur Griffiths, 'The Irish Board of Works during the famine years', *Historical Journal*, 13:4 (1970), 634–52.

54 Gray, *Famine, Land and Politics*, p. 120; Kinealy, *A Death-Dealing Famine*, pp. 61–3.

55 British Parliamentary Papers (hereafter BPP), 1846 (171) vol. 27, Instructions to the Committees of Relief Districts, extracted from Minutes of the Proceedings of the Commissioners appointed in reference to the apprehended scarcity.

56 Kinealy, *A Death-Dealing Famine*, pp. 62, 64.

57 Ibid., pp. 63–4.

58 Gray, *Famine, Land and Politics*, pp. 252–3; Kinealy, *A Death-Dealing Famine*, p. 77.

59 Poor Employment Act, 9 and 10 Victoria (1846), c.107; Kinealy, *A Death-Dealing Famine*, pp. 67, 71–2, 73. On the contested role and impact of Trevelyan see: R. Haines, *Charles Trevelyan and the Great Irish Famine* (Dublin: Four Courts Press, 2004).

60 Kinealy, *This Great Calamity*, pp. 90–106. For a detailed analysis of the numbers employed in public works, and the variation by region, see ibid., pp. 363–5.

61 *Times*, 12 March 1847; Kinealy, *A Death-Dealing Famine*, pp. 74–5, 79–80.

62 *Nation*, 27 March 1847, cited in Kinealy, *A Death-Dealing Famine*, p. 75.

63 But as Peter Gray has asserted, despite such efforts they still came in for considerable criticism in the British media: *Famine, Land and Politics*, p. 132.

64 Indian Relief Fund, *Distress in Ireland: Report of the Trustees of the Indian Relief Fund* (Dublin: J. Browne, 1847); Gray, *Famine, Land and Politics*, p. 257.

65 BPP, 1847 (761) vol. 51, Correspondence Relating to Measures for Relief of Distress in Ireland, July 1846–January 1847. On Baring's earlier involvement see: Kinealy, *Charity and the Great Hunger in Ireland*, pp. 22–3.

66 Murphy (ed.) *Annals of the Famine in Ireland*, p. 208 n.34.

67 Kinealy, *Charity and the Great Hunger in Ireland*, pp. 3, 63–83; Murphy (ed.), *Annals of the Famine in Ireland*, pp. 46–7, 207 n.30.

68 Gray, *Famine, Land and Politics*, pp. 257–8; Kinealy, *Charity and the Great Hunger in Ireland*, pp. 195–208, 219–20.

69 Ibid., p. 192.

70 National Library of Dublin, MS 2022, British Association Minute Book. For analysis of the donations see: Kinealy, *Charity and the Great Hunger in Ireland*, ch. 9.

71 Ibid., pp. 185–9.

72 *Cambridge Independent Press*, 18 October 1845.

73 *Wiltshire Independent*, 23 October 1845.

74 Ibid.

75 *Ipswich Journal*, 25 October 1845.

76 *Hampshire Advertiser*, 1 November 1845.

77 Ibid.

78 *Morning Post*, 30 October 1845.

79 *Taunton Courier, and Western Advertiser*, 24 December 1845.

80 *Leeds Times*, 27 December 1845.

81 *Sheffield Independent*, 6 December 1845.

82 *Bradford Observer*, 4 December; *Morning Post*, 10 December 1845.

83 *Western Times*, 8 November 1845. On the Anti–Corn Law League's campaigning see: Pickering and Tyrrell, *The People's Bread*, esp. chs 2 and 8.

84 As Charles Withers notes, though, policy responses and migratory consequences between the famines in Ireland and Scotland were similar: 'Destitution and migration: Labour mobility and relief from famine in Highland Scotland 1836–1850', *Journal of Historical Geography*, 14:2 (1988), 128–50.

85 This fractious, complex relationship was perhaps best typified by the fact that in the ACLL's hometown of Manchester it hired 'Irish thugs' to protect the League Platform *and* disrupt Chartist platforms: Janette Martin, 'Popular political oratory and itinerant lecturing in Yorkshire and the north east in the age of Chartism, *c.* 1837–1860' (PhD thesis, University of York, United Kingdom, 2010), p. 57.

86 The outstanding study is M. Chase, *Chartism: A New History* (Manchester: Manchester University Press, 2007). For an analysis of the work of Irish Chartists in England see: R. Swift, 'Thomas Carlyle, Chartism, and the Irish in early Victorian England', *Victorian Literature and Culture*, 29:1 (2001), 67–83.

87 *Northern Star*, 30 August 1845; *Northern Star*, 1 November 1845.

88 *Northern Star*, 15 November 1845.

89 *Northern Star*, 10 January, p. 4; *Northern Star*, 24 January 1846.

90 Chase, *Chartism*, p. 271. The idea that there was insufficient land in Ireland to support the level of population in the mid-1840s has been absolutely refuted; see: L. Cullen, 'Irish history without the potato', *Past & Present* 40 (1968), 72–83.

91 *Northern Star*, 14 February 1846.

92 Shipkey, *Peel's Irish Policy*, p. 321.

93 *Salisbury and Winchester Journal*, 4 October 1845.

94 *Salisbury and Winchester Journal*, 25 October 1845.

95 *Fife Herald*, 28 October 1845.

96 *Leeds Times*, 8 November 1845.

97 Ibid.

98 *Cambridge Independent Press*, 29 November 1845.

99 P. Gurney, '"Rejoicing in potatoes": The politics of consumption in England during the "Hungry Forties"', *Past & Present*, 203 (2009), 131.

100 *Hampshire Advertiser*, 1 November 1845.

101 *Hereford Journal*, 26 November 1845.
102 On the geography of Irish migrant settlement in Britain see: MacRaild, *The Irish Diaspora in Britain*, ch. 2.
103 Kinealy, *A Death-Dealing Famine*, p. 63.
104 *Hansard*, House of Commons Debate, 8 June 1846, vol. 87 cc. 129–94.
105 *Hansard*, House of Commons Debate, 24 April 1846, vol. 85 cc. 980–1022. For further reporting not detailed in *Hansard* see: *Bradford Observer*, 23 April 1846. An exception to this rhetoric was George Bankes, Tory landowner and MP for the 'family seat' at Wareham in Dorset. During the debate in the Commons on 8 May on the Corn Importation Bill, Bankes, an ardent supporter of the Corn Laws, stated that the 'distress' in Ireland ought be supported by 'public subscriptions and grants from the Exchequer' as opposed to 'aggravated by the sacrifice of one of the great interest of the country': Hansard, House of Commons Debate, 8 May 1846, vol. 86 cc. 226–99. The direct quotation comes from the Parliamentary report in *Liverpool Mercury*, 15 May 1846.
106 *Bristol Mercury*, 25 April 1846.
107 Ibid.
108 Ibid.
109 *Morning Post*, 10 April 1846.
110 Ibid.
111 *Morning Post*, 10 April 1846; Indian Relief Fund, *Distress in Ireland*. Also see: Gray, *Famine, Land and Politics*, p. 257.
112 Kinealy, *Charity and the Great Hunger in Ireland*, pp. 42–4. A subscription was also raised amongst the 'European and Native' residents of Kandy, Ceylon/Sri Lanka: *Freeman's Journal*, 2 June 1846.
113 *Standard*, 3 September 1846.
114 *Standard*, 15 September 1846.
115 *Morning Post*, 5 October 1846.
116 *Morning Post*, 12 October 1846.
117 *Standard*, 17 October 1846.
118 *Standard*, 13 November 1846.
119 *Freeman's Journal*, 20 November 1846. The surviving administrative records of the National Club are held at the Bodleian Library, Oxford: Dep. b. 235–40, c. 682–4, d. 754–7.
120 For instance see reports of schemes in: *Hull Packet*, 23 October 1846 and 25 December 1846; *York Herald*, 24 October 1846; *Standard*, 28 December 1846 (regarding a meeting at Liverpool to raise a general subscription); *Leeds Mercury*, 2 January 1847.
121 *Leeds Mercury*, 19 December 1846.
122 On the popular experience of the 'Hungry Forties' in England see: Gurney, '"Rejoicing in potatoes"'.
123 The best articulation of these geographies of working cosmopolitanism appears in the ongoing work of David Featherstone. For his most detailed exposition see: *Solidarity: Hidden Histories and Geographies of Internationalism* (London: Zed, 2012), esp. ch. 3.

124 MacRaild, *The Irish Diaspora*, pp. 163–7; L. Miskell, 'Reassessing the anti-Irish riot: Popular protest and the Irish in south Wales, *c.* 1826–1882', in P. O'Leary (ed.), *Irish Migrants in Modern Wales* (Liverpool: Liverpool University Press, 2004), pp. 101–18. On the culture of working xenophobia in rural England see: K.D.M. Snell, 'The culture of local xenophobia', *Social History*, 28:1 (2003), 1–30.

125 MacRaild, *The Irish Diaspora*, p. 54.

126 Gray, *Famine, Land and Politics*; Nally, *Human Encumbrances*, esp. chs 4 and 6.

127 One possibility is the systematic analysis of the Dublin-based Relief Commission's surviving papers held at the National Archives of Ireland, but given that the Commission was formally stood down in August 1846 and not reconstituted until February 1847 this source does not offer a systematic survey.

128 On the idea of compassion fatigue and ingratitude see: P. Bew, *Ireland: The Politics of Enmity 1789–2006* (Oxford: Oxford University Press, 2007), p. 210; Kinealy, *A Death-Dealing Famine*, pp. 13, 118; Kearns and Laxton, 'Ethnic groups as public health hazards', p. 31. The phrase 'monstrous ingratitude' was first used in a report in The *Times*, 22 September 1847.

129 The outstanding recent contributions are Nally, *Human Encumbrances*; and Crowley, Smyth and Murphy, *Atlas of the Great Irish Famine*.

130 T. Moore, 'Starvation in Victorian Christmas fiction', *Victorian Literature and Culture*, 36:2 (2008), 489–505; L. Scholl, *Hunger Movements in Early Victorian Literature: Want, Riots, Migration* (London: Routledge, 2016), p. 14.

131 S. Thompson, 'Famine travel: Irish tourism from the Great Famine to decolonization', in B. Colbert (ed.), *Travel Writing and Tourism in Britain and Ireland* (Basingstoke: Palgrave), pp. 164–80.

132 On this see N. O'Cioséin, 'Was there 'silence' about the famine?', *Irish Studies Review*, 4:13 (1995), 7–10; N. O'Cioséin, 'Approaching a folklore archive: The Irish Folklore Commission and the memory of the Great Famine', *Folklore*, 115:2 (2004), 222–32.

133 O'Cioséin, 'Approaching a folklore archive', 225.

Conclusions

Between 1 April 2017 and 31 March 2018 the Trussell Trust, the UK's largest network of food banks, distributed 1,332,952 three-day emergency food parcels, supporting an estimated 660,000 individuals in crisis. Whether they are afflicted by illness, disability, family breakdowns or worklessness, the peoples of Britain and Northern Ireland continue to be affected by hunger. As Emma Revie, the chief executive of the Trust, put it:

> As a nation we expect no one should be left hungry or destitute … and we owe it to each other to make sure sufficient financial support is in place when we need it most. It's hard to break free from hunger if there isn't enough money coming in to cover the rising cost of absolute essentials like food and housing. For too many people staying above water is a daily struggle.[1]

If austerity-era policies – including UK government welfare reforms like the so-called 'Universal Credit' – are the evident cause of a desperate rise in the number and use of food banks since the global economic crash of 2008,[2] hunger has never ceased to threaten those living near the breadline. Indeed, the continuing use of the term breadline – first used at the turn of the twentieth-century – is in itself an invocation of the importance of historical hunger politics in the present: a reference to the long-term centrality of bread to the diet of the poor and to the persistent idea that the most basic definition of poverty is being unable to literally subsist. Hunger persists because gross inequalities and inequities persist. Indeed, in Baroness Jenkin's notorious 2014 claim that 'poor people' went hungry because 'they do not know how to cook' – 'I had a large bowl of porridge today. It cost 4p. A large bowl of sugary cereal will cost 25p' – we see echoes of New Poor Law workhouse gruel-laden dietaries 'reforming' the poor and elements of Joseph Townsend's 1786 assertion that 'it is only hunger which can spur and goad them on to labour'. And in Tory MPs' praise of food banks as evidence of the compassionate nature of the British public – the Conservative dream of a social security net based on charity – we see echoes of poor law reformers' aspiration to reduce and ultimately eliminate statutory support for the poor.[3] The history of the politics of hunger matters because it is the not just the history of how we got to the current conjuncture but because it is the history of now. Indeed, throughout the developing world and in parts of the old Soviet bloc remarkably similar discourses around hunger and starvation to those of eighteenth- and early nineteenth-century England pervade public life.[4] It is with good reason that of the seventeen 2015 United Nations Development Programme Sustainable Development Goals, goal number two is to end hunger.[5]

In the early twenty-first century, as it was in the early nineteenth century, hunger remains a wretched everyday reality and persistent fear for millions of people in England. If perishing from want, thankfully, remains rare, the spectre lingers. It is this persistence that puts in the shade the fixation with famine that has so dominated considerations of the late eighteenth and early nineteenth centuries. Timing when the threat of famine lifted from the peoples of England is to consider, in biopolitical style, only the population rather than the individual; it is to deny the fear of death from want that remained throughout the period considered by this study and continues today. None of this is to deny the continued global devastation wrought by famines, arguably the cruellest and most persistent legacy of the entrenched global inequalities created by European imperialism.[6] Rather, it is to assert that it is the experience of, and response to, hunger that defines *everyday* experiences, both in Britain and across the globe. Famine, in its modern, widely used sense is occasional, whereas hunger, as felt, experienced and feared, lingers without leave. Indeed, some now archaic uses of the word (and concept) famine related not to excess levels of mortality caused by absolute bodily want but instead to a grinding and persistent hunger. For instance, the so-called Lancashire Cotton Famine of the early 1860s was not a famine as we would understand it, but rather a period of prolonged want and acute hunger, especially for those in and around Lancashire and Cheshire.[7] In the same vein, the 1840s represented a period of intense hunger for many, in the industrial towns and countryside alike, but not a famine. Just as in the 1790s and early 1800s, mass deaths from want and disease were averted because of a combined popular and political will. Charity and state-sponsored acts of relief prevented excess mortality. And this is the critical point. As Richard Hoyle in his survey of famine in Britain has suggested, by the mid-eighteenth century not only were markets sufficiently well integrated, with reasonably fluid and efficient mechanisms for the transhipment of (especially) grain nationally and in the North Sea region, but also systems of statutory relief and charitable giving meant that provided the political will was strong famine, would always be avoided.[8]

To claim, as Roger Wells did, that there were 'famine-like' conditions in the 1790s is thus at once correct – the situation was parlous in 1795 and again in 1800, one universal harvest failure or a lack of governmental will to intervene away from mass starvation – but also unhelpful.[9] To frame all historical analyses of responses to dearth, depression, market failure and political negligence (or wilful engineering) in terms of whether there *was* or *was not* famine is both to belittle the sheer hideousness of the famines that continue to destroy families and communities and to crudely conceptualise the spectrum of experiences and bodily states of need. One might even usefully argue that in placing so strong an emphasis on hunger – by way of extending our understanding of the spectrum of experiences and policy prescriptions – is in itself too limiting, a further act of conceptual obfuscation and denial of difference. To address this point, I would agree that simply asserting hunger as a universal, undifferentiated state of being is problematic. But, as the foregoing chapters attest, hunger was never understood in a neat, linear way. As related in chapter one, to ask whether 'hunger rioters' were ever really hungry might be an interesting intellectual exercise but it is to miss the point.[10] To engage in food rioting, and the associated protest practices, was an attempt either to preserve (and/or redirect) supplies, or to maintain fair prices and quality. It was an attempt to prevent hunger, or to prevent hunger becoming starvation. It was, as in the case of the skeleton of a cat nailed to a board before the start of the market at Lewes on Saturday 26 April 1800 with the tag 'Symptoms of Starvation' written above it, a graphic reminder of the responsibilities of the patrician class and a warning of what might happen were they to absolve themselves of their obligations.[11] The discourse was already established before food rioting became the defining form of popular protest in the early eighteenth century.[12]

The persistence of the dual discourses of hunger and starvation (which in itself was not automatically reducible to a famine discourse, for the word famine was not uttered in this way) speaks to the way in which poor consumers were able to articulate their perilousness. As noted in chapter one, protests during subsistence crises were motivated by a desire to avoid being plunged into a state of absolute, immediate calorific need. To protest was to survive: 'we might starve if we do not act, we might starve if you do not listen'. Of course, all forms of protest are discourses, repeated claims (whether spoken or unspoken, performed, inferred or threatened) that were understood by the plebs and patricians alike. Such language 'games', with their prescribed rules, followed by both sides, meant that pandemonium and bloodshed could be prevented. That hunger was at the heart of such language games during subsistence crises should hardly surprise us – whatever the remarkable silence of protest historians on this very point – but in the context of subsistence crises the rather mannered discourse of hunger was necessarily left aside for the visceral cry of starvation. The discourse of starvation was to amplify and make explicit the latent potential for misrule in all acts of protest. It was to scream of the destruction and terror that would follow – and would be justified – in the face of impeding bodily doom.

The discourse persisted because it spoke to a universal and genuine fear that grinding hunger was only ever one disaster away: a failed harvest; unemployment; illness; family tragedy; being socially ostracised and excluded. This persistence matters in other ways too. Claims that the food-rioting tradition died out in the early 1800s might well be true if we limit our conceptualisation of protest responses to subsistence crises to the relatively small number of crowd-based repertoires delineated in E.P. Thompson's 'moral economy' thesis.[13] Besides, after the crisis of 1800–1 subsequent dearths were not as severe, and our telling of the 'crisis' years of 1816, 1819–20, 1822 and 1829–30 has not been figured in terms of 'subsistence crises' but instead through conflations of socio-economic and socio-political crisis.[14] To draw on Sen's theory of entitlements, ultimately for the poor the issue remained access to food, or rather a failure of their entitlement to food.[15] Thus when the food-rioting tradition receded and subsistence crises were no longer reckoned with, the poor still figured their protests in relation to the discourse of starvation precisely because for individuals on 'the breadline' hunger was *the* visceral reality that bit hardest. When basic subsistence consisted of accommodation, clothes and food, of which food assumed (at least) three-quarters of rural labouring families' incomes, then food necessarily assumed the strongest possible political potency. It was the alpha and omega of labouring life. Thus if keeping fed defined so much of labouring life, it should come as little surprise that so many of the protest practices and performances of the poor were writ through with warnings about the consequences of hunger and about the dire threat of starvation. All was intertwined. The case of Sussex labourer Henry Dine, as detailed in chapter two, during the 1839 hop harvest is indicative. Not being paid in full by farmer Bourne was a threat to his sustenance, and his response that 'I will set a stack on fire, or steal a sheep or a duck for my supper' as he would 'much better off if transported than he was while running about the country in a state of starvation' is a perfect encapsulation of this interdependence.[16] To protest was an attempt to stay the threat and consequences of hunger.

If, as the wretched recent rise of the food bank suggests, the fear of hunger never really lifted for many of the peoples of Britain, the fact that the discourse of starvation stopped at some point after the 1840s evidently speaks to the changing ways in which protest was articulated and practised. Precisely when this happened is unclear. Indeed, we can only speculate as to the possible causes: the drawing in of many working communities to participatory politics; the shifting of the population from rural to urban Britain and the associated decline in the number of rural workers undermining established customs and protest practices; the collapse of the patrician system. Outside of the resort to trade unionism and the continued rise of participatory politicking, the 1850s and 1860s remain remarkably little studied in terms of the protests of the poor. We might assume, given the way in which radical polit-icking readily co-opted popular fears about hunger, and given that the New Poor Law acted to further politicise hunger, that the discourse of starvation remained live and well in the years beyond the 'Hungry Forties'. Indeed, so notorious was the fall in real wages in the 1860s that in 2016 Mark Carney, the governor of the Bank of England, claimed that the UK was then facing its 'first lost decade since the 1860s' in terms of real wages growth.[17] But this is to speculate, for these decades remain notable lacunae in our knowledge of the politics of everyday life in the English countryside, let alone in terms of our knowledge of hunger politics.[18] To further test the persistence of the discourse – and not just in terms of everyday workhouse resistances – we need to put aside neat categorisations and labels and, after Keith Wrightson, throw down the enclosures by time period, space and subject that continue to hinder historical investigation.[19] In so doing we need to be mindful of the fact that the discourse never fully disappeared, rather it was perhaps manifested in different ways, found skulking in conversations on street corners and dole queues, occasionally to find graphic form in 'hunger marches' of the 1920s and 1930s and during the 1984–5 Miners' Strike, when the tag 'hunger scabs' was given to those who returned to work when their resistance was broken by hunger.[20]

Such a shift necessarily also speaks to a changing relationship between hunger and public policy, or at least to a changing public relationship with hunger-related policies. We know that even after the Andover Scandal-induced remaking of the Poor Law Commission as the Poor Law Board, diet-aries remained not only essentially unaltered – the principle of less eligibility continued at the heart of workhouse governance – but also no less popularly despised. Hunger remained a key social policy tool and instrumental political battleground. Indeed, the Poor Law Board-led 'crusade against out-relief' instigated at the start of the 1870s acted initially, to further politicise hunger. Most of those denied out-relief refused the offer of entering the work-house: the 'deterrent' worked in no small part because of the dread created by dietary scandals, and they were forced to face their own fate unaided.[21] As one of the 'crusaders', Albert Pell, South Leicestershire MP and an ex-officio guardian of the Brixworth Union, saw it:

> The administration of the Poor Laws is a matter of police, not sentiment, and should be applied unswervingly in obedience to fixed principles, and not become the haphazard display of sentiment and a counterfeit charity … [otherwise] the incentives of industry are weakened; the fear of the consequences of cold, hunger and distress is diminished or vanishes.[22]

Whether, as Andy Croll has recently suggested of Wales, the poor in rural England became in time 'gradually reconciled' to the system is perhaps a moot point, but it is clear that hunger remained a critical social policy tool, a device to be channelled and made rather than something to be overcome.[23]

As chapter three detailed, social policy responses to hunger could be driven by humane intentions, a concern for bodily welfare – in the truest sense – rather than something that could be used to reform and transform the poor. Speenhamland-style payments were initially, and arguably until the 1810s, motivated by a clear-sighted need to support real wages in times of acute distress: to provide a net beyond the occasional support that charity might, or might not, offer. None of this is to say that such schemes, even from their inception, were never without other stipulations, for instance trying to morally reform the poor, but, on balance, such payments at first responded to genuine need, to a hunger already felt or imminent. The subsequent perversions and embedding of wage supplements into the economies of the cornlands during the 1820s and early 1830s, which became notorious thanks to the authors of the 1832 *Poor Law Report*, had nothing to do with preventing gnawing hunger but everything to do with self-interested responses amongst larger farmers and landowners at a time of crisis in the agrarian economy. And as costs spiralled so the logic of making all labourers dependent on the wider community of parish ratepayers begat universal pauperism, and thus emerged a sensibility and system that started to professionalise relief and began to figure relief in terms of minimum bodily needs. This also chimed with the turn to thinking differently about dietaries in a variety of institutional settings. Indeed, if the idea of the dietary had an important prehistory,[24] it was in the conjucture of the post-Napoleonic period that it was remade as more than a pragmatic attempt to manage costs, especially when issuing contracts. Instead the dietary became a biopolitical tool, a population-disciplining device. This was no less about hunger, for it calculated the population-at-large hunger point in making the poor as biological subjects, as things to be known only in the abstract, as points on the population surface. In short, hunger went from being a policy problem to a policy tool. It was not until 1906 that it became legal to institutionally feed at a level that went beyond 'less eligibility': the Education (Provision of Meals) Act allowed local authorities to spend public money on providing school meals, with the rationale not just to keep alive or to discipline but to aid pupils' education. Further, it was not until 1944 that local authorities were *obliged* to provide school meals, with central government funding available from 1947.[25]

Of course, such hunger policies were not confined to England and Wales but rather were explicitly exported to the near Empire – the imposition of the New Poor Law on Ireland in 1838 – and implicitly to the distant British Empire in the form of the making of black bodies as racially other and thus subject to even more brutal forms of bare-life bodily exceptionalism. We need, however, to be careful. There is a world of difference between racially othering to justify acts of remaking society and doing so to justify violent expropriation. Even Malthus, whose works were so influential in the process of making the English labourer as a racial subject, questioned the right and morality of the British state to create formal policies to remove indigenous peoples in North America and Van Diemen's Land. Even the seemingly ragged hunting and gathering savage – to use Malthus's own words – had a basic right to a prescribed (bare) life.[26] In short, hunger became a colonial project. Or as Vernon has put it, it was central to the making of the modern world, an uneven world shaped by policy and fashioned by British domestic consumption siphoning food from British colonies and colonial subjects.[27] As noted in chapter five, hunger was at once the necessary *condition* of the racialised population – hungry, haggard, dirty, desperate, different – that was to be controlled and remade, and also a biopolitical *device* in that very act of remaking. Yet arguably with the rise of neoliberalism in the late twentieth century we have turned full circle. To be hungry, again, was to be stigmatised and othered but also to be made as a different type of human being. The language is different from that of the early nineteenth century but still writ in racial terms.

Hunger was not only theorised by elites, by the makers of policy; rather, as the discourse of starvation attested, those who faced and feared hunger also imaginatively conceived and theorised hunger. Accessing the imaginative, intellectual world of those people who typically left little trace in the archive is necessarily difficult, but the persistence of this discourse attests to a vibrant, shared conception of how best to engage in the politics of hunger, an understanding that hunger was not a natural state of being poor but a false state brought about by economic and social dislocation. While such conceptualisations of sharing only extended so far – the culture of local xenophobia (to use Keith Snell's phrase) or nascent working-class racisms (to draw from Satnam Virdee and Ryan Hanley) acted to limit a deeper working solidarity across different peoples – the hunger of others, of those at a distance in Ireland and elsewhere, acted to reframe popular theorisations.[28] Hunger was not only experienced bodily and grounded locally in the spaces of everyday life, but was also something that happened elsewhere and to others, something that elicited a combination of sympathy, empathy and racialised enmity. But whereas enmity arguably had a deep history, for instance in one dearth-bound community stopping the export of goods to support another unknown but hungry community elsewhere, sympathy and empathy shown to hungry others acted to extend webs of reciprocity, to build new global communities that helped to forge popular humanitarianism and transnational solidarities.[29]

As the foregoing chapters show, to write the politics of hunger is to engage in telling a complex set of spatial stories. From the networked nature of emergent humanitarianism rooted in the spaces of uneven colonial relations, the local–centre dynamics of policy-making and implementation, through the disciplining spatial designs of the workhouse to the spatial metaphor of the surface central to biopolitical thinking, spatial plays are integral to our understandings of hunger. Besides, the experience or fear of hunger was necessarily a product of the political-economic geographies of commodity production, exchange and regulation. Arguably the hardest geography to understand relates to the changing interdependence between the agrarian and the industrial worlds. I use the word interdependence deliberately, for however much England (and ultimately Britain) remained economically, demographically, politically, imaginatively and iconographically an agrarian nation, not only was the demographic balance rapidly tilting towards the urban and the economic engine-house likewise moving from the fields to the factory, but the two realms overlapped and were mutually co-constituting. From the industrial workers of West Yorkshire bringing in the harvest in the East and North Ridings, to the commodity chains linking rural crafts and putting-out industries and urban factors and factories, mines and quarries amidst fields and forests, families consisting of agricultural and industrial workers, and the hybrid spaces of the urban fringe literally located betwixt and between, the rural and the urban and the industrial and agrarian were not hermetically kept apart. So, the townsfolk fearful for their food supplies often marched upon rural mills and granaries to secure stocks; rural labourers, in turn, often descended upon the towns to implore benches to force their parishes to relieve them or to engage in taxation populaire in the market-place. Likewise, the Speenhamland-style policies that responded to a crisis of the cornlands, of the south and east, had universal implications in terms of subsequent poor reforms and ultimately led to the downfall of the old poor law and the institution of the new, that centralising policy so bitterly opposed in the industrial towns of the Midlands and the north.

If the foregoing analysis speaks to these networked, hybrid spaces, the foci also reflect that the policies that responded to and refigured hunger in the period were born of the agrarian south and east. This is, then, another book whose focus rests on the totemic cornlands of the south and east, a continuance of the skewed historiography of the poor laws that Steve King correctly described in 2000.[30] But it is necessarily so given that, remarkably, Speenhamland-style scales and allowances have hitherto not received systematic treatment beyond Neuman's study of Berkshire,[31] while the subsequent perversions and impacts have likewise not been subject to a deep contextualised reading in the very spaces that experimented with scales and allowances in the first place. If workhouse (and poorhouse) dietaries – again, something that before now have not been subject to systematic study – had no evident regional geography during the old poor law, it is important to remember that the New Poor Law workhouse dietaries were a response to the 'issue' of labour discipline (and morality) in the agrarian south and east.

None of this is to say that the study of the spaces of the north and west would yield little in developing our understanding of the policy spaces of hunger. As Peter Gurney has shown for the period from the 1840s onwards and as the analysis in chapter one details for the period before 1800, the fear and experience of hunger was not something that just afflicted the laboring families of the south and east.[32] Downturns in trade, sometimes short-lived and sometimes prolonged, dearth, industrial supply issues – as in the Cotton Famine – and the uneven geographies of industrialisation and deindustrialisation in the north and west all combined to make, and to politicise, hunger. Indeed, wherever poverty stalked, hunger was necessarily an issue. Investigation of popular responses to the fear of hunger in northern and midland cities post-1800 would be of huge value, while testing whether the persistence of the discourse of starvation post-1800 also held true of districts such as the Welsh Marches and rural Cumberland and Westmorland, Lancashire, Northumberland and north Yorkshire would also help to deepen our understanding of the popular workings of the politics of hunger. Likewise, further analyses of the operation and reception of old poor law dietaries would also be welcome. There are other histories to be told. Arguably what might be of greatest value though are in-depth microhistories of hunger politics, grounded and deeply contextualised studies of moments when hunger came to the fore: a solitary food riot; the imposition of a workhouse dietary; a local relief scheme for the support of hungry distant others.

For far too long hunger as a frame of historical analysis has been ignored by scholars of eighteenth- and early nineteenth-century England who have been either too fixated on the hard absolutes of famine or too scared of being labelled as crudely reductionist. To borrow from Amartya Sen, 'the subject of hunger is dominated by preconceptions and often by attempts to understand a very complex problem in excessively narrow terms'.[33] Fine studies by James Vernon and Gurney for the Victorian era and beyond have shown the worth of taking hunger seriously.[34] It is a fallacy to think that any one era, whatever the wider economic and agricultural context, whatever the historiographical direction, might be skipped over as it was free from famine. This is perverse – doubly so, given the example of the power of taking hunger seriously in studies of the causes of the French Revolution.[35] Hunger was, for the period, more powerful, more pervasive, more engrained into the fabric of everyday life and more central to policy-making and political projects than we have admitted. Hunger defined popular protest and popular politics. But to adopt a 'history from below' approach would not have been enough, would not have done justice to the fear and force of hunger, for the experience was necessarily framed by local and central policy-making. Hunger was central to experiments in government; it was used to make new subjects and to assert bodily and racial difference between peoples. Hunger was critical in the making of humanitarianism and early forms of transnational solidarities. If this is the first study to make these connections, I hope not only that it provokes future studies – to dig wider, deeper, further – but also that it reminds us that we have a duty to our subjects to throw off of our disciplinary shackles and break free of neat historiographical bounds and instead follow our subjects' lives, wherever the journey may take us. I hope too that these pages are read not just as a telling of the past but also as a plea in the present. To be ashamed and sick that hunger persists. To listen to the voices of hunger and act. To redouble our efforts so that to be free from the fear of hunger becomes an unalienable human right.

Notes

1 https://www.trusselltrust.org/2018/04/24/benefit-levels-must-keep-pace-rising-cost-essentials-record-increase-foodbank-figures-revealed/, accessed 23 August 2018.

2 *Guardian*, 29 May 2017 ('Report reveals scale of food bank use in the UK'), https://www.theguardian.com/society/2017/may/29/report-reveals-scale-of-food-bank-use-in-the-uk-ifan, accessed 23 August 2018.

3 *Guardian*, 8 December 2014 ('Tory peer says poor people go hungry because they do not know how to cook'), https://www.theguardian.com/society/2014/dec/08/tory-peer-apologises-poor-hungry-do-not-know-cook, accessed 24 August 2018; J. Townsend, *A Dissertation on the Poor Laws*, ed. A. Montagu (Berkeley: University of California Press, 1971), p. 23.

4 For instance see: L. Kurtović, '"Who sows hunger, reaps rage": On protest, indignation and redistributive justice in post-Dayton Bosnia-Herzegovina', *Southeast European and Black Sea Studies*, 15:4 (2015), 639–59; J. Hanoman, *Hunger and Poverty in South Africa: The Hidden Faces of Food Insecurity* (London: Routledge, 2017).

5 The full goal is to: 'End hunger, achieve food security and improved nutrition, and promote sustainable agriculture': UN-DESA, 'Transforming our world: The 2030 agenda for sustainable development, Division for Sustainable Development Goals', https://sustainabledevelopment.un.org/post2015/transformingourworld, accessed 7 September 2018.

6 At the time of writing famines plagued South Sudan, Somalia, northern Nigeria and Yemen: A. Seal, P. Hailey, R. Bailey, D. Maxwell, and N. Majid, 'Famine, conflict, and political indifference', *British Medical Journal (Online)* 357 (2017).

7 On which see: D. Oddy, 'Urban famine in nineteenth-century Britain: The effect of the Lancashire cotton famine on working-class diet and health', *Economic History Review*, 36:1 (1983), 68–86; P. Gurney, *Wanting and Having: Popular Politics and Liberal Consumerism in England, 1830–70* (Manchester: Manchester University Press, 2015), ch. 8.

8 R. Hoyle, 'Britain', in G. Alfani and C. Ó Gráda, eds, *Famine: A European History* (Cambridge: Cambridge University Press, 2017), esp. pp. 141–65. On market integration see: J. Chartres, 'Market integration and agricultural output in seventeenth-, eighteenth-, and early nineteenth-century England', *Agricultural History Review*, 43:2 (1995), 117–38; K. Gunnar Persson, *Grain Markets in Europe, 1500–1900: Integration and Deregulation* (Cambridge: Cambridge University Press, 1999).

9 R. Wells, *Wretched Faces, Famine in Wartime England 1793–1803* (Stroud: Alan Sutton, 1988).

10 D. Williams, 'Were "hunger" rioters really hungry? Some demographic evidence', *Past and Present* 71 (1976), 70–5.

11 *Sussex Weekly Advertiser*, 28 April 1800.

12 On the point of the emergence of food rioting as the dominant and defining protest form see: A. Charlesworth and A. Randall (eds), *Moral Economy and Popular Protest: Crowds, Conflict and Authority* (Basingstoke: Macmillan, 2000).

13 E.P. Thompson, 'The moral economy of the English crowd in the eighteenth century', *Past & Present*, 50 (1971), 76–136.

14 For instance Malcolm Chase's wonderfully wide-ranging and contextually rich study of 1820 makes only one reference to the harvest of 1819: it was 'far from bountiful'. In truth, the harvest was uneven across England. In the East and North Ridings of Yorkshire the crops were unusually abundant and labour scarce, the usual influx of West Yorkshire mill workers failing to materialise despite the 'extraordinary want of labour in the manufacturing districts'. In other places late rains and hail stifled both the quality and quantity of the crops. The point holds, though: 1819 and 1820 were crisis years whatever the state of the crops. M. Chase, *1820: Disorder and Stability in the United Kingdom* (Manchester: Manchester University Press, 2013), p. 12. On the harvest see *Yorkshire Gazette*, 14 August 1819; E.L. Jones, *Seasons and Prices: The Role of the Weather in English Agricultural History* (London: Allen and Unwin, 1964).

15 A. Sen *Poverty and Famines: An Essay on Entitlement and Deprivation* (Oxford: Oxford University Press, 1982).

16 *Brighton Herald*, 23 March; *Brighton Patriot*, 26 March 1839.

17 *Financial Times*, 5 December 2016 ('UK suffering "first lost decade since 1860s" says Carney'), https://www.ft.com/content/c0c36268-bb0d-11e6-8b45-b8b81dd5d080, accessed 3 September 2018. On the context see: C. Feinstein, 'Pessimism perpetuated: Real wages and the standard of living in Britain during and after the industrial revolution', *Journal of Economic History*, 58:3 (1998), 625–58.

18 Note, for instance, the paucity of reference to this period in Barry Reay's fine *Rural Englands*. The gaps reflect the dearth of work on this period; Reay's *Microhistories* is a notable exception: B. Reay, *Rural Englands* (Basingstoke: Palgrave, 2004); B. Reay, *Microhistories: Demography, Society and Culture in Rural England, 1800–1930* (Cambridge: Cambridge University Press, 1995).

19 K. Wrightson, 'The enclosure of English social history', *Rural History* 1:1 (1990), 73–82.

20 P. Kingsford, *The Hunger Marchers in Britain, 1920–1939* (London: Lawrence & Wishart, 1982). On 'hunger scabs' see: J. Winterton and R. Winterton, *Coal, Crisis and Conflict: The 1984–85 Miners' Strike in Yorkshire* (Manchester: Manchester University Press, 1989), pp. 201–3.

21 M. MacKinnon, 'English poor law policy and the crusade against outrelief', *Journal of Economic History*, 47:3 (1987), 603–25; E. Hurren, 'Labourers are revolting: Penalising the poor and a political reaction in the Brixworth Union, Northamptonshire, 1875–1885', *Rural History*, 11:1 (2000), 37–55.

22 E. Hurren, *Protesting about Pauperism: Poverty, Politics and Poor Relief in Late-Victorian England, 1870–1900* (Woodbridge: Boydell & Brewer, 2007), p. 109.

23 A. Croll, '"Reconciled gradually to the system of indoor relief": The poor law in Wales during the "crusade against out-relief", *c.* 1870–*c.* 1890', *Family & Community History*, 20:2 (2017), 121–44.

24 C. Shammas, *The Pre-industrial Consumer in England and America* (Oxford: Oxford University Press, 1990), pp. 140–5.

25 C.E.L. Evans and C.E. Harper, 'A history and review of school meal standards in the UK', *Journal of Human Nutrition and Dietetics*, 22:2 (2009), 89–99. On 'collective feeding' see: J. Vernon, *Hunger: A Modern History* (Cambridge, MA: Harvard University Press, 2007), ch. 6.

26 A. Bashford and J.E. Chaplin, *The New Worlds of Thomas Robert Malthus: Rereading the Principle of Population* (Princeton, NJ: Princeton University Press, 2016).

27 Vernon, *Hunger*, ch. 1.

28 K.D.M. Snell, 'The culture of local xenophobia', *Social History*, 28:1 (2003), 1–30; R. Hanley, 'Slavery and the birth of working-class racism in England, 1814–1833', *Transactions of the Royal Historical Society*, 26 (2016), 103–23; S. Virdee, *Racism, Class and the Racialized Outsider* (Basingstoke: Palgrave, 2014).

29 D. Featherstone, *Solidarity: Hidden Histories and Geographies of Internationalism* (London: Zed Books, 2012).

30 S. King, *Poverty and Welfare in England, 1700–1850* (Manchester: Manchester University Press, 2000).

31 M. Neuman, *The Speenhamland County: Poverty and the Poor Laws in Berkshire, 1782–1834* (New York: Garland, 1982).

32 P. Gurney, *Wanting and Having: Popular Politics and Liberal Consumerism in England, 1830–70* (Manchester: Manchester University Press, 2015).

33 A. Sen, Hunger in the Contemporary World, Suntory and Toyota International Centres for Economics and Related Disciplines, Discussion Paper DEDPS/8 (London: London School of Economics, 1997), p. 2.

34 Vernon, *Hunger*; Gurney, *Wanting and Having*.

35 For instance see: S. Schama, *Citizens: A Chronicle of the French Revolution* (London: Viking, 1989), ch. 7.1.

Select bibliography

For secondary literature, see the references in the main text.

Archival

Berkshire Record Office

D/P22/12/4, Bradfield Overseers Accounts, 1808–1818.
D/P48/12/2, Drayton, Overseers Accounts, 1794–1821.
D/P 66/8/1, East Hendred vestry minutes.
D/P92/12/2, Peasemore Overseers Accounts, 1810–1830.
D/P110/8/1, Shinfield vestry minutes.
D/P116/8/5, Speen vestry minutes.
D/EX 1457/4/30, Scales of bread allowances, Sonning, 1819.
D/P124/12/3, Sulhampstead Abbots Overseers Accounts, 1800–1831.

Bodleian Library, Oxford

National Club Papers, Dep. b. 235–40, c. 682–4, d. 754–7.

British Library

Place Ms., 27,820, f. 374.
Add Mss. 40451, Peel Papers.

Cambridge University Library

Madden Broadside Ballad Collection.

Canterbury Cathedral Archives

U3/49/8/1, Hougham select vestry minutes.

Cornwall Record Office

R/5145, Scale for regulating poor relief, 1817.

Derby Local Studies Library

Broadsheet Collection, box 15.

Dorset History Centre

D124/242, Ilchester Papers.
PE/BF/VE 1/1 and 3, Blandford Forum vestry minutes.

East Sussex County Record Office

AMS/5567/1, Alfriston vestry minutes.
PAR 236/12/1/2, Battle vestry minutes.
PAR 237/12/2, Beckley vestry minutes.
DE/A1/3, Eastbourne vestry minutes.
PAR343/12/1, Framfield vestry minutes.
PAR 401/12/1 Icklesham vestry minutes.
PAR422/12/1, Mayfield vestry minutes.
PAR430/12/1, Ninfield vestry minutes.
PAR 440/12/1, Peasmarsh vestry minutes.
AMS 5995/3/12, Curteis Papers.
Q0/EW 32, East and West Sussex Quarter Sessions Order Book.

East Yorkshire Record Office

PE121/63, Howden vestry minutes.
zDDX131/1/6, Copy of Enclosure Award and plan relating to
    Goodmanham, 1777.
AP/3/24, Goodmanham Enclosure Act, 1775.
PC56/1, Lund Enclosure Act, 1794; IA/101, Lund Enclosure Map, 1795.

Hampshire County Record Office

43M67/PV1, Amport vestry minutes.
40M75, A PV2, Botley select vestry minutes.
30M77 PV1, Bishops Waltham vestry minutes.

57M75/PO16, 'An Account of Money expended in the House of Industry belonging to the united parishes of Bramshott, Headley & Kingsley', Headley Account Book 1795–1852.
6M77 PV1, Eversley vestry minutes.
PL2/2/2, Farnborough Workhouse Account Book, 1794–1822.
25M60 PV1, Fawley select vestry minutes.
90M71 PV1, Minstead vestry minutes.
44M69/J30/1, Printed scale for regulating parochial relief by the price of standard wheaten bread adopted in the Hindon (Wiltshire) division 5 March 1817.
75M91/E26/10, Porchester Papers.
15M84/Z3/61, Rev. Henry Wake, *Abuse of the Poor-Rate!! A Statement of Facts* (Andover, self-published, 1818).

Centre for Kentish Studies

P45/8/2, Brenchley vestry minutes.
Bromley Vestry Item 5.
P49/8/3, Brookland vestry minutes.
P88/8/1, Chevening vestry minutes.
P125/8/1, Dymchurch vestry minutes.
P145/8/1, Farningham vestry minutes.
P81/8/1, Great Chart vestry minutes.
P192/8/2, Horsmonden vestry minutes.
P202/8/1, Ightham vestry minutes.
P309/8/7, New Romney vestry minutes.
P/347/8/1, Staplehurst vestry minutes.
P399/12/8, Wittersham vestry minutes.
P408/8/1 and 2, Yalding vestry minutes.
PS/Ma/4, Malling Petty Sessions Minutes.
U951 C177/28, Knatchbull Papers.

Lancashire County Record Office

Lancashire County Record Office, DDLi, box 57

Lincolnshire Record Office

Burton upon Stather PAR/10/1, Burton vestry minutes.
Frampton PAR/10/3, Frampton vestry minutes.
Heckington PAR/10/1, Heckington vestry meetings.
HD/65/1/5, Holbeach vestry minutes.
Quadring PAR/10/3, Quadring vestry minutes.

Manchester City Library

Broadside ballads, BR f.824.04.BA1,Vol. 4.

National Library of Dublin

MS2022, British Association Minute Book.

Somerset Record Office

Somerset Record Office, D\P\Can13/13/6, Cannington overseers' correspondence.

Staffordshire Record Office

D3891/6/100, Kidderminster overseers' correspondence.

Surrey History Centre

6672/2/1, Coulsdon vestry minutes.
P25/3/1, Godstone vestry minutes.

The National Archives

Home Office, Assi 94/1387, 1856, 2073.
Home Office, 40/24.
Home Office, 41/12.
Home Office, 42/35, 49, 50, 51, 52, 55, 62, 65, 102, 150.
Home Office, 44/21.
Home Office, 52/7, 8, 10, 12, 26.
Home Office, 64/1.
Ministry of Health, 12/10661, 13076/3.
Ministry of Health, 32/39, 70.
State Papers, 36/4, 50, 52.
Treasury Solicitor, 11/943.

West Sussex County Record Office

PAR 153/12/1, Pulborough vestry minutes.
QR/W608, f.58, West Sussex Epiphany Sessions Roll 1795.

Wiltshire and Swindon Record Office

1719/6, Box vestry minutes.
2944/78, Mere vestry minutes (1819).
1551/48, Poulshot vestry minutes.
1489/9, Steeple Ashton vestry and select vestry minutes.

Printed primary sources

Annals of Agriculture, 24, 1795.
Anon. *An Account of the Several Work-Houses for Employing and Maintaining the Poor; Setting Forth the Rules by Which they are Governed, their Great Usefulness to the Publick, and in Particular to the Parishes Where they are Erected*, 1st ed. (London: J. Downing: 1725).
Anon. *The Case of the Poor Consider'd; or the Great Advantages of Erecting a Publick Manufactory, for Maintaining and Employing the Poor* (Edinburgh: J. Maclaurin, 1729).
Anon. *The Workhouse Cruelty: Workhouses Turn'd Gaols and Gaolers Executioners* (London: Printed for Charity Love-poor, 1731).
Anon. *An Account of the Several Work-Houses*, 2nd ed. (London: J. Downing, 1732).
Anon. *A Digest of the Poor Laws, in Order to their Being Reduced Into One Act* (London: P. Uriel, 1768).
Anon. *Essays on Agriculture: Occasioned by Reading Mr Stone's Report on the Present State of that Science in the County of Lincoln. By a Native of the County* (London: W. Richardson, 1796).
Anon. ('Marcus, One of the Three'), *The Book of Murder! A Vade-mecum for the Commissioners and Guardians of the New Poor Law … Being an Exact Reprint of the Infamous Essay on the Possibility of Limiting Populousness, with a Refutation of the Malthusian Doctrine*, 2nd ed., with a preface (London: John Hill, 1839).
Becher, J. *The Anti-Pauper System* (London: W. Simkin and R. Marshall, 1828).
Bentham, J. *Pauper Management Improved: Particularly by Means of an Application of the Panopticon Principle of Construction: Anno 1797, First Published in Young's Annals of Agriculture: Now First Published Separately* (London: R. Baldwin & J. Ridgway, 1797).
Brontë, E. *Wuthering Heights* (London: Thomas Cautley Newby, 1847).
Brooker, C. *The Murder Den, and Its Means of Destruction; Or, Some Account of the Working of the New Poor Law […]* (Brighton: William Woodward, 1842).
Burke, E. *Thoughts and Details on Scarcity, Originally Presented to the Right Hon. William Pitt, in the Month of November 1795* (London: F.C. Rivington, 1800).
Clark, W. *Thoughts and Management and Relief of the Poor* (London: R. Cruttwell, 1815).
Clarkson, C. *An Inquiry into the Cause of the Increase of Pauperism and Poor Rates* (London, 1816).

Davies, D. *The Case of Labourers in Husbandry Stated and Considered* (London: C.G. & J. Robinson, 1795).

Dent, J. 'The present condition of the English agricultural labourer', *Journal of the Royal Agricultural Society*, 2nd series, 7 (1871).

Dickens, C. *Oliver Twist, or, the Parish Boy's Progress* (London: Bentley, 1839).

Doubleday, T. *On Mundane Moral Government Demonstrating Its Analogy with the System of Material Government* (London: Blackwood, 1852).

Eddowes, J. *The Agricultural Labourer as he Really Is; or Village Morals in 1854* (Driffield:, 1854).

Gardiner, W. *The Adventure of Hodge and the Monkey: A Comic Tale* (London: T. Nonmus, 1852).

Gilbert, T. *A Scheme for the Better Relief and Employment of the Poor* (London, 1764).

Gilbert, T. *Observations upon the Orders and Resolutions of the House of Commons, with Respect to the Poor, Vagrants, and Houses of Correction* (London, 1775).

Gilbert, T. *Plan for the Better Relief and Employment of the Poor; for Enforcing and Amending the Laws Respecting Houses of Correction, and Vagrants; and for Improving the Police of this Country. Together with Bills Intended to be Offered to Parliament for those Purposes* (London: Wilkie, 1781).

Girdler, J.S. *Observations on the Pernicious Consequences of Forestalling, Regrating, and Ingrossing* (London: H. Baldwin and Son, 1800).

Gleig, G. *The Chronicles of Waltham* (London: R. Bentley, 1835).

Hardy, T. 'The Dorsetshire labourer', *Longmans Magazine*, 2 (1883).

Hicke, W. *The Agricultural Labourer Viewed in his Moral, Intellectual, and Physical Conditions* (London: Groombridge and Sons, 1855).

Howitt, W. *The Rural Life of England* (London: Longman, 1838).

Indian Relief Fund, *Distress in Ireland: Report of the Trustees of the Indian Relief Fund* (Dublin: J. Browne, 1847).

Jefferies, R. *Hodge and his Masters* (London: Smith, Elder, 1890).

Macaulay, T.B. *The History of England from the Accession of James the Second*, vol. 2 (London: Longman, 1849).

Malthus, T. *The Crisis, a View of the Present State of Great Britain, by a Friend to the Constitution* (London, 1796).

Malthus, T. *An Essay on the Principle of Population*, 2nd edition (London: J.M. Dent and Sons, 1803).

Malthus, T. *A Letter to Samuel Whitbread, Esq. MP, on his Proposed Bill for the Amendment of the Poor Laws* (London: J. Johnson, 1807).

Middleton, J. *General View of the Agriculture of Middlesex*, 2nd edition (London: G. and W. Nicol, 1807).

More, H. *The Riot, or, Half a Loaf is Better than No Bread* (London: J. Marshall, 1795).

Poor Law Commissioners, *First Annual Report of the Poor Law Commissioners for England and Wales* (London: Charles Knight, 1835).

Poor Law Commissioners, *Second Annual Report of the Poor Law Commissioners for England and Wales* (London: Charles Knight, 1836).

Poor Law Commission, *Report of the Poor Law Commissioners to the Most Noble the Marquis of Normanby, Her Majesty's Principal Secretary of State for the

Home Department, on the Continuance of the Poor Law Commission (Her Majesty's Stationery Office, London, 1840).

Porteous, D. *A Letter to the Citizens of Glasgow* (Glasgow: Robert Chapman, Alexander Duncan, 1783).

Roberts, S. *Chartism and its Causes and Cure: Addressed to the Clery and Others of Sheffield and Eccleshall* (Sheffield: Whittaker and Co., 1839).

Thelwall, J. *The Tribune: A Periodical Publication, Consisting Chiefly of the Political Lectures of John Thelwall* (London: self-published, 1795).

Tucker, H. *An Address upon the Condition of the Agricultural Labourer* (London: Longman, 1854).

Young, A. *A Six Weeks Tour, through the Southern Counties of England and Wales* (London: Nicoll, 1769).

Zouch, H. *Remarks upon the Late Resolutions of the House of Commons Respecting the Proposed Change of the Poor Laws* (Leeds: G. Wright, 1766).

Autobiographies and edited papers

Thompson, F. *Lark Rise to Candleford* (Oxford: Oxford University Press, 1945)

Vaisey, D. (ed.), *The Diary of Thomas Turner, 1754–1765* (London: CTR Publishing, 1994).

Coombs, H., and P. Coombs (eds). *Journal of a Somerset Rector, 1803–34* (Oxford: Oxford University Press, 1984).

Editions of primary sources

Ashby, A.W. *One Hundred Years of Poor Law Administration in a Warwickshire Village* (Oxford: Oxford University Press, 1912).

Bacon, F. *The Works of Francis Bacon, Baron of Verulam, Viscount St Alban, and Lord High Chancellor of England* (London: C. and J. Rivington, 1826).

Bentham, J. 'Tracts on poor laws and pauper management: Outline of a work entitled Pauper Management Improved', *The Works of Jeremy Bentham* (Edinburgh: W. Tait, 1843), vol. 8.

Board of Agriculture, *The Agricultural State of the Kingdom* (Bath: Adams and Dart, 1970/1816).

Calendar of Home Office Papers, George III, 1766–1769, vol. 2 (London: HMSO, 1879).

Cobbett, W. *Rural Rides*, ed. I. Dyck (London: Penguin, 2001).

Cobbett, W. *Cottage Economy* (New York: Cosimo Classics, 2007/1821).

Donovan, J., C. Duffy, K. Everest and M. Rossington (eds.). *The Poems of Shelley: Volume Three: 1819–1820* (London, Routledge, 2014).

Drysdale, C. *Life and Writings of Malthus*, 2nd edition (London: G Standring, 1892).

Eden, F. *The State of the Poor. Or, An History of the Labouring Classes in England, from the Conquest to the Present Period* (Cambridge: Cambridge University Press, 2011/1797).

Engels, F. *The Condition of the Working Class in England in 1844*, trans F. Kelley Wischnewetzky (Cambridge: Cambridge University Press 2010/1892).

Engels, F. *The Condition of the Working Class in England*, ed. David McLellan (Oxford: Oxford University Press, 1999).

Hampson, E.M. *The Treatment of Poverty in Cambridgeshire 1597–1834* (Cambridge: Cambridge University Press, 1934).

Heath, R. *The English Peasant: Studies Historical, Local and Biographic* (Cambridge University Press, 2011/1893).

Malthus, T. *An Essay on the Principle of Population*, vol. 2, ed. P. James (Cambridge: Cambridge University Press, 1989).

Marx, K. *Capital, Volume One: A Critique of Political Economy*, trans. F. Engels, ed. S. Moore and E. Aveling (New York: The Modern Library, 1906).

Parker, C.S. (ed.). *Life and Letters of Sir James Graham, Second Baronet of Netherby* (London: John Murray, 1907).

Shelly, P.B. *Ballad: Young Parson Richards*, ed. W. Heck (privately printed, Iowa, 1926).

Smith, A. *An Inquiry into the Nature and Causes of the Wealth of Nations*, vol. 2, ed. E. Cannan (Chicago, IL: Chicago University Press, 1977).

Sturt, G. *The Journals of George Sturt, 1890–1927*, vol. 2, ed. E.D. Mackerness (Cambridge: Cambridge University Press, 1967).

Townsend, J. *A Dissertation on the Poor Laws: By a Well-wisher to Mankind*, ed. A. Montagu (Berkeley, CA: University of California Press, 1971).

British Parliamentary Papers (BPP)

BPP, 1803–04 (175), vol. 8, 'Abstract of the answers and returns made pursuant to an act, passed in the 43d year of His Majesty King George III. Intitled, "An act for procuring returns relative to the expense and maintenance of the poor in England"'.

BPP, 1817 (106), vol. 84, 'Report from the Select Committee of the House of Commons on the Poor Laws'.

BPP, 1818 (400), vol. 19, 'Report from the House of Lords Select Committee on the Poor Laws'.

BPP, 1819 (529), vol. 2, 'Select Committee to Consider the Poor Laws'.

BPP. Commons, 1824 (392), vol. 6, 'Report from the Select Committee on Labourers Wages'.

BPP, 1825 (334) vol. 4, 'Select Committee on Poor Rate Returns: Report, Appendix (1824)'.

BPP, 1828 (494) vol. 4, 'Report from the Select Committee on that part of the Poor Laws Relating to the Employment or Relief of Able Bodied Persons from the Poor Rate'.

BPP, 1834 (44), 'Report from His Majesty's Commissioners for Inquiring into the Administration and Practical Operation of the Poor Laws Poor Law Report'.

BPP, 1846 (171) vol. 27, 'Instructions to the Committees of Relief Districts, Extracted from Minutes of the Proceedings of the Commissioners Appointed in Reference to the Apprehended Scarcity'.

BPP, 1847 (761) vol. 51, 'Correspondence Relating to Measures for Relief of Distress in Ireland, July 1846–January 1847'.
BPP (1851) vol. 43, 'Census of Great Britain, 1851, Tables of the Population and Houses in the Divisions, Registration Counties, and Districts of England and Wales; in the Counties, Cities, and Burghs of Scotland; and in the Islands in the British Seas'.

Newspapers

Bath Chronicle and Weekly Gazette
Belfast News-Letter
Berkshire Chronicle
Bolton Chronicle
Bradford Observer
Bridgwater & Somersetshire Herald
Brighton Guardian
Brighton Herald
Brighton Patriot
Bristol Mercury
Bury and Norwich Post
Cambridge Chronicle and Journal
Cambridge Independent Press
Chester Chronicle
Cobbett's Weekly Political Register
Cork Examiner
County Chronicle
Courier and Evening Gazette
Derby Mercury
Dublin Evening Post
Exeter Flying Post
Farmer's Magazine
Fife Herald
Financial Times
Freeman's Journal
Gazetteer and New Daily Advertiser
General Evening Post
Gloucester Journal
Guardian
Hampshire Advertiser
Hampshire Chronicle
Hampshire Courier
Hampshire Telegraph
Hereford Journal
Hertford Mercury and Reformer
Hull Advertiser
Hull Packet
Illustrated London News

Ipswich Journal
Keene's Bath Journal
Kent Herald
Kentish Chronicle
Kentish Gazette
Leeds Intelligencer
Leeds Mercury
Leeds Times
Limerick Chronicle
Liverpool Mercury
Lloyd's Evening Post
London Gazette
London Standard
Maidstone Journal
Morning Chronicle
Morning Post
Newcastle Courant
Northampton Mercury
Northern Liberator
Northern Star
Oracle and Public Advertiser
Oxford Journal
Reading Mercury
Rochester Gazette
Royal Cornwall Gazette
Salisbury and Winchester Journal
Salisbury Journal
Scots Magazine
Sheffield Independent
Sherborne Mercury
Sherborne & Yeovil Mercury
Southampton Mercury
Spectator
Standard
Star
Suffolk Chronicle
Sun
Sussex Advertiser
Sussex Weekly Advertiser
Taunton Courier
Times
Two-Penny Trash
Waterford Freeman
Weekly Dispatch
Western Times
Wiltshire Independent
Woolmer's Exeter and Plymouth Gazette

York Courant
York Herald
Yorkshire Gazette

Digitised sources (all accessed 30 April 2019)

Thorne, R. 'Young, Sir William, 2nd Bt. (1749–1815), of Delaford Park, Bucks.', in R. Thorne (ed.), *The History of Parliament: The House of Commons 1790–1820*, Vol. 5, https://www.historyofparliamentonline.org/volume/1790-1820/member/young-sir-william-1749-1815.
UN-DESA, 'Transforming our world: The 2030 agenda for sustainable development, Division for Sustainable Development Goals', https://sustainabledevelopment.un.org/post2015/transformingourworld.

Index

EU authorised representative for GPSR:
Easy Access System Europe, Mustamäe tee 50,
10621 Tallinn, Estonia
gpsr.requests@easproject.com

www.ingramcontent.com/pod-product-compliance
Ingram Content Group UK Ltd.
Pitfield, Milton Keynes, MK11 3LW, UK
UKHW031402170425
1818IPUK00010B/31